BROTHER TONY'S BOYS

THE LARGEST CASE OF CHILD
PROSTITUTION IN U.S. HISTORY
THE TRUE STORY

MIKE ECHOLS

Prometheus Books
59 John Glenn Drive
Amherst, New York 14228-2197

Published 1996 by Prometheus Books

Brother Tony's Boys: The Largest Case of Child Prostitution in U.S. History. The True Story. Copyright © 1996 W. H. (Mike) Echols II. All rights reserved. No part of this publication may be reproduced, stored in a retrieval system, or transmitted in any form or by any means, electronic, mechanical, photocopying, recording, or otherwise, without prior written permission of the publisher, except in the case of brief quotations embodied in critical articles and reviews. Inquiries should be addressed to Prometheus Books, 59 John Glenn Drive, Amherst, New York 14228-2197, 716-691-0133. FAX: 716-691-0137.

00 99 98 97 96   5 4 3 2 1

Library of Congress Cataloging-in-Publication Data

Echols, Mike.
    Brother Tony's boys : the largest case of child prostitution in U.S. history : the true story / Mike Echols.
      p.   cm.
    Includes bibliographical references.
    ISBN 1-57392-051-7 (cloth)
    1. Leyva, Tony, 1946–   2. Morris, Edward Rias. 3. Herring, Freddie M.   4. Pentecostal churches—United States—Clergy—Biography. 5. Evangelists—United States—Biography. 6. Child sexual abuse by clergy—United States. I. Title.
BX8762.Z8L484   1996
289.9'4'092—dc20
[B]   96-7059
                                                                                                                         CIP

Jesus said: "As for the man who is a cause of stumbling to one of these little ones who have faith, it would be better for him to be thrown into the sea with a millstone round his neck."

Mark 9:42, The New English Bible

Contents

Foreword
   Frank Fitzpatrick   11

Dedication   13

Acknowledgments   15

Preface   19

Introduction: "God's special way for
   His people to love each other . . ."   23

1. "He was first called on to preach when he was
   about a nine- or ten-year-old boy."   27

2. "He is truly inspired by sin!"   40

3. "If I'd a gotten close enough to that son-of-a-bitch
   that night, I'd'a done blowed his head off."   55

4. "He preached the Word of God and always took
such an interest in our children—especially the boys." 69

5. "... He's had many, many unusual experiences
in the Lord." 77

6. "... False prophets shall rise, and show signs
and wonders to seduce." 89

7. "I ain't never lived with my own father and
I thought that was what Tony's trying to be to me." 104

8. "Honey, when it comes to Tony Leyva,
I want to set the fire!" 130

9. "Back then, it felt good him calling me 'son.'
Nobody had ever done that before." 149

10. "At first my thinking was that Tony Leyva
was heaven sent." 160

11. "There were these government men that Tony knew.
He had us to have sex with them." 173

12. "It would probably blow people's minds to find out
just how many places Tony Leyva was run out of!" 184

13. "I told [the FBI] how from the time I was twelve till
I was about sixteen, Tony Leyva and the other ministers
did sex with me ... so many times I kinda lost count." 195

14. "I've been in full-time ministry since the night
of my twelfth birthday!" 211

15. "He said to me, 'Tony and me got a secret,'
the classic line." 225

16. "I believe Tony Leyva is the Antichrist . . .
   straight from the very pits of hell!" 248

17. "He probably asked for it . . . most of those boys did." 259

18. "I think he's where he belongs now 'cause he's hurt
   so many people in the name of God." 274

19. "The boys Gray sexually assaulted he came to know
   [when they were] thirteen to fifteen years of age." 290

20. "Brother Tony knew how to treat us and
   love us to get to us." 303

Epilogue: NAMBLA Revisited, the Author's Travails,
   Pedophiles, Pederasts' Assaults, and
   Helping and Protecting Children 321

Selected Bibliography 373

Foreword

Frank Fitzpatrick
Survivor Connections, Inc.

Throughout humanity's recorded history there have been footnotes about the continuing holocaust of adults sexually attacking children. But until recently, efforts to expose this devastating destruction of youngsters' minds and souls have been effectively squelched. From firsthand experience as a survivor of sexual assault in childhood, and from my dialogues via Survivor Connections with thousands of former victims from around the world, I know that the battles we, as adult survivors of childhood sexual assaults, face to protect other children from our own perpetrators, and others, are immense.

One great hurdle we must overcome is our isolation, which in turn fosters shame and fear that no one will believe us. Most survivors of rape occurring in their youth assume that they were the only victims of their abuser. Statistics, widely publicized cases (such as the Father James Porter case in which I was involved), and the dogged, inspiring work to expose the truth by investigative crusaders such as author Mike Echols, prove otherwise. The average pedophile has over a hundred victims before he or she is brought to justice through the criminal court system. Indeed, Survivor Connections distributes a bumper sticker that reads, "You know a sexual assault survivor."

And you do. Likely quite a few of us.

Because of Mike, and others who dare to speak the truth regardless of the personal consequences, there is now some hope that things may be changed, a faint but growing glimmer of opportunity. To expose these horrible crimes, shouting from the rooftops until someone is forced to listen, no matter how powerful the societal position of the criminals involved, is the only way to stop future attacks. Such necessary defiance by former victims and their champions is now happening.

In *Brother Tony's Boys,* Mike Echols powerfully tells the very disturbing, true chronicle of a not-so-well-hidden deviant world of a type that most of us would like to deny exists. The book contains sometimes graphic descriptions of sexual assaults on young children and teenagers. Some will find these depictions offensive. I, too, did at first, until I realized that such details are unavoidably necessary in order to bring home to a society that is generally in denial the nature and severity of the crimes committed by such predators as those described in this book.

In *Brother Tony's Boys,* denial, avoidance, and protection of the powerful are recurring themes. The devoutly religious who were fooled by the wiles of the preacher, the families who trusted without limit, those police and FBI offices that investigated accusations halfheartedly if at all—all contributed to the continuance of the regionalized holocaust against children that was Brother Tony Leyva and company. So many people knew, yet so many declined to take decisive action. Unfortunately, the story is a microcosm of what happens in so many other child abuse cases, including my own sexual assault and that of countless others by Father James R. Porter.

Parents and others who care about protecting children from the manipulations of sexual predators would do well to explore *Brother Tony's Boys* to understand just how such a master con-artist could inveigle himself into the confidence of so many families and worshipers. When Brother Tony put on his role of preacher, his followers put on their blinders. Sadly, the ploys and machinations of Tony Leyva will be all too familiar to survivors of sexual abuse by pedophiles. Mike Echols's depiction is right on the mark.

And as to organized rings of pedophiles, anyone who doubts their existence should be convinced otherwise by reading Mike's exposé of NAMBLA, the North American Man/Boy Love Association, in his Epilogue.

There is much, much more—including the monstrous betrayal of trust and the resulting monumental havoc on children's emotional lives. In reading *Brother Tony's Boys,* you will be outraged—maybe enough to join the crusade to protect our children.

Dedication

This book is dedicated to:

- My loving mother, Anne Brown Echols, and to the memory of my loving father, Walter Harlan Echols.
- The memory of Patricia Casey, a loving mother without whose courage this story would never have been told.
- The memories of the thousands of children who have been kidnapped, sexually assaulted, and murdered, especially Steve Branch, Christopher Byers, and Michael Moore, three eight-year-old friends murdered in West Memphis, Arkansas, May 5, 1993.
- The thousands of children and young people still missing today, in the hope that they may be found alive and well. The names of a few are given below (along with the location where last seen, birth date, and date when kidnapped):

Christopher Abeyta—Colorado Springs, Colo.—11/28/85—7/15/86
Walter Thomas Ackerson—Yachats, Ore.—7/6/73—3/24/90
Tammy Lynn Ackers—Roanoke, Va.—6/28/62—2/7/77
Sarah Elizabeth Avon—Joliet, Ill.—1/6/75—7/21/81

Dedication

Cherie Nicole Barnes—Kansas City, Mo.—7/30/84—1/7/87
Daniel Barter—Perdido Bay, Ala.—12/12/54—6/18/59
Tammy L. Belanger—Exeter, N.H.—2/24/76—11/13/84
Susan Robin Bender—Modesto, Calif.—11/27/70—4/25/86
David Michael Borer—Willow, Alaska—3/21/81—4/25/89
Gina Dawn Brooks—Fredericktown, Mo.—11/28/75—8/5/89
Tilwanda Denise Cheatham—Aiken, S.C.—12/4/80—8/11/89
Kevin Andrew Collins—San Francisco, Calif.—1/24/74—2/10/84
April Ann Cooper—Rancho, Calif.—5/13/79—12/13/86
Jon Dabkowski—Tarentum, Pa.—11/9/70—1/14/82
Michelle Lee Dorr—Silver Spring, Md.—10/12/79—5/31/86
Jaycee Lee Dugard—South Lake Tahoe, Calif.—5/30/80—6/10/91
Michael Wayne Dunahee—Victoria, B.C., Canada—5/12/86—3/24/91
Scott Christian Echols—Muscoy, Calif.—11/20/83—7/26/92
Robert Joseph Fritz—Campbellsport, Wis.—8/5/77—5/14/83
Thomas Dean Gibson—Glendale, Ore.—7/5/88—3/18/91
John David Gosch—West Des Moines, Iowa—11/12/69—9/5/82
Christopher James Harvey—Hinsdale County, Colo.—8/9/69—7/11/84
Mark Himebaugh—Del Haven, N.J.—5/23/80—11/25/91
Danny Randall Jackson—Gainesville, Fla.—8/10/77—8/25/89
Lloyd Eric Larsfolk—Caledon, Ontario, Canada—9/4/66—8/24/81
Marjorie Christina Luna—Greenacres City, Fla.—4/7/76—5/27/84
Eugene Wade Martin—Des Moines, Iowa—8/17/70—8/12/84
Gabriel Minarcin—Tarentum, Pa.—10/5/71—1/14/82
Toni Lynn McNatt-Chiappetta—Clairton, Pa.—5/31/66—11/5/81
Michael Lee Montelongo—San Benito, Tex.—6/22/72—7/12/77
Tiffany Jennifer Papesh—Maple Heights, Ohio—7/2/71—6/13/80
Monique Pebbles Santiago—Albany, N.Y.—9/11/78—3/29/90
Vinyette Teague—Chicago, Ill.—12/8/81—6/25/83
Jacob Erwin Wetterling—St. Joseph, Minn.—2/17/78—10/22/89
Angela Mae Rader—Roanoke, Va.—7/30/62—2/8/77
Cindy Jocelyn Zarzycki—Eastpointe, Mich.—6/7/72—4/20/86

If you have any information about the kidnapping or location of any of these people, please call the National Center for Missing & Exploited Children on their toll-free hotline, 1–800–843–5678.

Acknowledgments

First of all, I must thank the dozens of victims of evangelists Mario Ivan "Tony" Leyva, Edward Rias Morris, and Freddie M. Herring who, in my interviews with them, freely shared the painful experiences which they suffered because of these bogus preachers. Most especially I am indebted to the stellar in-depth assistance and interviews given to me by brothers Jason and Kenny Embert, two very brave young men.

I also thank the parents of many of the victims for sharing their very painful experiences and feelings involving their sons' seductions and sexual assaults by this trio of false evangelists. Most notably among them was the late Patti Casey. At the top of this list—for sharing her pain *plus* her heart, her family, and the extensive files she purloined from Tony Leyva's last office in Columbus, Georgia—is that "tough old bird," Macalynn Embert.

Strangely, many people within law enforcement chose not to help with—and in some cases actively attempted to thwart—my efforts to research and write this book. Notable exceptions, however, are Randy Leach, the Assistant Commonwealth's Attorney in Salem, Virginia; L. Garrick Hudson, a former deputy sheriff in Roanoke County, Virginia; Ann Miller, formerly with Children's Protective Services in Roanoke County; Emily Holden, a retired deputy sheriff in St. Tammany Parish, Louisiana; and Bonnie Beatty, a deputy sheriff and true victim's advocate who is in charge of sexual assault cases in Franklin County, Virginia. Each of them unstintingly gave of their time and knowledge of this case.

Acknowledgments

For years my journalistic eyes and ears in Roanoke were those of crack reporter Doug Pardue at the *Roanoke Times & World News*, now with *The State* in Columbia, South Carolina. After he departed, his journalistic cudgel for the Tony Leyva case was picked up by reporter Jan Vertefeuille, whom I thank for her assistance. And I also sincerely thank other helpful *Times & World News* staff members, particularly Mary Lynn.

For hearing me out and deciding to write and see through to publication the first national newspaper story about the case, I thank Ron Smothers of the Atlanta Bureau of the *New York Times*.

For her courage in talking to me in great detail and quite candidly about her ex-husband, Tony Leyva, his personality, her life with him, his charlatan's approach to being an evangelist and prophet, and his sexually assaulting boys, I thank his first wife, known in this book as Martha Robinson.

Even though they cannot be named because of their openness and candor in discussing and keeping me abreast of Leyva, Morris, and Herring since their imprisonment, I thank the several employees of the United States Bureau of Prisons for their assistance.

I am also most appreciative of the unusually forthright information given to me about Tony Leyva by his former attorney, Harry F. Bosen, Jr., of Salem, Virginia.

Lastly, I cannot omit Tony Leyva and his mother, Ada: Although they did so unwittingly, their providing me with information about themselves, their view of religion, and their particular and peculiar versions of Tony's "ministry" and sexual involvement with young boys truly added an important and previously missing facet to the telling of the true story.

For their help with the epilogue to this book, I wish to thank my longtime friend, former Executive Director of the Texas Boys' Choir, Jack Noble White; Greg Lyon, Jon Dann, and Craig Franklin of KRON-TV's Target 4 staff in San Francisco; and Detective Noreen Wolff of the Coordinated Law Enforcement Unit of the police department in Vancouver, British Columbia, Canada.

✝ ✝ ✝

Beyond the assistance I received in researching and writing this book, I must thank my dear Colorado friends Richard and Helen Love from the bottom of my heart for all of their financial and moral support for this project. God bless you both!

For his friendship, support, advice, and editorial assistance on my first

Acknowledgments

book, *I Know My First Name Is Steven,* and on *Brother Tony's Boys,* I thank my friend Norman Milford in Evergreen, Colorado.

And for his commitment to my work and the moral, material, and spiritual support he has provided to me over the past seven years, I thank my priest, the Reverend Father Carl R. Hansen.

Also, I must express my deep gratitude to two professionals at opposite ends of the continent who have been generous with their advice and unstinting in their friendship: Albert J. Boro, Jr., Esq., in San Francisco, and Paul Dinas, editing expert extraordinare, in New York.

And for their overall care, concern, and dedication to help kidnapped, missing, and sexually abused children, my hat is off to the folks I deal with at the National Center for Missing & Exploited Children in Arlington, Virginia: Ernest E. "Ernie" Allen, President; Ruben Rodriquez, Law Enforcement Liaison; and Julia Caughey Cartwright, Director of Media Relations.

Last, but not least, for his faith and courage in publishing this book I thank Prometheus Books' Editor-in-Chief, Steven L. Mitchell. And I thank Eugene O'Connor for his fine work editing this book.

Preface

In the 1980s I researched and wrote *I Know My First Name Is Steven*, the true crime story of the longest stranger abduction in U.S. history of a child who was safely returned: the 1972 kidnapping of seven-year-old Steven Stayner by convicted pedophile-kidnapper Kenneth Eugene Parnell. Until 1980 Steven was forced to live with Parnell while he subjected the boy to hundreds of sexual assaults.

In 1989 *I Know My First Name Is Steven* was the basis for an NBC-TV miniseries of the same title. In 1991 it was published by Pinnacle Books. Both the miniseries and the book helped many people finally understand the full scope of the dangers and horrors of child kidnapping and the sexual abuse facing our children, specifically those crimes committed by pedophiles, pederasts, and ephebophiles,* whose sick aim is to sexually abuse young boys.

Due in part to *I Know My First Name Is Steven*, the public is no longer

---

*A *pedophile* is a person who is sexually attracted to and who sometimes sexually assaults children of one or the other sex.

A *pederast* is a man who practices oral or anal sex with boys.

An *ephebophile* is a man who is sexually attracted to and sometimes sexually assaults pubescent (adolescent) boys.

Tony Leyva "crossed" categories: he became attracted to older teenage boys apparently due to the convenience and exciting danger it presented. But his preference was young adolescent boys.

complacent about these crimes. No longer does it find media coverage of them just another story, with which it cannot emotionally connect. For society the sexual abuse of children is real and disturbing, and something it is now ready to face head-on and do something about.

Although everything in *Brother Tony's Boys* is factual and based on my extensive taped interviews, many readers may find the events so incredible that they will have to suspend belief; as dyed-in-the-wool Pentecostals, the people who followed Brother Tony Leyva and his cohorts were involved in a personality cult in which they dismissed any thoughts that his ministry was not of God.

Today, parents, educators, counselors, and religious authorities are moving toward better protection of children from sexual abuse and assault, but we are still a long way from getting these problems anywhere near under control. Sadly, children remain at risk not only from crafty pedophiles like Kenneth Eugene Parnell, but, more insidiously, children are at risk from many of those whom society, parents, and the children themselves thought they could trust: policemen, teachers, coaches, scout leaders, doctors, and even priests and ministers. In his book *Scout's Honor: Sexual Abuse in America's Most Trusted Institution* (Rocklin, Calif.: Prima Publishing, 1994), p. 33, author Patrick Boyle quotes the FBI's top expert on child sexual assault, special agent Kenneth V. Lanning, as saying: "People seem more willing to accept a father or stepfather as a child molester than a parish priest, a next-door neighbor, a police officer, a pediatrician, an FBI agent, or a Scout leader."

As I did with my first book, I used my training and thirteen years as a social worker with emotionally, physically, and sexually abused children to do my research and conduct my interviews for *Brother Tony's Boys*. Almost all of my interviews with the victims, their parents, Leyva's first wife, and some law enforcement officials were conducted by me in person during several trips to the South in 1988 and 1989. All the subjects were agreeable to my interviewing them on tape about their knowledge of Tony Leyva, his so-called ministry, and his sexual assaults so as to assist in my telling the true story. Nevertheless, I have used pseudonyms in the vast majority of cases and where necessary altered descriptive information to protect the anonymity of innocent victims and their families, with the notable exception of Macalynn Embert; her sons, Jason and Kenny; Patti Casey and her husband, Jimmy Casey; William G. Gray, M.D.; and others who can be considered public persons.

Beginning in 1983, many FBI field offices across the South were contacted repeatedly by victims, their parents, and local law enforcement personnel, but for whatever reason the bureau failed to mount an investigation of pederast-evangelist Tony Leyva.

I did not receive any cooperation from the FBI in Roanoke, Virginia, or the U.S. Attorney's Office in that city. Indeed, both offices attempted to thwart my efforts to write this book. Whereas FBI agent John Terry did a modest job investigating the case, once he, U.S. Attorney John P. Alderson, and Assistant U.S. Attorneys Jenny Montgomery and Morgan Scott learned of my plans to conduct my own thorough investigation into the case—including their handling of it—they slammed every possible door in my face.

After Leyva, Morris, and Herring pled guilty in federal court and were sentenced to prison, the FBI learned that Leyva's former secretary had given me a box full of evidence against the trio, the same evidence that the FBI had earlier declined when it was offered to them. When I refused Terry's telephoned order that I turn it over to him, a pair of FBI agents came calling on me in Durango, Colorado, and demanded that I give it to them. I refused to do so and countered by offering to make copies of some of it for them. But I told them I would not hand over the originals unless they got a court order. They never did and I never did.

After a pause of several years, in 1992, I returned to work on *Brother Tony's Boys* and obtained additional material from my two lengthy telephone conversations with Leyva's mother as well as two letters from her and one from Leyva himself. Also, in 1992 and 1993, I conducted many telephone interviews with various personnel in law enforcement, the courts, a number of federal prisons, as well as with some attorneys, and reporters with the media, and did follow-up interviews with some of the victims and their parents.

Like my first book, *Brother Tony's Boys* contains an epilogue detailing the current unbelievable efforts by the pedophile group NAMBLA—the North American Man/Boy Love Association—to teach its members how to seduce and sexually assault boys and then get away with it; it tells of my recent personal struggles as an investigative journalist; it briefly details a few cases of horrendous sexual assaults and related murders of young boys; and most importantly, it offers encouragement and advice for what must be our national fight to drastically reduce child sexual assault by quickly and permanently identifying and isolating from our children anyone who perpetrates or attempts to perpetrate sex crimes against them.

With all of my heart I hope that *Brother Tony's Boys* increases active individual and collective public concern which leads to a hundredfold increase in efforts to prevent child sexual assault and incarcerate the offenders. While we may not be able to totally eradicate this damnable, insidious human aberration that subtly infects from generation to generation (i.e., turning many victims into future perpetrators), we can increase our vigilance and knowledge about recognizing and effectively dealing with it and thereby give boys and girls—ours, our neighbors', indeed *all* children—that degree of protection that a responsible, civilized society consistently provides all of its most vulnerable members.

Introduction

*"God's special way for His people
to love each other . . ."*

That most American of mountain chains the Appalachians cut grandly through the eastern third of the United States from the heart of the Deep South right up through New England's center. They start as gentle verdant undulations in north-central Alabama before crossing into northern Georgia where they gain substantial elevation with the occasional craggy peak nearly a mile high laced here and there with small jewel-like valleys alive with clear rushing streams teaming with trout. Twenty miles south of the town of Blue Ridge the famed Appalachian Trail begins its ascent into the Blue Ridge Mountains chain of the Appalachians. These storied hills and peaks barely nick South Carolina before their northernmost fingers become the storied Great Smoky Mountains at the Tennessee-North Carolina border and sport still higher fog-swirled peaks.

The trail defines a wiggly border between the two states which almost evenly divides the Great Smoky Mountains National Park between them. With astounding vistas the park is home to the nation's largest population of *Ursus americanus* east of the Mississippi and preserves one of the last vestiges of the original frontier of Colonial America. Northeast of the park the Smokies merge serenely back into the Blue Ridge and plunge into far eastern Kentucky and western Virginia and on northward through most of West Virginia and then spread and sprawl into portions of Pennsylvania and New York and Massachusetts and Vermont and New Hampshire and Maine before finally ending at the St. Lawrence River in southern Quebec one thousand-six hundred miles from north-central Alabama.

In western North Carolina the most scenic route through the Blue Ridge Mountains is the twisting pastoral Blue Ridge Parkway traveling the range's spine as it threads its way through forests velvet green in spring and rusty red-orange-gold in fall. The parkway was built by FDR's Depression-era Works Progress Administration and begins its northward meanderings on the Cherokee Indian Reservation in North Carolina just outside Great Smoky Mountains National Park. From there to the city of Asheville the traveler saunters along eighty miles of forty-mile-per-hour contour-conforming two-lane road through spectacular North Carolina scenery before reaching the historic city's outskirts and the unbelievably grand Biltmore Estate of nineteenth-century tycoon George Vanderbilt.

Nestled in hills bordering the French Broad River Asheville has long been popular with artists and musicians and writers. Famed novelist Thomas Wolfe called it home and spent his boyhood soaking up local gossip and watching local characters with whom he later peopled his first novel *Look Homeward Angel*. This set Haywood County agin' him and prompted his attempt to appease the hometown folks with *You Can't Go Home Again*. But this second novel failed to set things aright and Wolfe could only rest in peace once he was laid to rest in Riverside Cemetery near the grave of renowned short story author O. Henry.

A half-hour's journey south on Interstate 26 travelers encounter the exit for East Flat Rock and Flat Rock and Tuxedo which nuzzle each other in sylvan Henderson County. Most tourists head for Carl Sandburg's beloved pastoral farm Connemara where the famed poet and Lincoln biographer lived and wrote and where he died at age eighty-nine in 1967. This is the heart of the Cherokee Indians' ancestral homeland. Flat Rock itself got its name from the nearby large flat granite rock which the tribe considered sacred.

In Colonial America many settlers considered this large well-organized tribe "civilized" since its members lived in peace with most settlers and had adopted a republican form of government and Christianity and "modern" farming techniques along with a consuming thirst for literacy. Early in the nineteenth century this prompted the young United States to grant the tribe status as a sovereign nation and the protection attendant thereto. But in 1829 former Indian fighter Andrew Jackson was inaugurated president and gold was discovered on Cherokee land in northern Georgia. Three years later Jackson refused to enforce a Supreme Court decision favoring the Cherokee which presaged doom for this tranquil people.

By 1838 these events coupled with the westward push of settlers and sealed the tribe's fate. President Martin Van Buren ordered the United States Army to forcibly evict the Cherokee nation from the ancient homeland which these Native Americans had occupied for many centuries and to move them west by land and river over one thousand miles to the newly designated Indian Territory.

Beginning in May of that year and throughout the following winter troops under General Winfield Scott rounded up eighteen thousand Cherokee men and women and children and drove them westward like a huge herd of cattle on a brutal overland trek all the way to what is now northeast Oklahoma. With little food and almost no shelter, over four thousand died and their bodies were rudely dumped in unmarked graves stretching along the circuitous route from North Carolina through Georgia and Alabama and Tennessee and Kentucky and Illinois and Missouri and Arkansas. To this day the Cherokees still sadly refer to this infamous forced removal and the route traveled as the "Trail of Tears."

After spending several summers with his maternal grandparents on their Henderson County farm playing in the nearby lush woods, a precocious nine-year-old boy from Miami, Florida, stayed on to attend the fourth grade in Tuxedo. Back in Miami, on the night of his twelfth birthday, this lad told his deeply religious mother that he had had a vision in which Jesus Christ appeared to him and ". . . anointed me to preach the gospel."

One hundred and twenty-five years after the Cherokees were forcibly removed, this seventeen-year-old boy preacher, the son of a placid Cuban father and a domineering American mother, moved permanently from bustling Miami, Florida, to bucolic Tuxedo, North Carolina.

From that day forward, his pious Pentecostal-raised mother prompted him and then watched proudly as her first-born son went around Henderson County clutching his black Bible and proclaiming his vision and version of the Gospel of Jesus Christ as he pointed an accusatory finger at almost everyone unfortunate enough to be caught within eyesight and earshot of him, sinners all as far as an increasingly morally myopic Tony Leyva was concerned.

That fall Tony also began putting an end to the childhood innocence of ever-increasing numbers of young adolescent boys around Henderson County: After ingratiating himself with them, Tony then seduced and sexually assaulted trusting yet unwitting boys several years younger than himself. The majority of the boys he met at church, a pattern which "Brother" Tony—the Pentecostals' form of address for adult males in the Church—repeated hundreds of times during the next three decades.

Before he was finally stopped years later, Tony Leyva had been joined by other Pentecostal preachers who shared his voracious appetite for sex with young boys. Together these "men of God" wreaked untold emotional, spiritual, and sexual havoc on over eight hundred boys in thousands of oral and anal sex assaults on youngsters as the trio traveled through North Carolina, Virginia, Georgia, Florida, Alabama, Tennessee, and a dozen other states holding Holy Ghost revivals for the faithful.*

Before it finally ended, Brother Tony and his compatriots had created their own damnable "trail of tears" across the southeastern United States by seducing and sexually assaulting these naive, unsuspecting boys from simple, trusting Christian families, all the while repeatedly assuring the confused young victims that what they were doing behind locked doors was actually "God's special way for His people to love each other."

---

*In *Scout's Honor*, p. 32, Patrick Boyle states that experts "... know that molesters who have sex with nonrelated boys ("nonincestuous homosexual male pedophiles") have more victims, and abuse them more often, than any other type of sex abuser."

Boyle also quotes the FBI's Lanning as saying that such molesters are "the most persistent and prolific child molesters known to the criminal justice system. Depending on how you define molestation, they can easily have hundreds if not thousands of victims in a lifetime."

1

"He was first called on to preach when he was about a nine- or ten-year-old boy."

Mario Ivan "Tony" Leyva was born in Miami, Florida, on May 3, 1946, the first-born son of a curious couple from distinctly disparate worlds. His father, Mario, was a short, easygoing Cuban national from a quiet rural area on the island's coast one hundred miles southeast of Havana. As a young man out of work, Mario Senior had immigrated to the United States from Cuba during World War II to find employment in south Florida's wartime ship-building industry. While there he met, romanced, and married a young, attractive girl from North Carolina.

They were a strangely dissimilar pair: Mario, short in stature and easygoing in nature, spent most of his free time gathering with fellow Cuban expatriates at small ethnic Miami cafes to smoke hand-rolled Havana cigars and drink dark, thick Cuban coffee while catching up on the latest happenings in Havana. But Evelyn Sutton Leyva—who went by the name Ada—was tall and willowy, a determined, headstrong, very industrious woman who worked every day as a retail store clerk, homemaker, mother, and church member. Those who knew her found Ada to be supercilious and condescending, with a sharp edge only slightly tempered by an almost imperceptible sweetness.

By the early 1950s, Ada had given birth to three more children—two daughters and another son. And while Mario Senior truly loved his children, early on he had found the secret to maintaining his own marital harmony: he deferred all child-rearing decisions to his imperious wife. He was not given to argument, and even if he had been, Ada Leyva was a most formidable match for any man. But years later the younger Mario told his first wife that he had seen his father's lack of involvement with him differently. As she put it: "He said his daddy never had anything to do with him; he was always too busy." "Repressed" was the word Mario most often used to describe his father.

About Ada it could be said, to adapt a famous phrase, that hell hath no fury like a mother questioned about her motives for her offspring, for she had such set ideas about what her children should wear and eat and where they should go and not go, that not one was open to comment, much less discussion, even by her closest friends.

Her true pride and joy has always been her first-born, her "little Mario" whom she decked out in frilly dresses until he turned three, a fact substantiated by several family photographs. Ada went a step further to make certain that little Mario's outfits remained clean by decreeing that he should never, ever eat a candy bar, a rule so hard and fast that no member of her or her husband's family ever dared to challenge her. However, as a second grader the boy surreptitiously bought and ate a candy bar on the way home from school one day, but fearfully kept the fact from his mother as if it were a mortal sin. The first person he told was his wife twelve years later.

But Ada's real iron-clad intransigency lay in the area of religious training for all her children, something that she made very clear to her Catholic-born husband before even accepting his proposal of marriage. Ada had absolutely no use for his papist upbringing and made it infinitely clear that neither she nor any of "my" children would ever set foot inside a Roman Catholic Church. Instead, she would raise them in the same intolerant, hell-fire-and-brimstone, uncompromising Pentecostal atmosphere in which her parents had brought her up deep in the wooded mountains of rural western North Carolina.

Every Sunday, Ada took all four children with her to the nearby Pentecostal church for Sunday school and morning and evening services. On Wednesday nights they attended Bible study followed by another service, and they always went to the occasional week-long revivals that Ada loved so much. Ada also made certain that, starting as toddlers, her children learned and genuinely accepted her deeply held belief in accepting Jesus Christ as one's savior in order to achieve eternal salvation.

For Ada's children there were daily Bible readings and Bible study sessions at home, including memorization of selected passages of Scripture. Also, Ada had an entire litany of strict do's and don't's which she felt were required to live the "Godly Pentecostal life." And last but not least, Ada revered the crowning glory for any true Pentecostal: glossolalia.

Chapter 1

Though it is unkindly defined in dictionaries and by nonbelievers as "fabricated, nonmeaningful speech," Pentecostals and other fundamentalist Charismatic Christians consider glossolalia "the gift of tongues" as defined in Acts 2:4, when the Apostles gathered together in a room after Jesus' resurrection: "And they were all filled with the Holy Ghost, and began to speak with other tongues, as the Spirit gave them utterance." Ada proclaimed proudly years later, "All my children were saved and filled with the Holy Ghost at an early age. And Tony was just two when he begun to speak in tongues!"

With great ardor and zeal Ada Leyva was succeeding in thoroughly indoctrinating her children, most especially her first-born son, with her own peculiarly intolerant brand of Pentecostal faith. She fondly recalled: "Tony was definitely called to God! He was born a true prophet of God and that's followed him ever since the little fella was born . . . and even before he was born!"

But Tony—as his family began calling him by the time he started kindergarten—didn't view his mother very kindly in retrospect. According to Tony's first wife, "He told me that as far as his mother was concerned, she was never with him; she was always working. He don't want to hurt her, but from what he told me I think she's always been very overbearing to him."

Also—whether he can be believed or not is anyone's guess—Tony told his first wife that it was about this same time, i.e., when he was about five, that he experienced his first dark introduction to sex. If there was a perpetrator, Tony didn't identify the person to her. According to Tammy Sue, "He told me that he was molested in kindergarten. Just that he was molested in kindergarten and that he didn't want to talk about it."*

☦ ☦ ☦

Like most third grade boys, Tony enjoyed playing with his buddies after school; but unlike most of his peers, he especially enjoyed attending church and Sunday school since he saw how much his participation in both was a source of great pride to his mother. And Tony *always* did everything that he could to please his mama. In turn, Ada Leyva lavished most of her attention on her first born. For Tony, Ada felt and remarked to others, nothing was too good.

She was always baking special cakes and cookies for him, dressing him in the latest Sunday-go-to-meeting finery, and always making sure that

---
*Years later, Leyva would deny that he had ever been sexually molested.

his hair was neatly combed before they set out for church where, she said, "He was first called on to preach when he was about nine or ten years old."

But Ada delightedly dates the real genesis of her oldest son's preaching ministry to the night of his twelfth birthday. After he went to sleep—both Ada and Tony later claimed—Jesus Christ appeared to Tony in a dream and anointed him ". . . to preach the gospel." Of that vision his mother recalled, during a telephone interview in the summer of 1992,

> He come to me and he had a, you know, a special glow, and I just never seen it but just very few times on anyone's face. And he says, "Mama, the Lord called me to preach last night!"
>
> We'd been in a service the night before and after that vision he'd tell others about it and of course they's say, "Oh, yeah, he's going to be a missionary." But nobody really encouraged him. But I knew it and it just tickled me. I never did push him or never did, you know, persuade him in any way. It was all God! I just wanted him to be full as ever with the Holy Spirit!

But regardless of her insistence to the contrary, many family members and close friends recall Ada's constant stage-mothering of Tony as she relentlessly pushed him toward a Pentecostal pulpit.

✝ ✝ ✝

When school let out in early June of 1955, when Tony was nine, Ada accepted her parents' invitation for him to spend his summer vacation with them on their small farm near Tuxedo, North Carolina. Tony got to spend his entire vacation joyously climbing trees, tramping through the woods, and camping out with newly made friends. So, when his stay extended into September, requiring his enrollment in the fourth grade at Tuxedo Elementary, it didn't bother Tony one bit not to return to the frenetic city pace back in Miami. Truly, the lad felt that he had found heaven on earth for little boys like himself who so enjoyed being in the outdoors.

This was when Tony first met and became good friends with the girl who eventually became his childhood sweetheart, Tammy Sue Brown. "Tuxedo Elementary School; that's where we went to school together at in the fourth grade [and] that's where we met," she smilingly recalled. "Of course, we were going to church together then, too, in a little Pentecostal country church I was raised in."

Chapter 1

After finishing the fourth grade and staying on in Tuxedo the next summer as well, Tony had to return to his family in Miami. For the next few years, however, Tony returned to North Carolina and spent most of each summer vacation with his maternal grandparents, during which he would see and play with Tammy Sue. Said Tammy Sue, "Oh, yeah, every summer I saw him. And in between we wrote letters. I was supposed to be the only girlfriend he ever had. I don't know, I wasn't there. But we were childhood sweethearts!"

✝ ✝ ✝

During his early teens, Tony craved but failed to get the attention that all boys his age desire from their fathers—or, barring that, from the surrogate fathers whom many similarly deprived boys seek out. For Tony this deprivation became a void that was never filled.

Many would call Tony's father a henpecked husband: when he wasn't sleeping or eating he stayed away from home, and therefore away from Ada's opinions, dictums, and demands, usually going to his favorite cafe to join his Cuban friends. Sadly, by now Mario had become so set in his ways that he did not take notice of his son Tony's desperate efforts to establish a relationship with him. So, as do most such disinherited sons, Tony began searching for someone who would be a father figure to him. Someone who would validate his becoming a man, someone who would not just be a buddy to him, but take a genuine interest in him and treat him in a way Tony felt a real father should.

With such a plan in mind, Tony began actively looking for such a man. But, pitiably, he was downright unlucky.

Tony told his first wife that in the spring of 1960, when he was fourteen, he met a man who befriended him. A man whom he came to love and admire. But the relationship turned out to be one with a man who drew the emotionally needy teenager ever more deeply into his trust and confidence before coercing the confused adolescent into submitting to oral sex on a baseball field at his Miami high school.*

✝ ✝ ✝

---

*Once again, when confronted with this information years later, Leyva denied ever having been sexually assaulted.

From the time he was a baby, and continuing well into his grade school years, Ada Leyva bathed Tony and took great personal interest in dressing him for school, church, and Sunday school, and encouraging him to "always go a step beyond looking your best." As Tony grew older, this narcissism kept pace with his physical maturation as he strove always to be clean, well groomed, and well dressed, often to the point of very evident obsessive-compulsive behavior. Eventually this habit became an ingrained idiosyncrasy that many who have known Tony have seen in him throughout his life.

By the time this slightly buck-toothed lad had grown into a modestly handsome young boy of fifteen, it was at his mama's urging that he became "available" to preach at their own and other Miami-area Pentecostal churches, thereby completing the self-fulfilling twin prophecies of mother and son. For Ada, Tony's preaching in church was God's personal endorsement of her long-held wish for her oldest son.

About her son's preaching, Ada remarked: "Even my mother—a real saint of God—she said, 'Not because he's my grandson'—and this was when he was in his teens—she said, 'but I'd rather hear him than a lot of older preachers.'"

Thus armed with what she saw as a firm confirmation of her life plan for Tony, Ada never missed an opportunity to encourage her ever obedient son to foist what was actually her own view of scriptures and prophecies on unwitting preachers, church and family members, and even shoppers she and Tony caught by surprise when they went together to the grocery store in Miami. Thus Tony got an early taste of public ministry that stayed with him throughout his life.

By the time Tony turned sixteen in May 1962, he was going to church "every time they opened the doors." He always dressed in a suit and tie, regardless of how his peers dressed or how casual a particular church activity might be. Other church members now called him "Brother" Tony, the standard Pentecostal form of address for a male member of the church and a measure of respect which he greatly enjoyed and encouraged.

After all, church had become Tony's life's focus, the place where he preached, led Bible study, prophesied, spoke in tongues, and where he found that he could retreat into his religion and be safe from a world that he increasingly felt was dangerous, sinful, and hostile. Along with his black Bible, Tony's deep Pentecostal religion had become something that he always carried around with him, like a turtle its shell, everywhere he went.

Chapter 1

✝ ✝ ✝

In June 1963, Tony finished his junior year in high school. Many of his Miami friends and fellow church members alike breathed a collective sigh of relief when this self-ordained teenage preacher announced that he was moving to Tuxedo to live with his recently widowed grandmother and to help her around her farm. While most of Tony's peers acknowledged him to be a good Christian, his endless quoting of scriptures, incessant prophesying, and persistent preaching had worn very thin and even become an embarrassment to many.

But for Tony, fond memories of thoroughly enjoyable summers spent camping and hiking in Henderson County's back woods whetted his appetite for the move. But he also knew full well that among the local residents he would probably find greater acceptance of his intense, fundamentalist, Pentecostal approach to reading, studying, and quoting the Bible, and preaching "the Gospel of Christ crucified." Tony's ever-increasing habit of speaking in tongues and prophesying that he had indeed become "a true prophet of God" would appeal to many hardcore Pentecostals (and there were many there).

Once back in Tuxedo, "Tony hit the ground a-runnin'," his mother smilingly recalled as she talked about his preaching some of the regular services at the community's small country church as well as at some nightly youth services at other small Pentecostal churches in the area.

Initially, being preached to by this gangly teenage boy held a certain novelty for most members of the Tuxedo Pentecostal Church, but as he gained experience Brother Tony's appearances in other Pentecostal pulpits around Henderson County became more and more frequent. His sermons were filled with considerable adolescent exuberance, much scripture, but they had no focus. They featured his rote-learned, traditionally overwrought emotional delivery.

The compliments that church members gave Tony on his sermons encouraged the teenager to start preaching publicly around Tuxedo to try and save more sinners. He stationed himself first in front of the post office, then on downtown street corners, and next at the courthouse in Hendersonville where he was regularly seen quoting scripture, prophesying, and preaching to passersby.

Those who paused to listen to this local oddity quickly caught the teenage preacher's eye, much to their chagrin, and this in turn prompted him to begin wagging a scolding finger, upbraiding them for what he supposed were their sins. At this most quickly scurried away, learning, as one old-timer put it, "not to pay him no mind."

Tony soon discovered that the unchurched as well as the mainstream, traditional Christian Tarheels didn't take kindly to his raucous preaching around town any more than had those in Miami. In fact, some considered him to be a nuisance and complained to local authorities, but to no avail.

When Brother Tony preached he noticed that his self-evident narcissism experienced a tremendous rush from standing alone in a pulpit or in public at the center of attention. What fellow church members saw as his "brave witness for Jesus Christ"—on its own a good thing—Tony realized to be a pragmatic and confidence-building step toward achieving his and his mother's deeply held wish that one day he would be as famous an evangelist as was her idol, A. A. Allen.*

When he preached in public it didn't matter to Brother Tony whether his accusations of his listeners' sinful behavior were on target or not. Since the night Jesus Christ appeared to him in a dream at age twelve, Tony had convinced himself that just by preaching and waving his Bible in people's faces he was truly doing the Lord's work and that was all that he really cared about . . . *almost* all that he really cared about.

✝ ✝ ✝

As Tony had previously told his first wife, in the spring of 1960 he had been sexually molested as a fourteen-year-old. Since then, he confided to her, he had experienced an increasing urge to become sexually active himself. At first it was just a peripheral awareness. But as Tony's body matured, his sexual attraction to others grew; but he was initially frightened to realize that his sexual interests weren't like those of his peers: Whereas he occasionally had some sensual feelings for girls, Tony's primary sexual attraction was to young boys.

He knew this wasn't right or normal. And fear that somebody might discover it crowded his thoughts. Tony didn't know what to do. Telling his preacher about it was completely out of the question, for something that evil was not even discussed by Christians. But Tony's increasing attraction to young boys repulsed and panicked him since it so stridently conflicted with his strict Pentecostal upbringing and rock-solid beliefs.

---

*A.A. Allen was a famed U.S. Pentecostal tent evangelist of the 1940s and 1950s.

Chapter 1

Time and again Tony summoned all his might and courage to squelch his recurring urges for sex. He immersed himself in increased Bible reading. He prophesied more. He preached more. "Anything," he thought, "anything Christian that will mark me outwardly and inwardly as a true believer in Jesus Christ!" And then, like a mantra, Tony began saying to himself over and over: "I know that I am not a sex pervert! I am Brother Tony Leyva and God has ordained me to preach the Gospel of Jesus Christ!"

But as Tony inexorably moved toward sexual maturity, his desires to involve himself with young boys refused to go away. They presented themselves to his psyche day in and day out, and again and again with such ardor and frequency that the seventeen-year-old felt helpless to deal with them, and even briefly considered suicide.

These sexual desires had haunted Tony in Miami and shortly before the move to North Carolina, he worked hard to convince himself that things would indeed be different when he got there. But that did not happen, not even when Tony and his childhood sweetheart, Tammy Sue Brown, were reunited.

Ever since he had met pretty Tammy Sue in the fourth grade, Tony had felt some degree of emotional and sexual attraction to her. But when, like other teenage boys, he shut his bedroom door at night, lay on his bed, and occasionally masturbated, his erotic images were not of Tammy Sue or other girls, or even grown women. They were instead of boys of twelve, thirteen, and fourteen whom Tony had seen on the street, at the swimming pool, and in church where he found himself using them for his own version of spiritual inspiration, watching them while he preached.

Most of that summer, struggle as he might with this enigmatic juxtaposition of his strict Pentecostal upbringing with his ever-increasing urges to have sex with young boys, Tony's emotions were torn apart. He struggled mightily with what on the one hand he knew would feel good and on the other what his religious training very clearly told him was the right thing to do.

Tony was at a spiritual and sexual impasse with no satisfactory resolution to his dilemma in sight until finally, in August 1963, he began regularly and fervently praying to Jesus day after day, asking Him to "help me get right with God." After a week or so, God answered his prayers: He told Tony that he could indeed have relationships with these young boys as long as he kept them on a "strictly Christian basis."

Using will power and daily prayer to help, and with what he thought were the best of intentions—not to mention his personal charisma and charm—Tony Leyva began building relationships with young adolescent boys, relationships that he genuinely felt he could limit to Platonic, Christian friendships, even though these same boys were the subjects of his sexual fantasies each night when he went into his room and closed the door. Now, when Brother Tony saw a young adolescent boy whom he sensed craved his attention and love, he sidled up to him and assured the boy how much the Lord loved him and how uncommonly much he himself, Brother Tony—the Lord's on-site representative, as it were—loved him, too. And Tony was physically demonstrative about his love, freely offering the boy hugs, and embraces, and caresses.

Slowly at first, Tony drew the lad into a deeper level of trust by quoting scripture to him, teaching him the Bible, and prophesying to him, efforts which also engendered much parental appreciation and trust usually on the part of the boy's mother.

All of this happened in a simpler time, when children and adults took people at face value. And actually, most boys who knew Brother Tony back then remembered their initial relationships as being special, trusting, loving Christian friendships with someone whom they thought of as an older brother—a man of God who had come into their emotionally bereft young lives.

✝ ✝ ✝

That fall Tony enrolled in the twelfth grade at East Henderson County High School in Flat Rock to finish his secondary education, an academic career which continued to be mediocre at best. He didn't have time to read the poetry or biographies of Abraham Lincoln by Flat Rock's famed resident author Carl Sandburg; the classic American literature written by nearby Asheville's native son, Thomas Wolfe; or the acclaimed short stories by that city's adopted son, O. Henry. He didn't even learn the history of the area's legendary Cherokee Indians.

Tony's joining the Class of '64 held mixed blessings for his teachers and classmates. Tammy Sue Brown, however, was happy to have her boyfriend back attending school with her, noting how he provided her and her friends with regular, unorthodox class interruptions with his impromptu preaching: "Oh, everybody knew he was a preacher and they looked up to him," she recalled. "And they loved for him to get started in classrooms, 'cause if he ever got started talking about the Bible in classrooms they wouldn't ever have to have class that day. The other kids loved it!"

In an era before the U.S. Supreme Court was finally effective in removing religion from the public school classroom, the Bible was fair game for class discussions and Tony regularly used it. "Oh, then the teacher would get carried away for a while with him," Tammy Sue said, " 'cause, I mean, Tony was a talker. He really is. He can carry on a conversation till the cows come home! He's well versed in a lot of things. And he knows the Bible backwards and forwards. He's no dummy when it comes to the Bible!"

Between classes Tony would roam the halls looking for people to whom he could witness and preach, cornering teachers and students alike in his all-consuming desire to vociferously proselytize and preach his version of the Gospels—bits and pieces taken out of context and peppered here and there with admonishments to his listeners that they were "headed straight to hell" for their sins.

✝ ✝ ✝

As the autumn progressed, Tony continued to fool himself into believing that his friendships with adolescent boys to whom he was sexually attracted were nothing more than Platonic, Christian friendships and would remain so. Most were lads whom Tony had carefully chosen because they didn't have a father or, if they did, had a poor relationship with him. And he continued to ever so craftily engender trust in the boys' mothers.

Lavishing attention beyond his window-dressing teaching of the Bible—which in actual fact he rarely did anyway—Brother Tony fawned over first this and then that boy, doing small favors for the lad such as helping him with homework, buying him snacks and soda pop, and taking him to football games. And these attention-starved kids ate it up.

As the autumn air grew crisp and the surrounding mountain forests turned from deep velvety greens to shimmering reds and golds, Tony found it increasingly difficult to maintain a pretense of having nothing but wholesome Christian interest in these boys with whom he spent virtually every afternoon, evening, and weekend. These relationships and his obsessive dedication to the boys confused an already jealous Tammy Sue, although Tony repeatedly assured her that through these boys he was doing "God's work."

By November Brother Tony's desire for sexual intimacy with one or more of these young boys had become so intense that he knew his efforts to keep the relationships pure and wholesome were doomed. He also realized that to achieve his real goal of duping one or more of the boys into having sex with him would require his kindling in them an even deeper level of trust and intimacy.

So, Tony set to work concocting the perfect scenario, one whereby he could set a foolproof trap which would be inviting enough that, one by one, he could draw these boys into having sex with him. It didn't take Tony long to devise the ideal approach.

Remembering his own desire as a thirteen-year-old to learn how to drive a car, Tony realized that such an invitation would be an irresistible lure to any young adolescent. "Yes," he excitedly thought to himself, "I'll keep prayin' with 'em, quotin' the Bible to 'em, and prophesyin' to 'em. And then I'll promise to teach 'em how to drive! And then . . . !!" Brother Tony could hardly wait to spring his plan on one of the unsuspecting boys he had befriended and commit his first-ever act of fellatio on a child.

The next evening after supper, Tony told his grandmother that he needed to borrow her car "to go teach the Bible to this boy" and she was only too happy to lend it to her loving, devout grandson. Tony headed off to pick up his very first boy victim.

Arriving at the home of a church member who had just turned thirteen, Tony told the boy's grateful mother that he wanted to take her son out for "a soda pop and to help him memorize some scriptures." Of course, she said that would be just fine, and off the pair went.

But once in the car Tony told the boy that, if he could keep it a secret, he would take him out in the country and teach him to drive his grandmother's car. Smiling broadly, the boy happily accepted the offer. After a brief stop for sodas, Tony drove them up the highway, turning off onto a desolate mountain road he had craftily selected. Tony stopped the car and offered the boy the driver's seat. Gleefully the boy switched places with the young preacher and Tony helped his student shift into first gear and drive off to rendezvous with Brother Tony's now all but uncontrollable lust.

Fervently "witnessing in the Lord" all the way, Brother Tony continued his charade as Christian preacher, prophet of God, and "big brother," whose sole interest was the boy's salvation. But what the budding pederast and self-proclaimed prophet of God got when both arrived at road's end was a chance to slide the bewildered boy's jeans and underwear down, take the young lad's penis into his mouth, and then suck it until the trembling boy ejaculated into Tony's mouth—so, the preacher solemnly assured his trembling victim, "I can be filled with the power of the Holy Ghost to preach."

Then Tony pulled out the clean white handkerchief he always carried, cleaned up first himself and then, tenderly, the boy, and assured his shaken young guest that what he had done was "God's special way for His people to love each other." He quickly added that it was also "a secret God wouldn't want you to tell anybody about."

Brother Tony drove the confused boy home, hugging and kissing the youngster and reminding him of "our secret" just before letting the boy out. Then Tony drove back to his grandmother's house. Once there Brother Tony headed directly to his room, shut the door, undressed, lay down on his bed, and masturbated.

2

"He is truly inspired by sin!"

Tony soon had boy after boy accepting his offers to learn how to drive up remote dirt roads in the North Carolina countryside. He would teach them in his grandmother's car, spinning his mesmerizing one-on-one witnessing in the Lord, scripture quoting, and prophesying all along the way, and then, finally, teach the unwitting boy "God's special way for His people to love each other."

One such boy Tony seductively pulled into his web of deceit was Johnny Ray Williams, a thirteen-year-old living with his divorced mother, Betsy, and his seven-year-old sister, Melissa. Tony first spotted Johnny Ray with his mother and sister while preaching at the Tuxedo Pentecostal Church one Sunday. Leaning over the pulpit's edge as he drove home points in his extemporaneous sermon, the young evangelist espied his prey and from that moment forward couldn't finish his sermon fast enough.

With the last hymn sung, the grinning Brother Tony almost tripped as he rushed to the church door, keeping one eye on his prey as he smilingly greeted members of the congregation along the way. When he reached the exit, he made certain to stretch out his right hand directly toward the handsome young lad with long blond hair when he and his family approached.

Tony introduced himself to Johnny Ray's mother, and immediately asked her to introduce him to her son with, "What a fine looking son you have, Mrs. Williams!" Smiling even more widely, Tony reached out his hand right over Melissa's hurt gaze toward a beaming Johnny Ray.

Not noticing how he had singled out Johnny Ray, Betsy smiled back and introduced both her children to "the young preacher." After a quick "Hi!" to Melissa, Tony turned back to the still-beaming boy and asked his standard "Where's your daddy?"*

At this the boy's mood darkened; he lowered his head and mumbled, "He don't live with us no more." But to Brother Tony's face this brought an immediate, if somewhat smug, smile as the teenage preacher put a fatherly arm around the boy's shoulders, squeezed him comfortingly, and said, "Well, that's too bad, Johnny Ray. But I'll be your friend!" Right on cue, both mother and son beamed at the young preacher.†

For the next month Tony carefully fostered his new relationship with Johnny Ray, dropping by after school to take his new young friend out for soda pop and snacks, and then helping him with his homework. From the very start, Betsy saw how happy the teenage preacher's big brotherly attentions made her son and viewed the relationship as a most fortunate one for her older child.‡

Unlike most pedophiles and ephebophiles who seek such relationships, Brother Tony had a distinct advantage in being a man of God, a preacher, and among fellow Pentecostals, an acknowledged prophet of God. Most of his intended victims had heard him preach from their church's pulpit frequently and, therefore, he was someone whom his victims as well as his victim's parents trusted implicitly.

After a month of such contacts Tony was sure that Johnny Ray was emotionally in his thrall. When the opportunity presented itself, he progressed to another trick from his ever-developing bag by which he could access boys' bodies: One day Tony drove by school and picked Johnny Ray up after his seventh grade football team's practice. When he found the boy

---

*For many homosexual pedophiles, pederasts, and ephebophiles—i.e., men sexually attracted to adolescent boys—who cultivate seemingly benign relationships with boys, this is as much a gambit as the heterosexual male's opening line to attractive ladies in a bar: "Are you married?"

†In *Scout's Honor*, p. 86, Boyle points out: "With their gift of being able to reach and understand children, many pedophiles quickly pick up signals from the most troubled. 'Pedophiles are usually good at finding children who feel bad,' says Kay Jackson, counselor at [a New Jersey prison program treating pedophiles]. 'Pedophiles will tell you they can go to a playground and within two minutes pick out the lonely, vulnerable kids.' "

‡In *Scout's Honor*, p. 91, Boyle quotes FBI agent Kenneth Lanning as saying, "Very often, before you get far in the seduction of the child, you have to seduce the mother or father."

Further explaining this, Boyle, p. 87, states: "The next step [for men abusing boys] is to offer help, maybe take the boy off his mother's hands for an afternoon. [According to veteran California child abuse prosecutor Jill Hiatt] 'They're the ones who offer to take the kids away on weekends, who offer to babysit overnight for the parents.' "

limping from a pulled muscle in his thigh, on the way to the Williams's home he offered to "rub it and make it feel better." When they arrived, Johnny Ray's mother and Tony greeted each other warmly. She noticed her son's limp and remarked about it, at which the boy brightly remarked, "Brother Tony knows how to rub it and make it feel better." At this Betsy smiled and thanked the young preacher for his concern.

The preacher and his prey made their way to the boy's bedroom. With the door shut, Brother Tony had the boy undress down to his briefs and T-shirt and stretch out face up on the bed.

Brother Tony began massaging up and down Johnny Ray's leg, all the while carefully monitoring the boy's face for any sign of rejection of his progressive, tactile assault on the child.

Noticing nothing untoward, Brother Tony felt encouraged and asked the boy to roll over onto his stomach "so I can rub your back, too." Johnny Ray did so as the older teenager helped him to pull his T-shirt up and off. Then the real sexual assault began as Tony ran his hands up and down the youngster's back, purposefully letting them slip repeatedly down over the boy's brief-clad buttocks, the child molester happily seeing that this did not seem to concern his young victim.

In his own bed at his grandmother's that night, Brother Tony masturbated himself to sleep as he used his imagination to plan his final step in his progressive, safe seduction of Johnny Ray.

Later that week Brother Tony asked Johnny Ray out for a hamburger, fries, and malt at a local drive-in. While they ate in his car, Tony sprung his trap by offering to take the boy up into the mountains to a little-used road where, "I'll teach you how to drive the car." Just as Tony had craftily planned, it was a sure-fire lure for a boy like Johnny Ray: the lad excitedly took it hook, line, and sinker.

After a short drive Tony arrived at the desolate road, and told the grinning Johnny Ray to take his place behind the steering wheel, while Tony moved to the front passenger's seat. Jerkily the boy shifted gears and slowly drove off, but his preacher paid no heed. While adroitly witnessing to his otherwise engaged young guest about visions and prophecies and "my very special relationship with Jesus," gradually Brother Tony slipped his left hand from the boy's shoulder down his side to his thigh. Then—after noting the boy's continuing preoccupation with driving—he slipped his hand all the way down into Johnny Ray's crotch.

Brother Tony's witnessing had reached fever pitch, and he was beginning his pat little rehearsed speech about how Jesus had come to him in a vision and revealed to him "special things that He wants His people to know about." Seeing the awe on Johnny Ray's face, Tony proceeded to lay out the crux of what he had shrewdly crafted for his boy victims' introduction to fellatio.

"Johnny Ray, this is something *real* special that Jesus told me and He wants me to be *real* careful about who I tell about it." Right on cue Johnny Ray looked directly at him with wide-eyed wonder and responded, "Really? What is it?"

Tony smiled with pleasure at the lad's innocent curiosity and continued slowly drawing the boy in with, "Well, it's a secret . . . a *real* special secret. I don't know if I can tell you or not."

"You can tell me! I can keep a secret! Really, you can trust me!" Johnny Ray pleaded, almost running off the road.

Tony reached over and steadied the steering wheel as he smiled in erotic anticipation at the boy's enthusiasm, now that he saw the door open for him to have sex with the boy with little danger of Johnny Ray telling anyone. "I'll show you how to do it," Tony deliberately explained, and then cagily added, "But remember, it has got to be a secret between just you and me and God."

Feeling especially honored and privileged, Johnny Ray smiled broadly at the trust his Christian big brother was placing in him. "Yeah, Brother Tony! I'll keep it a secret! I promise! Cross my heart and hope to die!"

At this the lanky teenage preacher said, "There's a little road that goes off to the left up here. Turn down it and then pull off to the side and I'll show you all about how God wants us to love each other."

Excited at the prospect of learning more about Jesus and his special revelations to this mesmerizing "prophet of God," Johnny Ray Williams could hardly wait.

But once parked what happened failed miserably to measure up to the boy's anticipation. While Tony prattled on about how important this "special way of loving each other" is for "true Christians like us," Tony pulled the thirteen-year-old boy's jeans and underpants down to his knees and then did the same to himself.

Immediately the young preacher began masturbating his own penis with his right hand and took the startled boy's penis into his left hand and did the same. The evangelist murmured over and over to his trembling victim, "I love you, I love you, I love you," as he bent over the boy's lap.*

---

*In *Scout's Honor* Boyle quotes the FBI's Kenneth Lanning as saying: "There is no human being on the face of the earth easier to seduce than an adolescent boy in his early teens. They have an ease of sexual arousal. They're curious. They're exploring their sexuality. They sometimes have a need to be rebellious."

Afterward, Tony reassured the disquieted boy with considerable religious fervor that "this *really is* God's special way for His people to love each other." He further deceived the confounded boy by telling him that it had been necessary for the youngster to ejaculate directly into his mouth "so I can be filled with the power of the Holy Ghost to preach next Sunday."

Then Brother Tony pulled up his pants and told the thirteen-year-old to do the same. He reminded the perplexed Johnny Ray that since they were "God's special people," other folks wouldn't understand "what we did." Tony solemnly swore his young victim to total secrecy, dropping his voice conspiratorially: "You know, Jesus don't *ever* want us to tell anybody else about our secret."

While Johnny Ray tried with all his child's intellect to make some sense out of what had just happened between him and his Christian preacher-big brother, Brother Tony suggested that he start up the car and "drive down as far as the highway so we can get home 'fore your mother gets worried about us."*

✝ ✝ ✝

A cultural feature that played directly into Brother Tony's hands as he sexually assaulted boys in his church in Tuxedo, and later in similar congregations throughout the South, was that these lads had had ingrained in them the Southern rural male dictate that men and boys don't cry *and* that they keep whatever it is that's bothering them pent up inside and handle it all by themselves without tellin' *nobody* else, not even Mama or Daddy!

Also, Brother Tony was genuinely beloved and respected as a preacher and true prophet of God. He knew this, and used it to manipulate others—adults as well as children—at every opportunity, knowing full well that acknowledged prophets and their activities—no matter how strange they might seem—were sacrosanct to the faithful Pentecostal. He felt blessed and safe that he had found such an ideal environment in which to practice his twin, yet thoroughly incongruous, interests in life: preaching and having sex with young boys.

---

*Boyle writes in *Scout's Honor*, p. 44: "People generally don't think of molesters as seducers, but that's how they usually work. 'Pedophiles seduce their child victims pretty much exactly the same way men and women have been seducing each other since the dawn of mankind,' FBI agent Lanning says. They find someone they like, learn their interests, and 'begin to shower them with attention and affection and kindness. Or buy them presents and gifts. Gradually lower their inhibitions in ways that are fun.' "

Chapter 2

As Tony's first wife said, "I was supposed to keep my mouth shut. He told me, 'You're touching God's anointed if you say *anything* about me. Open your mouth and you'll be destroyed!' "

✝ ✝ ✝

Around Henderson County the number of boys keeping Brother Tony's secret about "God's special way for His people to love each other" steadily grew. By the spring of 1964 the special brotherhood walking in the halls of the Flat Rock Junior High School with this dark secret had reached several dozen. And all the while Brother Tony kept preaching more often at Tuxedo Pentecostal Church where the pastor became so pleased with the increased attendance—many to hear the teenager—that he began giving a small portion of the plate offering to Tony.

The farmers, blue-collar workers, widows, divorced ladies—especially single mothers with sons—just couldn't get enough of him, one recalling, "He preached the word of God and always took such an interest in our children—especially the boys."

It wasn't long before Brother Tony's popularity as preacher and prophet of God had spread to the point where he was receiving invitations to preach at revivals from the pastors of Pentecostal churches in surrounding communities, offers which frequently included sharing the standard plate offering on a fifty-fifty basis, the same share that regular traveling evangelists received.

In these new locales Tony ingratiated himself to one boy after another in what became an unbridled rush to find more boys to seduce, boys who didn't have a daddy, who were enamored of Brother Tony, and who for the most part were such devout Pentecostals that they wouldn't even *dare* question the actions of this true prophet of God, let alone tell his secrets to their parents.

Increasingly, Tony found himself spending little time cultivating these treasured relationships. Unlike before when he would patiently spend time prudently developing a friendship before exploiting the boy to satisfy his aberrant lusts, now he moved much more quickly, often having a new boy in bed within hours of meeting him. Unless, of course, his sensitive child molester's antennae detected some faint question, rejection, or a lack of trust in his latest boyfriend and victim-to-be.

✝ ✝ ✝

Immediately after graduating near the bottom of his class at East Henderson High in May 1964, it was an ambitious Brother Tony who, with his mother's encouragement, began a career as a small-time traveling evangelist by making the circuit of the scores of small Pentecostal churches scattered around western North Carolina.

Early that summer Tony's parents, brother, and sisters moved from Miami to Hendersonville, the county seat for Henderson County and just nine miles up the highway from Tuxedo. Even though at that time he had never held a revival more than two hours' drive from home, Ada Leyva bought her son a used car and proudly wrote to distant family and friends that Tony was traveling around "preachin' revivals just like A. A. Allen," comparing her eighteen-year-old son to the then dean of traveling Pentecostal evangelists. To hear Ada tell it, her Tony was a real expert on sin: "Not because he is my son, but he is anointed and he can teach against sin. He really teaches against sin. He is truly inspired by sin!"

Whether preaching one-day, three-day, or week-long revivals, Brother Tony's gravelly, charismatic voice and traditional rapid-fire delivery and command and recall of Bible scriptures drew ever-increasing crowds of men, women, and children to his host churches as word of this mesmerizing young evangelist spread. Said one mother, "He was like a breath of fresh air!"

For a full year Tony drove his car to communities like Brevard, Sylva, Mars Hill, Burnsville, and Rutherfordton to grace Pentecostal pulpits under the aegis of their resident preachers. Congregations that formerly had rarely topped thirty or forty on a typical Sunday morning now grew to over a hundred when dapper young Brother Tony took to the pulpit to preach one of his Holy Ghost revivals. As an added bonus, the collection buckets that normally gathered more jingling than folding money were muted by the number of greenbacks.

With the standard fifty-fifty split Brother Tony made a tidy fifty dollars or so if he preached on a Sunday morning, another forty dollars if he preached that night, and up to two hundred fifty dollars if he preached six or seven nightly revival meetings. Not bad in the rural South in the 1960s.

Brother Tony was happy preaching and prophesying and making good money holding revivals around western North Carolina, his narcissism fed by his respectability and acceptance by the area's Pentecostals. He especially enjoyed the covert fringe benefit of being able to select his next victim—though he never considered him as such—from the expanding pool of teenage boys in all the different congregations.

Having his own car made it easy for Tony to take his latest young friend in Forest City out to breakfast in the morning, pop over to Thermal City that afternoon to drive a twelve-year-old home from school, and still get to the church in Marion to preach at 7:30 that evening and to select a new boy.

About his charismatic effect on children at church services, Tony's mother, Ada, said years later: "You know, the children always called him 'Pied Piper' because, back at the very beginning of his ministry, it seemed like the children always flocked to him. They've always loved him. He's a very loving person."

But it was a vicious cycle: Brother Tony would preach and prophesy in a church and be praised and paid for it, all the while sizing up the boys in the congregation, deciding which one he would take as his next victim. After befriending them, he would take these virginal young sons of God's people alone in his car up remote dirt roads for a driving lesson, seduction, and sex. Then the cycle would begin again.

During that first year Brother Tony established one of the widest followings in recent years for any area revival preacher-evangelist, one that eventually carried him and his reputation well beyond the mountain communities of western North Carolina.

✝ ✝ ✝

After his first year on the road Brother Tony returned to Tuxedo with a tidy sum and, because it was the thing to do and the accepted lifestyle for a Pentecostal preacher, he courted and married his casual childhood sweetheart, Tammy Sue Brown.

Their honeymoon consisted of Tammy Sue's joining Brother Tony on his revival circuit as he preached and prophesied and—still unknown to her—continued seducing and sexually assaulting naive young boys while at the same time manipulating the boys' equally gullible parents for money in the form of gifts and donations to his ministry.

✝ ✝ ✝

Tammy Sue Brown was a thrilled, radiant teenage bride when she took to the road to cover the revival circuit with her new husband. She loved traveling through the gorgeous rolling mountains and lush forests of her native countryside with Tony by her side as they went from one revival to the next. She deeply respected and admired Tony as he spread God's word, preaching and prophesying to God's people.

Initially their itinerary included only modest independent Pentecostal churches scattered about the hills of western North Carolina. However, as Brother Tony's reputation steadily grew, they were soon ranging much farther afield and holding revivals in western South Carolina and southwestern Virginia as well.

Although she had heard Tony's sermons countless times, when they arrived at a revival site, Tammy Sue would again sit for hours on a hard wooden pew in the little country church, smiling and gazing lovingly at her new spouse as if it were the first time that she had ever heard his message.

In those days Tammy Sue was so filled with infatuation and adoration that she almost fell into a trance watching and hearing Tony speak in unknown tongues prompted by the Holy Ghost while the animated, spellbound congregation joined him. At times like these Tammy Sue felt that she might actually burst with pride at the realization that this really was *her* husband up there stirring up the Holy Ghost in these sinners who had come to be saved.

Raised up a Pentecostal herself, Tammy Sue knew full well how exceedingly influential and deeply esteemed such true prophets of God were. Indeed, the Pentecostal faith is as long on spontaneous bursts of uncontrolled emotion as the Roman Catholic Church is long on ceremony. And when her tall, dark, handsome groom began cavorting about the pulpit and aisles at a revival speaking in tongues and prophesying, Tammy Sue freely drank in her own portion of the praise and adulation his impassioned performance—there is no other way to phrase it—drew from the congregations assembled to see and hear this young phenomenon.

Seemingly, the people never could get enough of this upstanding, gifted, Spirit-filled evangelist she had married. "My husband" she murmured repeatedly to herself as she praised God for His allowing her to have such a mate for life.

After the revival services, Tammy Sue and Tony were frequently guests in the homes of various preachers and their wives. Tammy Sue was eager to learn from her hostesses what was expected of the perfect preacher's wife. As an observant guest she carefully watched and made mental notes about what these women did and did not do, said and did not say, adroitly perfecting and finessing her role as a wife to complement "God's anointed," her husband.

Chapter 2

In the early days, Brother Tony's Holy Ghost revivals were usually held in the sanctuaries of small Pentecostal churches. Typical was one he held in the Bryson City, North Carolina, Pentecostal Church in August 1965.

The church's regular attendance had flagged and the resident pastor contacted Tony to come and conduct a week-long revival in order to draw God's people back and to increase collections. The pastor had heard and liked the young man's preaching as well as his ability to stir up the Holy Ghost in his listeners which, he remarked to another preacher, was fast becoming a legend in the mountains of western North Carolina, not to mention the fact that having a phenomenon like Brother Tony would pull in folks from many other churches as well.

Allowing time for his mostly blue-collar congregation to get home from work, and then to get cleaned up and eat supper, the resident preacher scheduled the week of Holy Ghost revivals to begin at 7:30 on Monday night.

Fifteen minutes past seven, throbbing gospel music began greeting early arrivals. Freshly dressed in a three-piece suit and tie despite the summer day's lingering heat, Brother Tony strode confidently through the church's front doors with Tammy Sue following several respectful steps behind him.

His host's wife was playing the electric organ but it was the pair of fifteen-year-old boys accompanying her on guitar and drums that immediately caught Tony's eye. Beaming as if he had laid eyes on a couple of long-lost cousins, the evangelist strode expansively up to them. He began patting them both on the back and profusely thanked the grinning boys over and over, telling them how much "me and Jesus appreciate your gift of music here tonight." Only then did he step over to the preacher's wife and offer her a brief word of encouragement and thanks.

With the church's preacher following Tony around like a doting father, the evangelist walked to the pulpit, took the microphone in hand, and began pacing back and forth between the musicians and the pulpit as he made final plans for that night's sermon.

As more and more people filtered in, Tony pasted a perennially broad smile across his face and started strutting around the stage singing and occasionally pausing to greet some members of the congregation as they arrived. It was now 7:30—show time!

"He is able, He's a-a-ble, I know, I know He is able." Tony crooned in his gravelly though youthful baritone. Spotting a nicely dressed matron he waved politely and beamed, "Hello, Sister! So glad to have you with us tonight," before turning back to singing, hardly missing a beat, "I know the

Lord is able to carry me through. He healed the broken hearted, He set the captive free, He healed the sick, He raised the dead, oh, I know He walked on troubled seas...."

Soon Tony saw a well-dressed couple he knew and jumped down off the stage and smiled warmly, greeting them with, "Brother and Sister Jones, you just come right down here in front"—he patted the first pew—"so's you can hear real good."

Then jumping back on the stage he told the organist to pick up the tempo, and, with Tony singing, she swung into, "Glo-ry, Glo-ry, Glo-ry Hallelujah, since I laid my heavy burden down!" Bouncing on and off the stage, Tony put his microphone under one arm and began clapping in time to the music as he continued greeting arrivals and stirring up excitement.

The music segued from one booming gospel song into another as Brother Tony smoothly whipped the congregation to fever pitch. Soon the church was full and he was assertively encouraging them to "Raise up your hands and Praise the Lord!"

Noticing some reticent folks near the front, he ran over to them, microphone in hand, got right in their faces, and—as if they hadn't heard him the first time—smiled and shouted into the microphone, "Just lift your hands and shout your praise to God, brothers and sisters! Just lift up your hands and praise Him! Praise the name of the Lord!" Embarrassed and not knowing what else to do, they obeyed and a pleased Brother Tony leapt back onto the stage.

Pirouetting and shouting wildly "Praise Jesus! Praise Jesus! Praise Jesus! Praise Jesus! Everybody, let me hear you praise Jesus!" Tony got the congregation to begin loudly responding with their own "Praise Jesus" as he danced and twirled happily around the stage.

After ten minutes of this—satisfied that he had sufficiently primed his congregation—Brother Tony began delivering a rapid-fire, free-wheeling mixture of scripture and little sermons while prancing back and forth, his actions frequently underscored by heavy-handed riffs from the organist and guitarist with occasional rim shots from the drummer thrown in for good measure:

> Thou shall praise Him! If thou shalt turn loose of the praises! If thou shalt turn loose and worship me in spirit and in truth! If thou shall turn loose this night and glorify my name! If thou shalt praise and shake thyself in the Holy Ghost, saith the Lord thy God!
>
> For know ye that the Devil is angry, that he doesn't like revival, he doesn't like the love of God, that he would fight it, that he would discourage it!

But I'm sayin' to you, as the spirit of the Lord came upon Sampson, it comes upon you! Shake yourself! Shake yourself in the Holy Ghost! Come alive in the spirit tonight!

I'm lookin' for somebody to bless! I'm lookin' for somebody to heal! I'm lookin' for somebody to fill with the Holy Ghost! I'm lookin' for somebody to send revival to! I'm lookin' for a soul to encourage! Arise in the Holy Ghost! Put on the whole armor! Be thou victorious tonight! For I'm in the midst of travail!

I'll rebuke the devourer! I'll bring the deliverance unto thee! But praise me! Praise me! Praise me! Praise me! Praise me! Saith the Lord thy God! Wow-oooooooo! My God! My God! My God! Clap your hands in praise of God! Wow-oooooooo!

Taking advantage of the congregation's temporary rapture Tony had the organist, guitarist, and drummer continue building their crescendo, simultaneously reaching dizzying heights in volume and depths of musicianship. Then:

I want us to have a Holy Ghost Jericho march around the church. Right around the aisles. I want you to turn loose of the Spirit and praise God! Praise Him in the morning! Praise Him in the noontime! Praise Him in the afternoon! And praise Him in the evening time, tonight here!

Everybody, now, let's get up and let's march around and get the Holy Ghost all fired up! Praise Him! Praise Him!

Labo-sa-maca-da-sa-tini! Lomo-sa-ba-ta-macho-co-se! Labo-sabactini-lak-sa-di! Oh, we're marchin' in the Spirit, now! E-pago-sa-ba longo-sa-Lord! In the Spirit just praise Him! Let's all get in the Spirit tonight!

By this time, to the sounds of wild, frenetic clapping, almost everybody in the church boisterously was marching up and down the aisles in ecstatic "Praise to Jesus" and speaking in tongues.

Early in his traveling ministry Brother Tony had learned to lead off with bouncy, emotional renditions of gospel songs and hymns like those he now was using to build the Bryson City congregation's emotional intensity to a frenzy. In this way, over the course of the two- to three-hour service he could continue to be successful each time he passed the collection plate. Tony had also learned to break his sermon up into sections of gospel songs and witnessing. And he knew how to keep the congregants on the edge of their seats! As the service concluded that evening he told the congregation that—just like the old serials at Saturday matinees—"I will tell you the rest of this special message that God has sent me to share with you tomorrow night. Remember, that's at 7:30 tomorrow night!"

Night after night Brother Tony built the intensity of his singing, preaching, and prophesying and thereby enjoyed increased attendance through progressive services on Monday, Tuesday, Wednesday, and Thursday evenings. By the weekend, his was the best show in town and word of him had spread from the church's faithful to others throughout the area.

On Sunday morning the young evangelist preached for the last time. Delighting in seeing the dozens of youngsters scattered among the pews, he invited "the children to gather 'round me . . . 'specially the boys," one mother recalls. "He *always* seemed 'specially to want to meet all the little boys."

At the church door Tony reached out and pulled the church's young sons to him, as was his habit, totally ignoring their sisters. He held these boys to him, tousled their hair, and hugged them as if they were his favorite nephews.

Finally, after he had embraced the last boy—and noted down many of their names and addresses—the church's pastor and his family welcomed Brother Tony and Sister Tammy Sue to sit down at their table for a traditional Sunday dinner, the truest form of Southern gentility and hospitality.

On a dining table covered with a bright yellow oilcloth sprinkled with white daisies and set with Melmac and stainless flatware, each place had a tall, quart-sized tumbler of dark, sweetened iced tea and a large, fancy, folded paper napkin. The center of the table held huge platters and bowls of hot crispy fried chicken, deep-fried okra, homemade mashed potatoes, thick country gravy, blackeyed peas and smoked ham hocks, steaming ears of freshly boiled corn, and buttermilk biscuits. And, of course, there was homemade coconut cream pie for dessert.

As honored guest Brother Tony offered his fervent grace over the lavish spread, going on and on with such stilted eloquence and at such great length that the pastor's children sneaked peeks at the orator, hoping to see signs that the praying might soon end and the eating begin. Tony's interminable blessing finally ended, and with earnest "amens" all around, the feast began.

During the meal polite conversation ranged around such topics as gossipy news gleaned from church members after the service and discussion of Brother Tony's sermon, the various scriptures he cited, and the number and names of those people who responded to the altar call and accepted Jesus Christ as their Lord and Savior, each name accompanied by fervent acclamations of "Praise Jesus!" The pastor and Tony initiated and dominated the real discussions while their subservient wives smiled approvingly and added frequent supportive codas of "Amen" and "That's right, Brother Tony."

✝ ✝ ✝

Even though Tammy Sue's mother missed having her at home, it thrilled her to have her daughter married to such a fine, up-and-coming Pentecostal evangelist and prophet of God as Brother Tony Leyva. And she felt it an honor that her daughter did God's work by serving this respected young man as his wife.

As a dutiful, submissive, Christian, Tammy Sue also felt measured pride in her role as the obedient, devoted spouse, just as her mother raised her to be. And she kept telling herself that, just like Tony's preaching, her own role fulfilled God's will and purpose.

During her occasional visits home Tammy Sue continued assuring her family that she cherished her husband and that touring with him as he spread God's word and prophesies made her life spiritually meaningful beyond compare. But deep down Tammy Sue began to wonder why whatever she did for Tony never seemed to be enough. Why did he correct her when what she had done had been done in love and to the best of her abilities and training? Why was he so much more loving toward the young boys he encouraged to flock to him at the revivals than he was to her, his own wife? And why did he always get so upset with her—loudly reciting scripture to her to set her straight—whenever she meekly questioned these things?

When Tammy Sue visited her mother she addressed these concerns, but the response she always got was, "He's just under a lot of pressure doin' the Lord's work, honey. Love him and support him in what he does." When the Leyvas hit the road again for the next revival, praise for Brother Tony and for her, his wife, once again convinced Tammy Sue that quietly taking care of her husband was truly God's will. Time and again the churchwomen told her how much they admired—coveted, actually, but that was a sin to which they would never admit—her work as the wife of "such a fine preacher and true prophet of God."

✝ ✝ ✝

For Tammy Sue, her husband's intense attention to the young boys he encouraged to flock around him amounted to almost total neglect and had become almost too much for her to bear.

Throughout Tony's philandering with young boys, Tammy Sue had tolerated her husband's behavior since, like most strict Pentecostal couples, casual marital sex was not a priority. But now the religious aura that had surrounded their marriage was about to crack. As Tammy Sue put it, "So, I'm the subjected wife with an overbearing husband. He says, 'God talks to me! God don't talk to you!' He says, 'You gotta listen to me!' And I'm supposed to keep my mouth shut?"

But then, after a little more than a year on the road, two dramatic changes came into the couple's lives: In 1967, Tony got his first pastorate, a small Pentecostal church in Fletcher, North Carolina, twenty miles north of Tuxedo, and Tammy Sue learned that she was pregnant with their first child.

Being just twenty miles from her family gave Tammy Sue added comfort during her pregnancy. And Tony was thrilled to have his very own church pulpit. And soon he was blessed with a child of his own.

3

"If I'd gotten close enough to that son-of-a-bitch that night, I'd'a done blowed his head off."

It confused Tammy Sue when she and Brother Tony's baby son did not become her husband's top priority. She had thought that with her husband's extraordinary love for children—especially little boys—having one of his own would refocus his love and affection to within his now growing family and, Tammy Sue had hoped, herself. But shortly after Mark's birth his young father took an inordinate liking to eleven-year-old Anthony Grooms, the second son of Mary Lou Grooms and her husband, Percy, in Fletcher, North Carolina.

This happened soon after Tony Leyva's arrival in the area to put down roots and establish his unique, charismatic ministry as a pastor in his own right. And it wasn't long before Mrs. Grooms and all her children became enamored of this outgoing young preacher barely out of his teens, who always had time for the church's children and young people.

Anthony Grooms became the first of Brother Tony's child molestation victims to come forward and openly accuse the evangelist, an event that forever seared itself in both Anthony's and Tony's minds. In every sense a genuine North Carolina "good ol' boy," Anthony tells his story in a style that would remind you of comedian-actor Andy Griffith.

According to Anthony, "The first time that I can recall meetin' Tony Leyva was when I was twelve in 1966 in a tent revival of his that was bein' held in Fletcher there where we lived. Mom and Dad had heard him and really liked him at church up in Brevard or over to Hendersonville, I forget which.

"My brother Alexander was fourteen then and he was a musician and very talented for his age. And I don't know how the meetin' between him and Alexander come about or how he had come to ask Alexander to play the organ for him. Evidently, Tony had heard Alexander play at a church for somebody else, but Alexander played the organ for Brother Tony at that revival of his. We helped Tony—a group of young boys around the community there, myself and my brother and some neighbor boys—we helped Tony put up his tent. But that is the first time I can remember goin' to a revival meetin' of his and hearin' him preach, there at that tent revival.

"But it seems like it was a three- or four-week thing that that there revival was runnin' there in Fletcher. And we went a lot, Mom and us kids because, of course, Alexander was playin' every night. Then . . . Tony went from there to somewhere in South Carolina to set up his tent for another revival. I can remember goin' there with a neighbor friend's mother and her boy and Alexander to help Tony set up.

"Then shortly after that—it was within a six months' span—Tony opened up that little, small church in a vacant buildin' there in Arden that they used for a church right there between Fletcher and Arden. And it was when he set up this church of his that I got to know him better. And there was a little house-type buildin' on the premises that was detached from the buildin' they used for the church and that's where the first episode of him with myself ever took place."

But before that occurred, Tony, true to form, spent time carefully and steadily ingratiating himself with members of his new church's congregation, especially with those young families with male children. In his youth he had been somewhat brash in rushing into sex without laying a trusting foundation with his victim, and, he felt, that had almost led to tragedy a time or two. So, at twenty-one, Tony Leyva began to learn that patience was the key.

Alexander played the organ for Brother Tony's services while Anthony couldn't do enough for his idol as the preacher's adoring gofer. But it always seemed that while Tony had plans for the boys in the congregation, the girls—including Anthony and Alexander's younger sisters—were frequently disappointed at being left out.

However, Mary Lou felt very pleased that such a positive, Christian relationship was rapidly developing between the new preacher and her sons since her husband's drinking was becoming such a problem that she and her children made a point of avoiding contact with him whenever he got drunk, which was happening more and more often.

Anthony's initial impressions of Tony were that "he was real attentive toward the young people in respect to tryin' to have them involved in his services . . . mostly the boys, as I recall. He had youth groups and youth choirs and things like that and showed them special attention. And he sent out little flyers or mailers about special events comin' up and sometimes we kids would help him collect up information. Everybody got involved, or seemed to be allowed to be involved in the things that went on at the church."

For Anthony this was an opportunity to get away from his less-than-positive home environment, which made him feel good about himself. "I had a very disruptive life at home with my dad," he painfully recalled, "so that sorta made me feel important and a part of it when Tony would do things with me. That was the way in which he would find kids that had some problems at home with their parents or the parents didn't get along . . . things like that. Those were the vulnerable ones that he took to.

"But in any event, at home it was a situation where a lot of drinkin' and stuff like that was goin' on with my father. When we were younger there was a time when he wasn't drinkin', but then it would be from one extreme to the other. When I was eight years old, my father began to drink again and there was never no closeness with him after that. Usually he drank just beer, but he would drink anythin' he could get a hold of. But he would buy just beer.

"There was not a whole lot of violence in that situation, but some, you know, as far as the physical aspect. And as an eleven-year-old, I didn't have no relationship with my father. In fact, I was scared to death of him. Not so much for myself, but we was all scared to get him upset because the end result was that Mama would catch the brunt of it. You know, we'd get a spankin' or somethin' like that, but not what you'd say was bad physical abuse or nothin'. He wasn't violent towards us, but he was just real violent towards her. It was his way or no way."

After several months cautiously grooming the ever-increasing trust and admiration of his young friend Anthony, Brother Tony felt that he could make his move, so seemingly innocuous that Anthony recalled, "Honest to God, I can't remember how I come to be there [at the church] that particular day! But it wasn't uncommon for one of us boys to be up there around the church mowin' the yard or sweepin' or cleanin' up or somethin' of that nature or for Tony to stop by the house and say, 'Boys, you ain't got nothin' to do tomorrow. You want to go with me and help clean up at the church?'

"Nobody ever suspected anythin' or was concerned because he had a unique way of gettin' over to the people and gainin' their trust, even the adults. Otherwise I don't think people would have been so easily misled or would have let their kids go with him. And he had me alone with him when this happened.

"It was around tax time in the spring of 1966 and they was gonna audit him and he was dealin' with a lot of figures. He was tryin' to get all of his deals and donations together for tax purposes. And there was this house that was with the facility that was the church and it had been converted and it was one or two rooms for like Sunday school and then there was an office set off in one corner. And it was in this office where I was workin' cleanin' up and he was askin' did I want to help him do the totalin' of these figures.

"And he was at his desk and had me sit beside him at the desk with an old mechanical, button-type addin' machine where you push the buttons and pull the lever. And he was callin' out figures and I was pushin' the buttons and pullin' the lever and we was addin' all these figures up. Then he asked me to move around a little closer to him. He made some sort of excuse that he wanted to make sure that I was totalin' up the numbers right. So then we ended up real close and side by side with him still callin' out the numbers and I would put them in and pull the lever.

"And, uh, that's how the situation began. And we was still sittin' there and he put his hand on my leg and started feelin' into my groin area and he didn't say why it was that he was doin' that. Then he just got up and locked the door that come into the office with a slide bolt and came back and sit back down beside me and proceeded on with the figure thing. And then I guess he was becomin' more and more excited with himself and he said let's get up and sit on the couch there and rest awhile because they had like a couch in that office like you got in a livin' room along with a couple of settee chairs.

"And then that's the point where he began to pull my jeans and underwear down. And he didn't explain anythin' to me and I didn't ask him anythin'. I pretty well knew at the time that I was there by myself 'cause I don't recall seein' anybody else there that day. And I was pretty much scared, to tell you the truth. I didn't know what was goin' on.

"I trusted him and I thought the world of him at that time. I had heard talk of people bein' called weirdos and queers and stuff like that back then, but I never heard him called that. Unt-uh! I had just heard that term before, but at that time I didn't know beef from bull about it! I was probably more concerned that I would do or say somethin' wrong and offend him because I really did look up to him. He was always somebody who made everybody feel important, especially somebody who didn't have anybody, like me . . . anybody to show him some attention . . . and he did show me some attention. So, I guess that's why I let it happen.

"He said let's just rest awhile and then, uh, then it began when he undid my jeans and pulled them down and my underwear down. And then he said, 'Just lay down here and rest. It's a little hot in here.' And I was layin' down there on the couch and then that's when he performed the oral sex on me.

"But while he was doin' it, some instance happened. I can't recall exactly what it was. Either the phone rang, a car pulled up in the driveway, somebody knocked on the door, or somethin'. He was into the act as far as my penis penetrating his mouth, but no ejaculation had taken place. . . . But the situation just interrupted him there for a split second for him to see what was goin' on and I got up and put my pants on and got out of there.

"But, as far as he bein' finished, no he hadn't; but I got up and unlocked the door and ran out of there and went home. And he didn't say nothin' to me till later when he made the clear comment to me not to make no mention of what had happened to anyone.

"So, I didn't say anythin' to my mother right away, but it was a short time later—I would say two or three weeks or somethin' like that—before I did because I started not to attend church or any of the little youth group meetin's or Sunday school programs that he held. And at first I just told my mother, 'I just don't feel like goin'.' And Mom asked, 'What's wrong?' And I guess she could see that there was somethin' other than just my gettin' tired of goin' to church behind the scenes there, so I finally told her the situation of what exactly had happened to me.

"And she was furious! She must have contacted him by phone 'cause a few days later he did come by with his wife, Tammy Sue, to our house to apologize. But he never came right out and made any apology about what he had actually done to me. It was just an act. He just said, 'I apologize to you and your family and your son for whatever problems I've caused.' But he never did say nothin' about 'I'm sorry that I molested your child' or nothin' about that.

"On the day that he came to our house to make his apology my dad wasn't much [for] any of that mess, you know. And there was a cousin of mine there who had been made aware of the situation—and I can't name his name—but he was there with the intent if Tony got out of hand, it was the situation that my cousin intended to kill him then and there.

"But before all that happened Mom had talked to an attorney in Hendersonville about prosecuting him for this thing, but he just basically—from what Mom told me—the attorney said that there ain't no way you can beat this: 'He's an upstandin' Christian preacher in the community, well known and well liked.' It would be your boy's word against his.'

"And he told Mom, 'You and your son come from a pretty rough family and we know Brother Tony comes from a good family.' And the attorney made me look like the villain. And he said that it would be very hard to prove, and that's not countin' the court expense to prosecute it. And that was just basically it.

"And after that Mom never did go to church as much as she used to."

✝ ✝ ✝

In April 1989, Mary Lou Grooms met with me at a restaurant in Hendersonville, North Carolina. She was racked with emphysema and worry over her terminally ill husband whom she had left alone at home, but she was insistent that she meet with me so that I could interview her and get her story. Said Mary Lou, "I want to give you my two cents worth about that son-of-a-bitch!"

During my brief meeting and interview, Mary Lou said, "Back when he done that sex stuff to my boy Anthony, I wanted to take a gun and blow his brains out for what he done to my little boy. And then when he and his wife came over and he tried to apologize for what he done—and there ain't no apologizin' for that kind of stuff—but he thought he'd try anyway, and my husband had to stop me from takin' his pistol out of our bedroom and blowin' his head off."

Suddenly seized by a terrible coughing fit, Mary Lou reached under the table and struggled to raise her huge handbag, finally plopping it down on top of the table. Still coughing, she reached into the bag and began pulling out the biggest, meanest-looking pistol I've ever seen. Then as I looked about nervously to see if anyone might be watching, she summoned all of her strength to stop coughing and flourished the heavy pistol in her hand as she said in a rasping voice: "But if I'd gotten close enough to that son-of-a-bitch that night, I'd 'a done blowed his head off and he wouldn't 'a ever again molested no more kids!"

When I shared this story with Anthony in 1993, he said apologetically, "When she gets emotional like that she's not very stable and she's difficult to deal with. She can't think of the right thing to do and she may do the wrong thing."

I assured Anthony that what his mother said showed not only that what had happened to him as a child all those years before still hurt her deeply but, also, and more importantly, revealed the continuing, deep love of a mother for her child.

Thinking of his mother, who was at that time terminally ill, Anthony lowered his voice and replied softly, "I know, I know. She's a good mama."

✝ ✝ ✝

Anthony also recalled that he wasn't Tony's only victim around Fletcher: "I'm certain that there was a lot more boys he abused there, but I was the only one who'd really talk out about it.

"Now back there in about 1966 there was also this young teenage boy from Asheville. His parents had evidently heard Tony in previous services and they began attendin' and their son played the accordion for Tony. I don't know if Tony ever did anythin' to him, but he did travel a lot with Tony when he went elsewhere from the church to hold revivals. And then, all of a sudden, the boy he quit a travelin' with Tony and he wouldn't talk as to why.

"At that time they wasn't doin' a lot of revivals, but my brother, Alexander, did travel some with Tony in a tent revival. They had those travel trailers they stayed in at the tent and Alexander stayed with Tony. But Alexander says that Tony never done anythin' to him."

Though the subject was a very tough one, listening to Anthony's accent and masterful storytelling made you feel like putting your feet up in front of a fire in a cabin way back in the Blue Ridge Mountains and letting the inky night outside drift by. A salt-of-the-earth fellow with a loving wife and children of his own, Anthony approached what had happened to him as an impediment, yet not a roadblock to leading a full life as husband, father, and friend.

"But then there was a family of Myers"—David smoothly shifted tales—"and they was like four boys and four girls. And they had come to know Tony even before we did. And this Myers lady had some trouble with her husband and they separated and Tony went down there to Georgia and physically moved this lady and her children up here to North Carolina. Their family situation was a lot like ours, but probably more severe since it justified her movin' away from her husband.

"And I know for certain that Tony was sexually involved with all of the Myers boys. There's no doubt in my mind about that! He was involved with those boys and he moved them up here to get better access at those boys. There is no doubt in my mind, because after Tony left Henderson County all of that stuff about them brothers as well as other boys livin' 'round here came out. And that mother and her children lost faith in Tony and they moved back to Georgia.

"And the reason I know this is when I was about fifteen Mrs. Myers hired me to help her move them back to Georgia. On the way the oldest boy done told me what Tony . . . done to him and his brothers. He said that Tony fondled them all and tried to have oral sex with him and his brothers."

✝ ✝ ✝

In 1993 I asked Anthony how he had managed to handle what Brother Tony had done to him through the nearly thirty years that had passed since that spring day in 1966, and he said:

"Well, I don't know if I dealt with it in the proper way. I think that probably I should have maybe had some counselin'. But, like I say, I know that it was discouragin' to Mama and to find out what the lawyer told her, you know, that this kind of thing is virtually useless to pursue and not to say anythin' about it.

"But, all of us kids were pretty much on our own 'cause if you had a problem you had to deal with it 'cause of the situation at home. I know that Mama probably done all that she could do for us, as best she could do. There was four of us kids she had to look after and so this just made that much more of a burden for her.

"And I feel that because of what happened to me I've always had to keep people at arm's reach. Now, I try very, very hard to talk to my children, honest and open about anythin' they want to talk about, from drugs to sex to problems at school, hopin' that they won't feel that they can't come and talk to me. Now, I can't say I wasn't afraid of Daddy beatin' me or anythin' like that, but [back then] I was just afraid of him and just couldn't talk to him.

"Oh, what happened to me shook me down and I've still not got over that. I attend church some, but nothin' like a person should devote . . . to a church and their belief. . . . I've always been lax about tryin' to get involved again with any church, which is wrong. That's not right! It shouldn't be used as an excuse. I just spent most of my life tryin' to forget it."

✝ ✝ ✝

Tammy Sue Brown remembered Anthony, the hell he went through, and her own struggle with forgiving her young husband for his indiscretion, remarking to me in 1989: "The little Grooms boy . . . was the first one that Tony molested after we moved to Fletcher. He helped Tony at the church; supposedly, helped Tony do some stuff at the church, and that's how he come to be alone with Tony and how come Tony was able to [have] done those things to him. And he's the one that Tony told that God let him do that because he needed release.

"And I liked to have died havin' to go over to the Grooms place with [Tony]. But after we got back, Tony got down on his knees and begged me to forgive him. He said that he'd never done nothing like that before, that he didn't know why he done it then, and that he never would do anything like that again.

"And like a fool, I believed him and forgave him."

✝ ✝ ✝

Soon Tony discovered a new way to deceive his ever-growing numbers of followers: fasts. For weeks he would announce in church that he was going on a "forty-day fast in the wilderness, just like Jesus done," and ask the congregation to fill his "special fast envelopes" with money for his ministry.

Then when the appointed day arrived, with great fanfare Brother Tony departed for a trailer or cabin back in the woods, proclaiming that "nothing but water will pass my lips!"

But once ensconced in his hideaway, he drank fruit juice, soda pop, malts, shakes, and as several former supporters admit—occasionally ate catered steak dinners provided by his wife and others. (One time, a follower said, he got mad when she brought him a complete steak dinner including a baked potato, but forgot the sour cream. "Boy, was he pissed," said the woman.)

Tammy Sue even dealt with several of Tony's fasts, recounting to me: "Well, I'd been married to him for a year when he had the first one. He had a vision from God about it and then went on this forty-day fast.

"I had to go and live with my mother. I wasn't allowed to be around him. I was his wife but he said God told him that I couldn't be with him during his fast. And he had this travel trailer parked back up in the woods. He said that he didn't eat, okay? He really didn't that time. He drank fruit juices and water. I'm serious, 'cause he lost a lot of weight.

"But me, his wife, he couldn't have me around, but he could have little boys come see him while he was on this fast. And this was when he first molested boys [after we were married], but I didn't know this until later. I believed in Tony then. Back then I thought Tony Leyva was a saint of God!

"And besides them little boys that went to see him at first, I come to find out that he had a bunch of other little boys traipsing out there to visit him at that trailer while he was on this fast: Melvin Morse, Jimmy Powell, Lenny Jessup. They all lived on the river down there!

"But he had them all come out to that trailer and take off their clothes and then's when he molested them. . . . And here he was, a preacher of God out there fastin' and molestin' little boys!

"But I can't tell you about all the bad things what happened in that trailer 'cause I wasn't allowed to go around there for them forty days." She added sarcastically, "I was just his wife, ya know."

✝ ✝ ✝

One of the many stories Brother Tony's victims kept hidden for years dates back to 1966, and took place in Tuxedo when this victim was thirteen.

He was one of the boys Tony attempted to seduce and sexually assault that year while on one of his fasts at an old weather-beaten cabin back up in the mountains outside of town. But the boy successfully resisted Tony's efforts and got away.

Five years later, in 1971, Tony came by the then nineteen-year-old's house one Friday afternoon while the older teen was at work and offered to take his thirteen-year-old brother "out campin' and to study the Bible" over the weekend at an old, remote cabin up in the mountains. The boys' mother—not knowing what had almost happened to her oldest boy five years before—was quite happy to allow her youngest son to go off with this fine young preacher and evangelist about whom she had heard so many good things and whose preaching she had felt so blessed by on several occasions.

So, Tony and his young guest left for a weekend together soon after the lad got in from school. But when the older brother returned from work a few hours later and learned that Tony had picked up his kid brother "to go off campin' for the weekend," he knew immediately what the reason for the trip was and where they had gone: the same cabin where Brother Tony had tried to molest him as a thirteen-year-old.

Telling his mother that he and his thirteen-year-old brother had made other plans for the weekend, the young man wasted no time rushing off in his pickup in a steady rain to fetch his little brother from Tony Leyva's clutches.

Chapter 3

The old one-room cabin was so far back in the thickly forested Blue Ridge Mountains that the road ended before he got there, forcing him to walk the last half mile. By now the weather had turned even nastier, with a slanting rain mixed with hail pelting down from lowering clouds.

The young man parked his truck. Although on the drive up he'd planned to arm himself with it, he left his shotgun on its rack because of the wet weather. Pulling his collar up around his neck, he began slogging uphill.

When he got to the gray, weathered cabin, he could hear nothing other than the drumming of rain and hail. He ran around to the shack's only window and peered inside. Dimly visible on the floor was a large blanket covering a lumpy mass on an old mattress. Then the mass started moving up and down. The young man jumped onto the front porch, jerked open the cabin door, ran inside, and snatched the blanket back.

In the middle of this lumpy, stained mattress was his brother face down with Brother Tony—Bible in one hand—on top of the boy. They were both stark naked. Cursing and swinging, the older brother kicked the preacher away, grabbed the boy, and told him to get dressed. While Brother Tony backed toward a corner apologizing and begging forgiveness, the young man let the evangelist know in no uncertain terms, "I'll cut off your nuts if you ever so much as phone our house again."

Clutching his hastily dressed little brother to his side, the trembling youth rushed out of the cabin and the two ran through the whipping rain and hail down the hill to their pickup. On the way home, they agreed never to tell their mother the truth about Brother Tony and what he had tried—on separate occasions and five years apart—to do to the both of them.

✝ ✝ ✝

During the next two years Brother Tony engineered scores of more successful secret manipulations of Anthony's friends and other young boys from Arden, Fletcher, Skyland, Mountain Home, Hoopers Creek, West Haven, Mills River, and many of the small surrounding communities close enough for their families to attend this "fine young preacher's church." Unknown to many of these families, the preacher moved stealthily through the area's pool of prospective "candidates" and became increasingly emboldened with each successful seduction, feeling ever more self-confident in his quest to surreptitiously single out naive young adolescent boys as his victims.

Before long, parents were vying for the privilege of having Tony take their young sons out on his increasingly popular camping trips deep into the surrounding Blue Ridge Mountains "to study the Bible," treks on which he became so audacious as to commit oral sex with two and three boys at a time.

All the while Brother Tony continued to explain to his victims that their sex was "God's special way for His people to love each other," warning that "God wouldn't want you to tell" until he felt Henderson County held no more safe youngsters from whom he could pick. With this he felt compelled to select fresh victims from the Pentecostal congregations outside of Henderson County that were now inviting him to preach.

✝ ✝ ✝

In addition to needing new boys, Brother Tony realized that tithes and plate offerings at his little Fletcher church could never meet his increasing desire for the finer material things in life and that he could do much better on the revival circuit. Therefore, much to his wife's chagrin, in 1969 Brother Tony packed up his little family and hit the road once again.

Over the next few years Pentecostals from Virginia to Florida came to know and appreciate Brother Tony as an evangelist and prophet of God, a reputation he took pains to enhance at every opportunity. Previously he had preached under other evangelists' tents, or rented one, but soon, just like P.T. Barnum over a century before, he purchased his own big top—"like a circus tent," Tony himself told me in 1989—to begin spreading his wings and holding his Miracle Restoration Revivals in Bible Belt towns throughout the South.

Having his own tent enabled Tony to keep all of his collections, paying out only his own direct expenses: a plus considering his twice- or thrice-a-night collections—depending on the frenzy into which he could whip the crowd.

Of course, this necessitated Brother Tony's buying a truck to carry his new tent as well as an assortment of used crutches, wheelchairs, braces, and even hearing aids and spectacles as thick as the bottoms of pop bottles. These were the props used by the ringers Tony hired to achieve instant "cures."

Although Tony had also purchased a used motor home for himself and his family, which now included just-born daughter, Rachel, the life of a religious vagabond did not appeal to Tammy Sue. She and the children rarely accompanied him. Undeterred, Brother Tony went on his own to join that strange band of charlatans, con artists, faith healers, and preachers of loosely identified, nondenominational Pentecostals traveling from town to town around the country holding revivals wherever the financial take and, in Leyva's case, the selection of attractive, gullible, young teenage boys was sufficient to satisfy his desires.

As Tony learned, erecting and striking a tent as he moved from site to site required unskilled laborers, and so he adroitly satisfied his labor and sexual needs in one fell swoop by gathering about him a tent crew of four or five emotionally starved boys, no older than fifteen. Once the tent was up and the revival about to start, Tony pressed these boys—immature and untrained though they were—into handling his sound system, lights, and the myriad other duties such a road show entails.

As for the lads' parents, they were almost universally pleased when this wonderful preacher and prophet of God asked permission for their sons to join him on the road to help spread the gospel and so that he could "teach them God's word." With Tony's encouragement, his followers soon began calling these youths "Tony's boys," but it quickly became a troubled group which saw constant turnover as a result of the nights its members were forced to spend in bed with their preacher in his travel trailer, motor home, or motel room.

Some of these lads were throwaways. Many were failing in school and had discipline problems at home. Most were fatherless. But their parents felt truly blessed, as one mother said, "to have Brother Tony bring my boy up straight in the ways of the Lord." After all, Tony was a charismatic Pentecostal preacher and a "prophet of God," and he had an attractive wife, a handsome little son, and a beautiful baby daughter. Indeed, for all appearances, they were the ideal Christian family!

✝ ✝ ✝

Then the bottom all but fell out of Tony and Tammy Sue's marriage when Tammy Sue learned that a young boy she knew extremely well had been sexually assaulted by Brother Tony. Now as a fifteen-year-old he made it clear to Tony and Tammy Sue that he would tell. And that wasn't all: The boy's two younger brothers had also been molested and were ready to tell, too.

Tammy Sue vividly recalls how it happened: "In 1969 when we was visiting my family in Hendersonville, all of a sudden Tony just got up and left me. We had been married for three years and I couldn't understand why he was leaving me.

"Then, he goes to Florida and calls me after he's there and says to me, 'Come on down here to Florida where I'm at.'

"And I said, 'No, you left me here so you'll have to come get me back up here in Hendersonville.' But, you know, that was strange for him to say for me to come down there to Florida by myself, 'cause he never let me go anywhere by myself and here he was going to pay mine and my kids' plane tickets down to Miami, Florida. He didn't want to come back up here.

"Then is when I found out about Tony's problem. Right after he called me is when this boy came and told me that Tony had molested him. He said, 'When Tony done took me out camping he had me take off my clothes and then he got me to do bad things with him.' And he told me that Tony had molested him more than once. And that Tony had molested his brothers, too. They all came to our house and told us, and Mom and Dad like to have died!

"So, the reason he left me was he knew that these boys were going to tell. . . . But not everybody else knew he did that, and they couldn't understand why he was leaving me. I thought, what have I done wrong, ya know, for all this stuff to be happening to me.

"And I refused to fly down there 'cause, once I'd found out about what he'd done to these boys, and that I'd have to approach him about it for their sakes, I just could not live with him. . . .

"But you know, when these boys told me about it, I said, 'Explain to me what you're talking about.' Back then, I never knew gay people existed, okay? I never knew this! Much less, you call it molesting a child. I was thinking Tony was homosexual. I wasn't thinking he was a child molester.

"I said, 'I'll be there in a few days.' Then, he didn't understand why I wouldn't come. So, he writes me a letter telling me he's coming and I said, 'Okay, God,' ya know, I'm praying all of this time. Being a Christian family, we're fasting and praying about it and asking God's guidance on what to do, 'cause you gotta forgive and forget. That's the Christian way!

"So, we are praying about this and he tells me he's coming. About an hour before he's supposed to get there, I sit down and I wrote it on a piece of paper exactly what I'm gonna tell him.

"When he got there, I said, 'Tony, I want to go into the bedroom so we can all talk.' So we went in there and we all talked and I explained to him the situation—about these boys telling me about him molesting them—and he wept . . . cried like a baby and asked me to forgive him and said he wouldn't do that with any boys no more.

"I said, 'Well, that's good. We gotta go out here and talk to Mom and Dad about this, too.' So, we got out there and he wept and cried before my mom and dad and asked their forgiveness and they forgave him. And then he asked my forgiveness and I forgave him. And so, me and my little kids packed up our little duds and we hit the road, again, with him."

4

"He preached the word of God and always took such an interest in our children—especially the boys."

With over two months of revivals scheduled from West Palm Beach, Florida, to Tylertown, Mississippi, to Salem, Virginia—with many stops in between—Brother Tony, his wife, and children were back out on the road again in the fall of 1969. It was with no small measure of trepidation that Tammy Sue committed herself to this trip with her husband so soon after learning that he had molested these boys who were well known to her and her family.

Before they pulled out, Tammy Sue's better judgment had told her that she should remain at her family's home rather than travel with Tony. But she felt moved by his apology and tearful pleas for forgiveness. Her ingrained, fervent Christian belief in the sublime power of confession, repentance, and forgiveness to efface sins even as heinous as Tony's overruled her head and she forgave him. But Tammy Sue always found it difficult to forget what he had done.

But at Tony's very first revival back on the road, she saw something which made her feel that her husband had really not changed his ways: Fifteen minutes after the service ended, there he stood in the middle of a clutch of twelve- to fourteen-year-old boys chatting amiably and smiling and hugging each in turn, totally oblivious of everyone else.

As Tammy Sue watched, she realized that her husband's actions were a familiar prelude to his picking and choosing the boy or two whom by week's end he would invite to travel with them to help set up the tent and operate the sound system and . . . Tammy Sue didn't even want to think about the "and," so she turned and walked sadly back to their motor home parked beside the little country Pentecostal church. There she relieved the kindly churchwoman who had watched her children during the service, kissed her sleeping babies goodnight, and without undressing crawled disconsolately onto their bed. Hearing Tony's booming, gravelly voice in the near distance happily jabbering and laughing with *his* boys, punctuated here and there by the boys' own piping responses, she drew a deep breath, turned her face to the wall, and cried herself to sleep.

As a teenage preacher, most of Brother Tony's early Pentecostal revival ministry consisted of preaching at small churches whose pastors recognized that his youthful approach to preaching, prophesying, and gospel singing attracted not only backslid church members but prospective new members as well. In small southern communities a week-long revival is often the best show in town and an ideal way for the host church to bring in more contributions since, instead of tickets, the price of admission is confrontation by a collection plate and peer pressure to contribute two or three times an evening.

Now, with a few years' revival experience behind him, his own motor home, revival tent, a couple of hundred folding chairs, portable stage, sound system, electronic organ, and a truck to carry it all—usually driven by one of the older "Tony's boys"—Tony Leyva was his own boss, selecting communities and towns big and small where he could set up and preach his Miracle Restoration Revivals, scooping proceeds from his twice-to-thrice-a-night collections into his private purse.

His own master, Tony planned his schedule two months in advance of his departure from North Carolina and sent out notices to those local preachers and faithful on his mailing list in the selected areas—the life blood for an evangelist like him—telling them when and where he would preach his revival, encouraging them to come and "bring a friend," for his Miracle Restoration Revival would be in their town soon!

Some places Tony had preached in before; other locations were recommended to him by people on his mailing list, and still others he poached from the printed schedules of older Pentecostal evangelists with years on the road, or else schedules he received in the mail, had handed to him by his own followers, or filched from the bulletin boards of churches he visited on his travels.

Finding suitable locations to pitch his tent did not present Brother Tony with a problem: For a nominal fee or often nothing at all—"Thanks,

Brother, you're really serving the Lord by doing this!"—Tony and his troupe never wanted for a place to pitch his tent: fields alongside country churches; rural county fairgrounds; or lots owned by Pentecostal businessmen, farmers, and homeowners who readily identified with his Holy Ghost revival approach to worship.

And if renting land on which to set up his tent came cheap, electricity for Tony's organ, sound system, and floodlights required little more than running a couple hundred feet of heavy-duty extension cord to his temporary landlord's nearest outlet and paying the small estimated cost for electricity out of his collection proceeds.

By their very nature traveling evangelists like Tony Leyva operate on a strictly cash basis. Their incomes come almost exclusively in the form of nontraceable coins and dollar bills, along with some fives, tens, twenties, and—"God bless you *real* good, Sister!"—even occasional fifties and hundred dollar bills. Checks and money orders were mailed back to the ministry's "home office" in Hendersonville, where Tony's mother, Ada, processed and deposited them, using this money to pay the postage on her son's newsletters, revival schedules, and impassioned pleas for still more donations which constantly went out to hundreds, and eventually thousands, of faithful followers in dozens of states.

As his operation grew, Tony earmarked funds for major, traceable ministry purchases such as office machines, sound equipment, more folding chairs, and—for Brother Tony's newest money-making scheme—recording equipment, tape duplicators, and blank cassettes so he could make and sell recordings of his sermons. Tony began training his boys to operate the tape duplicating machines. The blank cassettes he bought by the case for twenty cents each were quickly sold for five dollars apiece, which he then slipped into his bank bags. "A donation of five dollars for each would be appreciated, brothers and sisters." Then, to close the sale, Brother Tony would add, "By getting one of my tape-recorded sermons and giving it to a shut-in or sick, suffering person, you can join the Army of the People of God who will receive their blessings in heaven!"

With the sizable portion of his funds arriving as cash, who—other than Tony and the ever changing flock of "Tony's boys" who helped count it—ever knew whether last night's revival service take was $150 or $1,500, or if the collection buckets last Friday or Saturday night brought in $300 or $3,000? Therefore, when it came to buying himself new clothes, or fashionable tennis shoes, or jeans or shirts, a Walkman or hard rock tapes for that special boy who granted him such favors in bed last night, Brother

Tony just pulled the requisite cash from one of the zippered bank bags he carried as a woman does a purse.

Also, as a religious enterprise—"a church"—the Tony Leyva Evangelistic Association, Inc., didn't have to report its income or expenses to the IRS or even to those people gullible enough to support it. What was the association's was his, Tony smugly thought and smiled, "Who's the wiser about what I do?"

With this continuing lack of accountability, it was easy for Tony to hide giving a twelve-year-old boy a roll of quarters in exchange for a blow job, a twenty dollar bill to a thirteen-year-old for allowing the preacher to take nude photos of him, or the rare fifty to a disgruntled victim to keep him quiet when he just didn't understand that what Brother Tony had done was "God's special way for His people to love each other."

Just like a traveling carnival or circus, after the last performance of a week-long revival stand, the current "Tony's boys" would load up his stage, sound system, organ, and chairs, strike the tent, and load it in the truck. As early as possible the next morning, with Tammy Sue and their two young kids usually still asleep in the back, Tony climbed behind the wheel of his motor home and drove out, followed closely by his truck being driven by a boy barely old enough to drive, with a couple of younger boys sitting beside him. At the next location a preacher friend or other faithful follower made final arrangements by picking up several excited youths to help raise Tony's tent and set up the sound system. Typically, within a couple of hours of Brother Tony's arrival, the scene around his gospel tent resembled that of a small circus setting up for a performance in some backwater town, except that there were no lions, tigers, or elephants.

What one found under Tony's big top were rows and rows of folding chairs, a platform stage with a pulpit, a portable electronic organ and sound system with auditorium-sized speakers, floodlights, and wiring running everywhere. The collection of wheelchairs, crutches, leg braces, and hearing aids remained out of sight in his truck until just before service time. Then a couple of his trusted boys outfitted the ringers hired for the night at twenty dollars or more each. In the usually poverty-stricken areas Brother Tony drove through and operated in he rarely had a problem finding faux "believers" to employ as mutes or invalids for the night, using his props to maximum effect.

Brother Tony preferred week-long revivals since that gave him not only the time to build his attendance through word of mouth but also time enough to size up the selection of available boys proudly introduced to him by faithful parents. In this way he could find out about their family situations, snow their parents, and then—a day or two before his departure—issue a warm invitation to that special boy (or boys) to join him on the road and become one of "Tony's boys."

Tony had learned that, when made to the right boy and parent, the offer could not be refused: Affection, love, good food, travel, working for the Lord, and studying the Bible were enticements beyond compare—not to mention (which Tony never did) learning "God's special way for His people to love each other" from the master teacher.

To make sure that he had not missed any available boys, at the close of each service Tony smiled especially broadly and issued his own version of an altar call, urging "all the young children to come up here so I can meet 'em and show 'em God's love. Remember, Jesus said, 'Suffer the little children to come unto me.'" Their parents came up, too, beaming happily and unaware that the charismatic evangelist was a cunning pederast who—Tony confessed years later—specifically used these altar calls to begin his well-planned selection process for certain types of boys to become his victims, intentionally overlooking their sisters and other children parading by.

Remarked a Virginia victim's mother: "He preached the word of God and always took such an interest in our children—especially the boys!"

✝ ✝ ✝

But Tammy Sue's shock at learning about her husband's sexual assaults of boys she and her family knew personally was soon matched by what happened during their current travels. "Right after he admitted to me that he had molested those boys, and asked my forgiveness—and I'd forgiven him—me and the kids went back out on the road traveling with him. And we'd been gone for some time when we ended up in Salem, Virginia, where he preached a two-week revival at this independent Pentecostal church.

"We had our motor home parked at this KOA (Kampgrounds of America) campground there in Roanoke. It had a top bunk and a lower bunk and our kids slept on the lower bunk while Tony and me slept on the top one.

"Well, Tony wanted this boy he really liked down in Florida to come stay with him, so he calls this boy. He phoned down there and asked this thirteen-year-old boy to come up and help him with the revival, help set up the tent or do the sound or something like that. A thirteen-year-old boy!

"Well, Tony talked to this boy's mother and told her that he'd pay the boy's way up to Roanoke and she said, 'Sure! Fine!' And she was real happy about him coming and all that. And then Tony sent the boy a ticket and he come to Roanoke and we picked him up.

"So, he come and stayed with us there in our motor home, and when he got there Tony told me that I had to sleep on the floor . . . his own wife! While he and this thirteen-year-old boy slept together in the top bunk, I was put down there on the floor!

"And I asked Tony why and he just said, 'The boy needs me to comfort him.' So, I'm the subjected wife with an overbearing husband who's a prophet of God and preacher that the people love and Tony says to me, 'God talks to me and tells me things I gotta do. God told me to have this boy come up and stay with me so I could comfort him.' And then Tony says, 'God don't talk to you, ya know, so you gotta listen to me on this.'

"And while I was down there on the floor I didn't hear nothing going on with them up there in the top bunk 'cause I didn't want to hear nothing. I just sorta tuned things out. . . .

"But the fact that he put me on the floor and put the boy up there in the bed with him, with our kids right up under him, I didn't like that one bit! But, just like always, if I said anything to him, I was touchin' God's anointed prophet. I was supposed to keep my mouth shut and not say anything about what he did. And he did whatever he wanted to do. Tony didn't have to listen to nobody else but God!" Pointing to an old photo of Brother Tony preaching at one of his revivals, Tammy Sue sneered, "Just like that little beautiful picture right there . . . God's anointed!"

Tammy Sue also seethed over Tony's constant insistence that his own children be seen and not heard. "When we lived and traveled together my kids were always in Tony's way. When we were together it was, 'Hush! Be quiet so Daddy can read the Bible. Hush! Be quiet so Daddy can preach. Hush! Be quiet so Daddy can sleep.' That's just what they had to do and I got tired of it and they got tired of it."

For the time being, Tammy Sue continued to travel with her husband and remained faithful to him because of her Pentecostal upbringing, a divorce being anathema to her family and faith. But being made to sleep on the floor while he bedded a young boy so angered her that once they had returned to Henderson County two weeks later, she told Tony that she would never travel with him again.

When Tammy Sue told her parents back in Tuxedo what her husband had done in Roanoke with the young boy from Florida, they were aghast and scandalized beyond belief by their son-in-law's continued blatant involvement with young boys. Tammy Sue's mother and father avidly supported her decision to separate from Tony for good and rear her children by herself.

✝ ✝ ✝

Soon Tony left on yet another long revival trip. Now traveling alone, he was free to more openly select and bed his latest victim from the sons whom parents continued to parade up to meet him at his services' close. Just like a "John" in a whorehouse choosing from the available ladies, Tony would set his eye on a particular boy, size him up for safety's sake, and then convince his parents—usually the boy only had a mother—to allow the lad to spend the night with him, help him count his collection money, "and teach the Bible and the Lord's ways to your fine son."

No longer was there any extended "courtship" or cultivation of a relationship. Tony's sense of which boys would "put out" quickly and which would not had been finely honed by years of practical experience as a successful pedophile. These days he lost no time taking his prospective victims to bed, still being careful, however, to advance on his chosen bedmate stealthily and cautiously until the moment was just right.

✝ ✝ ✝

After completing this trip Brother Tony went to his in-laws' home where Tammy Sue was staying with their children. For one last time he tried to get her to travel with him "for appearance's sake and for the ministry." And just as he had done when Tammy Sue learned of his sexual abuse of the young boys known to her family, the preacher turned on all his charm, became weepy, then tearful, and finally got down on his knees to beg Tammy Sue's forgiveness "in Jesus' precious name!" But his wife would have none of it and stood firm in her decision to remain in Tuxedo.

Realizing that this time his tears and pleading would not work, Tony returned to his traveling revival ministry with ever-increasing vigor and brazenness in the pulpit, healing the sick, pleading for money, wooing and bedding boys.

✝ ✝ ✝

Although she had doubts about doing so, Tammy Sue still allowed Tony to have unsupervised visits with their children and, occasionally, let Mark travel alone with his father. "Tony was always real generous at providing for the kids' needs," Tammy Sue recalled, "and he liked to take Mark places with him.

"Then, when Mark was seven years old, he went with his daddy one summer to Indiana . . . but when Mark came back . . . he said, 'Mama, why does daddy hold the other boys' hands?' And he said, 'I've never hurt so bad in all my life as when my daddy would put me in another bed at night and let another boy sleep with him.' "

Fearing the worst, Tammy Sue gently delved deeper into what had happened during the trip: "Mark told me that he was upset because his father didn't love him the same way he loved the other little boys. And my blood ran cold when he said that, but I just had to ask him what he meant by that. And then Mark told me all about what went on.

"Well, then, of course, me and Tony had it out when I told Tony what happened. I just said, 'Mark, I hate to tell you this, but this is a problem your daddy has. I didn't know that it was happening again, but this is his problem.

"And Mark just cried. He was so brokenhearted. And he never did go with Tony again. Not by himself. And not even with somebody else along. That was in June of 1974. And then in August of 1974 is when I filed for a divorce.

"After I told Mark what I told him, I got my brothers to talk to him, 'cause I didn't have nobody else I could trust to talk to him, and he seemed to pretty much accept things as they were. It was sad, though. Real sad for him, 'cause he'd lost his daddy."

5

". . . He's had many, many unusual experiences in the Lord."

During the early 1970s the United States was experiencing the height of sentiment against the war in Vietnam. The West Coast, the Northeast, and the Midwest saw violent confrontations between the pro-war, pro-America establishment and the anti-war protesters, most of them young people who were being sent to do the fighting. In the South, however, it was only the rarest local against the war who felt at all comfortable in letting his feelings be known publicly, because almost assuredly his neighbor's pickup carried an "America, Love It or Leave It" bumper sticker, which was a mild expression of the owner's true feelings on a black or white subject.

In the fall of 1972, a motor home with a freshly painted, used bobtail truck following behind—both emblazoned with patriotic slogans—left Hendersonville, North Carolina, headed south on U.S. 25 on a planned odyssey crisscrossing southern highways from Virginia to Alabama to Florida and the states in between. Gracing the sides of the truck were four huge, brightly painted U.S. flags. Between them the preacher's name was emblazoned in foot-tall western script in bright red and blue against a white background.

As if an afterthought, above the fancy curving letters of his name—"Tony Leyva"—the leader of this two-vehicle caravan had added three-inch-high plain black lettering identifying the vehicle as part of "Miracle Restoration Revivals." Along the bottom, in still smaller letters, ran quotes from the Bible:

> For as by one man's disobedience many were made sinners, so by the obedience of one shall many be made righteous. Moreover the law entered, that the offense might abound. But where sin abounded, grace did much more abound. That as sin hath reigned unto death, even so might grace reign through righteousness unto eternal life by Jesus Christ our Lord (Rom. 5:19–21),

and

> I Jesus have sent mine angel to testify unto you these things in the churches. I am the root and the offspring of David, and the bright and morning star. And the Spirit and the bride say, Come. And let him that is athirst come. And whosoever will, let him take the water of life freely. (Rev. 22:16–17)

The back doors of the truck were decorated in a similarly garish religious motif so that motorists caught behind the usually slow-moving vehicles clearly knew that up ahead traveled a Bible-thumping, Pentecostal evangelist's road show.

In the driver's seat of the heavily laden truck a tall, skinny, pimply-faced seventeen-year-old boy clung tightly to the oversized steering wheel as though he were piloting a sailing vessel through a hurricane. Next to him, a mop-headed fifteen-year-old boy fiddled with the truck's radio dial and pounded on the dash as he cursed his inability to tune in any rock music traveling through this rural backwater area of southern Georgia, "th' fuckin' boonies," he called it.

By the passenger window sat a disconsolate fourteen-year-old youth with long, stringy blond hair staring straight ahead and grinding his teeth so noisily that, when the mop-headed boy gave up and turned off the static-filled radio, he heard the gnashing above the road noise and truck engine's roar.

"Hey!" he shouted at his troubled seatmate, "What's wrong with you?" but got no answer and the grinding continued.

"How much did he give ya?" the driver nonchalantly asked the youngest boy.

Silence except for the truck, the road, and the boy's grinding teeth.

"Ten dollars?" the driver prompted. "Twenty?"

Still no response.

"What, then? He gave me two whole rolls of quarters the first time I slept with him."

Still choosing not to respond, the blond boy continued grinding his teeth, only harder, as he stared into the back of the motor home just ahead.

Like a dog with a bone, after a few seconds' silence the driver prodded him again with, "I asked you: What'd he give you? What'd you do for him? Did he want you to come in his mouth?"

Again silence but evidence of smoldering anger, too.

"Did he play with your nuts? That's what he done to me," said the driver.

Chimed in the boy in the middle: "When he got me to do 'it' with him, really, 'it' wasn't so bad, ya know, 'cause when we were in Jacksonville last week he bought me these new jeans and this shirt"—he pointed to his clothes—"just for one night with him. And I only did 'it' twice. That's not so bad. It's really not. And I remember when I first met him . . ."

"Shut up! Shut up, you goddamned mother fuckers!" the blond boy exploded at the other two so violently that he sprayed spittle all over them, and caused the driver to jerk reflexively and swerve the right front tire onto the road's shoulder. "That asshole calls hisself a 'preacher' and 'man of God,' but he ain't no such fuckin' thing! He's a queer, that's what he is! A fuckin' queer, the way he be playin' with my balls and ass and all. And then he wants me to suck him off and all, says he'll buy me some new tennies when we get to Chattanooga. Well, fuck him!! I don't want no goddamned fuckin' new tennies! Not ever! Not from that mother-fucker, I don't!"

✝ ✝ ✝

Up ahead sat Tony Leyva in the captain's chair of his motor home: a neatly dressed, well-groomed gentleman in his mid-twenties. Smiling often and self-assuredly to himself in the rear-view mirror, the Pentecostal preacher and evangelist began to worry about his one apparent physical defect which of late seemed to him to be getting even more pronounced: his buck teeth. Again he smiled at himself in the mirror and his protruding teeth smiled back at him as he studied them yet again.

Across from Tony sat his "copilot for the day," the thirteen-year-old son of one of the single mothers who, for nearly a year, had been one of the growing legion of followers receiving his newsletters and revival schedules by mail at least once a month.

Brother Tony replayed in his memory his favorite scene from the revival in Bainbridge the previous night:

Barbara Jean Harris lived a truly hardscrabble existence on the banks of the turgid Flint River in southwestern Georgia. After the service had ended, she came up to Tony and began telling him about how she was having to struggle so hard to raise her seven children, "now that my husband done run off with another woman. One that ain't got no kids to tend to."

The preacher nodded in preacherly understanding and Barbara Jean continued: "My thirteen-year-old, Curtis Wayne—You've met Curtis Wayne, ain't you?"—The preacher smiled at the recollection—"Well, he's done been suspended from seventh grade again just this week for the third time in a month. As usual, it's for his fightin' and I don't know what I'm gonna do with him. I really don't know what's gonna become of Curtis Wayne if he can't get along and stay in school like the other kids!"

The preacher listened compassionately to how Barbara Jean had all she could handle taking care of the cooking, washing, and cleaning for her other six children. He did his best to commiserate with her so she would feel better, say good night, and let them both leave for home and a good night's rest.

But Barbara Jean had just gotten her second wind. "What with my three-year-old twins underfoot there at the house, I just can't stand havin' to satisfy Curtis Wayne there at the house, too. He's so unhappy at home, but he keeps on gettin' in trouble at school. And when he's at home, Lord knows, Curtis Wayne . . . well . . . Curtis Wayne ain't no good when it comes to helpin' me and lookin' after the twins. Somebody's gotta look after him and keep him out of devilment!"

At this a familiar light snapped on in the preacher's mind: He knew just who might be able to take care of Curtis Wayne, but he had to carefully plan just how to innocently suggest that to the boy's mother. About this time Curtis Wayne himself sheepishly walked up his mother in that way children do when they know that they are being talked about. The preacher smiled a greeting from ear to ear, his problem solved.

During the past couple of years the preacher had pitched his tent around rural Decatur County several times. Each time Barbara Jean had managed to come to his services bringing along her Curtis Wayne and her other children, except, that is, for the two youngest she always dropped off at a neighbor's.

Just as Barbara Jean had witnessed at their previous meetings, she saw this "special loving look" spread across Tony's face as he greeted her son, reached out, and drew the boy close and hugged him while he stroked the lad's hair. Instinctively and immediately, Curtis Wayne wrapped an arm around the man, looked up into the preacher's beaming face, and smiled broadly.

Chapter 5

Barbara Jean didn't know it, but at their first meeting Brother Tony had memorized the ages and names of her and her children, especially noting and mentally filing away visual information about Curtis Wayne, this handsome young son of hers who just couldn't understand why his daddy never paid him much attention. And now, according to his mother, the boy had become angry and confused because his daddy had run off for reasons he couldn't understand.

On each of their previous two meetings, Curtis Wayne had looked up to this friendly preacher who always noticed him and playfully tousled his hair and hugged him tightly, little things even his own daddy had never done. But Tony had always felt the time wasn't quite right for him to make his move.

It had at first embarrassed Curtis Wayne to have his friend the preacher hear what his mother was saying, but—Tony smiled to himself again in the mirror—it had all worked out. For Curtis Wayne, embarrassment quickly turned to shocked thrill when this warm, loving man suggested that he, Curtis Wayne Harris, not worry about going to school for a while and instead travel around helping him set up his big revival tent while living on the road with the other boys who helped the preacher with his revivals. "And I'll teach him the Bible real good, every night, Mrs. Harris. I promise," Tony nearly forgot to add.

Before, when Curtis Wayne had watched the boys traveling with Brother Tony help him erect his tent, he didn't think he would ever have a chance to go on the road and do this, too. First of all, he wasn't very strong, and second, his mama was always careful about where he went and whom he went with. But seconds after the preacher's proposition, Barbara Jean accepted on her son's behalf, then turned to her son and added as an afterthought, "That is, if you'd really like to go, Curtis Wayne."

"Yeah, Mama! I wanna go! I wanna go!" he bounced up and down with glee, the likes of which Barbara Jean rarely saw in her son.

So it was all arranged: Curtis Wayne Harris would travel with Brother Tony as one of "Tony's boys," helping to set up his big top revival tent in western Georgia, Tennessee—"I've never been to Tennessee!" Curtis Wayne excitedly thought when he heard Tony mention it—and then come back down through Alabama before arriving back home in three weeks.

As soon as they got back home that night, the boy's mother got down her old tan tartan suitcase and gave it to her son for him to start packing. But at two o'clock the next morning the light in Curtis Wayne's room still burned brightly as he sat on the edge of his bed, so excited about traveling with this preacher man who always acted so loving and nice toward him that he just couldn't concentrate on what he should pack. It was a dream come true: He was going to get to go to Tennessee! Be part of a big-time revival ministry! And all the while this kindly, father-like preacher was going to teach him the Bible and how to get right with God!

✝ ✝ ✝

To Barbara Jean Harris and the thousands of other believers in the Holy Ghost Pentecostal faith, the Reverend Mario "Tony" Leyva still held himself out to be "a married man with a wonderful Christian wife and a young son and daughter waitin' for me back home in North Carolina who I miss dearly."

Technically—at least for now—Brother Tony spoke the truth: the divorce was not yet final. On the road Brother Tony made a great deal out of his being a loving father who missed his own children back home; consequently, he was transferring and showering his fatherly affection for his children onto their children.

Brother Tony's self-promoted cachet as a highly respected evangelist, prophet of God, and preacher served him well as a moral letter of credit for trustworthiness among fellow Holy Ghost Pentecostals. Therefore, fathers and especially single mothers, readily allowed him access to their young sons and, in most instances, even actively encouraged their boys to establish relationships with him, and let them stay with Brother Tony overnight or travel with him for a week or a month.

But a persistent question lurked in the minds of many of his followers: "Why is it only the boys he pays attention to?"

✝ ✝ ✝

Tony again checked his smile in his rear-view mirror before directing it toward his young guest. Curtis Wayne, swiveling around and around in the captain's chair, didn't catch Tony's momentary frown before his omnipresent charm returned and he cast his lustful eyes up and down the slender young body before him, mentally undressing the boy as he went.

"Ah, Curtis Wayne," Tony sweetly sought the lad's attention. "What would you like to have for supper tonight?"

"I dunno," the boy slowly answered.

"Ya know, we can stop and eat at a restaurant and have just about any

Chapter 5

kind of food you like. Would you like a steak? With French fries and a soda pop?" Tony coaxed.

"Yeah, that'd be good. But ain't we gonna eat dinner first?" the typically ever hungry boy was already thinking about the fast-approaching noon meal.

"Yeah, son," Tony assured his young friend, "we're gonna stop up here in Columbus and you can have the biggest old cheeseburger you ever done had, an' French fries, an' a malt. Ya' like chocolate?"

Curtis Wayne nodded, "Uh huh."

"Good. That's what I'll get for ya."

Then Tony shifted mental gears: "And after we have that steak dinner tonight I'd like for ya to stay with me in my room at the motel so's you can massage my neck for me. Ya know, drivin' all day like this sure does make my neck sore. And I got this vibrator thing that I'd like to have you use on me tonight, if you would."

"Sure, Brother Tony!" Curtis Wayne innocently assented, "I'd be happy to!"

"Fine! That's just fine! I'll really appreciate that." The preacher smiled at Curtis Wayne, and then at himself in his rear-view mirror as if to validate for himself his success at laying the groundwork to accomplish the deflowering of yet another unsuspecting young boy.

Then Brother Tony let his mind flow freely as he planned his first evening with this handsome youngster. He settled back in his captain's chair and daydreamed about what he would make happen that night: getting into bed with an almost naked Curtis Wayne, having the boy run the vibrator on his neck, his taking and running it over the boy's back and buttocks, hugging and cuddling the boy's body close to him, telling the thirteen-year-old how Jesus showed him this special way for God's people to love each other, peeling the lad's and his own briefs off, lying on top of him, head to crotch, gently caressing the boy's buttocks, then his lips. . . .

"*Watch out, Brother Tony!*" Curtis Wayne's scream scared the hell out of Tony, as he reflexively slammed on the motor home's brakes.

Lost in his sick erotic fantasy, the pervert preacher had almost rear-ended a slowly moving semi-truck and trailer rig. He had slammed on the brakes just in time, throwing Curtis Wayne to the floor.

"You okay there?" Tony anxiously inquired.

"Yeah, I guess so," the boy tentatively responded as he eased himself back into his seat.

✝ ✝ ✝

Experience had taught the revival truck's driver to keep a good distance between himself and the motor home in front, therefore, the preacher's sudden braking didn't come as a total surprise.

"Ya think he's got the new kid givin' him a blow job?" the fifteen-year-old snickered.

"Fuckin' A, he probably does," the driver half gleefully agreed. "I saw that look in his eye this mornin' before we pulled out. I didn't think he could wait till we got to Rome tonight and I guess I was right!"

"Fresh meat!" the mop-haired fifteen-year-old giggled, "It'll do it for Brother Tony ever time!"

But the fourteen-year-old riding shotgun just seethed and ground his teeth together all the more, his sole consolation being that tonight it wouldn't be him sharing a bed with the preacher and prophet of God.

✝ ✝ ✝

These were heady days indeed for Brother Tony. He had reached a point in his ministry where he did what he wanted when he wanted to do it. He felt invincible, and why not? God himself had blessed him. God let him do all these things, he had convinced himself, because he, the Reverend Mario Ivan "Tony" Leyva, was special: Just ask the thousands of folks who flocked to his tent revivals, received his newsletters, dropped thousands of dollars into his tent revival collection buckets every week, and then sent him checks and money orders totaling thousands more every month!

Almost constantly on the road with his ever-changing band of "Tony's boys," it didn't take long for Brother Tony to get over his separation from Tammy Sue. Indeed, when he had to appear in court in Hendersonville in 1975 for the divorce proceedings, all he could do was complain about the time it cost him away from the revival circuit and his boys.

The demand from charismatic Holy Ghost Pentecostals from Florida to Indiana wanting to hear and watch the mesmerizing Brother Tony preach, prophesy, and heal the sick seemed never to stop. Said his mother, Ada:

"He got to where he was preaching two and three times a day, six and seven days in a row, year in and year out. My son is a real man of God and he loves the Lord so much that he wouldn't take any time off, hardly. There was just so many hurting people who wanted to hear his message.

"Oh, he traveled for many, many years. He was definitely called to God and he loves the Lord with all his heart. He is a very anointed preacher and teacher in God and he's had many, many unusual experiences in the Lord. And, as a man of God and a prophet of God, quite naturally, the devil fights him.

"And, you know, the children always called him 'Pied Piper' because back at the very beginning it seemed like they always flocked to him. They've always loved him. He's a very loving person."

By no means did Brother Tony's hoodwinking of these thousands of dedicated, mostly poor folks flocking to his revivals remain limited to his almost daily sexual assaults of their sons, grandsons, brothers, and nephews. In an equally bizarre deception he continued expanding his collection of crutches, braces, canes, wheelchairs, hearing aids, eyeglasses, and even a stretcher, all to be used at specific services.

There were spots where Brother Tony had preached before, and where he was so loved and adored that he could hold sway over those assembled and in short order whip them into a trance-like state of emotional frenzy, thereby assuring him that there would be ample "cures" among the true believers in the congregation.

However, when he traveled to a new location and took to the stage for a revival filled with gospel singing, preaching, prophesying, and speaking in tongues, he knew from experience that it helped to salt the congregation with two or three well-trained hired "healees" to get the impassioned Holy Ghost revival off and rolling.

In some of these towns Brother Tony turned to fellow preachers whom he knew he could take into his confidence to locate "safe" people to convincingly play "healees" at his revival services. But for many of his new revival sites Tony personally selected and hired transients he had found a town or two back, men who desperately needed the money, who would not be known to local residents, and who would stay with him and perform at several revivals over a period of a few days to a week. Men who would keep quiet about his duplicity because they wouldn't get a dime until Tony dropped them off in a distant town.

Those entering this "service in the Lord" (as he assured them it was) were coached by this fundamentally fraudulent man of God, had their meals provided along with a place to sleep—usually a motel room floor—and were paid ten to twenty dollars for each successful healing. Of course, Brother Tony's latest loyal believers had no idea that the crippled old man they saw take off his braces and throw away his crutches had been walking down the highway without so much as a limp the day before when the evangelist hired him.

One of Brother Tony's favorite farces was an elaborately staged re-enactment of one of his favorite passages from Mark 2:3–5, which tells how Jesus healed ". . . one sick of the palsy, which was borne of four . . . [and] they let down the bed wherein the sick of the palsy lay. . . . I say unto thee, Arise, and take up thy bed, and go thy way into thine house. And immediately he arose, took up the bed, and went forth before them all. . . ."

Tony truly went to great lengths to duplicate this scene. For his followers it was so real that after a performance it could be said of them as in Mark, ". . . insomuch that they were all amazed, and glorified God, saying, We never saw it in this fashion."

In Brother Tony's version, at a prearranged point during his sermon, four of "Tony's boys" would start shouting and making a commotion at the entrance to the tent, and then rush in carrying a stretcher with a ringer lying on it. As they set the violently shaking man down in front of him, Tony would stop his sermon, approach the man, and—frequently speaking in tongues—begin commanding that the demons leave the man's body. Suddenly the ringer stopped shaking, went into a trance, then jumped up and danced around shouting, "I'm healed! I'm healed! I'm healed! Praise Jesus, I'm healed!" before running wildly out of the tent and into the night where he disappeared into Tony's motor home until the coast was clear.

But even this wasn't the limit of Brother Tony's chicanery: Nightly, with a traditional rural Pentecostal preacher's quiver in his gravelly voice and cash receipts already bulging in his collection of zippered bank bags, Brother Tony lied, cried, and pled poverty to the faithful, claiming that unless he received an *especially* large offering "this very night" he couldn't pay his "way past due bills" and would be forced to fold his tent and "quit preachin' God's word!"

At one such taped tent revival service, Tony cajoled those assembled into a true giving frenzy with a performance that is vintage Tony Leyva:

> Half of you want to shout tonight, and the other half wants to stand and look or sit and look. But we're gonna all do something tonight. I do not come to entertain. This is not a show. We come to worship God. My body's as tired as everybody else's. I work through the night to daylight every morning doing office work. But I love to praise God when I come to church.
>
> Now you can just sit there and dry up or you can turn loose and let

God bless you. If you do nothing, you get nothing. And if you give nothing, you get no blessing back. God wants you to give. It ain't me that wants you to give. It's God that wants you to give. Everybody's got problems. The devil's fighting everybody. But the way to get the victory is to fight back. And praise God. And you can fight back against the devil by giving to help this ministry.

Now in case somebody hasn't been getting the touch tonight, we're gonna have another offering now. And I say, "Lord, loose them, and give them anointing tonight." In Jesus' name!

[The congregation shouts "Amen!"]

In Jesus' name!

[Louder yet the congregation shouts: "Amen!"]

In Jesus' name.

[And still louder the congregation shouts: "Amen!"]

In Jesus' name I want everybody to get ready to march up here and give! If you're not crippled you're able to march up here and give thanks to God for not being a cripple. And he knows what you've got in that wallet, brother, or that purse, sister, and he wants you to praise Him with what he has given you.

We're gonna praise God here tonight. I fight for revivals and for your help to make those revivals happen. I don't believe in dead services. And I don't preach to dead people. I preach resurrection. I said I preach resurrection!

[The congregation shouts "Amen!"]

I said I preach resurrection!

[Louder still the congregation shouts: "Amen!" as throbbing gospel music flows from the electronic organ.]

Everybody just march up here right now tonight and give in Jesus' name! Amen! Amen! Amen!

As always, the faithful came through and filled Brother Tony's coffers to overflowing. As a former member of "Tony's boys" recalled, "Some nights Tony'd take in as much as sixteen thousand dollars . . . and sometimes people'd put their rings and watches in the buckets"—which he had obtained free from Kentucky Fried Chicken franchises—"and one night some dude put a Rolex watch in the bucket and Tony was thrilled to death . . . till he took it to a jeweler in Atlanta and found out it was a fake. Boy, was he pissed off! He swore to God that he'd never preach in that town again!"

But instead of sending money to "my" orphanage in the Dominican Republic as he claimed nightly in his sermons—only a partial lie for he did give the administrator money whenever he traveled there and had sex with its young male residents—or buying his much-touted "Bibles for Cuba," Leyva had other "charities" in mind. He gave his revivals' collection of quarters to his favorite boys for video games—two fistfuls the going rate for a good oral performance in bed, one boy recalled—and put the folding money in his bank bags for daily expenditures for himself and Tony's boys like movies, amusement parks, steak dinners, stereo radio/cassette players, jewelry, and new clothes.

Tony Leyva himself dressed like a pastel peacock and probably would have chosen brighter hues in keeping with that bird's natural plumage if the tailors he frequented in Palm Beach and Atlanta had only had such swatches available. But he settled for flashy enough three-piece numbers in colors like powder blue, peach, and shimmering green . . . "so he'd stand out and people'd notice him," laughed one of his former employees.

6

*". . . False prophets shall rise,
and show signs and wonders to seduce."*

Inconceivable to all but a mere handful of his adult followers, Brother Tony's remarkable, ubiquitous, unscrupulous ability to successfully select, charm, court, and ultimately bed one young adolescent brother or cousin after another established him as an unknown avatar of the safe, successful pedophile life by the late 1970s.

Without pause through the rest of that decade and well into the next, family after family suffered as Brother Tony visited his scourge like a plague on the sons and brothers of faithful Pentecostals from Virginia to Florida to Louisiana to Ohio and on out into the Caribbean. Like all adult male homosexual pedophiles or ephebophiles, Leyva's quest for sex with specific boys ended once their bodies matured into young manhood. Then his only concern for his former victims became "Will they tell?" as, one by one, they reached the age where they no longer felt so frightened to reveal what the preacher had done to them in secret.

As with all such obsessive-compulsive sex perverts, Leyva's lust for new sexual conquests came from his deep-rooted narcissistic need to have power over those weaker than himself. Therefore, his list of victims grew exponentially from relationship to relationship: he was never sated by his ever-spiraling surfeit of young conquests.

But rolls of quarters for pinball machines and cash to buy flashy tailor-made suits were not the only iniquitous uses to which Leyva put the money conned from pensioners, widows, and blue-collar workers. Usually, twenty dollars would suffice to buy silence from a miffed fourteen-year-old after a sexual overture went awry. But then there were sumptuous post-revival steak dinners for Tony, his current tent crew of adolescent boys, and his special boy guest for the evening, not to mention the latest in teenage male fashions, first-run motion pictures complete with a run on the concession stand, and amusement parks like Six Flags in Atlanta.

After a full day driving to a new location, setting up the tent and sound system, and an evening preaching and healing and collecting money from the unaware, evangelist Brother Tony Leyva and his boys retired to a suite of motel rooms. Once safely in his own room with his newest tent crew applicant, the evangelist put this aspiring "helper for the Lord" through his version of the casting couch. Yet, almost unbelievably, Leyva's reputation as a charismatic Pentecostal evangelist continued to grow steadily throughout the South and even began spreading north as he started conducting revivals in New York, Pennsylvania, Ohio, Indiana, and Illinois.

Of course, occasional rumors from this or that town concerning Brother Tony's indiscretions with teenage boys threatened to besmirch what he saw as his exalted reputation as evangelist, prophet, and preacher; one intuitive former supporter frequently speaking out against him backed up her statements by quoting the scripture, ". . . false prophets shall rise, and show signs and wonders to seduce" (Mark 13:22). However, Tony imperiously one-upped these scandalmongers by quoting one of his own favorite passages: "Touch not mine anointed, and do my prophets no harm" (Psalms 105:15).

If this didn't quiet these "totally un-Christian rumors," Tony simply dropped that particular town from his itinerary and added another. After all, there were thousands of other towns where his message and revival services were welcome, each with faithful Pentecostal families with young sons among whom he could select those emotionally needy enough to go to bed with him. And if he found that his latest guest for the night did indeed acquiesce to his sexual advances behind closed doors, then he had another candidate for his Miracle Restoration Revivals attrition-prone tent crew of teenage boys.

✝ ✝ ✝

Interestingly, in 1978 Brother Tony became concerned about carrying large sums of cash—or, perhaps, he more likely feared some irate father, mother, big brother, or uncle. For whatever reason, he bought a .38 revolver "for protection." After that, occasionally as a treat, Tony would take especially favored boys back into the woods and let them fire it at tin cans, bottles, and pine cones. But several of his young victims recall his using it to vaguely threaten them when they refused his advances or, more often, if they told him that they were going to tell folks about what he had done to them in bed.

✝ ✝ ✝

Since giving up his church in Fletcher, North Carolina, in 1969, Brother Tony traveled the revival circuit constantly, only pausing briefly to rest every few months at his mother's home in nearby Hendersonville. But in 1976 the Reverend Tony Leyva put down roots of his own and established the Tony Leyva Evangelistic Association in a run-down church complex that he leased on Southern Boulevard in West Palm Beach, Florida. He renamed the small collection of buildings the Bible Days Revival Center and began preaching regular Holy Ghost services there as well as continuing frequent Holy Ghost revival trips throughout the Southeast and all the way north to Illinois, Indiana, and Ohio.

As 1977 began, Brother Tony announced to his fledgling flock in West Palm Beach and those attending his revival meetings on the road, "God called me to set a world record for preaching His word!" This intensified over the next month as he began inviting one and all and even newspaper reporters to come and hear him. Just before the planned date for his performance he presented a singular request to his local congregation: "God told me that he wants all you brothers and sisters to put extra money in the collection tonight so you can be part of this great preaching to defeat Satan. And remember: When you do this, God will give you extra special blessings for doing your part to help spread His word!"

This trick caused the cash to come rolling in, and so at 7:00 P.M. on February 10, 1977, Brother Tony climbed onto the roof of his revival center and began his much-ballyhooed "preachathon" by telling members of his flock assembled in great numbers below him, "I'm gonna preach till Jesus tells me to stop 'cause I'm wrapped up, tied up, tangled up with Jesus! I love Him to death!"

Over the next three days specially selected and trained groups of teenage boys brought him food, and water, and erected screens so that Brother Tony could relieve himself privately or doze for five minutes here and there. Miami-area newspapers and radio and television stations carried progress reports day by day, and an estimated five thousand people came to watch the stunt.

Not one to miss such an opportunity to enrich his coffers, Brother Tony strategically positioned several large washtubs for donations on the ground below and had members of his flock constantly circulate through the crowds with collection buckets. Finally, at one o'clock in the afternoon of February 13, 1977, Tony Leyva hoarsely boasted to over one thousand faithful and curiosity seekers gathered below: "God just come to me in a vision and said for me to end my sermon because it's now a new world's record!"

In short order Brother Tony sent off the required documentation to the *Guinness Book of World Records* certifying his record sixty-six-hour sermon as the world's longest, a record which he held for several years.

On through the late 1970s and well into the 1980s, Brother Leyva made his headquarters in West Palm Beach as he added cities and towns all over southern Florida to his revival schedule, in addition to more frequent stops in other states and even occasional trips overseas to Haiti, the Dominican Republic, and for the first time, his father's native Cuba. His personal wealth and congregations both at home and on the road grew right along with his never-ending sexual exploitation of constantly growing numbers of teenage boys.

✝ ✝ ✝

In 1976 Brother Tony discovered a rich lode of faithful Pentecostals with comely young adolescent sons in Roanoke County, Virginia, and began mining it with frequent, regularly scheduled revivals, eventually holding many of his meetings in the county seat's Salem Civic Center which held seven thousand. Although Brother Tony's revivals never drew more than three or four thousand, his thrice-nightly collections often brought him upwards of twenty thousand dollars for a single performance.

Traditional Pentecostals attending these revivals found themselves put off by the evangelist's habit of flamboyantly parading around the stage calling himself "Super Christian" wearing a custom-made Superman-like costume complete with cape. Some observant congregants couldn't help but notice how his act attracted scores of young boys to the foot of the stage. But Tony didn't worry about this; after the service, "Tony's boys" as well as some adult supporters would hawk his vanity press autobiography—also entitled *Super Christian*—and sell paperback copies to the faithful and their young sons along with gaudy "Brother Tony Leyva" prayer cloths, plastic Bible covers, "Super Christian" book marks, and scores of other cheaply produced souvenirs that earned him net profits as high as five hundred percent.

One family drawn into the evangelist's thick web of fiscal and sexual deception lived in a small community east of Roanoke near Lynchburg, home to nationally known Baptist preacher and Moral Majority founder Jerry Falwell, his Thomas Road Baptist Church, and his extremely conservative Liberty College.

I interviewed Susan Plunkett, the Pentecostal matriarch of this family, in her rural red rock home on October 12, 1988. Her daughter, Tina Myers, sat in on my interview. The night before, I had extensively interviewed Susan's sons from her first marriage—Bobby and Timmy Earls, both victims of Leyva's—for the first time.

Susan said that she first became aware of Tony Leyva when he preached a revival in Roanoke in the late 1970s, when Bobby and Timmy were about eleven and nine and therefore rapidly reaching an attractive age for Brother Tony.

"My children come from a broken home," said Susan. "I got married when I was a young teenager and my first husband was a drunk . . . he always mistreated me; he never provided for the children the things that they needed. And this is Bobby's and Timmy's real father. Okay? So, I divorced him after more than a dozen years of marriage.

"So, I didn't have any money and I had to put my children with a neighbor lady and find a job before I could get my children back, which I did. I divorced my first husband and I went to work and got my children all back home within six months' time. Then, it was about a year later that I married their first stepfather, David, and the older kids, they rebelled against him; they didn't approve of him; they weren't satisfied with him.

"But Bobby and Timmy were smaller and they really thought a lot of him and they loved him. Me and David were married five years and then he had a heart attack and he died. He died with my son Bobby beside him and Bobby seen all of this. He was eight years old when David died. So, since Bobby seen all of this he always had this on his mind; it was something that he could never get out of his mind.

"Then I married Jimmy Wayne Plunkett, and he tried to be good to my children, but by then the youngest ones were so upset over their real father's way of treating them and then their stepdaddy David's dying, that they didn't even want to give Jimmy Wayne a chance. . . . They resented him coming into the family so soon after David had died."

While David was alive he and Susan had attended several of Brother

Tony's Miracle Restoration Revivals at the Salem Civic Center. Bobby and Timmy were mesmerized by the attention lavished on them and their peers after the service by this fun-loving, frequently costumed, affectionate evangelist. Susan told how, as her two youngest sons' resentment of Jimmy Wayne grew, so did their attraction to Brother Tony.

"The way I came to know Tony Leyva," Susan said, "was that it was posted on papers that were passed around that he was gonna have a revival at the Salem Civic Center, so we had went. There had been other evangelists there, but he was different 'cause he just won the people over; I mean, he was sincere in that he looked and acted like he was really dedicated to God and was the man of God doing God's work. You would just fall in love with him! You felt so comfortable being there at his revival meetings 'cause you could feel the spirit of the Lord moving; you would feel so much love!

"I mean, it was just altogether different than any of the other meetings that I'd went to, such as this Ivy something evangelist from Ohio that came in quite a few times; and he'd say, 'Well, I'm just not getting enough money from the people to pay my room here and my traveling expenses. I don't guess I'll be back to Roanoke again.'

"I said, 'Well, if that man just come here to get the money and not teach us the word of God and tell us about the word, heck with that, I'm not ever going to his meeting again.'

"But then Tony Leyva comes in. I mean, he just swept everybody off their feet, 'specially the children. And before Tony Leyva came, I would not watch a TV, I didn't read the newspapers; and when I read, I read my Bible. And I prayed. I was really dedicated to God. Back then, the Pentecostal movement was all new to me. But I'd never really experienced it before until just before Tony Leyva started coming to the Civic Center.

"Then when Tony Leyva came in, I mean, he just really swept everybody off their feet! You'd hear about his meeting that was coming up and everybody would get so excited that they just couldn't wait to get to his meeting.

"At first we went to worship the Lord and to learn more about the Lord and Brother Tony would tell us different things; how the Lord would bless him, what the Lord was doing for his ministry; you know, just different things so that you really didn't pay any attention about him attracting all these young boys around him at his meetings."

A very personable, handsome young man today—married and with two young sons of his own—Bobby Earls candidly told about meeting Brother Tony Leyva:

"I first met Tony Leyva through my mom. She always went to his meetings when he was over to Salem and she knew how he loved kids. I was twelve years old when . . . I went to his revival for the first time. I wasn't religious or nothin' like that, I was just tryin' to be with it by going with all the other kids who went to his revivals. And Tony wanted me to come stay the night with him then, but I didn't till later.

"But the first time I heard him preach I thought he was like a king! He preached good and everybody liked him. And he really did pay attention to us kids, my friends and me. I really admired being around him! After that we kept going to hear him and see him and every time somebody mentioned he was comin' in again I was up there!

"That was when we went to his revivals with my first stepdaddy; but then he died and my mom got married again to Jimmy Wayne, my second stepdaddy. And just before I stayed overnight with Tony Leyva the first time, Jimmy Wayne had just got in the family. He was tryin' to pay me and my brother attention, but the problem was, I think, we was resenting him being there between our mama and us. But when it came to Tony Leyva, I didn't resent the attention he gave me. Naw, I guess I didn't resent it at all."

Susan Plunkett told how it finally came to pass that she allowed her son Bobby to spend his very first overnight with Brother Tony Leyva, and how the evangelist himself craftily engineered the event:

"[O]ne night Tony Leyva come to me wanting my son Bobby to go with him, ya know, stay the night with him. He said that he would work with him . . . take care of him, tell him about the Lord and try to bring him to the Lord. But at that time Bobby was just twelve and I felt that my son was too young to go and I told Tony Leyva no.

"So, Tony Leyva would still come back in to the Salem Civic Center and hold his revival meetings for a full week every few months, and we'd always go and after the services he'd tell my son he could spend the night with him if my son would come ask me himself and I would say yes. So, after a while, after my son asked several times, I finally agreed and let Bobby [then twelve] go and spend the night there with Tony Leyva at his motel over in Salem. See, after he asked that first time, Tony Leyva never did come right up and ask me again about my son spending the night with him. But he'd always put Bobby up to asking me.

"After I'd gotten to know Tony Leyva and was going regular to his revival meetings, I kinda thought, ya know, maybe his attention to my son will kinda get this worry off of my boy Bobby and bring him out of what he was going through after his stepdaddy died. So, I let my son go spend the night with Tony Leyva in his motel room.

"But that same night I had a vision when I was asleep that my son was gonna be hurt in some way. And I woke up in a cold sweat and I told my husband, Jimmy Wayne, I said, 'Jimmy Wayne there's something wrong.' I said, 'God showed me, that something was going to happen to my Bobby and he was going to be mistreated and it's about Tony Leyva.'

"So, my husband says, 'Susan, you can't go by things like that, you just can't because the devil puts things into your mind and he can give you dreams, also.' He said, 'Ya know you're not supposed to touch God's anointed and Brother Tony is God's anointed!'

"But, then, after Bobby got back the next day after spending that first night with Tony Leyva, . . . he had a hundred-dollar bill. A twelve-year-old boy and he had a hundred-dollar bill in his pocket! And I said, 'Bobby, where in the world did you get money like that?'

"And he said, 'Brother Tony give it to me.'

"I said, 'Why?'

"He said, 'So I can buy me a minibike. He felt sorry for me, 'cause he knew I couldn't buy it.'

"And I says, 'Something's wrong.' I mean, you don't just give a boy that much money. Still, I'd go back and talk to my husband and it was the same old thing over. He didn't suspect nothing with the money. That's how Tony Leyva had everybody deceived, you know. They thought so much of him that they couldn't even imagine him doing anything wrong."

Of course, Susan's suspicions were absolutely correct, just as her son Bobby confirmed in his detailed account of what happened that fateful first night he spent with Brother Tony Leyva:

"When I first stayed the night with Tony Leyva he was holdin' a week-long revival at the Civic Center over to Salem. There was a lot of people there at the revival . . . I'd say at least several hundred or so every night, and lots of 'em were kids. And we was goin' to his services ever night he was there.

"That was in about 1981 when I was thirteen years old. We went to two or three of his night services that week and then one night he told me to go ask my mom if I could stay the night with him. And for some reason my mom didn't like the idea and so she said no.

"But the next night he was preachin' about how important it was to be teaching kids about God and stuff like that, so she heard him and she kinda trusted him . . . 'specially when he came to her afterwards and told her how he was really wanting to talk to me about God. Then my step daddy, Jimmy Wayne, went up to Tony and asked him if he was gay, and he said, 'No.' So, after that my stepdaddy trusted him and so then my mom said yes and . . . she let me go spend the night with Tony Leyva at his motel.

"First off, he took me to eat at Country Cookin' over on Melrose Avenue where they had all-you-can-eat chicken and steaks and stuff like that. Then we walked up to the Embassy Motor Lodge . . . and he gave me money to go play video games while he done his bookwork.

"After a while I come up to his room and it kinda bothered me that there was just this one bed. It was just me there in the room with him so I got in bed with all my clothes on 'cause I was scared to take 'em off.

"So, I went to sleep and it was later on that night that he woke me up ticklin' me. He told me I'd be more comfortable without my clothes on and he finally got me to take all my clothes off, 'cept for I left my underwear on. . . .

"But right after I done that he started playing with me . . . you know, my dick . . . then he pulled my underwear down and started suckin' on me down there. And I didn't understand what was goin' on 'cause I was only twelve years old then. And I was shakin' and stuff and he started crying and telling me how much God loved me and how much he loved me and cared about me . . . sayin' how much he liked layin' there with me. . . . You know, it's really hard to explain the way he does . . ." (Bobby trailed off emotionally).

"Afterwards, after he'd finished doin' sex to me, I asked him does he think it was right for him to do that to me and he said, 'yeah,' that he didn't see nothin' wrong with 'it.' And I just had to trust him 'cause I'd never knew nothin' about sex up until then . . . and him being a preacher and all.

"But it was kinda funny 'cause he asked me not to say anything about what he did. He said some people will think bad about what he done. But I didn't think to ask him why 'cause at that time I trusted him 'cause he was a preacher. So, I just took his word for it.

"Then the next morning he got me into [the] shower with him. While we's in there he started rubbin' on me with a bar of soap in his hand and then he got down on his knees and had oral sex with me for the second time. And when we's dryin' off and dressin' he reminded me not to say nothin' and then he gave me a hundred dollar bill for letting him do sex with me. Ya see, for Tony Leyva, money was the only thing that really talked for him.

"But thinking back to when I went with him that first time, I'd thought, 'He's gonna teach me the Bible and stuff about God.' But he never did."

That first night Bobby Earls spent with Brother Tony at the Embassy Motor Lodge was but a prelude to regular stays at that location, a rendezvous the evangelist made certain to arrange whenever he would come to the Roanoke area, said his then new victim:

"Tony Leyva came back to the Salem Civic Center in about three months. He'd always come in about every three months. And again he had me come stay the night with him in the same motel and sleep in the same bed he did. And he did oral sex on me again. And he didn't teach me no Bible or stuff about God then, neither.

"Then the third time he got me to get my friend James Cash to come and stay the night along with me. James was the same age as me and we was good friends. And that time he had two beds, but he had me and James to sleep in different ones. First he done oral sex with me, then he done it with James in the other bed. Same every time, except after a while he started doin' masturbation, too, with each boy in each bed. Just one time with each of us, though, then he'd go on to the next one.

"With me it was always '69.' That's about all Tony Leyva wanted and that's the way he liked it with me, but I always quit on him before he'd come. But he'd always have me come in his mouth 'cause he said that's the way he got the power of the Holy Ghost in him so's that he could preach.

"All together, he did it to me about two hundred times total, I guess it was. And he masturbated me with his hand, too. And lots of times while he was doin' it to me he was into self-masturbation, too, right at the end when he was gettin' ready to come.

"And when I was about thirteen or fourteen, he talked about tryin' anal sex with me when he was feelin' all over my butt. But I didn't like the idea and he said that it hurt him too much when somebody did it to him, and I said, 'Well, I don't want nothing to do with this,' and so he didn't even ask me again."

About his little brother getting to know Brother Tony and coming to "stay the night," too, Bobby Earls said: "The fourth time I stayed with Tony Leyva was about a year later and that's when my brother Timmy come and stayed the night with him for the first time. Since I didn't tell my mom about it 'cause I was ashamed, my mom didn't know what Tony was doin' and so she let Timmy come. And he done the same thing to Timmy, too, that he done to me."

Timothy Earls himself talked about being seduced and sexually assaulted by Brother Tony Leyva, and then being used to recruit the evangelist's next young victim:

"I first met Tony Leyva when I was about ten, but I wasn't old enough to stay overnight with him like my big brother. It was at least a year after my brother Bobby started stayin' with him before my mom would let me stay, too. Not till later when I was twelve. That night when I first stayed with Tony Leyva, after the service he took me and my brother out to eat at a real nice place and let us order whatever we wanted.

"But then he took me and my brother back to his room and had my brother Bobby sleep in one bed and me and him sleep in the other one. And Tony Leyva had sex with me that very first night I stayed with him at that motel in Salem.

"When I first stayed with him and he done that, I didn't know what he was doin' 'cause me and my brother never talked about it with each other. You see, my brother never told me nothin' beforehand. And that very first time, just like my big brother, it was oral sex that Tony Leyva done to me.

"He acted like it was natural, just like that was what I was supposed to do . . . I was there in that bed with him by myself and I hadn't had no experience with sex or anythin' like that before. I was frightened and scared. I didn't know what to think. . . ." (Timmy sighed and paused briefly).

"At first, he just played with me. Then he put his mouth on me and did 'it' to me while I just laid there. I was so scared that I didn't move, but then I started shakin' and he tried to calm me down and told me that it was okay for us to be doin' that.

"Then he went right ahead and jacked himself off and put my hand down on him afterwards. And when he got through he said that other people might not understand the way that he did and that I ought not to say anythin' about it. And I didn't, neither.

"The next time he asked me to come stay the night with him he got me to bring along Jonathan Cash, James's brother. Me and Jonathan went to school together, and we was the same age then. And startin' then, usually, we both stayed with him together on the same nights.

"That first time that he got me to bring Jonathan, he took us to some nice steak place to eat. (He'd always take us out to eat. . . . Usually it was an all-you-could-eat place. I mean, it was more or less good food for a cheap price.)

"Then we went back to where he always stayed [the Embassy Motor Lodge on Melrose] and we went up to his room. When we got there there was two beds and he had us undress and get in different beds, just like he done that first time I went with my brother to stay with him. That's when he done oral sex with Jonathan for the first time, then he come to my bed and did it again with me.

"With Tony, he called us his boys. . . . 'Tony's boys' is what people called us. And he said it made him feel good when we was around. He said that he never got to be around his son that much. We was supposed to be taking the place of his son, I thought, and he was takin' the place of my stepdaddy that died."

Remarked Timmy's mother, Susan, "We knew that Tony Leyva was divorced and that he had two kids. He told us that. But he blamed the divorce on his wife. He said that she was of the devil and because he wouldn't have anything to do with her, she turned against his ministry. He said that it was her that was of the devil 'cause she said he wasn't preaching God's word. And on different occasions, I guess to make people think he was normal, Tony Leyva would mention in his meetings that some woman in his services in another state was trying to put the make on him, but he said he was too busy preaching God's word and holding his revival meetings to have any relations with a woman. So, he had us fooled about that."

But Timothy vividly recalls Tony Leyva's rationale for sexually abusing him: "When it came to the sex, he said he had asked God about it and God had never answered him about it, so, as far as he knew, it was all right for him to do it. Therefore, with him bein' a preacher and a prophet an' all, we knew better than to question him about it so we just done what he said and never questioned him about anything."

Robert Earls picked up the story: "The next time he came to town, James, Jonathan's brother, was there again and Tony Leyva done 'it' with all three of us . . . me, Timmy, and James; once each, right in front of each other. Most times he'd do whoever was sleepin' with him first and then he'd go to the other bed and do 'it' with them. It was sorta like, ya know, 'He's gonna come over to my bed next,' so we'd just lay there and wait."

Apparently on a cathartic roll, Robert Earls continued detailing his experiences with the evangelist: "Finally, he got to where he had others come spend the night, so many boys that he'd have to have more 'n one room at the motel and that's when he got to where he switched around: There was me and James and Timmy and Mark and Jonathan and some others, and he'd go from one room to the other doin' 'it.' It was just like one of us would lead Tony Leyva to another one and then that one would lead Tony to another one and they would all come and stay the night with Tony Leyva at that motel in Salem.

"First time he took nude pictures of me was one time when just my friend James Cash and me spent the night with him. First he got James to go in the bathroom with him and stand there naked and use the bathroom while he took pictures of him standin' up an' pissin'. Then he had us both lay on the bed, face up on our backs without any clothes on and he took a few pictures with us regular [i.e., without an erection]. Then he got some pictures of us with hard-ons. Then right after he took them pictures, he had oral sex with both of us."

"Startin' soon after that, when I'd stay the night with him, in the mornings he got me to gettin' up with him. He'd tell me to go take a shower, then after I was in there he'd come get in with me, sayin', 'We's in a hurry. We's goin' to a meetin' and so I gotta take a shower with you so's we can hurry up.' But he wasn't in no hurry 'cause then when he got himself in there with me he'd try to play around with me and have sex with me.

"It wasn't long before we was always coming around and stayin' with him. He'd call us on the phone all the time and let us know when he'd be up here and we'd go over to Salem and stay the night with him...."

✝ ✝ ✝

On a hot July day in 1983, in Salem, Virginia, Tony Leyva took four of his boys to the Salem Civic Center to set up his sound equipment for that night's revival. All four were set to spend the night with him afterward. After the sweaty work at the Civic Center Tony drove them back that afternoon to his favorite local haunt on Melrose Avenue, escorted them to his room, dramatically remarked about the heat, stripped naked in front of them, and announced that he was going to take a cold shower to cool off, suggesting they do the same.

Present were Bobby Earls, his brother Timmy, and James and Jonathan Cash. Of that afternoon Bobby Earls recalled: "First he showed us some nude pictures of his kids from overseas ... from that orphanage he said he was givin' money to over in Haiti. And he says that that's the way he likes to remember his kids."

Bobby's brother, Timmy, agreed. "He showed off a bunch of nude photos he had took of naked boys over in the Caribbean and says that's the way he likes to take pictures of his boys ... naked. Then he took off his clothes and said he's gonna take a shower an' we ought to take one, too."

Bobby continued: "Then after he got us to undress and we was takin' turns gettin' in the shower—'cause we couldn't all get in there at once—he came in with his Polaroid camera and said that he wanted to take some pictures of us naked so he could keep somethin' to remember us by, too. And we said 'okay' and let him 'cause we thought it was interestin'."

But that wasn't the end of it. Eric finished describing this sad episode by recounting Brother Tony's insatiable rush to take still more nude photographs of his young guests that night: a rush so all-consuming that the evangelist couldn't get away from his revival soon enough.

"When we got back to the Civic Center he rushed through his sermon and finished up real quick and it was after nine. He didn't spend no time visitin' with people that night. He just hurried up and stuffed his collection money in his money bags . . . so we could leave and get back to the motel, is what he said.

"Then me and Tony and James and Jonathan all got in his limousine and he started drivin' all over Roanoke tryin' to find a store that was still open so he could buy some more Polaroid film.

"Finally, he found a People's Drug Store, but they was just closin' and so he jumps out and run up to the door with his money bag and starts bangin' on the door. And he was yellin' at the guy who he was and that he needed to get film for his revival. The guy let him in and when he come back he had a whole bag full of Polaroid film for his camera. Then he took us for hamburgers and fries and such, but he kept on wantin' us to hurry up and eat.

"When we got back to the motel that night he had us take off our clothes and take showers again. Then he had us suck on each other's dicks while he took, roughly, probably, 'bout thirty to forty pictures of us doin' it. An' he was just eatin' up that film 'cause it was ten pictures to the roll!

"He said he was takin' 'em so he would have somethin' to remember us by, but that just didn't sound right. But like before, we was more or less not askin' him any questions. With him we just kinda learned it was better not to ask.

"When he was finished he gave us twenty dollars each and we went and played Pac Man while he stayed in his room and done his book work. We come back later and went to bed, but then he done what he always done, had sex with us after we got in bed.

"But that day was the *only* day that he took nude pictures of me . . . and he took 'em twice . . . once just naked but the other time of us suckin' one another off."

For Timothy Earls this became a sad, vicious, abusive circle as he kept coming back to stay with Brother Tony, not liking what happened, but apparently attracted both by the attention—"any attention's better 'n no attention"—and the money . . . lots of money to this very impressionable young teenage boy from rural Virginia: "Later on he always gave me lots of money. He never did buy me no clothes or nothin' like that. But in the thirty times or so that he had sex with me, he gave me lots of money. All together, ever since I've known him, I'd say probably about three thousand dollars. Maybe even four thousand.

"About twenty out of the thirty times that Tony Leyva did 'it' with me, Jonathan was there with me and he had sex with him, too. But after it was over Jonathan and me never would talk about it . . . even with each other. We'd just keep it to ourselves."

Then the young man paused and reflected sadly, "But I feel real, *real* bad about the sex stuff that happened back then . . . 'specially them pictures I let him take. I still cuss and party and drink, but I don't do that kind of sex anymore 'cause I know it's real bad now."

7

"I ain't never lived with my own father and I thought that was what Tony's trying to be to me."

Susan Plunkett became even more troubled when she noticed how her sons all but worshiped at Tony Leyva's feet. In Bobby's and Timmy's eyes Brother Tony could do no wrong, even though their mother felt ambiguity in their oft-repeated denials to her that anything was wrong. And still she experienced the mysterious and appalling dreams of Tony Leyva committing unspecified malevolent acts with boys. Nevertheless, she had failed completely in her efforts to find evidence of anything morally amiss with the preacher: every time Susan brought the subject up, her husband, her sons, and even her relations told her to be careful, that her dreams and visions were dead wrong and came from the devil. But then Tony Leyva's involvement with her boys reached distressing new highs.

"Tony Leyva come to me wanting my son Bobby to go out of town with him," Susan remarked with an edge to her voice, "to *travel* with him and help him to set up the tent and sound equipment for his revival meetings. And Bobby really begged me; he said, 'Mama, please let me go with Brother Tony! It's something I wanna do! . . . I can get to see other sights and all.' My husband, Jimmy Wayne, was all for it; but I was not! But, against my better judgment, I let him go.

"That first time Bobby went out of town with Tony Leyva, he went to join him on the bus. And Tony Leyva sent the money for the ticket. My Bobby was just thirteen years old then!"

Said Bobby, "By the time I was thirteen I was having trouble at school and at home, and my stepdaddy let me travel with Tony and help him with the tent and his sound system at the revivals. And altogether I traveled on the road with Tony Leyva for a total of about seven or eight months. I traveled all over with him . . . Georgia, and Indiana, and Florida, Alabama, Illinois, Arkansas, Louisiana . . . and Mississippi, I been there, too."

"But," interjected Susan, "later that same night that Bobby left on the bus, I had another vision. This one was that my son was on this bus and the man that he was going to meet was gonna mistreat him and that there was something desperately wrong with Brother Tony. But my husband, Jimmy Wayne, said I was wrong and to go back to sleep.

"So, this sort of thing just kept stirring in me and kept worrying and worrying and worrying me. I'd went to my sister and said, 'I feel so uneasy. God's trying to show me something concerning this man Tony Leyva and my Bobby.' I said that something's not right.

"But she just turned her head away and she said, 'Well, you know, you're not supposed to go against God's anointed; we're not supposed to put him down; we're not supposed to talk about him.' So, everybody I would try to talk to would just say the same thing. Then, I got to thinking; 'Well maybe, the devil *is* putting this stuff in my mind. Maybe I'm just being suspicious and overprotective of my son.'

"So, when Bobby got back, I talked to my son and said, 'Bobby, what do you and Tony Leyva do? What do y'all do while you're away and you're staying in the motels with him?'

"And he said, 'Mama, we watch TV. Tony reads his Bible and prays.' That would be all he said."

In spite of her tremendous maternal intuition to the contrary, Susan Plunkett allowed first her son, Bobby, and soon thereafter his brother Timmy to join Tony Leyva on the road, leaving behind the safety of their home and family.

Timmy Earls recounted: "I was fourteen the first trip Jonathan and me took with Tony Leyva. He picked us up in Roanoke and drove us in his limousine to Indiana. We stayed in an apartment up there right beside a church. And each night we drove from there to some place in Illinois, right there across the water, where he preached in a church there for a whole week.

"Up there, it was basically the black people he preached to, more or less from what I seen. And at the services he'd just be huggin' on the black boys, but he never brought any of them 'round to the apartment to spend the night. Like, when me and my brother and friends traveled with him, he never brought none of them back from the services with him.

Only time I knew him to do anything with black kids was taking those nude pictures of 'em at that orphanage he had over in Haiti.

"But with white kids it was different. There was so many young people and 'specially boys at his meetings and services that he was always having somebody stay with him in his room. He didn't have no trouble with that! After I started travelin' with him, lots of times it was some new boy he'd done met at one of his revivals there on the road. And that was fine with me 'cause I knew that that night it would be him instead of me in bed with him.

"I remember this boy that stayed with him up in Indiana. His first name was Lloyd, but I don't remember his last name. And he was about me an' Jonathan's age, thirteen, and he went to the church that was by the apartment where we stayed at. But I remember Lloyd tellin' me that Tony Leyva asked him to let him do anal sex with him. Then they went into Tony's room at the apartment and the next day Lloyd told met that he let Tony do 'it' and then Tony gave him fifty dollars. Tony Leyva was always pickin' up boys like that, 'specially if they'd let him do what he wanted to with 'em.

"But in the motels on the way to Indiana and on the way back, just like always when me and Jonathan went with him, he had two beds. He would have one of us sleep in one bed and the other sleep in the other. Then he'd go get in bed with one of us and have oral sex and then he'd go get in bed with the other one and do 'it' with him."

From Indiana they drove south to Marietta, Georgia, where Brother Tony got word that some law enforcement officials from out of town had been checking around his church in West Palm Beach asking questions about his whereabouts and activities. Tony's informant wasn't sure what was going on, but for the time being Tony felt it best to lie low in Georgia for a while.

Within days of his party's arrival in Marietta, local organist and evangelist Edward Rias Morris had begun rapaciously pursuing Tony's boys and having sex with a couple of them, Timothy Earls among them; so the boy sadly learned still more on this, his inaugural trip with the deviant prophet.

"When he finished up preachin' in Illinois," Timmy recounted, "we drove down to Marietta, Georgia, and on the way we went by Roanoke and picked up Jonathan's brother James.

"Back then Tony Leyva was stayin' temporarily at the Skyview Motel in Marietta and when we got there his [Tony Leyva's] young relative Danny Perez was there. He'd been staying there with this other evangelist that Tony knew, a guy by the name of Ed Morris. And Danny Perez was just ten, and the very first night we got back Tony slept with Danny and had sex with him. Danny told us about it.

"Atlanta . . . is where Ed's wife lives, but they really live separately. They always talked like they were living together, but they always lived separately and never in the same home. And after Tony Leyva come to Georgia he met Ed and after that most times Ed was Tony's organist and he was always travelin' around with Tony. I knew Ed was gay. Everybody knew it, even if he never did say it," Timmy remarked.

Over the next week Tony's boys learned more about the ne'er-do-well Ed Morris, and it certainly didn't fit his stated role as a Pentecostal evangelist and regular church organist. According to Robert Earls, "Ed was a jokester. . . . Even when he was up front preachin, he'd tell his jokes. And Ed Morris had a dirty mouth. A *real* dirty mouth. He wouldn't use it when he was preachin', but away from that he was always calling people 'motherfucker' and 'SOB' and stuff like that. But then both him and Tony Leyva cussed when they were not preachin'."

Robert's brother Timmy added, "You ain't kiddin', he had a dirty mouth! But I just overlooked their cussin', 'cause I did it myself. When you do stuff yourself, you don't think of it as bein' that bad."

Added to this, Leyva and Morris were soon trading their young victims back and forth and going from one boy's bed to another's at the motel. But when it came to the boy who happened to be one of his special favorites in bed, Tony Leyva drew the line.

Robert recalled, "Tony Leyva warned me about Ed Morris. He said that he liked messin' around with kids. That he wanted to keep me to himself and he didn't want Morris moving in on me. So, I stayed away from Ed as much as I could. It was kinda funny, though, comin' from Tony Leyva, 'cause the way he talked it was like he was jealous of Ed, like I was gonna start hangin' around with Ed instead of him. In a way, I thought probably Tony was stickin' up for me. That he was caring for me . . . tryin' to help me. And in a way, that made me feel real good.

"But Morris took me out to a movie once in Atlanta and while I sat and watched the movie he started talkin' 'bout sex shops, stuff like that, mainly. And I wanted to go back to the motel 'cause I was going out with some friends of mine. That was when I was workin' on Tony's big revival tent rig for a while.

"But Ed always come around a lot when Tony was gone. He'd come over a lot to see us boys and he'd wanta take us out to eat or somethin'. At first, I never thought anything of it, I just thought he was a jokester. He always joked with people. But then Tony warned me about him and made sure I was never alone with Ed Morris."

But Tony Leyva didn't have the same affection for Robert's brother, Timothy, and so—with Leyva's blessing—Morris freely moved in on and started sexually abusing Timothy with no compunction.

As Timothy recalled it, "When we was down there Ed had me have sex with him. Actually, Tony Leyva's the one who got me to do oral sex with Ed. Tony did 'it' with me and then he told me to do 'it' with Ed, and so I did.

"Ed usually give us money after he had sex with us. And, of course, Tony did, too. But with Tony it was always like a friggin' slot machine. You couldn't lose with him!"

According to Susan Plunkett, "I had no dealings with that Ed Morris; never met him. But I heard my sons talking about him and Robert would say that Tony Leyva would leave him with Ed Morris while he went off to another revival meeting somewhere and I said, 'Well, Robert, that wouldn't be right, 'cause Tony Leyva took you with him. He's supposed to have kept you with him at all times.' But Tony Leyva didn't. So, my sons are with this man Ed Morris that I have never met and I had the same feelings of concern about him as I did about Tony Leyva."

On their long-haul revival trips with Brother Tony, Timothy and Robert Earls had many experiences as tent crew members on the Miracle Restoration Revivals. They observed the evangelist's own style of old-time religion on stage, gospel singing, preaching, speaking in tongues, prophesying, and performing miracles. Up close they learned his skill with collection buckets, milking the last dime out of the poor yet truly believing souls who attended his services.

As to Tony Leyva's "performing miracles," he put on a good show that even Susan Plunkett could remark on: "There was this lady by the name of Sister Waters who went to Tony Leyva's meetings over at the Salem Civic Center. She had a daughter named Kathy who started coming to the services with her mother and she wasn't a Christian; she was a young girl, confused by living a wild life.

"So, Sister Waters wanted Tony Leyva to pray for her. Her daughter didn't want him to, but he come up and put his hands on her anyway; and she cussed him and she spit in his face. He grabbed hold of her and he shook her, and he started praying for her and demanding the demons to come out of her. I mean, she was throwing just one heck of a fit with him! Then, all at once, she got real calm, ya know, just real peaceful-like. And with a lot of the people at the meeting it was like, 'Hey, he really did cast out that demon that was in her!' At the time I believed. But now—after all that come out about him—I suspect that Tony Leyva had that arranged.

"And my son Robert told me that in some of Tony Leyva's revivals in the tent down in Georgia he set things up to appear like that. Robert says, 'Mommy, you wouldn't believe what went into Tony Leyva's sermon.' He says, 'Mommy, you can't believe that Tony Leyva cast this devil out of this person because he set it all up beforehand.' He says, 'Mommy, it looked like it was amazing! But it wasn't real. A person like Tony Leyva could never do something like that for real!'

"And you know, if he was doing things like he was to little boys, as far as I'm concerned, the sky's the limit. He'd do anything to trick the people!'"

Another dark facet of Tony Leyva emerged when he became angered at some of the hard-working adolescent members of "Tony's boys." As Susan recalled: "My boys told me that sometimes Tony Leyva would get real angry with them. . . . [I]f Tony would get real upset with one of the boys on the tent crew, he would beat him up. Also, my son Robert said that he got angry with him a few times, but he wouldn't tell me what Tony Leyva would do. He would just say that Tony Leyva got angry with him.

"I recall a couple of times when my Robert looked really worried and concerned, and I said, 'Robert, what's wrong?'

"He said, 'Mama, I ain't got time to talk. I've gotta hurry up and set this [tent] up. Tony Leyva's really upset.' I said, 'About what?'

"He said, 'I just don't wanna talk about it, Mama, he's real upset about something.' And Robert wouldn't tell me what had happened or anything; just said Tony Leyva got real upset with him. And Timothy was always the same way, so I never knew the details about what upset Tony Leyva or what, specifically, he would do to the boys about it."

As for the money that constantly flowed into Tony Leyva's pockets, nobody but Brother Tony has any idea about just how much cash his wheedling and cajoling of the faithful brought in through the years. But Timothy Earls could remark on the amount of money people gave: "When I got older, about fourteen, and went to travelin' regular with him, my brother and me always went out on the road together. That's the way our mom wanted it, so we could look out after each other.

"And one night soon after I went on the road with Tony Leyva, he had us takin' up his collections and people was givin' so much money that we was havin' to empty out th' washtub after we'd dump just one collection in it. Then later, after all three collections that night, we was countin' his money for him and noticin' that it looked like he coulda' robbed a bank! And several times when I was countin' his money I seen for myself that he cleared, easy, ten thousand dollars in just one night!

"At some of his tent revival meetings he would attract close to about seven, eight hundred people. But at some of the small churches he went to, like in Truman, Arkansas, there was only about two hundred that came. But it was worth it to him to preach in places like Truman from a money standpoint 'cause it seemed, just like almost everywhere he went, even if he had a light crowd, they always seemed to give him at least five thousand dollars 'cause they believed in his ministry that strong. And the reason they believed that strong was all the miracles that he'd do.

"And I asked him what he done with all his money and he says, 'I'm puttin' it in a Tony Leyva Evangelistics bank account.' He said he didn't get much of it, that all of it had to go into the bank. But I never seen him put any money in any bank. He was just tellin' us that he did. All I ever seen him do was put it in those bank bags he carried around with him and then spend it."

Robert Earls added, "I've always seen Tony with lots of money in those big bank bags of his. He'd have a bunch of 'em to where everyone would be three to four inches thick with bills. And he'd take all the quarters and give 'em to us to play video games with. I never seen him take any money to a regular bank, far as that goes.

"And when we went out to eat, he'd buy us all big steak dinners and pay for it with cash money out of those bags. Same when we'd go to a motel or when he'd keep his limousine and truck up or buy gas for 'em . . . and when he'd give us our money. He always dealt in cash for everything.

"Also, lots of times people'd want to help him so much they'd take off their rings and jewelry and stuff and drop it in the collection buckets. And he always kept this little box with all those diamonds, gold rings, watches, and other stuff in it. He said they was all gifts people gave him when they come to his services, and I guess so 'cause I seen them put that stuff in the collection buckets.

"And he was always tellin' people that all his clothes was gifts, and everything else he had, too. But there was some over-a-thousand-dollar suits that he wore. *Real* expensive suits! But nobody give 'em to him 'cause I seen him buyin' them himself with that money he got from all his collections!"

Timothy described yet another angle to the evangelist's total plan of deceit: "Yeah, one night when I was travelin' with him I was noticin' that he was gettin' all these rings and watches and stuff and I asked him about it and he said, 'I get 'em all the time.' Then he pulled out that little jewelry box he carried around and showed it to me. And it had a bunch of 'em in it already and he says, 'I collect 'em and when I get enough I sell 'em and get the money out of 'em.'"

Comparing her experiences attending revivals conducted by Tony Leyva with another evangelist she saw in Roanoke, Susan Plunkett, said: "I never personally saw anybody at Tony Leyva's revivals putting jewelry in his collection. But if they had, I wouldn't of thought anything about it because a preacher by the name of David Jones had come before Tony Leyva and at his meeting I saw hundreds of people take off their watches, their rings, their necklaces, money, whatever, and put it in a big old bucket that he had sitting in there.

"But at Tony Leyva's revivals it kinda bothered me when he would stand up there and say, 'God wants you to give, even if it's your last penny! Even if you can't pay your rent! Even if you can't buy your groceries and that's all of the money you got, you're still supposed to give it. 'Cause if you don't, God can't bless you.'

"And I'd seen people standing up there at Tony Leyva's revivals that didn't have anything and they'd give their last penny; that's how deceived they all were. That worried me; that really concerned me. I said these are poor people and I knew that they didn't have it to give, but they still gave. They'd do without just to give to Tony Leyva's ministry. And my sons would come home and say how much Tony Leyva would take in, thousands and thousands of dollars at almost every revival he preached."

"But," Timothy sarcastically remarked, "what Tony Leyva really collected was kids 'cause they would just come up to him as soon as he come into the church. He'd send out his newsletters tellin' their parents that he's coming and to bring their kids and that's how everybody always knew that he wanted kids comin' to his services."

Susan remarked: "Up until about 1986 we always got regular mailings from Tony Leyva about the places he was going to preach revival meetings. Part of this was because of my sons and part of it was because my husband was a licensed preacher through Tony Leyva's ministry.

"What happened was that after my sons and their friends had stayed with Tony Leyva again over in Salem we'd begun to hear rumors about sex-type things going on over there with the boys at the motel. So, I pushed and pushed Jimmy Wayne to find out if Tony Leyva was a homosexual and abusing my boys that way.

"But what Jimmy Wayne finally went and did was ask Brother Tony again to his face if he was a homosexual, which is not the way I would've done it. And Tony Leyva told Jimmy Wayne he wasn't a homosexual. But then, my husband said, all of a sudden Tony Leyva slapped his forehead and told Jimmy Wayne that God had come to him in a vision and told him to ordain my husband as a minister in his evangelistic association."

Susan proffered her husband's certificate. In fancy calligraphy at the top was written "Tony Leyva Evangelistic Association, Inc., Ministerial Fellowship." The certificate read as follows:

This is to certify that Jimmy Wayne Plunkett of Roanoke, State of Virginia, upon the recommendation of ministers, is hereby recognized as an ordained minister in good standing with the Tony Leyva Evangelistic Association, Inc. Ministerial Fellowship, with full authority to perform all ordinances of the church, with the approval of the Board of Directors of said Ministerial Fellowship.

"And so," Susan continued, "right here on Jimmy Wayne's certificate it says that he's an ordained minister and it's signed by Tony Leyva. And I find that kind of funny 'cause Tony Leyva isn't even ordained himself! ...

"And there's quite a few others around here that got licensed through Tony Leyva. My extremely close relative Patti Casey's husband, Jimmy Casey, got licensed through him. And if I'm not mistaken, that also happened when Jimmy asked Tony if he was funny. And I think Barbara Grisham was licensed through him. Her son Matthew traveled with Tony Leyva, too, and was one of them that was molested by him.

"But then, no matter what anybody else said, there was something bad wrong and getting worse with Tony Leyva. I watched as he started bringing in more and more boys . . . and you could tell there was something wrong with the boys . . . the way they talked . . . the way they acted . . . the way he started bringing them in to play the piano or setting up his equipment.

"He'd never pay attention to the little girls, ya know, the young girls . . . or prayed for them special like he did the boys; it was always the boys . . . always. . . . I'd say, 'Jimmy Wayne, don't you think it's strange that he's always got all these young boys around him?' But by then my husband was one of his ministers, so what was he going to say to Tony Leyva?

"But, just like I said to my son Robert, something's just not right. A person like Tony Leyva just don't give money to boys, unless there's something wrong.'

"He said, 'Mama, there's nothing wrong. Tony's a good preacher. He believes in God. He preaches good. He prays. He reads his Bible.'

"So, that would make me still more confused, you know, of the feelings that I have. I thought maybe it really is the devil putting these things in my mind.

"But then I started to notice that Tony Leyva never hardly read his Bible in his services until maybe the last year we went; then he would start opening his Bible in the services, because before then he never preached out of the Bible. That always concerned me, too.

"See, he had it all memorized. He'd come out with maybe a scripture or two or a verse or two out of the Bible and then he'd start off on something he did in another meeting, witness to this or that testimony, you know, different things; he would always go away from the Bible. And that would confuse me.

"Tony Leyva just had us all so deceived, that's all. My husband was really deceived by him. Just like I said, I had my doubts and I kept on having these feelings; but, my husband still had his trust in the man, because Tony Leyva would call him out at his services and he would prophesy to him. He would prophesy to others, too; 'Hey you, this is going to happen!'

"But he would always prophesy to them about what was going to come into their lives regardless. Nothing hard for anybody to know. Like one lady at a revival service of his put it to me, 'Any fool could have told me that!'

"And when Tony Leyva would call our home, it was always to talk to my sons. It never was to talk to me or my husband. When he would call, he'd say, 'Praise the Lord, Sister, how ya doing? Are the boys around?' And then he'd get on the phone with them and talk to them. But the boys would never want to sit in the same room with us and have a conversation on the phone with Tony Leyva. They went to their rooms and picked up the phone and talked to him. It was never in front of us and I suspected that, also.

"But, still, my husband said, 'It's just boys, ya know. They want their privacy.' But every time Leyva talked to my boys, it was always secretive.

"There was some letters that Tony Leyva had wrote my son Robert. I don't know what . . . they said because soon as I started reading them, my son walked in the room and he took them away from me and I don't know what he did with them. That one letter I saw Tony Leyva wrote him did say, 'I love you so much' and 'I miss you so much' and then signed his name on the end of it.

"But, that letter of Tony Leyva's also said something about how he was doing in his meetings and wanting to know when my Robert could come to where he was at again; that he needed my son with him so he could preach about the Holy Ghost; stuff like that.

"Just like I said, my boys wouldn't tell me anything about what was happening. Timothy is the type of boy that wouldn't tell on anyone; I mean, not until the very last bit would he talk about what happened between him and Tony Leyva. And when Timothy would come back I would question him about it and he'd say, 'Well, Mama, all I ever see him do is read the Bible and pray.' But they'd always talk about how he took them out to different fancy places eating, riding in the limousine, out to the movies, riding the rides at amusement parks . . . different things like that. Didn't sound like no evangelist to me!"

☦ ☦ ☦

As local Pentecostals in Roanoke had flocked to Brother Tony Leyva's revivals in 1976, so did they now—though on a much smaller scale—in 1984, in the small town of Truman, Arkansas, and it became a favorite stop for him. According to Timothy Earls, "I remember every time we went to Truman [Tony] always had boys at his revival meetings hang around afterwards and then to stay overnight with him. Every time we went to Truman! Never seen him have any little girls hang around him there, though. Never. Not any place else, either. If a little girl come up wanting to give Brother Tony a hug or something, he'd just try to get rid of her . . . actually push her out of the way!

"One time there was this boy younger than me come up to him there in Truman after the service and Tony was talkin' to him forever. Then he took the boy back to the motel to spend the night with him in his room while we stayed by ourselves. . . . It was just Tony Leyva and this new boy in his room. But the next mornin' the boy was gone and Tony woke us up real early and wanted us to hurry up and leave. We never did see that boy again and Tony never did talk of him so I don't know what happened between him and Tony. And I don't recall goin' back to Truman after that, neither."

☦ ☦ ☦

On one road trip to Atlanta, when Tony Leyva preached a two-week revival at the State Fairgrounds, he had a larger than usual crew of "Tony's boys" to help him and put them up in a nearby motel. One day when he left the Earls brothers alone there, they made a frightening discovery. For some time they had watched as Tony carried a large black metal footlocker around with him into his motel room, back out to his limousine, but never opening it, at least not in front of them.

Curiosity finally got the better of the brothers and they decided to find out what was inside. Timothy recalled, "When me and my brother was on the road with him down in Atlanta, we picked the lock on his chest . . . like a foot locker, down at the motel while he was having his revival at the fairgrounds. When we opened it up there was thousands of pictures in there of naked boys. . . . Polaroid pictures of naked boys having sex with each other, and a bunch of magazines with more pictures of naked boys doin' all kinds of sex with each other. Then there was a whole bunch of pictures of naked black and brown boys . . . I guess from his orphanage overseas. Some of 'em was just standin' there naked and others of 'em had hard-ons."

Remarked Timothy's brother, Robert, "He never really come right out to show us what he had in that chest of his. He had showed us a few of them pictures of naked kids from overseas before he took them nude pictures of us in Salem.

"But when we got nosy and picked the lock on his chest and seen them thousands of his naked pictures of boys and boys havin' sex, and them magazines of boys doin' sex. . . . Well, Tony always talked a lot about his overseas orphanage kids, but he had a bunch more pictures than that. I mean, he had a whole trunk full of his own pictures of boys standin' there naked and havin' sex, includin' the ones he took of us!

". . . So, we ain't never seen nothin' like that before and we got scared that he'd find out we picked the lock, so we just shut it all back up and never said nothin' to him about it. But I was real scared at what I seen!"

Timothy remarked about their never-to-be-forgotten discovery: "I never understood why he had all them pictures of naked boys in that chest. That one time he showed us them naked pictures of his boys from overseas and said he took 'em just to remember 'em by . . . well, that wasn't it. It was lots more'n just that in that chest of his!"

✝ ✝ ✝

After eight years operating out of his church-office complex in West Palm Beach, Tony Leyva actively began looking for another city in which to locate his self-promoted "Super Christian" image and related revival ministry aimed primarily at young teenage boys. Although he spent most of his time on the road preaching revivals under his tent or in small churches or the occasional auditorium, Brother Tony's frequent trips back home to West Palm Beach involved bringing his latest collection of adolescent male tent crew members with him.

Every time the boys returned from a revival road trip it was obvious to the facility's neighbors as well as to passersby on Southern Boulevard, it being impossible to hide the presence of a handful of boisterous teenage boys, especially when they were not in school and spent their days playing video games, or else shoplifting and committing other petty crimes.

Local police made repeated visits to the ever-smiling evangelist about his young charges, but were always met with relatively convincing reassurances that he was as distressed by the boys' behavior as they were and that he would speak to the lads and rein in their objectionable activities. But for several years local law enforcement had been receiving occasional, yet increasingly strident, complaints from parents of teenage boys staying at the center overnight, complaints that the evangelist was luring their sons into committing fellatio with him and then paying them for it.

However, so embarrassed were the young victims that they usually declined to cooperate and help authorities with prosecution. Coupled with that was the fact that most of the officers hearing these complaints found such sexual activity so disgusting they did not want to pursue it in the first place, and with their insufficient evidence they let things drift along until, finally, enough had become enough.

The West Palm Beach Police Department's file on Tony Leyva grew through the years with information from parents and, increasingly, their young sons that the preacher was seducing and sexually molesting young boys for whom he professed such care and concern. True, they received most of their information through anonymous phone calls, with only the occasional victim or victim's parent being brave enough to give a name; but this was incriminating enough.

Previously the peculiar Pentecostal evangelist's greatest single affront to local mores had been his preaching night and day from the roof of his church to set a world record back in 1977. However, by late 1984 the police felt compelled to confront Brother Tony and in the strongest possible terms insist that he leave town right away.

Having gone through this before, Brother Tony decided to try to quietly relocate as far away as possible without leaving the South. However, when Brother Tony stood on his pulpit and announced his plans to his local

Chapter 7

flock, he spoke with duplicity and pointedly avoided any mention of visits paid him by the local constabulary: "God came to me in a dream and told me that I have to move somewhere else to spread His word. He hasn't revealed just where yet, but I trust in the Lord that He will."

✝ ✝ ✝

In 1984 the citizens of New Orleans were involved in massive plans and expectations for the upcoming 1985 World's Fair, "The World of Rivers—Fresh Water as a Source of Life," and it was on New Orleans that Brother Tony set his sights. He would not only relocate his headquarters there, but in the process of shopping for real estate would enjoy a world's fair in one of the most exciting cities of the world, all the while remaining in the South and among his constituency.

In early 1985 Tony made the acquaintance of a salt-of-the-earth, small-time yet straight-shooting evangelist preaching in one of the seamier areas of New Orleans, one Jack Martin. Carefully working his way into Martin's good graces, Tony got the toehold he needed to advance his plans to relocate to the Crescent City. By the May 12 opening of the World's Fair, Brother Tony had arranged it so that his preaching revivals took place on a regular basis "at Jack Martin's invitation" in his host's venue, a leased former porno movie house, the Happy Time Theatre on Magazine Street in a truly "bad" part of the city. With an anticipated 12 million visitors to the New Orleans Fair, mostly from the South, Brother Tony was in an excellent position from which to preach to crowds, grow in stature and respect among southern Pentecostals, and rake in money while at the same time searching for a perfect local facility to buy and move into.

A month after the fair's opening, Tony Leyva was well on his way to sweeping off their feet the local teenage boys who hung around Jack Martin's ministry. One of the lads initially mesmerized by the traveling evangelist was R. C. Roundtree, a poor, skinny, thirteen-year-old.

R.C., who lived in a housing project, had been going to the theater to attend Martin's church for several months, attracted by this straight-shooting gospel preacher, a fatherly man who cared genuinely about R.C. and the other poor and down-and-out who attended his services. Jack Martin knew nothing about Tony Leyva's reputation as a pederast, and he began occasionally inviting the evangelist to conduct monthly revivals at the Happy Hour Theatre. Soon, young R.C. had become a special favorite of the out-of-town preacher.

"Until I met Jack Martin," said R.C., "I had never been into a church and it was, like, I would always work the sound equipment for Jack Martin and Tony Leyva. That's what I did for Tony when I was on the road with him. And when I traveled with Tony Leyva, on one occasion I knew him to take in seventeen thousand dollars in his revival collection! Sometimes people would write checks for the ministry and the next morning before we would leave that town he would go to the bank and get cash for them."

At least the boy ate well while he was with Tony: "We eat at places like Shonie's, Steak 'n' Ale, places like that. He'd always go expensive when he ate. We'd eat the same thing as him, like steaks and such. I was saying, this is a man with some money, but that's about it."

It was R.C. himself who made what amounts to a poignant contrast between the high-living preacher to the poor, fatherless teenager when he said: "He [Tony] had a very nice van. All of his clothes were real nice. He bought me a pair of shoes once, that's about it. They were about a ten-dollar pair."

Then, over the course of the first year that he knew him, R.C. would spend about one night a month with Tony Leyva at his motel when the evangelist returned from the road to New Orleans to conduct revivals at the Happy Hour Theatre. During this time the only idiosyncrasies R.C. saw were the fact that "He always took vitamins. I remember he had about twenty-five jars of vitamins and he took them tablets two to three times a day." And R.C. recalled seeing Tony drink prodigious quantities of NyQuil: "He used to drink it most every night. Lots of it."

R.C.'s relationship with Tony Leyva began innocently enough: "It was summer and they was having church and Chris Felix and Perry Sims asked me to come back with them to the motel and go swimming. That first time, it was just I was going with them to go swimming. Then it went on from there, you know, 'cause Brother Tony asked me to come spend the night with him on and on, every time he come to New Orleans. He stayed in a motel out on the highway towards Slidell.

"I'd say about two weeks after that Tony asked me to spend the night. Just me. But nothing happened, even though he had me sleep with him and there was two beds in the room. He didn't say why. He just always wanted to sleep in a bed with somebody. And he just talked about how much he loved me and all this stuff about God, you know, all kinds of what I found out to be bullcrap.

"At that time I looked up to Tony like a father. I ain't never lived with my own father and I thought that was what Tony's trying to be to me."

R.C. made one long road trip with Tony. "We had started in Alabama, and we was working back towards Louisiana while he preached that he was on a mission to get forty-eight thousand dollars to buy a [new] truck for his tent. But in his revivals he used to preach about needing money for all kinds of things.

"But then when I really found out about him was when we was in Pascagoula, Mississippi. Me and him was the only ones in the motel room and he asked me did I want him to take a shower with me. I told him no. When I got out of the shower he was in the bed and he was talking about he wanted to show me how much he loves me, ya know, and he started feeling on me. I told him, I said, 'Look, man, I'm gonna be a man for the rest of my life! I don't know what you are.'

"I told him that he would have to ride me home the next day, 'cause I seen the way he was acting. Then he apologized for it and everything and so I stayed with him another week. Then when we got back to Slidell, Louisiana, we had got back to the motel about eleven o'clock that night and I was gonna stay the night and go home to New Orleans the next morning.

"So, that night, he asked me would I please sleep with him. I told him, 'Man, I'm not sleeping with you!' So, me and Chris slept in the same bed. I was real tired so I just fell asleep. While I was asleep Chris got up and went to the bathroom and Tony got in the bed with me . . .

"When I fell asleep, I wasn't worried about him. But at about two or three in the morning I woke up and found him sucking my penis. He'd pulled my underwear down while I was asleep and just started doing it!

"So, that made me mad and I hit him hard. He jumped up and started cursing and hollering and screaming and all this. Then he leaned down and started crying and praying and I felt a little guilty; but I didn't worry about it.

"The next day, he was bringing me home and he gave me about sixty dollars and said, 'Here, this is money for you for being with me.' Then he told me that if I told on him, God will punish me."

✝ ✝ ✝

Shortly after Brother Tony began preaching revivals at the Happy Time Theatre, housewife and mother Marsha Markham from suburban Kenner, who had heard about Tony from a friend, decided to go downtown to hear him for herself. She had been raised Roman Catholic but had drifted away from the church after becoming involved in the growing charismatic movement within the church, a cross between traditional Roman Catholicism and the Pentecostal faith.

This movement was a real stretch for most Roman Catholics, particularly for older priests and communicants, and Marsha soon ran afoul of the pastor at St. Anthony's Church: "I wasn't in the church at the time I got saved," said Marsha, "but I was at the lowest point in my life. After I had gotten saved I started going back to the church then. [My son] Rusty was about four or five years old and that was about when I started writing little prayers up and putting them in the pews. Then in church one Sunday the monsignor tells the people, 'Whoever's laying all this trash in my pews, don't do it no more!'

"I went up to him after church and I said, 'I'm the one that's leaving trash in the pews.' See, the prayer I'd written and the one that he said upset him was [based on] the St. Teresa Prayer.*

"And he picked it up and said, 'The picture's pretty, but the prayer is trash.' Well, I almost had a nervous breakdown over that! I went home and just sat in my recliner for about forty-eight hours, just sitting there. I couldn't believe it 'cause those prayers was what was keeping me going. I said, 'I'm not going to sit there in St. Anthony's no more!'

"The monsignor didn't like charismatics. I mean, he treated us so cold! Al Hirt's daughter had an experience with the Lord and became charismatic and when she went up to receive Communion with her hands lifted up, the monsignor told her to put her hands down, that he wasn't gonna give her communion like that . . . and she wasn't even doing anything wrong! In other words, he was just very anti-charismatic! But I never got close to [him] so, I came out of the [Catholic] church and then's when I started going to Tony Leyva's revivals.

Over several years—from 1984 until 1987—Marsha and several of her sons became ever more deeply involved with Tony Leyva and his revivals, all four of them heading off to attend whenever he came to New Orleans. In fact, of her three sons who were still young enough to be attractive to the pederast (and became acquainted with him), the eldest, Chris Felix, seventeen, began working for Brother Tony as one of his many chauffeurs. Then her two youngest boys, Perry and Rusty Sims, started spending nights and eventually traveling on the road with the evangelist.

Among the fundamentalist Pentecostals and charismatics, religious

---

*St. Teresa of Avila, a Carmelite nun of sixteenth-century Spain, is considered a major mystic of the Catholic church. She exposed with unequaled clarity the secrets of the mystical and interior life and her relationship with God through two major books. She was inspired by God to establish thirty-two reformed Carmelite monasteries along with her helper, St. John of the Cross.

emotions—what one feels coming from God or Satan in dreams, prayers, an other interactions individually or in groups—play an extremely big part in what is and what is not to be believed. "[T]he very first time I met him," Anne recalled, "I had some bad feelings about him and I told him about that. He said, 'The devil's trying to put ideas in your head, sister.'"

Like Susan Plunkett, Marsha Markham was given to revelations in her dreams. And as it turned in the end, she and Susan had been on the right track all along. Marsha recalled: "I had a dream about him and I told him about it and he got really upset. What it was was that I saw Tony was in Atlanta, Georgia, in the tent and up on the platform preaching. Then I seen two men walking up towards him with guns and I told him that they had them pointed right at him while he was preaching. And I got right in their way. I put myself in the way so he wouldn't get shot. Then Tony says, 'What?'

"And I said, 'Yeah, it was over a little boy.' At that time I didn't even know of this business of him having sex with boys and when I said that to him he just turned white.

"Then I told him that I had another dream and I said to him, 'That dream was that you was preaching again. But, in back of the platform there was curtains and somebody was hiding behind them waiting for you to come out.' I told him, 'They wanted to take your life.'

"And he says, 'Oh, yeah, there's a lot of people that wanna take my life because they're very jealous of me.'

"But you see, God was trying to show me it then . . . even in dreams. And these people at his services told me, 'Satan's trying to put bad ideas in your head.' But I couldn't put it together, you know. And for a time, I wouldn't go to his services. Then I said, 'I got to go to his services.' And in fact, my husband and I, we almost broke up because of [Tony Leyva]. It was like tearing me up!

"At one point, [my son] Chris got to where he wanted to kill Tony! He said that he seen a man walking up the aisle with ghosts, and the ghosts was walking straight up the aisle and he walked right in the back of Chris. I was taking him home and I said, 'What's wrong? Why are you looking the way you are?'

"He said, 'Oh, I had a bad experience today at the theater. A man was walking in the middle of that theater, came right up on the platform, walked right through the screen and walked back there by me.' That really scared me. I said there's something strange going on there.

"Then, another time, Chris was up there and he said he'd seen a jackal running down the side aisle. And Tony Leyva said, 'Ya seen that? I seen the same thing!' Ya know, they were talking about jackals running around the theater and such stuff. I really didn't want to go then, but I wanted to seek this thing out.

"So, I started gettin' people to go with me, ya know. I said there's something wrong. I said, 'We're gonna have to get together and check this thing out.'

"One day down at the theater I walked upstairs and [Tony] was in the office and he was laying on the sofa and his face was swelled up like a demon. I mean, he didn't even look like Tony Leyva! And I said, 'What is wrong? Let me take ya to the hospital!'

"And he says, 'No, it's gonna pass. Just leave me alone. It's gonna pass.' But I was really worried, ya know?

"Then, another time that happened was in Houma [Louisiana]. They were working on the tent getting ready for a revival and all of a sudden he started swelling up: his hands, his face, and everything started swelling up real, real bad. I rushed him to the hospital and the doctor said that I got him there just in time, he would have died. His throat, ya know, swelled up.

"I don't know what it was and neither did the doctor, but to me he looked like the devil!

"And I'd say, 'Lord, take these feelings I have for Tony Leyva away and let me serve you.' And the more I prayed, the more I wanted to get away from him. I'd be crying and depressed all of the time and I told my kids, 'I want you all away from that theater!'*

"But, all together, I guess I went and listened to Tony preach about two hundred times, because he was here for the World's Fair and I went almost every day."

Marsha recalled how there always seemed to be some sort of political intrigue or turmoil swirling around Tony Leyva. One incident she recalled involved a lady named Sylvia Collins who had given Tony a travel trailer; as part of the deal, Tony allowed her to travel with him and his revival troupe and stay on the tent grounds.

But when Pass Christian, Mississippi, preacher Bobby Ray Hopkins and his wife, Katie, showed up driving a bus bringing children to the revival services, Tony kicked Sylvia Collins out and put the Hopkinses in the

---

*The mystical, emotional nature of the Pentecostal faith prompts many adherents to believe in such apocryphal sightings of animals, symptoms of illness, and strange interpretations of these events.

trailer, and the squabbling began. Said Marsha, "Oh, it was a mess; it was like a three-ring circus! I mean, serious! I wasn't familiar with this sort of thing!"

Marsha's son Rusty was only eleven when Tony Leyva first seduced and sexually assaulted him. I interviewed him in his Kenner, Louisiana, home in April 1989, over two years after the last of—Rusty estimated—the more than two hundred molestations.

Rusty Sims was then a very handsome, soft-spoken, engaging sixteen-year-old with clear blue-gray eyes and neatly trimmed blond hair. After some pleasant chitchat with me about school, his girlfriend, and his obviously loving, supportive family, Rusty began recounting his experiences with Tony Leyva during his hundreds of sleepovers with the man.

"I guess I was close to seven or eight when I first met him at a civic center in St. Bernard [Louisiana]. The first time I met him, I had an idea in my head that he was weird 'cause I was brought up from a Catholic point of view and never did see a preacher jumping and hollering around the stage. I just thought it was quite odd. And then after the service he hung onto the little boys like me and hugged us.

"But when I got to know him, I realized that he acted like a Pentecostal-type of preacher behind the pulpit. When I got to be about ten, he always asked for me to sleep over and the monsignor never did that. No priest ever asked me to sleep over, ya know. I was never used to any of that, even just the idea.

"The idea I had in my head the first time that I was gonna sleep over there at his hotel was that a preacher is the most holy man. I thought that I was gonna go home with him and probably talk about the Lord. Just like my mom, I thought that I was gonna get more spiritual.

"To tell you the truth, I was really counting on it because I thought it was a big thing. I was really looking forward to learning more about God! But when I got there, all of my intentions and thoughts were wrong. I'm sitting there curious about the Lord and sitting in the hotel room I would ask him something 'bout the Lord and I would say, 'Tell me, what do you believe about the end times?'

"And I'd ask him, 'Tony, what does the Bible say about these last days?' Because that was my interest, the last days. But he was very quick to get off the subject. I mean, in all the years I knew him, I never did see him study the Bible . . . never once! Never seen him read the Bible. And of all the times I asked him about the Bible, he never, ever sat down and talked to me about it. He didn't want to talk about the Lord for some reason.

"The only time I ever seen him open the Bible was when he read the same scriptures and preached the same sermons over and over again at his services. He'd preach certain sermons in one area and then he'd go to the next area and preach the same exact sermons.

"My first incident with him was in 1984 and after 'it' I was so ashamed. I was scared to tell anybody because I thought he was truly a man of God! He just had weird motives and did weird things. But he just kept on doing it and wouldn't stop. Back then I was all confused and always afraid to tell somebody.

"I thought it was weird [but] I didn't know any better. At that age, I never knew too much about relationships and, so, what was I to do but to believe someone from a pulpit? I don't know why I didn't stop it. I guess it was because he made it sound like he was teaching me something. . . . like I was doing something right.

"He says, 'Don't you feel like something wants to come out?'

"I said, 'Yes.'

"He said, 'Do you know what that is?'

"I said, 'No, I don't.'

"He goes, 'It's white stuff. I'll show you what it is.' Then he just sat there and played with himself in front of me.

"Then he said, 'Why don't you touch me and put your mouth on it.'

"I said, 'No, I won't put my mouth on it!' And he sorta like mainly put my hands on it. And he said that it would make him feel good and he would enjoy it.

"He did it to me orally, I guess, close to about fifteen to twenty times. . . . A lot of time I spent the night with him he didn't do anything to me, but sometimes I'd wake up in the morning and didn't have anything on . . . he'd just take my underwear off during the night."

As this bright, likable young man recalled the abuse he had suffered, his normally cheerful expression changed to heart-rending, painful sobs that racked his body and sent tears streaming down his face, the deep betrayal and hurt caused him by Tony Leyva spilling out: "And when he did it he always told me, 'I love you so much and this is the way I express my feelings. My love for you is so strong [and] I have no other way to show it.' Then, when he finished he always repeated, you know, 'Don't tell nobody! Don't tell anybody!' "

With copious tears running down his face, Rusty paused to wipe his face before haltingly continuing: "I was so young . . . I never knew what was going on. I'll tell you what, for a crime like that, somebody shouldn't get years, they should get death! Because, you can kill somebody physically, but you can also kill somebody mentally. It just tears me apart inside. ... I mean it! It's something I gotta live with the rest of my life!"

✝ ✝ ✝

Instead of the bright, happy, fun memories one would expect a then-twelve-year-old to treasure of the 1985 World's Fair, Rusty Sims was haunted by dark, bizarre ones. During the exposition Tony Leyva rented an apartment in New Orleans at the Oakbrook Village Apartments, and it was there that he; Ed Morris; Ed's friend from Georgia, fellow pederast Freddie M. Herring; and the trio's preacher-pederast friends from around the South entertained and assaulted various boys between visits to the fair.

Said Rusty, "When the World's Fair was down here you could say Tony Leyva attracted a ring of preachers, more or less, taking the kids like me and using us like we were prostitutes: There was Freddie Herring, Ed Morris, and Bobby Ray Hopkins ... and Freddie was always talking about weird things in a girlish voice, like, 'Oh, the guys down in the French Quarter do 'it' this way or that way.' You know, all kinds of comments about gay sex, and here we was kids."

At this apartment Rusty said that Freddie tried to rape him: "This was in the apartment at Oakbrook Village. I was upstairs sleeping. It was like an afternoon [and] he came in and laid down next to me and I never thought nothing of it. So, I was half-way sleeping and all of a sudden I felt him pull my underwear down and I just got up and out of the bedroom and left.

"I looked at him and he was just sitting there naked, looking at me [and he had] ... an erection. He never said anything, just looked. I guess, he was quite stunned that I just got up and walked out of the room. And nobody ever had anal sex with me!"

In many ways a typical middle-class lad from suburbia, Rusty told of his experiences with the first inner-city youngster he ever knew in life: "R.C. Roundtree came out of the projects and Tony got him out of trouble [that R.C. was in] ... paid for his thefts and took care of his money situation. Then when Tony tried something on him, R.C. just went crazy on him.

"I can't remember what state it was in—Alabama or Mississippi—but this lady had a revival there in a little tent and Tony was up there speaking. ... That night at the motel room is when it happened. I was there, but I was outside throwing a football. R.C. hit Tony inside the motel room and then he came out and he was very, very mad at him.

"So, that's when I started believing Tony really did do it to other boys, because my incidents had happened before his. Before I was too scared to tell anybody and ashamed because I thought I was the only one. I was always asking questions about this of the Lord . . ." Rusty's voice softly trailed off into sobs.

"Then when Tony did it to R.C. again and we did go and tell the sheriff in Slidell—it was R.C., my mom, and my brother Perry—and they didn't believe R.C., evidently because of his background. . . . They said he lied on the polygraph test, like on some stupid answer; . . . they asked if he liked chocolate and he said no when he did.

"So, the law didn't do anything [and] that's when we went to the church where Tony was preaching and confronted him about it. I was very embarrassed. I never wanted to see him again because I felt the shame and the guilt."

✝ ✝ ✝

By fall 1985, Brother Tony had been preaching revivals at the Happy Hour Theatre and the World's Fair for a number of months while secretly spending his spare time away from the pulpit prowling the numerous gay bars and clubs along Bourbon Street as well as dark, dangerous back alleys, picking up older teenage boys for visits to his apartment or fifteen minutes in his van.

Tony repeatedly told local supporters in New Orleans that he wanted to move permanently to their city since "I've found so many sinners here in need of being preached to." He did not, however, tell them that in truth it was actually the attractive young male sinners down along Bourbon Street—as well as the young boys in their families whom he led astray—for whom he felt such affinity.

For both his publicly acknowledged and private reasons Tony Leyva then set in motion his plans for relocation of the Tony Leyva Evangelistic Association to New Orleans. He had discovered the old Soulé College at 1410 Jackson Street. Built in 1856 as a family home by Henry Sullivan Buckner, this grand mansion covers a good portion of a city block. From 1923 to 1983 the massive structure had been a young ladies' secretarial school, and Tony felt that it would make an excellent site for relocation of his Bible Days College. It would, he thought, make the ideal headquarters for his revival ministry as well as a boarding school for teenage boys.

Undeterred by the million-dollar purchase price and no credit history,

Tony announced a new mission for his Association, to raise "a million dollars to teach God's word!" And he even temporarily inveigled moral support from an evangelist whose headquarters were in southern Louisiana near New Orleans.

On occasion Tony had been allowed to use some of the evangelist's property on which to pitch his tent and preach. But according to Tony's former supporters, on at least two occasions the pederast squired this man around New Orleans and pointedly drove his guest past Soulé College while elaborating on his plans for the landmark. Further, one of these occasions included a stop by the two men, accompanied by three of "Tony's boys," at a Bourbon Street club featuring female impersonators.

But if the evangelist wasn't quite into underwriting pederast Tony Leyva's plans to open a boarding Bible college for young teenage boys, he was apparently agreeable to spending an evening helping Tony show the lads the sinful sights and sounds of the Crescent City. As the young guests of that evening tell it, they were taken out on the town and visually shown sins they had never known before, all in the name of "scarin' us into obeyin' the Lord."

The party traveled to the club in Tony Leyva's limousine driven by Chris Felix. While watching the young men in pumps, skirts, and low-cut blouses bump and grind and strip down to G-strings and less on stage, the two evangelists kept pointing out the comely young male performers' moves to their young guests, remarking that this is how they wanted them to perform when they got back to Tony's motel.

After this bizarre night out on the town, Brother Tony had Chris drive the party back to his motel near Slidell, Louisiana, near the Mississippi state line. There, in his room, Tony placed his black footlocker containing his kiddie porn collection in the middle of the room, tuned a boom box radio to Neville Brothers music with a throbbing beat, and one by one encouraged the three teenagers to mount the impromptu stage and strip naked in time with the music. According to the boys there was no sex, no touching, and no picture taking. Just plain simple voyeurism . . . featuring a trio of young teenage males performing for the two adult male evangelists.

When the dancing ended a bit past midnight, the other evangelist left, while Tony bedded down with one of the boys and let the other two share the room's other double bed.

But during the night Tony reprised his previous bed-hopping routine. Tony's thirteen-year-old bedmate awoke to find the preacher with his hand down his undershorts fondling him. The boy jumped out of bed and spent the remainder of the night huddled in a corner of the room.

"When Tony got up that next morning and went to the bathroom,"—said the boy breathlessly, even though it was years later when I interviewed him—"I told the others what happened and they told me that Tony done the same thing to them. And when I found out he was doin' it to everybody that was with him . . . that's when I decided to come out and tell that lady deputy in St. Tammany [Parish] what he done to me."

Before Tony emerged from the bathroom, the three boys had slipped out of the motel room and gone to a pay phone in the lobby, where they phoned the mother of one of the boys and the St. Tammany Parish Sheriff's Office. Within minutes a uniformed deputy responded and took the boys to the sheriff's substation in Slidell to interview them and to await the mother's arrival.

It being a Sunday, the boys recall that once the mother picked them up at the substation they all drove to the church in Slidell where Brother Tony was preaching that morning. "After the service we all talked with Brother Tony and he admitted that he did it," the victim said. "And he was tellin' us how sorry he was and askin' us to forgive him.

"So, we went on back home and talked about it some. Then, the next day my friend's mother took me back to the sheriff's office in Slidell and I talked to this lady deputy [Emily Holden] and told her what Tony had admitted doin' to me, so she had me to take this lie detector test. Then she got me in her car and drove over to Tony's motel to confront Tony and have him come in to take his own lie detector test.

"That lady deputy told Tony to follow her back to the sheriff's office, but when they got to the Interstate, Tony got up on the Interstate and took off fast towards Mississippi. He skipped town and the law never talked to Tony Leyva."

Now retired, Emily Holden remembers the story in a somewhat similar fashion: "The young man came to our office and told me what Leyva did to him sexually, and one of the deputies went out and asked Leyva to follow him in to the office to take a polygraph. But he never did show. He was supposed to have followed the man because he knew [Leyva] from a previous time when Leyva used to have those tent churches down in Chalmette [Louisiana] and he would hire this man as his security. So, the man trusted [Leyva] to follow him.

"But when our man got to the office and Leyva didn't show, I told him that he should have been driving directly behind Leyva and not in front."

Emily Holden described what she found during the ensuing investigation: "All together there was three boys staying at the motel with Leyva . . .

besides the boy that was supposed to be his employee, the one that drove the van. But there was these three young boys with him and he left them all here in Slidell.

"We went back to the motel looking for him [Leyva], but he didn't find him. He hadn't checked out and he had left a suitcase in his room, but he never did come back to get it. And it was then that I found out that that old rascal had some money!

"But I can truthfully tell you that it amazed me the way those boys' parents would allow these people to take their kids off and didn't know where they was going and how long they'd be gone before they'd be back. And it hasn't stopped because the little bit of work I do in the DA's office now, you find that happening still with these tent preachers today. I don't like preachers! If there's a born-again atheist, preachers taught me the trick!"

8

"Honey, when it comes to Tony Leyva, I want to set the fire!"

After being rebuffed for financial support by the Louisiana evangelist, and failing to get sufficient contributions to buy Soulé College in New Orleans, in late 1985 Brother Tony Leyva held a number of revivals in and around Atlanta, Georgia, met a number of like-minded Pentecostals, and continued to network and meet a few with his same sexual attraction to boys. Then he put down roots in the area by establishing his new headquarters at the Moonraker Apartments, located in a wooded area in suburban Marietta, Georgia. "This," he deceptively told his supporters, "is where the Lord wants me."

Brother Tony moved into an especially commodious four bedroom apartment lock, stock, and teenage boys, one of whom was Timothy Earls: "When Tony moved his headquarters from West Palm Beach to the apartments in Marietta, he brought me and Jonathan and James Cash down there to help him move in. We stayed for two whole weeks and one night he took us to see this sex movie with teenagers having sex with each other at a picture show in Atlanta . . . a preacher taking kids to see a X-rated movie!

"Then that night when we went back to his apartment it was all four of us together: me, Jonathan, James, and Danny Perez. And he had sex with all of us there in his apartment right after takin' us to see that movie.

"When I was there in Georgia that time I basically tried to stay away from Tony [Leyva], but he was like, 'All right, you're sleepin' with me tonight.' And I was like, 'Oh, this is great, you fuck-head!' And I would just try and sleep in another room. But some nights it was just like musical chairs 'cause he would go from one bedroom to another in the middle of the night and have sex with whoever he wanted.

"Most of the time when we was there and come in after helpin' with the sound and collections at his services he'd go do his paper work and we'd go to bed soon as we got in and that would be about it.

"Then it would be real late, about one or two in the morning, and Tony'd get down on his knees and pray to himself like he done every night before he went to bed. After that he'd go get in bed with one of us in his underwear at first, then after he'd been in bed with us for a while he'd take his underwear off and start rubbin' on us then pullin' our underwear down and suckin' on us.

"I mean, we were really basically tired and wore out—'specially if we'd been workin' settin' up his tent—and we didn't really feel like arguin' or nothin'. It was like, we had to get it over with. Morning would be here soon."

Soon after Brother Tony established his headquarters at the Moonraker Apartments, another tenant duly noticed the comings and goings of all the handsome young teenage boys and came over and introduced himself to the youngsters: it was Ed Morris's friend who had visited Brother Tony in New Orleans, the Reverend Freddie M. Herring, an effeminate Pentecostal preacher and evangelist who had a small congregation at the Lighthouse Assembly Church in Douglasville, Georgia, about twenty-five miles west of Atlanta.

For years Freddie had secretly prowled Atlanta's gay bars and "meat racks" for older teenage boys and young men. While he kept a fancy town house at the Moonraker, Freddie also had a home in Douglasville—a strange, spooky place, many of the boys said: Even though located in a small rural town, it had bars over the windows. It was where Freddie would sometimes take boys for an afternoon tryst or an overnight stay.

A man whose silver hair and dark, conservative business suits belied his sexual lifestyle until one observed him in action whenever a teenage boy or boyish young man in his twenties walked by, once Freddie Herring discovered the activity at Tony Leyva's apartment, nothing would keep him away. Soon Leyva began preaching occasionally at the Lighthouse Assembly as well as sharing some of his boys with his acquaintance, while Herring shared some of his own local finds with Brother Tony.

Timothy Earls recalled: "I met Freddie Herring through Tony. We was at his church in Douglasville, Georgia, and Tony introduced me to him and said, 'This is the preacher of the church here and you need to go and stay with him at the motel.' And so I did and that's when he first had sex with me.

"Freddie Herring usually did '69' with me, but what he really wanted was anal sex. But that happened just once. You know, he got it in and I made him take it back out, 'cause I said I had to go to the bathroom. I went to the bathroom and nothing else went on that night. We didn't have another time of that. It was just that one time.

"Most people think that Freddie is this little ol' sweet innocent man. But if you knew him . . . ! Sex was about all he was interested in . . . sex with boys and young men.

"But when he finished he always gave me money. Lots of money. And Freddie has all this gold and diamonds and fancy jewelry. And he even has a diamond necklace he wears himself! He gets his money from his church's collection and when he's out travelin' and preachin' with Tony he spends lots of it on gold and diamonds and jewelry."

Then Timothy's brother, Robert, explained: "I've always known Freddie to have a lot of gold. He buys it all the time with the money he takes from his church and his preaching. He had all kinds of diamond rings and stuff like that on his altar at his home. He took his money and put it into rings and gold and jewelry. I seen all kinds of rings that he has. And then when he bought suits, he didn't buy something that just looked expensive, he bought expensive!"

With his headquarters established in Marietta, Brother Tony Leyva and his Miracle Restoration Revivals resumed road trips with week-long revivals as far away as Arkansas, Ohio, and the ever popular Salem, Virginia, which was only logical given the fact that the area had contributed so many of "Tony's boys." Timothy Earls said: "Back when I started travelin' regular on the road with Tony Leyva and helpin' him set up his tent and sound at his revivals, he had this older boy, Jimmy "Bubba" Gordon, who drove for him. I think Bubba come from somewhere down in Mississippi. Tony met him at one of his revival meetings down there.

"Bubba would drive Tony in his Cadillac Fleetwood limousine while another older boy drove the truck with the tent and other stuff in it. Sometimes I'd ride in the limousine and sometimes I'd ride in the truck. Bubba wrecked one Cadillac limousine, but one of the people who always went to his revival meetings got Tony another brand new one.

"But I was on the road with Tony and his revivals, off and on, for two whole years. I quit school and started travelin' with him. My mom thought it would be better in a way for me to go with him. She trusted him to take care of my schoolin' and all. He was supposed to take care of it and everything, but he didn't.

"I guess I was too young to know just how wrong and bad it all was; I didn't know about anything really bein' wrong with the sex part. And after the first couple of times I pretty much knew what he's gonna do.

"But Tony said he loved us and all. And he said that 'it' was a special way for God's people to love each other. And I guess we was likin' the attention he gave us. And he always gave us money . . . lots of it. I guess we was excited, too, 'bout all that money 'cause we didn't . . . say nothin' to nobody else back then.

"We knew together what was goin' on, but none of us ever understood it all and we was keepin' it to ourselves. It just ain't something that you go up and say, 'Mom, there's somethin' I gotta tell ya. . . .'

"But, still, it bothered me havin' to take my clothes off and sleep with him and stuff. But after a while it was just like it become natural 'cause he didn't even have to talk me into it. We'd just get into bed together and he'd do it just like that . . . like that's what he expected me to let him do . . . and I did . . . and then it was over and I'd go on doin' what I'd normally do.

"Between when he first had sex with me when I was twelve and when I turned sixteen he did *it* to me a good thirty times, at least. Each time, it just more or less happened when he was there and when he was through I was glad it was over . . . something that, like he told me not to do, I just didn't talk about outside the room."

All the while, whenever Brother Tony Leyva was asked about his wife and children, he had a ready, pat response, said Robert Earls: "Tony Leyva told us that his wife left him 'cause he traveled so much to go out and spread the word of God and because of that she was turnin' his own kids against him. And he said that he loved on us 'cause he couldn't love on his own son. But I believe that he was really out travelin' and preachin' to take money from people and take in young people . . . young boys for sex.

"It's kinda hard to explain, the way Tony works, but people would trust him 'cause the way he works on 'em. They would trust the way he talked 'cause he talked like he made sense. Everything he said. You see, in public Tony always acted like he was really holy."

† † †

As Robert's and Timothy's involvement with Tony Leyva increased, Susan Plunkett became increasingly concerned about the evangelist's exclusive use of boys in his ministry until many around her considered it a type of fanaticism. But this only made her more convinced than ever that it boded ill for her sons. When she first manifested concern about Tony Leyva's interest in her sons the preacher tried to beguile her with his charismatic persona as a loving, dedicated preacher and prophet of God. But she was already past that having any effect on her. She couldn't exactly put a finger on any facts to back up her deep suspicions, but before long she knew more about who he was, a great deal more!

And it also seemed to Susan that Tony Leyva had begun to throw caution to the wind when it came to those he allowed to travel with his Miracle Restoration Revivals: "Toward the last of Tony Leyva's ministry there were so many different questionable men that were supposed to be ministers coming around and traveling and staying with the boys. There was a Reverend Bobby Marston. He was at most of Tony Leyva's meetings and he traveled with him a lot and he'd also get up there on the stage and witness that he went to the various boys' homes with Tony Leyva and he'd tell everybody how the boys was in so much need and how much good Tony Leyva did for them.

"And then there was this guy that drove his limousine for him, Bubba Gordon. And the way he acted, he bothered me being around my boys . . . always hugging them and squeezing them. And another one was named Lawrence Bounds. He came and spent the night at my relative's home and he also spent the night at Harriet and Larry Myers's home with their son in his bed and you could tell exactly what that man was! I told [my husband], 'Jimmy Wayne, that man is not right. Something's wrong there 'cause when we went out to McDonald's with him and my relative's brother, Jonathan Cash—who was twelve then—this guy Bounds was putting his arm around Jonathan and hugging him and kissing him and, honest, Jonathan was acting just like a little girl!'

"And I said to my husband, 'Now, Jimmy Wayne, this is terrible. Can't you see through this guy? I'm calling [my extremely close relative] Patti and I'm telling her to beware of this.'

"And Jimmy Wayne says, 'I don't know, Susan. I just don't know what to tell you.'

"I says, 'Well, open your eyes and look! This is not normal! There's something wrong!'

So, Lawrence Bounds come home to my house with Jonathan [Cash], James [Cash], Robert, and Timothy and spent about an hour in my home, which I didn't approve of at all, 'cause I could see right through him.

"Then I called Patti, but she let Bounds come into her home 'cause then he took Jonathan and James back home and he spent the night there in Patti's house with Jonathan right in the same bed! Then he went over and spent the night with Larry Myers at his home after that.

"But, you could see through the guy. You could tell what he was. And this was the type of people that Tony Leyva was starting to bring into his services at the last, you know, right when I stopped going. And then later my boys talked about it. When it all came out, my two boys said that Morris and Marston and Bounds and even that fella Herring were just like Tony Leyva and did the same sexual things to boys as Leyva did!"

By late 1986 Robert and Timothy had quit traveling with Tony Leyva; bit by bit, they began telling Susan what had really gone on between them and Brother Tony over the years. It became so much that it all but destroyed Susan's belief in evangelists: "Finally, when my son Robert was seventeen, he quit going with Tony Leyva. And I wouldn't go to his meetings no more, either, because right there I knew definitely there was something wrong with Tony Leyva. And all the way from when my sons first went off with Tony Leyva, I saw them changing. I did wonder and tried to talk to them, because they always kept things about Tony Leyva secretive.

"And then, just like I said, all the confusion started. He really had us deceived. All the doubts. It really has hurt my Christianity. It really has.

"But now my husband is so hurt over it because he put a lot of trust in Tony Leyva. I guess that's why God says don't put your trust in man.

"But, like I said, at first it seemed as though the man had something about him. But, well, you know, God says that wolves come to you in sheep's clothing; so, I guess that's what Tony Leyva really was: a wolf."

✝ ✝ ✝

The majority of the parents of the hundreds of boys whom Tony Leyva "successfully" seduced, assaulted, and then swore to secrecy, likewise wondered just what it was that enabled this man, whom they saw as a charismatic evangelist, dynamic preacher, and especially blessed prophet of God, to so swiftly and effortlessly establish such a close relationship with their sons in the first place, a bond which then developed into a strong emotional hold over the boys long after the first sexual encounter.

But these parents could not understand why it was that their sons so facilely and gullibly continued to maintain a relationship with this man once they had learned the true reason for the evangelist's deep interest in them. However, on reflection many of these parents realized that at the same time their sons were engaged in their deepest fealty to Brother Tony, they themselves were openly praising the preacher's godliness and Christianity, holding him up as a prophet of God. Further, only a handful of parents ever openly questioned why this man of God had such a penchant for and attraction to young teenage boys. In fact, only a very few parents recall having had at the time even the most fleeting thought about anything unsavory behind Brother Tony's gushing affection whenever he first met a new boy—always a boy he immediately viewed as a new sex partner for his bed and cheap labor for his revivals' tent and sound crew, not as a child in need of genuine love, care, protection, and religious training.

Most of these boys' fathers were absent, so their mothers considered it a true godsend when this man of God took such deep personal interest in their sons. With few exceptions, they never paused to reflect on why such a man would be so preoccupied by and in pursuit of young boys to the exclusion of girls, men, and women. But years later, when they finally came to painful grips with this horrible realization and acknowledged to themselves that this respected and admired preacher had in reality been a slick, sick, sexual predator, their overriding question was: "Just how do people like Tony Leyva find their victims in the first place?"

Indeed.

✞ ✞ ✞

From the hundreds of boys whom a typical predator-pederast like Brother Tony Leyva intentionally puts himself in the path of and remains in contact with year in and year out, he very quickly learns to identify and single out those particular boys who are actually or emotionally fatherless, and who are thus most in need of and frequently actively craving the attentions and affections of an adult male who will act as a surrogate father.

Understandably, such boys are thrilled and quite blinded by what they genuinely perceive as their good fortune when such a man acknowledges them and shows an interest in them. And such boys are naturally naive—more so if they have not had previous positive experience of a father's or father figure's affections, and therefore, they are not likely to question a pederast's motives until too late, if at all.

Having thus identified such relatively safe prey, pederasts ingratiate themselves with these boys by taking them out to eat, to play video games, to movies, to sports events, and hiking or camping: exactly the same things done altruistically by screened big brothers and other men whose genuine selfless interest is to provide positive adult male relationships and role models for such boys. And in truth, pederasts like Tony Leyva very often masquerade as these benevolent souls: *True wolves in sheep's clothing!*

Further, pederasts have learned well and count on the fact that boys who crave this attention, contact, and affection from an adult male invariably seek it out on their own if they do not get it at home or from a screened individual. And once a clever pederast has identified his prey and begun his quest, he further increases the malleability of his chosen, impressionable boy victim by being sycophantic in the extreme, thus nurturing the friendship with a congeniality and patience that would make Job look like a piker.

Finally, after very carefully cultivating and currying his selected boy's fealty, the seasoned pederast takes his young guest—alone or with other similarly emotionally starved boys—camping or on an overnight trip requiring a stop at a motel or at the pederast's home to spend the night with him, thereby concocting a situation where he is able to sleep with the boy in the same bed or even the same sleeping bag: to the pederast the ideal exigency to involve the boy in a sexual liaison.

True—and this *cannot* be overstated—with the exception of this last activity, these are the very same things that loving fathers do. But the important exception is that once alone with a boy, the skilled pederast—unless he detects reluctance on the boy's part—craftily yet progressively encourages and engages his young guest in skinny-dipping, posing nude for photographs or videos, nude wrestling, mutual showers or baths, strip poker, circle jerks (i.e., mutual masturbation), and sleeping together before he finally graduates his young victim to fondling, fellatio, and anal penetration. By the time these last activities occur, the young victim usually totally trusts this wonderful man who has come into his life.

Practiced pederasts know well what they must do to attract, foster, and then loyally hold such susceptible young boys in lasting emotional relationships in which their own principal objective is seduction and clandestine, self-gratifying sex. The pederast's frequently voiced justification for his actions is that otherwise the boys would have had no meaningful relationships with a father figure

With some success this was how I explained Leyva and his actions to some of the victims' mothers, and occasionally their fathers. Many of them recalled that this was precisely how Brother Tony filled the voids in their sons' lives, all the while using as special cover his respected reputation as a Pentecostal evangelist, preacher, and prophet.

Initially, Brother Tony benevolently met the needs of the young boys who came to know him; but once they were within his emotional thrall he exposed them to the dark, hidden side of his personality as he insisted on sexual favors. Most certainly they felt betrayed by him, yet at the same time they were deeply fearful of being embarrassed should they tell anyone about his sexual behavior. And—as is frequently seen by social workers—many of these boys allowed Leyva's abuse to continue since to them it seemed such a small price to pay to finally have a loving, attentive father figure in their lives.

Finally, like all young adolescent males, physiologically these boys possessed a growing sexual curiosity and drive along with a natural sexual naivete. Sometimes they were willing to accept and, in a few cases, even enjoyed his advances, particularly the fondling, the masturbation, and, to a degree, the oral sex. Remember, these were almost exclusively boys who did not have a father to guide them along the path toward sexual maturity by providing healthy parental sex education.

In short, Tony Leyva connived to fulfill these boys' natural, pressing, and deep emotional needs to be loved, cared for, and thus validated by having an adult male involved in their lives; someone who made them feel important and worthwhile. From 1967 to 1988, he selected in his respected role as preacher and "man of God" boys whom he would dote on and hire to pitch his tent and handle his sound system, and then—when the revival was over—take freely into his bed and clandestinely assault, sometimes over a period of many years.

✝ ✝ ✝

As I spoke with Robert and Timothy Earls's mother, Susan Plunkett, and their sister, Tina, they struggled to understand how the boys had fallen under Tony Leyva's spell. After hearing my social worker's explanation of why it had happened in the first place, Tina remarked about her mother's marriage to her father: "When Mom finally realized what went on with my dad, his [physically and emotionally] abusing us kids as well as her, she got out of it. I have no resentment toward her because she did something about it. But Robert and Timothy was just ten and eight then and they knew what my dad was like, beatin' on Mom and us. And I know that it affected them bad because it affected me bad, too."

Susan finally swallowed her pride and took responsibility for having failed to recognize the warning signs that Brother Tony's relationships with her sons was not right: "Sister Sharp [another victim's mother] came forth and told me and the other people right out loud at the meetings ... what Tony Leyva really was and what he did to her son. But nobody believed her; they all put her down, which I knew myself back then to be true and ... I regret right now that I didn't stand beside the woman. I knew in my heart what was going on, and I knew before she ever knew it.

"So, you see, God couldn't get me to come out with it, so He used her and it still didn't get nowhere to do something about it.... God was trying to bring it out the whole time, but He wasn't getting the right people to bring it out. We were all afraid, just like I was afraid.... Oh, God, did I have the urge several times to stand up in one of Tony Leyva's revival meetings and say, 'There's something wrong! Tony Leyva's not right! He's messing up these boys' minds! He's doing bad things to them!'

"If I'd just done it.... But you see, I was afraid. I thought to myself, 'Hey, they're gonna put me down. They're gonna throw stones at me!' They all *loved* Tony Leyva! And if I'd said something against him they'd of done me just like they done Sister Sharp! They put her out of one of them meetings! They said she wasn't no good! They said that she wasn't living a Christian life 'cause she had no right to talk about Brother Tony like that. That's just how deceived the people were!"

Thinking back on her and her close relative's initial involvement with Tony Leyva's ministry, the fact that at the time both had abusive husbands who didn't relate positively to their sons, and the recriminations after the evangelist's sexual abuse of the boys became openly known, Susan remarked: "But then, ya know, my close relative's husband said to her ... 'I don't understand how them boys could just let it continue. How could they just keep going with Tony Leyva and lettin' him do all those things to them over and over and over? ... I don't believe it and I don't see how they could continue doing such things with that man!'"

Susan added: "And even I have a hard time with that 'cause those boys of mine cared so much about Tony Leyva that they would fight over him! I mean, really fight over which one of them was gonna go with him ... and yet they just kept on goin' out on the road with him!" Shaking her head she concluded, "I still just plain can't understand them doing that!"

✝ ✝ ✝

Later, on the same day, I spoke with Martha Sharp, an ample, motherly woman every bit as colorful in manner and speech as the beautiful Blue Ridge Mountains in which she lives way back in a hollow in a rustic, rural, picturesque home. In 1983 her son, Darrell Wayne, was a thirteen-year-old boy yearning to know God who became emotionally and sexually involved with Brother Tony.

One of the most articulate and outspoken of the victims' mothers, when first asked about the evangelist, Martha all but breathed fire as she spat: "Honey, when it comes to Tony Leyva, I want to set the fire! I want to light the candles! He did harm to my boy and my family that will never heal! And it's 'cause of that man that I don't trust preachers no more!

"I'll tell ya, Tony Leyva and them others of his brood of vipers done so much damage to me and my family that I don't think that in a few hours ... even a few *days* I could tell it all! And you know, I'd sure hate to be in his shoes when he gets to them Pearly Gates 'cause there is gonna be some almighty shakin' and thunderin' goin' on when he's sent down there!" she exclaimed as she glowered sharply and pointed toward Hell.

After she had calmed down just a bit, Martha told how she first got acquainted with Tony Leyva: "... One day back in '72 Dad was listening to the radio and he heard Brother Tony preachin' and that's when I first heard of his name. Which I wish I had never of done! But anyways, after that Dad asked me would I ride him and Mom in my car over to the Salem Civic Center to hear this Tony Leyva 'cause he was going to be there preachin' a big revival meetin'. And so I did and I took my children with me. I never left my kids at home. I always took them to church with me.

"Paul Eustace ... was only two and a half years old when he first met Tony Leyva in 1972.... The reason I remember it all so well is that that was when Paul Eustace was first in glasses and he had tape over his glasses 'cause he had what the doctor called 'the lazy eye.' And at that first revival meeting of Tony Leyva's he prophesied to Paul Eustace that his eyes were gonna be straightened and he'd soon be out of his glasses.

"But Tony Leyva never had no contact with Paul Eustace, other than just shaking hands with him. Apparently, Paul Eustace didn't appeal to him. And I know that my daughters never did appeal to him! He proved that with what he done to Darrell Wayne and all the other boys! Never the girls, but always the boys!

"So, that's the first time I went to one of Tony Leyva's revival meetings. After that, on through the seventies, every now and then whenever he'd come back over to the Salem Civic Center, I'd usually go to hear him one or two nights. And I'd take all my kids, too. But I never attended his meetings regular. He'd be there for a week or two, but we'd just go a couple of times 'cause of the drive over.

"And every time we went over to the Civic Center to hear Tony Leyva he would prophesy to people that, I guess it was, had plenty of money 'cause these folks always seemed to be givin' him lots of cash. But I never had plenty of money . . . in fact, I have very little. Anyway, he'd come 'round to me saying, 'Pack your bags, Sister Sharp! You're goin' overseas!'

"And I thought, 'Either you're dumb or I'm the dumb one 'cause I ain't got the money to go overseas.' Anybody with common sense knows it takes money to go overseas! I guess he thought I had a lot of money, but I didn't have no money. I'm just what I am! I've been a poor person all my life and I'm not out for money. Never have been!

"But during the time since we'd first gone to hear him in '72, I'd gotten to know him pretty good, I thought. Then, way long after Dad had died—this was in the summer of '83—Tony Leyva come in for . . . I don't know if it was a week's or two weeks' revival, but I'd invited him to come stay with us when he came to preach next time. And he showed up at my house with all these young boys that was traveling around with him, and they all stayed here in my house and I cooked for 'em. Those boys was just about Darrell Wayne's age then [fourteen], and like all boys that age they sure could eat!

"Anyhow, he was preaching over there to Salem and we were all going over there to hear him. It was just after my husband had gotten saved here at home. And one night Tony Leyva come up to me and my husband there in the Civic Center and he said to us, 'I'd like to talk to y'all if ya don't mind.' So, we went to sit down in his limousine with him and we was talking to him. He said, 'Darrell Wayne wants to go with me to help set up the tents and things with the other boys.'

"Well, see, Darrell Wayne had always helped preachers around here locally, but he'd be at home when he done it. He never had stayed away from home like that. And before then Darrell Wayne had said that he wanted to work with an evangelist with a tent, but he didn't say who that was.

"Well, me and my husband thought Tony Leyva was an upright, godly man. So, I looked at my husband and he looked at me and I said, 'What do you think?' . . . 'Cause, we didn't even think then about Tony Leyva bein' the one asking us and not Darrell Wayne asking us 'bout his wantin' to go out on the road with him. So, when Tony Leyva confronted us and told us that Darrell Wayne wanted to go with him, we said 'Yeah.'

"Ya see, back then Darrell Wayne didn't know the type of man that Tony Leyva was. None of us did! . . . And before he went off on the road with him, Darrell Wayne had only spent one night with Tony Leyva, the night he stayed over to the [Embassy Motor Lodge] over to Salem and helped him at the Civic Center.

"So, we trusted Tony Leyva and we let Darrell Wayne leave to go off and go travel the road with him and his bunch of young boys. And when they left, Darrell Wayne was in good spirits. But it was Tony Leyva [who] asked us about Darrell Wayne traveling with him. Not Darrell Wayne himself. . . . But I guess he'd seen that Darrell Wayne was a vulnerable young guy who wanted to work for the Lord, ya know, and so he used that against him . . . he used that to get to Darrell Wayne, like. And so then Darrell Wayne traveled with him off and on for well over a year.

"But I can tell you from my experience, when Tony Leyva and them little boys were here at my house, there was no ladies involved in his ministry. But back then that never dawned on me. I just thought that he was such a good man 'cause he quoted the Bible all the time and preached just like he knew what he was doin'." Martha sighed sadly to herself and slowly shook her head.

After pausing reflectively she continued: "Harriet George—she's a Myers now—well, she and her husband and her son, Larry, came up from Georgia and spent the three months of that summer in Roanoke. And that was during the same time that Tony Leyva and his boys came and stayed with me. Then later that summer, after Darrell Wayne had left with Tony Leyva, Larry Myers and his parents tried to upgrade Tony and his ministry by telling people 'round here that while he was here he was on a forty-day fast.

"But he had just pretended to be on a forty-day fast, trying to pull the wool over the people's eyes. I told the people that: 'No, he didn't go on no fast here for no forty days and nights!' And I said that I could prove it! I told 'em that I was here at home frying them chicken and cooking them roasts and baking them pies the whole time when he was preachin' over to Salem! I cooked and cooked and cooked for him and them boys every night and day they was here!

"Then when Larry and his folks went back to Georgia, they told Tony Leyva a bunch of stuff about what I was saying about him. So, that was when Tony Leyva wrote me his first threatenin' letter. And at the time he wrote it he had already molested my son Darrell Wayne . . . but I didn't learn about that until later.

"But it was 'cause of his stay here at my house that I did find out a lot about him and how he was, you know . . . about telling the truth. The Myers didn't want to tell me the truth about Tony Leyva, but I found out a lot just by watchin' and listenin' to what he and that bunch said while they was here. Also, I found out about as much by what the Myers said and didn't say about him.

"Later on I found out that Larry Myers would do anything for Tony Leyva—lie for him or anything else. Back then he was traveling with Tony Leyva and later on I found out that Tony Leyva done the same sex things with him that he done with my boy Darrell Wayne.

"But, I'll just tell ya, Tony Leyva had us all fooled . . . but not no more! I'll be careful of preachers from now on! I mean, Tony Leyva was a con artist pure and simple! There ain't no doubt in my mind now about that! He was just out conning people for their money and molesting their boys! There weren't no good in him at all!"

Then Martha went on to explain that Tony Leyva wasn't the only one in his ministry with an abnormal interest in her son: "When Darrell Wayne was fourteen, Freddie Herring wanted him to come back down to Georgia and help them in the ministry. Freddie began to call me and beg, 'Won't Darrell Wayne come down here?' Well, I didn't know the real reason why he wanted my boy to come down there. I just thought he wanted him to help them with the tent and the sound equipment at the revivals.

"So, we let Darrell Wayne go on back down there. Freddie Herring wired the money to us for my boy to fly down to Atlanta. . . . [T]hen Darrell Wayne traveled around and worked on their tent crew and doing the sound for the revivals for two solid months. And later on I found out that starting the first night he got there, and for the whole two months—maybe a little longer—that Darrell Wayne stayed down there with Freddie Herring and Tony Leyva, they both done all sorts of sex with my son!

"Then a short time later we drove down there to Georgia in our camper for a summer camp meeting that Tony Leyva and his bunch was having. It was also Darrell Wayne's birthday and we took our other children and they stayed in our camper. But I become suspicious of some things because Darrell Wayne was staying at Freddie's house when we got there and that's out in Douglasville. But the windows were barred, the doors were barred just like I done seen in the city. And the boys was never left alone, none of them, to talk to their parents. And I should have . . . known something was wrong then!

"We wanted to talk to Darrell Wayne, but we was never allowed to be alone to talk to him. And while we was there one of Tony Leyva's preachers, Ed Morris, made a statement to me personally under Tony Leyva's big tent. He said, 'Sister Sharp, Brother Tony is afraid to let the boys come home because of what they might tell.' And I'm not talking hearsay—All right?—and so that made me real suspicious and then I began to look into things.

"As to Ed Morris, when I first laid eyes on him when we drove down to Georgia, I asked Darrell Wayne, 'Is he a *funny* guy?' . . . And Darrell Wayne says, 'I don't think so, Mommy.' And at that time Darrell Wayne didn't know, either, 'cause he hadn't met Ed but briefly one or two times before then and Ed hadn't got his chance to have sex with Darrell Wayne yet. But later, after we left to come home, my boy begun to spend some time around Ed Morris and that's when Morris started molesting Darrell Wayne and doin' the sexual things with my son. . . .

"We left that camp meeting and come home by ourselves in our camper. But shortly after that Freddie Herring finally flew Darrell Wayne back home from Atlanta to the Roanoke airport. But they did not send that boy home alone. Along with him they sent another preacher that has the same condition that Tony Leyva has . . . that done the same dirt to those boys that Tony Leyva done and his name is Bobby Ray Hopkins. . . .

"I never thought much about Freddie Herring 'cause I didn't know nothing 'bout his molesting Darrell Wayne till much later. And I hadn't been around him but once. The thing is, though, just like Tony Leyva, I heard that after all of his revival meetings he was very much interested in the boys but not . . . in any of the girls. . . . After one of Tony Leyva's revivals at the Salem Civic Center, I went to Hardy's Restaurant with Sister Barbara Grisham and two other sisters who had been to Tony Leyva's revival meeting. And while we was there here comes Freddie Herring bringing a whole bunch of young boys with him. And he bought all of their meals for them. But none of us wondered about it then. We thought that he's just being nice to the boys and nobody seen through it! Honestly, back then if somebody had come up and told me that Tony Leyva or Freddie Herring was that kind of a man, I wouldn't have believed it!

"But that's just about the way you can sum it up. I mean, Tony Leyva and his bunch just had everybody fooled! And I'll tell you one more thing: My dad was hard to fool and Tony Leyva fooled him!

"And as to my husband, he'd kill Tony Leyva in a minute! . . . It would never do for Tony Leyva to even set foot anywhere near 'round here or for the two of 'em to meet out and about! Or for him to meet my oldest son, either, 'cause he'd blow Tony Leyva away! I'm honest about that, I am!

"Ya see, far as I know, Darrell Wayne was not sexually abused on that first night he stayed with Tony Leyva over to Salem 'cause he got took to the hospital with his foot [which he had hurt in the motel swimming pool] before Tony Leyva could get the chance to do something to him. But then there's a lot Darrell Wayne hasn't come to me and told me since then, 'cause he said, 'Mommy, Tony Leyva and them is just so nasty that I just can't tell you all about it.' But, there is a lot that he had told me. . . . He has shared a lot with me. . . .

"Now me and his daddy and him are closer to each other than I guess any family could be, because of what Darrell Wayne went through. We talk about it; we don't hold it in. We don't bottle it up. If he's got anything he wants to say, he'll talk to me.

"But you know, Brother Tony was sitting right here with his feet under my supper table the same day when I first found out what I know now . . . 'bout the sex he done to my son, Darrell Wayne. And then Tony Leyva come back here and tried to act nice and all like nothing had ever happened!

"First off, I couldn't believe it! But when I did finally believe it he'd done gone . . . done left. And when he drove out of here that day it's a shame that one of them deers didn't pop up in front of his limousine when he drove off and cause him to run off in the creek! [Martha laughed heartily.] Yeah, I'm being' honest about that too! I mean I can laugh about it now, but I've cried a river and I've shed many a tear over what that so-called man of God done to my boy Darrell Wayne and to me and to my family! . . .

"But, see, Leyva and his bunch used things that I would not have even dreamed of preachers using. They were smooth as sailors! They used a smooth approach to them boys. They knew how to sell a bale of goods to them boys and their parents and they done it! They used the Lord . . . they used the Bible to do all of those things and a lot of people were blinded to it. And some folks are still blinded to it!

"When my eyes were finally opened, I quit going to his services. . . . But since then I have received lots of mail from Tony Leyva, including these threatening letters he sent me. And he kept on signing 'em 'Bro. Tony,' like we was still acquainted with each other or something." She spat in disgust.

"If I'm such a threat to him—see, in the letter I got right here he's accusing me of destroying his ministry—then why'd he keep on writing to me? Why didn't he just leave me and my family alone?

"But ever since September of '85 Tony Leyva's been sendin' me these threatening letters . . . mostly just different copies of the same ol' 'I'll kill you' letter. But here just a few months ago I received this here letter, a different new one from him specifically threatenin' me and my family."

Martha Sharp showed me a letter that Brother Tony had mailed to her as well as to other former supporters once they had learned of his assaults on their young sons and had gone to various law enforcement agencies around the Southeast. It is a strange, rambling letter laced with many thinly veiled threats and rife with shibboleths primarily identifiable to Pentecostals:

Dear Sister Sharp:

A few weeks ago I was in Roanoke for a one-night miracle service. Twenty-four hours before I went to Roanoke, I had, what I call, a warning dream, that something was very wrong. I dreamed of a man, with whitish hair, flashing a badge at me, like that of a policeman. I saw some hands over his shoulders pointing to me, and then running out a back way. In the dream, I was instructed not to answer any questions but to hear everything that was being said. The vision came to pass twenty-four hours later.

I was never so hurt, and even sick to the stomach in my life. I begged God to show me the source of all of this. A week later I dreamed again, and saw *you* come up to me and kiss me on the cheek, and step back, and the same man walked up to me laughing and grabbing my arms.

After a few days, I did some checking, and found that this, too, was a true vision. It hurt me even more when I heard that some of my good friends, Rev. Freddie Herring and Rev. Ed Morris and the Hopkinses . . . were being implied on [sic] the filthy tales that were being told.

I remember once sitting in your dinning [sic] room, when you told me with tears that *God* showed you that all these tales were not true. How Pentecostals change their mind about what God said all the time.

While I was in Communist Cuba a few days ago, a terrible dream came to be, and I was told to send a warning in the Spirit about touching Gods annointed [sic]. It hurts me to ever have to warn things like this. As, while you may consider me enemy because of the deception, I still love you all very much. You see, I can't cut love off and on like cold and hot running water, like so many people do. I love you all very much, and am praying for you all.

Finally, I make this statement to you: I am not now, nor have I ever been a Homosexual, or child molester. I do not believe in such; and I preach against such sins and spirits.

I have always loved Darrell Wayne like a son (and still do), and had to even reassure him of your love for him when he was feeling used and abused. No matter what you may think or say against me, and this ministry, my Love and prayers are with you all—please, be very, very careful. (What I dreamed was very bad, and I plead the blood of Jesus over you all constantly.)

[signed] In Him
Bro. Tony (emphasis in original)

However, this letter did nothing to deter Martha Sharp in fact it only served to strengthen her resolve to see Mario "Tony" Leyva prosecuted to the full extent of the law for sexually molesting her son and the other boys, and then put behind bars "for as long as God is in His heaven!"

✝ ✝ ✝

Throughout most of the 1980s many of the boy victims' parents continued to revere Leyva as being "anointed by God." Although some of the boys were reluctant to do Leyva's bidding, if he really lusted after the lad he surreptitiously plied him with NyQuil, the 25-proof patent cold medicine that the evangelist bought by the case and drank daily to indulge his apparent alcoholism. Then, once the boy was sound asleep, Leyva carefully stripped him naked and raped him. More than one boy tearfully recalled how he awoke nude to find Leyva sodomizing him.

And if a boy was disquieted by the sex—which more and more frequently included painful anal intercourse—Leyva got down on his knees and prayed tearfully with the boy, asking God to forgive them both for what "they" had done, thereby using the pederast's oft-proffered stock-in-trade of getting his innocent young victims to share his guilt.

But Tony Leyva's ever-increasing popularity nearly did him in. By 1984 some of the parents of "Tony's boys" had become so enraptured with the evangelist that they traveled like groupies to distant revival sights and, while there, many of them heard dark tales about Leyva's purported sexual activity with teenage boys. But the preacher told them "that's nothing but the devil talking" and craftily devised a scam to deflect such tales, just as he had done with Timothy Earls's stepfather, Jimmy Wayne Plunkett: questioning parents were turned on the spot into ordained ministers in the Tony Leyva Evangelistic Association.

Once confronted, without delay Leyva dramatically slapped his forehead and said, "Brother, I just got a vision from the Holy Ghost Himself and he wants me to ordain you in my ministry so's you can preach God's word!" Then, Leyva opened his briefcase, produced, and solemnly filled in the blanks on the pocket card and an identical but much larger certificate "suitable for hanging" from the grandly titled Tony Leyva Evangelistic Association, Inc., Ministerial Fellowship.

Plunkett reported how Leyva then handed the documents to him. He was so awed after that, "I really didn't want to believe nothin' bad about the man. After all, he was a preacher and prophet and all!"

Unbelievably, the evangelist successfully used this scam again and again over the next five years.

9

*"Back then, it felt good him calling me 'son.'
Nobody had ever done that before."*

Brother Tony's rapacious appetite for sex with adolescent boys caused a constant turnover in his tent and sound crew, but that seemed to serve his purposes beautifully since he loved the thrill, the excitement of seducing and setting up new youngsters to take to bed. By 1986 the venues from which he could select his next victim included hundreds of towns and communities throughout nearly twenty states, especially the South and Southeastern United States.

However, had one looked at the *Rand McNally Road Atlas* Brother Tony used to plan his revival circuits, one would have seen hundreds of towns underlined in yellow with many of those also highlighted in orange. The orange marks denoted the locations (like Roanoke, and New Orleans) where he had scored big in terms of numbers of boys or where he found himself especially enamored of this or that boy's charms once he had the lad in bed.

By now all but two states south of the Mason-Dixon Line had a plethora of towns and cities from which Tony Leyva felt he could safely and successfully meet new boys and preach a revival. However, anyone privy to his revival schedules would have noticed a slowly increasing pattern whereby he would suddenly drop a town where he had previously held a number of revivals. If parents of one of his devoted followers asked why, he explained that the money there—the "take" as evangelists call the money, jewelry, and other valuables the rubes drop in the collection buckets—had become "poorly" and then haughtily remark, "Them people are sinful and they don't want me preachin' to them about God!"

But more often than not, the truth was that a boy he had bedded in that town had told his parents, and the local authorities were aware of the "secret" that he and Brother Tony shared. Then the county sheriff—or in some cases the boy's father or older brother, backed up by a gun—got the message to Brother Tony to "get the hell out of town before the sun sets and don't *never* come back!"

Increasingly, situations like this were turning Brother Tony's "Two-Week Holy Ghost Revivals" into one-night stands. On many of these occasions Tony folded his tent and faded away into the darkness—as often as not, with threatening townspeople in pickups and marked county cars in hot pursuit to make certain that he left.

In the early 1980s, Tony Leyva had learned that southern Florida offered him ripe pickings when it came to spiritually searching Pentecostals in tune with his brand of religion, many of them single mothers with handsome young sons to fill out his sound and tent crew and share his bed. When his headquarters were in West Palm Beach, Brother Tony took advantage of the area's numerous small communities with their populations of blue-collar fundamentalist Christians by frequently holding his revivals there.

One night in April of 1983, Macalynn Embert, a twice-divorced single mother who had recently moved from Delaware to Florida, accepted her friend Joyce Norman's invitation to go hear a dynamic preacher from West Palm Beach preach at a revival service in the Fort Pierce Civic Center. This woman had grown up Pentecostal and, although as an adult she occasionally attended other denominations, she continued to search for her vision of the perfect Pentecostal church with the ideal preacher and a faithful like-believing congregation.

Beginning in October of 1988, I have extensively interviewed Macalynn and her sons both in person and by phone. I have been a guest in Macalynn's home several times and she and her sons have traveled with me. In conversation Macalynn occasionally tries to disguise the fact that she comes from a troubled blue-collar family, but once she gets to know a person she candidly discusses her troubled childhood. Growing up she never could do anything good enough to suit her demanding, demeaning father. "I didn't have a good relationship with my family," she said. "I never have. I went through a terribly bad life as a child. And since I'd grown up it just seemed like everything I tried to do got destroyed."

Macalynn cited this disturbing example of family violence she witnessed: "One of the times that I had to run like the dickens to get out of my house was [one day] when I came home from school and my dad had a hatchet and my mom had a hammer, and they was swingin' at each other!"

Her failed marriages only served to reinforce her father's negative opinion of his daughter. By 1983 she had had enough and so decided to pull up stakes and head south to Florida. Macalynn felt that the move offered not only plenty of sunshine and warm weather but a chance to get away from her dysfunctional parents, "so I could try and make something for myself and my boys."

Of that momentous spring night in 1983, when she drove with her friend from Indiantown, Florida, to Fort Pierce and met the man who would so change her and her sons' lives, Macalynn recalled: "I was impressed with his preaching style. I was also impressed with the fact that he didn't know me at all and yet he was able to minister over me in the way that he did. It really impressed me!"

So overjoyed was she that she could hardly wait to bring her sons to the next revival to meet this wonderful man who, it seemed, had been sent to her as her own special gift from God. A couple of months later, Macalynn drove to the West Palm Beach Civic Center to attend another of Tony's revivals. Afterward she proudly marched her sons, Jason, age ten, and Kenny, fourteen, up to meet this charismatic preacher.

As Macalynn recalled: "After the service Jason walked up to where Tony was sitting playing the piano and the very first thing Tony did was to stop playing and ask Jason to turn around for him just like a model. Then he smiled at Jason and put his arm around him and asked, 'Where's your daddy?' Jason told him that he didn't have one and at that Tony just lit up like a Christmas tree!

"At the time it didn't dawn on me what Tony was doing or what he was really saying to Jason, but I'll never forget that moment!

"From that time on, my relationship with Tony started growing and Jason and Kenny's relationships with him started growing, too.

"After that, Tony started talking to me and we would spend a lot of time together and we'd go out to dinner all of the time after his services. And we'd do things together like we were a family. Before the summer was over he took the boys by themselves for two weeks over at Pastor Kelly's place out of town."

But at Pastor Kelly's, Tony wasted no time in slickly yet strangely ingratiating himself with his two young guests. He required them both to sleep with him in the same bed, a move that didn't last long for the older boy. Although he had been half asleep, Kenny snapped fully awake when he caught Tony fondling him through his underwear. The young teenager jumped up and spat at the preacher, "Hey, man, I'm not queer!" and left the bed to warily stake out a corner on the bedroom floor. The pederast told Kenny, "I'm sorry," and then nonchalantly crawled back into bed with the apparently still sleeping younger brother.

With Kenny on the floor the preacher pulled down Jason's underpants and fondled him—a test, apparently, to see what, if anything, the boy might say. Although confused by this, Jason lay still and said nothing. "He thought I was sleeping," Jason said, " 'cause the next morning he asked me was I awake and I said no."

True to form, all of this occurred during one of Leyva's two-week revivals. Kenny recalled that at meeting the next night Tony gave him a note which said, 'Don't tell nobody, but what I did is God's way of loving you.' To which Kenny replied, 'No, I don't believe you!'

"Then [Tony] said, 'Just don't tell nobody,' and I said, 'Okay . . . fine by me.' I figured, well, heck, I've read about it and heard about it, and I'm not gonna say nothing. I'm not gonna bring a man's ministry down. I thought maybe it was some sick childhood disease that he had, so I didn't say nothing about it. Not even to my mother. It was kind of scary, but him being a man and me being a child, there's not much that I could do . . . not then, anyway."

For the balance of those two weeks Kenny spent the nights curled up defensively on the floor of another bedroom while Tony emotionally and physically forced himself on Jason, requiring the fifth-grader to share both his bed and body.

Jason bitterly recalled how each night Brother Tony would "put his vibrator on and start giving me massages, . . . then he would put me on top of him on my stomach and start rubbing my back and holding me and telling me how much he loved me. And not even my own father had ever did that. And hearing him telling me over and over, 'I love you, I love you, I love you' made me real confused and all. Then he would just pull my underwear off and start sucking me and stuff until I ejaculated . . . and when he finished he'd keep on saying, 'I love you, I love you, I love you.'

"I didn't like it the first time. I don't think anybody would. But, you know, most of the time he acted like a dad to me. He'd do things for me. He'd take me places. He acted like he really cared about me." The blond youngster lowered his head and shook it sadly.

By the time the boys returned home to Macalynn after two weeks,

Chapter 9

Jason had been assaulted orally half a dozen times and Kenny had withdrawn even more as he fought hard to keep his more mature knowledge of Tony Leyva secret from his mother. In the end neither boy said a word about it, in part, they later said, because their mother appeared so happy about this new preacher who had come into their lives. Instead, they both decided—each in his own way and for his own reasons—to internalize what they knew about Brother Tony and to keep quiet about what had happened—and what continued to happen to Jason.

Always searching for her ideal vision of religion and an opportunity to fulfill her secret desire to "preach God's word," Macalynn thought she had found "it" when, shortly after Tony Leyva had added her sons to his list of sexual conquests, he grandly ordained her in his ministry.

Soon Brother Tony began arranging and conducting frequent revivals in the Indiantown area, inviting Macalynn to preach at some of them, and staying the nights in a rented trailer with Jason in bed beside him whenever, Jason recalled, "I hadn't been able to get him to let me get out of bed and lay down by the coffee table in [the] front of the trailer. I only stayed with him in the same bed when I had to. But after he'd do 'it' I'd have trouble going to sleep and I'd just lay there and think about what he did and stuff. But I didn't ever understand why I let him do 'it' to me in the first place. But, I guess . . . I was only ten or eleven then."

Macalynn glowed when she recalled how during this time "the relationship with Tony grew real good and I went to work with him as the tent manager for his revivals on the road. Some nights we would stay in the same camper together all night, but we never had sex. I believed that was because he was a prophet and he was keeping himself clean. And I was keeping myself clean. Since my last marriage, I hadn't fooled with a man.

"Tony considered me and the boys to be his family and said that God was giving him a second chance, another family. We went to Disney World together. He would talk to me and tell me things that he wouldn't tell other people. There was a lot of trust between the four of us. We trusted each other. I trusted Tony with all my heart! We really was as close as a man and woman can be without having sex!"

On and on Macalynn went with genuine fervor: "He'd never trust a woman to sleep all night with him, and yet, he did with me, although there never was any sex. I don't know how to tell it other than no other woman that had had anything to do with him since his wife Tammy Sue left him was as close to him as I was.

"And Jason and Tony would go out in public and people that didn't know them would ask Tony, 'Is this your son?' And he would smile and say, 'Yes, he is!' He'd always let the people think that Jason was 'our' son and that we was man and wife. They'd say, 'Well, you have a good lookin' family, Brother Tony!' and Tony'd just smile, you know, and Jason'd walk up to him and say, 'Hi, Dad,' and Tony would hug him."

Said Jason, "Back then, it felt good him calling me 'son.' Nobody had ever done that before! But sometimes when he called me that, my mind would go back to the sex, too. But I was afraid to say anything to him about the sex 'cause then I might lose him as a father. And I'd think, 'Thank God, I've got a father now! I've never really had one before!' "

Like many pedophiles and pederasts, this was exactly what Tony Leyva counted on to hold his young catamite in his sway.

✝ ✝ ✝

In 1988 Macalynn said that during this time there were signs that she should have recognized pointing to Tony being sexually involved with Jason: "When I sent him off with Tony, or when he stayed the night with Tony in his room, he went with clean underwear. But when Jay got back, they were all dirty . . . his underwear was stained. But I thought that was, you know, just that Jason was having wet dreams because he was at that age and not out of that stage yet."

To her horror the pieces of this dark puzzle increasingly fell into place although she continued to deny what she knew. "I always washed Tony's clothes and there was always stains on his underwear. Always. And on the sheets, too, after he had had Jason over. But, at the time I figured that Tony was, you know—being a man—that he was masturbating himself. I knew he used a vibrator on himself, but then whenever I'd go in and change the sheets on his bed—even after Jason had stayed the night with him—there'd be stains on the sheets and the vibrator was always in the bed. Who did he think he was fooling? I should have realized then what was going on, but I didn't! I don't know why, I just didn't!

"But I went ahead and let Jason go with Tony because he wanted to go so bad. Off and on I heard rumors, though. When Tony first started taking them I had talked to a couple of people. [One preacher] said, 'No, don't let them go. I don't feel good in the spirit about it. Don't let the kids go with Tony.' "

In spite of that, at the time Macalynn felt she was living in truly religiously inspired bliss being around Brother Tony; but the activities at his revivals on the road circuit she and her sons traveled with him almost defied description. In reality, it was not unlike the troupe of a third-rate carnival playing small towns in rural America: a huckster's fake religious road show featuring one tent, a couple of hundred battered metal folding chairs, a portable electronic organ mounted on a plywood stage, and a rather sad-looking trio of female gospel singers who traveled with the show. Instead of a garish carny-style collection of side shows, an evening's entertainment under this big top consisted of a long rambling sermon delivered by Brother Tony.

Tony's revival sermons were a replay of his carefully practiced, word-for-word delivery imitating the late Pentecostal evangelist, A. A. Allen.* Said Macalynn, "Tony claimed that A. A. Allen was his spiritual father and he preached the same sermons that A. A. Allen had preached. Naturally Tony was preaching them because he had all of A. A. Allen's master tapes! I'd hear Tony preaching the same thing as A. A. Allen did at his revivals . . . just like it was on those A. A. Allen tapes I watched him practice to!"

During this time Jason's and Kenny's education suffered tremendously in spite of Tony's repeated promises to Macalynn that her boys would receive top-notch Christian home schooling. The truth of the matter was that hardly any of those making up the motley collection of adults around Brother Tony had much of an education themselves—Tony being the only one with a high school diploma—and none of them had any training to teach children. Besides that, the sound and tent crew was composed of teenage boys who were dropouts and misfits.

By the time he had turned eleven, Jason's abuse by Tony had become frighteningly repetitive, yet the boy kept it all stuffed down deep inside himself. However, he could not understand why his mother had allowed him to go with this preacher in the first place without checking on him or really knowing anything about the man's background. Never having known his father or the protection that a good father provides his children, Jason had looked to his mother for this but he felt terribly let down by her.

"When he'd ask me [to spend the night] I'd always tell him, 'You gotta check with my mom.' And I would always hope that she would say no, but she never did. With Tony she always said yes," he bitterly recalled. Tony was Macalynn's employer, and Jason knew that in order for his family's income to keep coming in—and for his mother to be happy—he had to please her and, sadly, Tony as well. This caused Jason to harbor an inner anger toward his mother that smoldered for years.

---

*For A. A. Allen, see footnote to p. 34.

But Kenny—always a quiet loner—was spared sexual abuse by Brother Tony after the preacher's first aborted attempt. Unlike Jason, he enjoyed being out of school and having only a handful of friends, usually adults he met on the revival circuit. Said Kenny, "When we were with Tony, I mostly involved myself with adults. I got a few friends, but I'm the kind of person that'll pick two or three friends out of a whole bunch of others. I prefer that there's just two; like now, I've got just two."

Although Kenny began limiting his church attendance after his exposure to Tony Leyva, the taciturn teen remarked that even after his experience he still believes in God: "You know, not all of 'em is like Tony. After that happened I went to a church, a Pentecostal Apostolic Faith Church in Florida, and that preacher was all right. He was a great preacher. . . . I'll give him that much credit! . . . He never did anything wrong. He was no problem. He was a good man."

But it was years later before Macalynn was finally forced to acknowledge what had been done to Jason and Kenny by this man she had idolized. One thing Macalynn did discover early on about Tony was his terrible temper which, she felt, came from his father: "Tony had a Cuban temper that was out of this world! He hated it and despised it when I'd come in and corner him about a lie. The thing is, at the revivals I knew when he was lying to the people and I knew when he wasn't. I cornered him about it and we got into some heavy fights over it. He threw a vase at me one time and missed me that much.

"And Tony never was very truthful. Everything he preached, the visions he claimed he was having and everything, he received from listening to those A. A. Allen tapes. It was all a show."

As his reputation grew, Brother Tony expanded the "International" part of his ministry's name by frequently traveling to Haiti, the Dominican Republic, and Cuba—even though the United States did not allow its citizens to travel there—since he was the son of a Cuban national and had family on the island. He said that during his trips he was allowed to preach, however, no independent verification of his Cuban ministry could be found. After his first trip, he later claimed, he was contacted by the CIA and debriefed by an agent. But, as before, no independent verification of this could be obtained.

However, there is evidence that on his last trip to Cuba, Tony was given the bum's rush by Castro's men, whether due to his alleged spying for the CIA, or because he was discovered *in flagrante delicto* with some young Cuban boys.

Years later Tony wrote about his experiences in Cuba in one of his religious tracts. Filled with his typically flowery, fractured syntax and Pentecostal preaching style of storytelling, it offers an interesting insight into this man, his ministry, and his efforts to build himself before his followers:

> Over the years, in my travels into many foreign countries, I have been invited to meet with AMBASSADORS, eat in their homes; and have even lead Bible Studies and Prayer Group meetings in their homes (or embassy).
> One such meeting took place in Havana, Cuba, in 1982; my first of three journeys to that country during the 1980s. I was preaching in a church pastored by Marcial Miguel Hernandez Salazar, called Iglesia Evangelica Libre (Free Pentecostal Church). As I concluded ministering the Word of God, the Holy Ghost began to move upon me in THE GIFTS OF THE SPIRIT. Eventually, I was drawn by the Spirit to a lady that was blind. Now, I didn't have to be told by the Spirit that she was blind; she was led into the church, had on the typical black sun glasses, that matched a plain black dress that she was wearing; however, upon approaching her, the Holy Ghost revealed to me how she was blinded, and when. God never reveals anything except that he has intentions of doing something about it. As she stood to her feet, I removed the dark glasses from her face, led her to the front; and everyone could see the "scummy-film" or "fleshly-scales" that matted her eyes tightly closed. As the Spirit of God came upon me—I took out a handkerchief and gently began to wipe away the scales IN THE NAME OF JESUS! She began to shout: "I can see; I can see; Praise God, I can see!" The Pastor later told me that while the woman had come often to his church, he had no idea who she was—she generally arrived late, and departed early, and was a mystery.
> Only a couple of days before, I had been to Fidel Castro's office, seeking an audience with him (leaving a fifteen-page letter, just in case it never materialized—he *did* receive the letter). However, on the morning following the healing of the little blind lady, the telephone rang in my room in the Hotel Sevilla, in the old quarters of Havana. The manager was informing me that my limousine had arrived. "What limousine?" I answered. I didn't even know they had limousines in Cuba. I did remember that Fidel Castro has a black Mercedez Benz [sic] limousine; however, after the Spirit O.K.'ed it, I went down the ancient caged elevator, piloted by an equally ancient but kind woman in uniform; and cautiously entered a modern Cadillac limousine, after passing the inspection of the somber-faced chauffeur, who never said one word the entire ride. I had absolutely *no* idea where I was being taken (only that the Holy Ghost said that it was all right).
> After about a thirty-minute ride, we arrived at a district that reminded me of millionaires' row in Palm Beach, Florida, and I was quite taken back by this scene. This was where "Mafia" figures, etc., once lived

during the "BATISTA REGIME,' and many multimillionaires; but was now partially multi-family dwellings, elitest [sic] of the Castro Regime, and foreign embassies, with youthful Cuban soldiers wielding their Soviet AK-47's strapped to the shoulders, lazily patrolling under the hot tropical sun. "EMBASSY OF SIERRA LEONE, WEST AFRICA," it read; and now I was even more confused. "I knew no one from Sierra Leone," so I thought. In total customary-dress (multi-colored robe and beads, sandals, etc.), standing a towering 6'4", and 350 lbs., was MR. AMBASSADOR himself, his excellency, A.Y. Cecilia Komer, and to his side, a woman I seemed to recognize—the lady that was blind but now could see, from last nights [sic] crusade service. I was shocked.

My modest, humble upbringing had not quite prepared me for such a regale [sic] affair. The red carpet was rolled out, the native music piped in softly, servants scurried about speaking reverently of last-minute details, as I was taken on a tour of the Embassy, which reminded me of a beautiful museum, filled with their arts, crafts, furnishings and artifacts. Then I was taken to a table spread in banquet fashion—only, the table was only about 24 inches tall, and there were no chairs, but thick carpets and pillows that were beyond description in their beauty—and—removing our shoes (I was so glad I wore clean socks), we sat around this native banquet of delicacies that I still know not what some of the many items were (I only knew they were not liver and buttermilk, so it must be ok!). I was asked to say grace, and the feast began. I carefully watched all their moves, and found it delightful but strenuous, not wanting to do anything disrespectful or of bad manners with their tradition (I never did get the *burp* down pat!).

The conversation soon turned to his wife, the night before and "HOW DID *YOU* DO THAT?!" It was time to witness to this Moslem, the name of Jesus Christ. He, his entire family, and every servant received Christ as Saviour that hour; and prayer was made for every sick and infirm under the roof with one hundred percent victorious results. JESUS WON THE DAY IN THAT EMBASSY AND FAMILY!

I soon confessed my unworthiness of such an elaborate stately affair—in the home of an AMBASSADOR; and his responce [sic] humbled me even more—"But sir, I consider *you* an AMBASSADOR; an AMBASSADOR of a much higher Kingdom than mine; and *you* have represented that Kingdom well!" My only answer could be "TO GOD BE ALL THE GLORY!"

An AMBASSADOR represents his country (or, Kingdom) in his *conduct*—whether it be personal conduct, or conduct of stately affairs—of this Paul, the great "AMBASSADOR" stated in (I Corinthians 11:1—'BE YE FOLLOWERS OF ME, EVEN AS I ALSO AM OF CHRIST)."

Chapter 9

And an AMBASSADOR is AUTHORIZED with specific POWER and AUTHORITY in the representation of his country (or, Kingdom).

He took a very rambling, circuitous route, but Brother Tony eventually refocused his story back to what seemed his principal message: that a Christian is an ambassador of Christ. But, as Macalynn, Kenny, Jason, and hundreds of other parents and boys learned sadly through the years, Tony Leyva was not an ambassador for Jesus Christ. Indeed, he was far from it.

10

"At first my thinking was that Tony Leyva was heaven sent."

Susan Plunkett's extremely close relative Patti Casey said she first heard of Tony Leyva in the late 1970s "after I had come to the Lord. When I would come in from North Carolina to visit my parents, they would go out to the Salem Civic Center to see preachers and some of these evangelists there [and] that's where I met Tony Leyva. My mom and dad had been killed in a car accident two years before that and I was raisin' my three brothers, and I took my brother Stephen with me. He was just eleven then and he was just overtaken with Tony Leyva's ability to show so much love.

"Tony Leyva would walk into his revival meetings and it was just like sunshine flooding in . . . he had that type of thing about him. And Stephen was so overcome with the way that Tony would give him attention and express kindness to him. Stephen would get water and take it up to him during the services."

"Then one time after one of his services Tony Leyva told me that he believed that Stephen was troubled. Stephen may have been troubled, but if he was, I sure didn't know it. He was an awfully good boy. He never gave me or my parents any trouble! But Tony Leyva was insistent that Stephen was troubled and he said he would like it if he could take Stephen with him and talk to Stephen and help him, you know, encourage him in the Lord.

"I said, 'Okay.'

"Then Tony said, 'Well, Sister, why don't you let him stay at the motel with me tonight so I can have an opportunity to talk to him and discuss things with him.

"I said, 'All right,' that I would. And . . . Stephen did.

"But when Stephen came back, he was different. He *was* troubled then! Oh, when Stephen first went with Tony Leyva, . . . he was so full of life like most little boys his age. But . . . when he came back from being with Tony Leyva that first time, Stephen had the eyes of an old man. He started resenting everything about Tony Leyva whenever Tony was preaching over at the Civic Center. In fact, Stephen wouldn't even go with us. Then, when Tony Leyva would leave town and go out on the road again, Stephen would come out of it for a while [but when] Tony Leyva would come back to the Civic Center[,] Stephen would get right back into resenting him again. . . .

"After that, my brothers James and Jonathan started going to Tony Leyva's services with me and even started going out on the road with Tony Leyva. I didn't like it particular, but my husband, Jimmy, insisted that I let them go. He didn't spend no time with my brothers, tryin' to be a father to them or nothin' like that, but he thought the world of Tony Leyva and his preaching and prophesying.

"Then after a watching his brothers go off with Tony Leyva, Stephen wanted to go with Tony Leyva again. And he did go to stay with him . . . even traveled with him on the road like his other brothers was doin'. And that was when Stephen was about twelve years old.

"But after some more experiences with Tony Leyva, he left home. . . . He was a habitual runaway. . . . He got into drinking. He got into drugs. And I never did understand the why of it all."

Patti Casey said that she and her second husband, Jimmy, became increasingly concerned about her brother Stephen's behavior, but, "We thought that Tony Leyva could help keep that sort of thing from happening, and so I let Stephen go out with Tony Leyva on the road just like his older brothers had done.

"I still suspected that something was wrong [and] that something had happened to Stephen that first time with Tony Leyva. . . . At that time the Lord even gave me a questioning feeling about things and so I would go to Stephen and say, 'Stephen, I feel that there is something wrong with this man. Will you please tell me? What does he do? . . . Has he bothered you? Has he done anything to you? 'Cause, there is something wrong and I feel it!'

"And Stephen'd say, 'No, Sis. There's nothing wrong.'

" 'Well,' I'd say, 'What *does* he do? Just read the Bible and pray?'

"And Stephen'd say, 'Yeah, Sis, that's all he does.'

"And I'd say again, 'Are you *sure*?'

"And Stephen would just say again, 'I'm sure, Sis, that's *all* he does!' "

Patti shook her head sorrowfully as she recalled all that had happened: "I went to Stephen and my other brothers many, many times and talked to them about this, but they would never tell me anything bad about Tony Leyva. And then when I mentioned it to other people, like Jimmy Myers—[who] is Larry Myers's stepdaddy; and it came out later that Larry was also involved with Tony Leyva—why, his stepdaddy said, 'Sister, we had better watch what we say or think about Brother Tony because it's possibly the Devil causing us to question him and we could be touching God's anointed!' "

All the while Jimmy Casey became more and more mesmerized by the charismatic preaching and prophesying of Tony Leyva; so blinded, in fact, that he didn't want to hear anything negative about this man he acknowledged as a true prophet of God. But Patti was persistent in her concern.

"Jimmy would still want to go to Tony Leyva's services," she remarked, "but every time we'd go I'd feel so uneasy about it. Then I told Jimmy, 'I'm gonna listen very carefully to his teachings and I'm gonna see if there's anything wrong with them.' And Jimmy wouldn't like that, but I would go to Tony Leyva's revivals with that intent.

"But I couldn't find anything wrong with his teachings. And most of my boys—excepting Stephen for that time there—still wanted to stay with him. They would beg me. They would say, 'Mama, there's nothing wrong with him! He's all right! Please let us stay with him! He loves us and he's teachin' us the Word!' ...

"Even though I felt that the Lord was still dealing with me that something was wrong, eventually I figured it was probably the Devil speaking to me and that I had no right to say anything about it 'cause the kids had denied anything was wrong. And so I let my boys go back to stayin' with him nights here in Roanoke and even to travel on the road with him."

Patti Casey's only son, Mark Crump, was her only child from her first marriage, and for several years he had heard his uncles talk about Brother Tony and how nice and kind he was. Finally, in 1978, Mark talked his mother into taking him to hear Brother Tony preach at the Salem Civic Center. Unknown to Patti, however, by that time her young brothers were some of the evangelist's most favored catamites.

After the service that fateful night, at Mark's insistence, his mother somewhat reluctantly took her young son up to meet Brother Tony. As the preacher shook the boy's small hand he remarked to Sister Casey, "Why, your boy is handsomer than your brothers!" as he smiled benevolently at the eight-year-old and squeezed the boy's shoulder.

Chapter 10

An hour later, as Mark fell asleep at home, in a motel not far away Brother Tony coerced the boy's young uncle James, then fourteen, to crawl into bed with him for a night of sex.

And Mark's memory of Tony Leyva from that first meeting? "He seemed like a nice man."

✝ ✝ ✝

Frequently Patti and her extremely close relative Susan Plunkett, noted the competition between Susan's sons and Patti's brothers as to who would be invited to go on the next road trip with Tony or who traveled with him the most. Then, when they returned, there would be "Can you top this?" challenges between the boys about the cash and gifts Tony had given them.

Added Patti, "When Tony would call on the phone he would never talk to any adults. When he would call my house it would always be, 'Praise the Lord, Sister! Is one of my boys there? . . . Is one of *my* boys there?'"

Given these lavish gifts, it struck Patti as odd the way Brother Tony would plead poverty at his meetings. But his pleas unfailingly elicited a response from those gathered. "We would go to see other evangelists and they would have a hard time taking up a collection . . . a *hard* time! You know, people just wouldn't give. But with Tony Leyva we would sit there in the auditorium and when he would walk in that back door at the Civic Center, you just knew that God was there!

"It was like the whole place lit up and you felt like this wave of love was flowing through everything. People were just totally overtaken with him! He had this magnetic power about him that he could stand up there and it would take your mind off all your worries.

"And then when he would take up an offering, people gave! I mean, they gave and gave and gave! I just couldn't believe the size of the collections! He would flash that smile and you just wanted to get in there and give him everything you had!

"But, as soon as the service was over, he would spend great amounts of cash money on the boys . . . mine and the others.

"At the time, I didn't question him on it. But I did talk with my close relative Susan about it. She was suspicious also, [and] it was along about this time that she come to me and said, 'Patti, there's something wrong with him. . . . He's taking all this money and spending it for foolishness on these boys and there's no reason why anybody would have an interest like he has in those boys unless there's something wrong about his attraction to 'em. Why else would he let those boys come home with such great amounts of money and all those gifts?'"

About Brother Tony's Cadillac limousine Patti said: "It was just beautiful. And he was really proud of it. But about his limousine, people would say . . . 'A preacher shouldn't go around in a Volkswagen.' Like Jim Bakker said, 'God wouldn't want His people to go second class.' And people who supported Tony Leyva felt that God wants the best for his people so he blessed men like Tony Leyva because they're in a ministry and, 'Why should they have to do without when they can drive these big cars?'

"There was this thing about prosperity for God's people going around, this 'name it and claim it.' And I'd hear Tony Leyva asking people to give him their jewelry and gold. So, every time I would bring that up—which the Lord had shown me quite differently—that's the way the others of Tony's people would come back to me on it."

Patti said that this mind-set of his was quite similar to what she had heard from other preachers: "I heard Jim Bakker say on television that someone could lay down at his feet and die of starvation and he would step over them and not give them nothing if they didn't believe in God. And that man drove Rolls-Royces, lived in a mansion, and he was not doing anything for the poor!"

Even though scandals involving Jim and Tammy Bakker as well as Jimmy Swaggart occurred prior to Tony Leyva's being "found out," Patti strongly dismissed the suggestion that those public disclosures influenced her efforts at exposing Brother Tony, "because I had begun to really see what God had to say about him instead of what man had to tell me and teach me. I went straight to the Word of God to get my answers from Him to find out what was going on and what was happening and see what God thought about different situations.

"But," she said, "the Lord showed me very plainly that in these last days He is cleaning house, He is cleaning it out, and I knew that that was going on. I knew that God was going to bring forth a body of believers that were going to preach the pure Word of God who was going to live according to His word and not this 'name it and claim it' junk. They were not going to have sin in their lives. God was fed up with what was going on and He was putting a stop to it!"

Patti then continued her story of her family's involvement with Tony Leyva: "When Susan found out that my brothers and Mark were fixing to go out on the road again with Tony Leyva, she said, 'Don't let them go! I'm warning you! Don't let them go!' And I said, 'I think that it would be good for them to get away from Jimmy for a while.' And at that time Jimmy was wanting them to go with Tony Leyva."

Patti clearly noticed—as did most other parents in her religious circle, but most especially those with daughters—that it was always the young boys that Brother Tony fawned over. "His comment on this to me that cleared that up in my mind," Patti recollected, "was one time when he said, 'I love these little girls just as much as I do the boys, but I can't take them to the motel with me and talk with them and counsel them in the Lord because people will say things. You just don't take little girls to a motel! So, I have to do it with just the boys 'cause then there won't be any gossip when I try to help them.' "

For years Patti fought hard to keep her son, Mark, from being sucked in by what she believed to be a strange yet still unidentifiable spell that Tony Leyva had somehow cast over her brothers.

"For some reason," Patti said, "I was able to keep my baby boy from goin' off with Tony Leyva. You know, I'd already let my brothers stay nights with Tony Leyva and even go out on the road with him. But when Mark would come ask, I'd say no. And when Tony Leyva would ask me specifically for Mark to come stay with him, I'd tell him, 'No, Brother Tony, he's not going to.' And Tony didn't ever seem to take no on that. He just kept on asking and asking."

But when Mark was eleven his mother took him to yet another Tony Leyva revival service at the ever popular Salem Civic Center and afterwards acquiesced to the preacher's request to briefly take her "mighty handsome boy" out to his midnight-blue Cadillac limousine for a short talk.

Once there, however, the evangelists' hands were all over the startled fifth-grader, fondling his crotch through his clothes and covering his lips, cheeks, and neck with kisses while he whispered "I love you, I love you, I love you" over and over and over into the confused boy's ears.

The man's adulation startled and yet held a strange attraction for this affection-starved boy. But even though Mark was frightened by the man's behavior, he didn't say a word about it to his mother until years later.

☦ ☦ ☦

In the early 1970s—before his marriage to Patti—Jimmy Casey had been imprisoned for sexually assaulting a young girl. Patti knew this when she married him, figuring that his interest had been in girls, not boys. Besides, as a loving Christian she felt that Jimmy had been both punished for his crime and forgiven his sin, therefore, it was with open heart and considerable love that she married him and brought him into her life and the lives of her brothers and her young son.

According to Mark, Tony Leyva knew all about this aspect of Jimmy Casey's background. This just might account for the curious affinity the two men had for each other. Indeed, Jimmy became one of Tony Leyva's closest followers in the Roanoke area.

As Mark described it: "Jimmy acted like Tony Leyva was his pastor. Every time we went to Tony Leyva's meetings, Jimmy would go and him and Tony would meet privately.... Him and Jimmy would be in the limousine or the van.... It would be after dark but the light would be on inside and you could see through the tinted windows that the two of them was alone talking."

✝ ✝ ✝

By Mark's fourteenth birthday, Jimmy Casey had become increasingly angry about having to share *his* house with Patti's brothers and young son and—in a fit of rage—kicked Mark out of the house for the first of many times. Ostensibly, it always happened because Mark would not submit to Jimmy's authority or comply with his stepfather's extremely strict rules. And it all happened in spite of his mother's strong objections.

"You see, Jimmy wasn't involved with me and my uncles," Mark remarked both nonchalantly and with bitter sarcasm. "He was just ... just there. I mean, we all hated him 'cause he was a pain to everybody. He had us all under his thumb. We lived in the same house and he made us live in the basement for a while, and whenever he wanted me or one of my uncles he would stomp on the floor. He lived upstairs and he'd stomp on the floor and yell at us to come up and then he would treat us like dogs.

"He whipped us a lot with a leather belt ... actually, it was a leather razor strap with a handle he'd put on it. He'd take a little incident and treat it like it was somethin' real big and beat us with it. Lots of times me and my uncles had marks on us from it. He'd make us undress and then he'd tell us to bend over and then he'd whip us. And usually when he did it he'd hit us no less than fifty times.

"And that all started as soon as Mama first married Jimmy. I was just seven or eight back then. And Mama couldn't say nothin' about it 'cause, if she did, she'd get it, too. He'd cuss her out and take after her and beat her up. And it went on up until I was moved out when I was fifteen."

Roanoke County Deputy Sheriff L. Garrick Hudson found himself trying to deal with this once when Jimmy Casey kicked Mark out of the house and Patti called the authorities. But when he talked to the teenager the boy said very little about the later well-documented physical abuse that he and his uncles suffered from Jimmy Casey. "It was a control issue with Jimmy Casey," says Hudson. "According to Jimmy, Mark had run away from home, but, of course, I soon found out that Mark had actually been thrown out of the house by his stepfather. But I thought that Mark had a lot of potential and that he was a very nice young man."

Patti recalled: "I did everything to please my husband, and Jimmy insisted Mark leave our house when he resisted him. Jimmy was very cruel to the kids and in his punishments. He beat them with a strap and he mistreated them a lot; we had many fights over it. I'd take up for the kids and I would catch it. I wanted the boys to have somebody as a daddy who would love them, who would really care for them, ya know, this male companionship that they didn't get from Jimmy. . . .

"Supposedly, Jimmy Casey was a religious man. I mean, he read the Word of God, he confessed the Word of God, and he loved to go and hear Tony Leyva preach. So, I thought that these problems with his behavior were just problems that God would clear up in his mind later.

"But, as far as really being a Christian, no, he wasn't. . . . At that point in time, I guess, I wanted to see him as one because when he would beat the boys he would tell me that the Bible said, 'Spare not the rod.' He would always bring the Word [of God] against me if I complained about his beating the boys. He would say, 'You're going against God when you go against your husband in correcting the children. You're not letting me correct the children so that they will come up properly.' And, I think, more or less he had me confused and I didn't know what was right.

"But using a leather strap on the boys, that wasn't right!" she declared. "I know that now and I should have known it then.

"At first, my thinking was that Tony Leyva was heaven sent . . . to take the place of the father my children never really had. That Tony Leyva—being a man of God—would give the boys what was lacking at home. So, that's why I permitted the boys to go with Tony Leyva; mostly, it was to keep them away from Jimmy . . . his mistreatment . . . the beatings . . . the total lack of attention that he gave them.

"Before I knew anything for sure about Tony Leyva doing anything sexual to the boys," Patti said, "I had heard rumors that started with Martha Sharp about her son, Darrell Wayne. . . . It started spreading for a while, with Mrs. Sharp going and standing up at church meetings and such and telling people that Tony Leyva had done bad things to her boy.

"That's when I finally said, 'No, I'm not letting these boys go with him anymore.' And that made Jimmy mad, really angry with me 'cause he still believed real strongly in Tony Leyva and he told me that he didn't believe that he would do anything like that. And Jimmy warned me that I was going against God by believin' what Mrs. Sharp was saying against Tony Leyva."

✝ ✝ ✝

By 1986, Martha Sharp's brave efforts to expose Brother Tony in churches nearby had caused him such a huge loss in area followers that he could no longer afford to rent the Salem Civic Center. Increasingly he found himself in small Pentecostal churches where he had to settle for collections measured in the hundreds rather than the thousands of dollars.

While it also concerned him that his secret life as a pederast might indeed be discovered, Tony Leyva found it impossible to control his constant erotic drive to seduce young boys. As he later admitted, he often argued with himself about what his sexual desires and exploits were doing "to God's people."

However, Brother Tony frequently found such arguments with himself falling on deaf ears, such as the night in April 1986, when then fifteen-year-old Mark Crump showed up at one of his services at a small independent church in Roanoke where Brother Tony was appearing as the guest evangelist that night. He arrived with two of his uncles and their girlfriends, homeless for the night, having been kicked out of the house by his abusive stepfather. So Mark was quick to accept Tony's invitation to stay the night with him.

✝ ✝ ✝

According to a good friend of Brother Tony's in Roanoke, the Reverend James R. Carter, shortly after Martha Sharp's revelations about his pederasty, Tony Leyva would show up to preach at his little church with "probably seven, eight, or as many as a dozen boys with him. A lot of times the boys would just hang around outside. They weren't interested in what he was preaching; they were just interested in what they could get out of him. . . .

"It troubled me the type of kids he always had with him. I spoke with him about that, but he would just say he didn't want to be rude to them. He said he didn't want them to think he was trying to shun them or anything [and that] they were just there for him to be good to them! And then, after the service, he'd take them all out with him down to a big restaurant and get a big long table and they'd eat and he'd pay for all of their meals so they got stuffed.

"And when people were first talking about him and these kids, I warned him on a couple of occasions. I told him them kids was nothin' but trouble looking for a handout. And them kids was like any other criminal, if you get close enough to 'em, you get stabbed in the back!"

✝ ✝ ✝

When Mark presented himself to Brother Tony after the service and explained his situation, Tony immediately began making plans to take care of the boy for the night. But, Mark swears, he did not know at the time that that would include his being coerced into sex.

Once again, the evangelist's urge to have sex with a boy manifested itself as a force he could not control. By the time the last worshippers had filed out of the little church glowing over the inspired message they had heard, the true prophesies revealed to them, and the glorious blessings they had received, it went without saying that the object of their adulation would sexually violate yet another young boy before a new day had dawned.

After a late supper with Mark, Rev. Carter, and his wife, Eunice, the preacher drove Mark back to his room at the Holiday Inn in northwest Roanoke. Once they arrived it happened just like it had so many times before with so many other boys in a motel room with two beds.

"I had my pants on and my shirt on," Mark said. "I was sitting on the bed and he told me to take them off, 'because you'd be more comfortable without them.' And he's already in just his underwear.

"And so I got undressed down to my underwear, but when I tried to get in the other bed, he told me to get in bed with him. In a way I wondered about that, but I really knew what was goin' on so I just went ahead and didn't argue and got in bed with him. Then he started fondling me by sticking his hand down in my underwear and playin' with my penis till I caught an erection.

"He played around with me a little bit more and then he pulled down my underwear and started sucking my penis.

"When he got through he didn't say nothin' to me. He just rolled over and went to sleep.

"I started getting mad at myself for going with him and letting it happen, but I didn't have no place else to go!"

✝ ✝ ✝

A couple of months after the incident at the Holiday Inn, Mark had another fight with his abusive stepfather, which led to his being kicked out of the house yet again. For a time he lived under a bridge like a true homeless person, scrounging for food while being soaked by spring rains. So, in spite of the sex abuse he had suffered at the hands of Tony Leyva just a month earlier, Mark called the preacher collect and begged for a place to stay.

Inexplicably the teenager claimed that at that time he had forgotten all about the night four years earlier when Tony had aggressively fondled and kissed him in his limousine. And Mark now rationalized the recent incident at the Holiday Inn as a once-in-a-lifetime aberration.

Now this modestly handsome, naive, willing lad was turning to the man who had raped him for a place to live, food, clothing, and comfort on a full-time basis, thus effectively presenting the pederast-evangelist with an opportunity about which he had only dreamed before. Even with the object of his lust three states to the north, Tony considered Mark Crump as good as in his bed. As soon as Brother Tony got off the phone he drove to the Greyhound Bus Station to send his new acquisition a ticket to Atlanta.

Patti Casey remarked: "Mark never did stay with him until Jimmy kicked Mark out of our house. And because of Jimmy, there wasn't nothing that I could do about it. Back then, Mark had to have a place to live, and it was Tony Leyva that gave him that place."

✝ ✝ ✝

When Mark arrived in Atlanta, a smiling Ed Morris picked him up at the Greyhound station in Tony's van and transported him to the virtual boy-brothel that he, Leyva, and Freddie Herring were operating at the Moonraker Apartments in Marietta.

"The minute I come in on the bus, Morris was waitin' right there to pick me up. He had Danny Perez with him and right away he took me out and got me some new clothes before we went back to Tony's apartment down to the Moonraker Apartments. There Tony Leyva had this bedroom that I shared with him. . . . Whenever I was with Tony, I was his little pet, as you'd call it, and I stayed in his bed with him. Just the two of us.

"But that first night when Ed Morris met me at the bus station and took me to the apartments, Tony was gone somewhere to preach a revival. I'd just gotten there and I'm sittin' on the edge of what they had said was my bed with Herring and Morris and they was talking to me. And I had just met Herring and he moves over beside me and starts fondlin' me right through my pants. Then Ed Morris leaves—to give us a little privacy, I guess—and shut the door as he went out and this was like a signal to Freddie to get all over me.

"At that point I *knew* that there was something going on, but what was I gonna do about it? I'd been kicked out back home and I'd been sleepin' out under the bridge. And I'd done asked Tony to bring me down there to Georgia so I could work for him and have a place to live and somethin' to eat an' all. . . ." Mark plaintively pled for understanding before his voice trailed off.

". . . I was stuck there with Ed and Freddie. And until then I didn't know Herring. And then all of a sudden he's feelin' me up through my pants and all. And before he done 'it' he didn't say nothing to me about it, really. And then when he done 'it,' he didn't say word one to me, either. He just done 'it.'

"But . . . well . . . when he started he just pulled down my pants and he pulled down my underwear and then right away he just leaned over and started sucking on me right where I was sittin' down just like it was all perfectly natural!

"He, um . . . he finished me off an' just rolled me over and tried anal sex with me right there on the bed! And he got a little ways in and I told him that I was feeling sick and I had to use the bathroom. So I got up and went to the bathroom and locked the door and just stayed in there till I was pretty sure that everybody'd went to sleep.

"And this was the way that my first day with Tony Leyva and his bunch went. But there was nothin' I felt I could do!"

After a few more weeks sexually assaulting the new arrival, Freddie Herring propositioned Mark in a manner that he apparently felt the boy from Roanoke couldn't resist. Said Mark: "After I'd been doin' it with Freddie for a while he made me an offer that if I would stay with him I could have everything I wanted, as in diamonds, gold, silver . . . anything I wanted as long as I lived with him and had sex with him regular. And it had looked dirty to begin with before he even said that, so, after it had gone on for a while longer between us I said, 'Uh, uh!' and I left him. Got away from him completely and never had nothing more to do with him."

✝ ✝ ✝

But what had been a rude awakening for Mark at the hands of Freddie Herring when he initially arrived at Tony Leyva's apartment now became a continuing nightmare when Tony returned.

"When Tony got back," Mark said, "a day, maybe two days later, then he wanted me to sleep with him in his room. He said, 'You needed a place to stay, I sent you a bus ticket. Now, you come sleep with me.' Then when he got me in there he started the same thing he did at the motel up in Roanoke. He said he wanted to love me . . . all that type of stuff . . . the same old jazz.

"He didn't waste no time. He made me get butt naked and started right in playin' with my ass and my balls and fondlin' me while he got me to do '69' with him. And from then on it was like that every single night!"

11

"There were these government men that Tony knew. He had us to have sex with them."

Preacher Freddie M. Herring's lavish lifestyle didn't stop with a home in Douglasville, a classy townhouse in suburban Marietta, and his gold and rings and jewelry. He had a flashy car to go with it all: "A pink Cadillac," said Jason Embert, "and he always wore hot pink socks! He liked pink so much that he tried to get Tony to paint his revival bus pink, too, but Tony never did that."

When permitted by Brother Tony—or more often, when Tony went off to preach by himself somewhere—Freddie would load up the available boys at Tony's Moonraker apartment and drive them out to his home in Douglasville. One time he and Ed each took their own preferred boy— Jason Embert went with Ed in Tony's van and Freddie and Mark Crump got in the pink Cadillac along with Danny Perez—and drove out to Douglasville for the weekend. Neither Jason nor Danny would sleep with the men; but Mark spent the night in bed with Freddie, and Jason caught the two "doing 'it' with each other," he said.

"Freddie was a diabetic and had to take insulin several times a day," Jason recalled, "and that next morning I was just walking around . . . me and Danny were just looking around Freddie's house and stuff when I walked past his room and the door was open. Freddie was laying on his bed naked with Mark and Mark was still asleep. And I knew something was going on and so I hollered out or something and Ed jumped up in his room and ran into Freddie's room and real quick Freddie jumped up and put his robe on."

Shortly before this, Jason said that Freddie had made his one and only attempt to put the make on him: "That's when we were in Okeechobee. Freddie went down there to preach and I went down there with him. I was staying in this camper and 'cause it was cold and there was no TV, I went to Freddie's apartment.... And after I'd finished watching TV he told me, 'If it gets too cold, just come over here and lie down with me.'

"But I just ignored him, ya know. I knew he was gonna try and have sex with me 'cause I had found dirty pictures of men and boys doing 'it' in his briefcase.... So, I went to sleep on the floor but Freddie woke me up a bunch of times asking me if I didn't want to come sleep with him and keep warm. But I stayed on the floor and slept [by] myself."

✝ ✝ ✝

When Jason spent the summer of 1987 with Tony at the Moonraker Apartments, the evangelist reprised his early 1980s shower tryst with some of the resident boys: "Mark, Danny Perez, and Brother Tony all took a shower together and they came out smiling. I said, 'What happened?' Danny told me that Brother Tony sucked him off, then Danny said he did it to Mark, and then that Mark did it to Brother Tony.

"By the time I left that summer to come home, Danny and Mark were taking showers together and doing 'it' all the time. But I never did 'it.' I'd never touch a guy with my mouth like that. I don't even know why I let Tony Leyva do 'it' to me! I really don't!"

After his initial nearly two-month stay during which he was repeatedly assaulted by Freddie Herring and Tony Leyva, Mark returned to Roanoke for a short visit and an unsuccessful attempt at reconciliation with his stepfather. He was back at the Moonraker by midsummer.

And what about school? "The whole time I was with Tony," said Mark, "none of us was in school.... There was no concern about that. I mean, they really didn't bother with it. In fact, I quit school right before I went to Georgia the first time. I guess Tony was too busy foolin' around with us...."

✝ ✝ ✝

Unknown until my 1989 interview of a certain older teenage boy—let's call him Brad—who in 1983 was one of a score or so of boys from the greater Roanoke area involved with Tony, Leyva pimped his victims not only to preachers outside his "ministry" but to others as well. This boy's surprise response truly opened the proverbial can of worms: "Other than Tony and Freddie and Ed, I wasn't involved with any of the other preachers except two; but there were these government men that Tony knew. He had us to have sex with them." This boy nonchalantly detailed this entirely new aspect of Brother Tony Leyva's sexual abuse of young boys.

"That was in Roanoke. Tony Leyva took us to the airport to meet them. As I recall, it was about March of '87 that these government men flew in to the airport. It was a little jet, you know, nothing big and fancy, but . . . [it] said 'United States of America' on it in blue letters on the side. And it had a little round seal on it, too, . . . like the United States seal.

"We went out [to the airport] in the limousine. I started out sitting in the limousine while the plane came in and then Tony called me over and introduced me to them. Then they was talking about some type thing that was about to happen and Tony looked at me and said 'Go on back to the car,' like he wanted to get me away from it.

"And as I started walking back to the car Tony looked at them and said, 'Well, we're going to have to work something out on this. I'm going to have to make some more on this.' And then I couldn't hear no more. But to me it was like Tony was getting boys for them."

Brad couldn't identify which branch of the government the men were from nor did Tony tell him or any of the boys. "They were dressed fancy, like preachers," Brad said. "Suit, vest, and tie. And all Tony said was that they was friends of his and that they could protect his ministry and that we should go with them." Asked if he suspected anything when they picked up the men at the airport, Brad sighed, "I thought it might be for sex."*

Brad described how he and Danny Perez as well as a boy about fifteen named "Pete" who, according to Brad, "was kept kinda tipsy with alcohol . . . [we] spent the weekend with these three men and they done sex with us. Blow jobs . . . same stuff as Tony Leyva done."

According to Brad, this was the first of two occasions that Tony Leyva required him and other boys to spend the weekend with these "government men." The second time, Brad thought, was in May of 1987.

---

*Beginning in 1983 small law enforcement agencies scattered from Louisiana to Florida to Virginia made occasional calls to their local FBI offices advising them that young teenage boys had come to them complaining that traveling evangelist Tony Leyva had sexually assaulted them. These local agencies told the FBI that they did not have the manpower or money to go chasing after Leyva, but in virtually every case they were told that the FBI would conduct an investigation. And, strangely, it was in 1983 that Brad and other boys recall Brother Tony first pimping them to "government men."

"Once it was at the Embassy Motel over on Melrose. The other time it was out at a preacher's [home]. I don't remember the man's name. But he wasn't there. He just let Tony Leyva use his house. I don't think he knew what [Tony Leyva] was doing."

Asked if they were the same "government men" both times, Brad replied that two of the three men were different. "But it was the same kind of plane both times."

In a remarkably calm voice Brad detailed his stay with one of these "government men": "I had to get naked in the bed with him. He got naked, too." He described the man he slept with as being about thirty-five years old while the other two were "maybe about fifty. . . . well, maybe not fifty, but older than Tony Leyva." And he said that he remembers well what these men looked like: "I'll never forget them!"

Brad's story led me to "Pete," whom, when I interviewed him by phone in 1993, I found to be an alcoholic living on the streets in a small southwestern Virginia city. Pete nervously filled in some details of the story before he realized that I knew that he, too, had submitted to sex with the "government men" in Roanoke:

"We went out to eat and these men went with us. Ed Morris and Larry Myers was with us. . . . We all sat around and ate and then Tony gave us one hundred dollars and sent us off to play videos while he talked with them. So, then we went and played videos for a while and that was about it." When asked if "something sexual" had occurred, Pete disingenuously replied, "There wasn't actual sex. Just a shot at it."

The boy became extremely upset and defensive when I told him that I knew about the sex with the "government men." At first Pete repeatedly tried to deny that anything had really happened. But I was insistent.

At this point, Pete broke down and tearfully admitted that he had had sex with the "government men." He also expressed the fear that telling what he knew could get him killed by one of Leyva's followers or someone else beholden to Tony Leyva. He had already received death threats and said, "You don't know Tony! He plays for keeps!"

After being repeatedly assured that he would not be identified in this book and encouraged to help reveal the truth about the full extent of Mario Ivan "Tony" Leyva's illegal activities, the teenager's sobbing suddenly became muffled, as if he had lowered his head and buried it in his sleeve. After a brief pause he composed himself and began telling me his story of what had gone on with the "government men" during a bizarre yet very believable interview, which went like this:

"Oral sex?" I asked the boy.
"Yes," Pete softly replied.
"Anal?"
"Yes."
"Did Danny Perez, too?"
"Yes."
"Did Larry?"
"No."
"Why didn't Larry?"
"I don't know. Tony had him leave with Ed Morris."
"Where was the sex?"
"At the Embassy Motel and this preacher's home."
"How much time did you spend with these 'government men'?"
"A couple of days."
"Did the men sleep with you and the other boys?"
"Yes."
"Did they have any clothes on?"
"No, they was naked."
"Did you have any clothes on?"
"No, the man had me take off my clothes."
"Were you in the same room as the other boys?"
"No."
"Do you know what happened with them?"
"Yes."
"How?"
"They told me. We talked about it."
"Did Tony tell you why he wanted you to be with these men and have sex with them?"
"He didn't say 'have sex' . . . he just said for us to go with them. He said that by doing it we would help protect his ministry."
"Did these men appear to be well educated?"
"Yes."
"How old were they?"
"Thirty to fifty."
"If you ever saw pictures of these men, could you identify them?"
"Yes, sir."
"Who did you think these men were?"
"I really did not know."
"Did you care?"

"Not really. In a way I did."

"In what way?"

"In a way I wanted to know what was going on. In my mind I thought . . . well, Tony had me believing that doing it with him and with these men was okay. But in my mind, I knowed it was wrong."

"Did they take any pictures of you?"

"Yes."

"Have you seen any of those pictures since then?"

"No. But Tony said he had."

✝ ✝ ✝

During my initial investigation in 1988 and 1989, around the Moonraker Apartments in Marietta and other Georgia areas where Tony Leyva had operated during the 1980s, it was not hard for me to find still other boys with their own stories of being sexually abused by Tony Leyva, Ed Morris, and Freddie Herring, as well as other pederasts with whom he came in contact.

One such Georgia teenager—who will be called Billy—says he was thirteen when he first met Tony through Ed Morris in 1986. Ed had picked the boy up for sex several times in Atlanta. "One time he took me around with him [when] he was playin' at one of Bro. Tony's* revivals and they asked me if I'd like to help out with the tent and sound and stuff. So, I went out on the road with 'em."

Over the next year Billy became increasingly involved sexually with Tony, Ed, and Freddie Herring. "At first, Ed was real nice to me," Billy said. "He gave me money for video games. He took me out to eat. And he had me to stay the night with him at his motel room. He rubbed on my back [and] he started feelin' 'round on me, you know? Then he touched me between my legs, you know? Well, I was . . . [pause] . . . I was gettin' hard and, well . . . he took down my underwear [and] then he started playin' around with me, jerking me off. He acted like it was all natural."

Sadly for Billy, involvement with Ed Morris was not the extent of it, for soon all three evangelists considered the young teenager an all-around boy toy. And Billy saw Tony's collection of child pornography, remarking, "It was kinda' scary, but I knew what Bro. Tony and them was doin', the same stuff in them pictures, and so I just tried to put it out of my mind."

---

*As did a few of the other boys traveling as "Tony's boys," Billy used the slang abbreviation "Bro." for Brother Tony.

Brother Tony also introduced Billy to his preacher friend Bobby Ray Hopkins and soon Billy found himself coerced into sex with him as well: "It was on the road somewheres. It could have been here in Georgia, or maybe it was over in Alabama. It was in a motel someplace. When he got through he gave me some money to go play videos."

"Then," Billy sighed and went on, "there was one time that I had to do it with some friends of Bro. Tony's. He said that they was government men. They looked real important and they come into Atlanta airport on a little jet plane. They was all dressed up like they was going to church . . . but, naw," Billy laughed, "they didn't come to go to church!"

Asked how he knew details of their arrival, Billy replied, " 'Cause Bro. Tony took us out to the airport in his van to meet them and I saw it!"

"Us?" I asked him.

"Me and this other guy from Columbus, this guy that Freddie knew by the name of Randy Lee and this little boy that was related to Bro. Tony, Danny Perez, went along.

"It was one of them little jet planes," said Billy, "the kind only holds about six people, you know." He described it as being painted white and having "United States of America on it . . . just like one of them big planes I seen on television when the president flies off somewheres. I heard that they come from Washington. That's what Bro. Tony said." But the boy had no idea what branch of the government they worked for.

Billy's experience virtually matched that of Brad, but he met the "government men" at Hartsfield International Airport in Atlanta instead of Roanoke. And this time the boys were taken to the Moonraker Apartments, where Billy said Brother Tony told him "they was some important government men who was gonna help protect his ministry. . . . I weren't no fool! I knowed that he wanted us to have sex with 'em 'cause that's what he done when he put me with that guy Hoppy [Hopkins], or whatever. Bro. Tony wanted us to sleep with 'em and let 'em fool 'round with us. And that's what we done, James and Danny Perez and me."

A street-wise kid with considerable chutzpah, Billy claims that to this day he could identify the man he slept with. "He was sort of tall and had a good build on him . . . near 'bout the same as Bro. Tony. . . . The man Danny Perez slept with gave him fifty dollars. I know 'cause he showed it to me! But I just got forty dollars. Later Bro. Tony said 'thanks' for helping him and just like regular not to say anything to nobody 'bout it 'cause they wouldn't understand."

When I spoke with him again in 1993, Billy told me that in 1988, when an FBI agent investigating Brother Tony interviewed him, he volunteered information about the incident with the "important government men. But I didn't tell him much 'cause he didn't want to know about it."*

Asked if he found that strange, Billy nonchalantly responded, "No, not really. Besides, it wasn't somethin' I 'specially wanted to talk to him about 'cause he seemed real upset about it when I told him. I thought I . . . ought to keep my mouth shut."

Looking back on it all Billy said: "I don't like what happened. It just happened. I thought it would stop after a while, but it didn't. They didn't do it all the time, but it just seemed like every now and then it happened again. And it just went on and on forever. But back then I didn't have no regular place I could stay . . . and Brother Tony and the rest of 'em bought me clothes, fed me, gave me a place to stay."

Talking to Billy led to yet another Georgia teenager who had been sexually abused by Tony Leyva, his preacher friends, and "government men" who flew into Hartsfield International Airport on a plane bearing the legend "United States of America." And his story was virtually the same.

✝ ✝ ✝

After Mark Crump's failed attempt at reconciliation with his stepfather, Jimmy Casey, and his return from Roanoke, to Brother Tony's headquarters cum boy-brothel at the Moonraker Apartments, it was already the beginning of the end for evangelist Mario Ivan "Tony" Leyva.

Said Mark, "A couple of times Tony asked me to forgive him . . . he told me it wouldn't happen again. But then he'd do it again the next night like he ain't said nothin'.

"Finally, I got mad. I just said, 'I don't want it no more.' I said, 'I don't like what's goin' on.' But he kept gettin' me to let him do sex with me. And so did Freddie when Tony wasn't there."

During Mark's last month in residence with the three pederast-evangelists, one or another was always bedding him, or at least trying. Mark remarked how Freddie considered him fair game whenever Tony Leyva wasn't around. Once Mark went with Freddie to a revival meeting in Al-

---

*FBI Behavioral Sciences Unit Supervisory Special Agent Kenneth Lanning at the FBI Academy in Quantico, Virginia, regularly teaches new and experienced agents how to investigate cases of child sexual abuse; but, he says, it is very difficult to get male agents to investigate such cases aggressively when the perpetrators are men and their victims are boys, since "in a way that is an assault on their own masculinity."

abama, and while there Mark was attracted to a girl in the congregation. He sat with her during the service while Freddie preached, or, rather, tried to preach, so distracted was he at seeing the lad he thought of as his new squeeze snuggling with someone else.

"Then I sat there with that girl and talked to her after church and that *really* peeved him off," laughed Mark. "He was pretty mad! He wouldn't even speak with me when we drove back. I slept all the way and then when we got back I went into the bedroom and went to sleep by myself. The next day . . . he was still pretty well mad 'cause of what happened in Alabama and 'cause I wouldn't do nothin' with him that night. And Tony Leyva warned me that Freddie Herring was a very jealous man."

But that same summer things would begin to unravel for Tony Leyva. Mark continued, "Then Tony himself went off to Alabama with Mike Page [his revival's business associate] one weekend to preach a revival and I stayed home at the Moonraker by myself. I'd been talking to [my uncle] Jonathan . . . on the phone and he said something about a black box with pictures of naked kids in it. . . .

"So, I went and found it, picked the locks, and opened it up and looked through it. It had a whole big bunch of different pictures of mostly brown and black-skinned kids in it . . . all boys and all of them naked. . . . Some boys he'd get 'em doin' sex with others; some was just standin' there, naked. They were mostly all Polaroid pictures, like he took before of my uncle James and Bobby Earls. . . .

"I figured that [the pictures] were mostly of kids overseas. He'd said he'd worked with a lot of kids overseas and that he had an orphanage in the Dominican Republic, I think it was. And one time he said he was gonna take me to Jamaica, but my mama wouldn't let him.

"And I found that video movie *Mikey Likes It* . . . the one he tried to get me and Jason and Danny Perez to watch early that summer. It was a good tape—I mean, it was a long tape—but I didn't watch but about five minutes of it. It was all these guys 'bout my age havin' oral sex with each other. Tony kept sayin', 'Sit here and watch it with me.' I left, but he sat there and watched it while I went into the other room and went to bed."

Mark then described a home video that Brother Tony took during one of his trips to Cuba. "He showed it to me once. It had Fidel Castro in it and he's supposed to be completely against religion. Later Tony told me that the government back in Cuba got pretty mad about it and he said that they broke into his apartment right there in Marietta and took it back with them. He said this happened after he'd showed it in church once to a bunch of people. Bubba Gordon [Brother Tony's one-time chauffeur] was supposed to have made a print of it, but he never did."

Getting back to the photographs, Mark said, "I never did discuss [those pictures] with him 'cause it was his business and I just wanted out of there. When I found that he had this footlocker full of pictures of little boys naked and having sex . . . well, at that point I was, you know, 'I'm fed up with this. I know what's goin' on now.' . . . So, that's when I called Mama and told her about some of the things that were happening sex-like and about the pictures and such that I didn't like. That's when I first asked her when could I get back home, but I had to stay there for a while longer till after my birthday. I didn't get to leave and come back to Roanoke till sometime in August."

Before Mark could leave, however, he was victimized by Ed Morris. "I don't know why," Mark recalled, "but that first day when he picked me up, Ed didn't mess with me. But startin' about, I'd say about two or three weeks before I left, he got all over me. Sometimes he'd stick behind like me and Jason and he'd watch us while we was there and Tony was gone. And then at night he'd come to one of us and say, 'Okay, you come sleep with me tonight.'

"So, he got me to go to bed with him. He operated just about the same way as Tony. He didn't really ask, he just started feelin me and then forcin' me into doin' '69' with him all of a sudden. And bein' right there with him and Tony and Freddie and all, I was afraid to say anything to him so I just kinda went along with him, you know.

"Just like Tony, Ed had his ways of, well . . . if he wants you to do 'it' then you do 'it.' He's real forceful about 'it.' But Ed would hold me down, like when I'd tell him 'I don't want to,' he'd just hold me down and act like he was playing with me and then he'd undress me and just go ahead and do 'it.' Tony'd never do that, though. He'd talk you into it . . . kinda like that was what he expected you to do."

After his call home in late July, Mark's mother talked to L. Garrick Hudson at the Roanoke County Sheriff's Office who had been involved with Mark and Patti during the incident with Mark's stepfather almost two years earlier. Said Mark, "She got a hold of Detective Hudson to talk to me on the phone and I told him all that was goin' on, and then they arranged for me to get a bus ticket back to Roanoke."

By the time Mark left Georgia the final time, Tony Leyva had heard about Mark's phone calls and tried to frighten him with thinly veiled threats: "After I got the ticket back to Roanoke, Tony Leyva didn't want to put me on the bus the next day. That night before, I told him, 'Either put me on the bus tomorrow or I call the FBI and have 'em here pickin' me up and arrestin' you . . . one or the other.' So, I thought he was gonna cooperate, but then he goes, 'What if somethin' were to happen to you on the way back to Roanoke? What if God would not allow you to live on the way back?'

"And I said, 'Well, God ain't in the middle of this junk! He never has been the whole time I've been here after it started happenin' to me!'

"And soon as I got back to Roanoke I had a blood test, I mean, I wanted to make sure I didn't have AIDS or anything from them. I didn't know if any of them had it or not. Tony Leyva said he'd had a blood test and that he didn't have AIDS, but I doubt that. Later [FBI agent] John Terry told me that he doubted Tony had had the test, too."

Patti also took her son for a complete physical exam: "I took him to a medical doctor to examine him and the medical report that that doctor made came back saying that he had never seen a more sexually abused child in his life.

"I tell you, when Mark would talk with the authorities, I would leave the room. I really don't know all the details of what happened. Mark was willing to talk; but I guess at that time I wasn't ready to hear."

12

"It would probably blow people's minds to find out just how many places Tony Leyva was run out of!"

Accolades must go to Mark Crump's mother, Patti Casey, for having the courage to step forward in 1987 to expose Tony Leyva's, Ed Morris's, and Freddie Herring's sexual assaults on her son, which prompted an intense reexamination of all of the rumors about sexual assaults on teenage boys that had circulated in the Roanoke area for a number of years.

Seventeen-year-old Mark showed considerable intestinal fortitude by chronicling first to his mother and then to authorities the details of what had been done to him in the name of religion, an effort that became the most difficult task of his young life. Even though he understandably suffered much trauma, Mark never buckled under the strain caused by the physical and emotional abuse by his stepfather at home and then by Brother Tony.

Plaudits must also be given to Roanoke County Sheriff's Detective L. Garrick Hudson and his partner from Roanoke County Children's Protective Services, Ann Martin, who spent thousands of hours on this investigation, one of the most massive in their careers. Without their extreme concern and attentiveness in dealing appropriately and seriously as well as sensitively with this case, the trio of pederast-evangelists might still be visiting their own brand of hell on believers young and old. Indeed, without their efforts, this investigation could well have ended up just another "get out of town before sundown" message passed to Tony Leyva and his fellow pervert preachers.

When I interviewed him in 1993, Detective Hudson said, "It all started when Patti called and I went over there to talk to her. Tony Leyva was in Marietta, Georgia, at the time and Mark was with him. And Patti started telling me all that Mark had told her was happening—the sex and all—and that's when we called Mark and talked to him on the phone.

"I really liked Patti Casey as a person. She was . . . honest . . . and we had a good relationship and I considered her a friend, even. I knew what she was telling me was true. A lot of people would have been put off, but from working other child sex abuse cases . . . nothing surprised me at that point. I lent a lot of credence to what Patti Casey told me about Tony Leyva and his bunch. I took it all very seriously right from when we first talked [in the summer of 1987] and we started making plans on getting Mark back from Georgia.

"I talked to Mark several times long distance while he was still down in Georgia. A couple of calls were where he gave me a number where he could go to another phone and I called him back. He was getting really paranoid about it then. He said, 'They don't allow us to make phone calls and they monitor the phone.' So, we had to play it under the table there for a while just to get him back safely. We weren't getting any help from the FBI, so we made up some kind of excuse for him to tell Tony and sent money to him to get back up here in Roanoke.

"I told him to tell Tony he was sick or whatever and that he just wanted to come back home. I met him at the bus station in Roanoke and took complete statements from him about the sexual assaults right away.

"Mark was really scared by the time we got him back. I mean," Hudson breathed deeply, "he had been down there with a bunch of child molesters and they had threatened him. But when I started talking to him he just let it rip; just no holds barred.

"At the time," Hudson went on to explain, "Mark's uncle Jonathan was encouraging Mark not to say anything about Leyva because, I was under the impression, that Mark's uncles were getting money from Leyva. Leyva would send them money, you know, and Mark would call it 'hush money,' for them to be quiet. But Mark wouldn't hush!"

Ann Martin also heard about payoffs being made to some of the victims by Tony Leyva to try and keep them from testifying. "We had heard that," she confirmed. "Mark was one of the ones who let us know that that was indeed occurring. But after a while so did a couple more of the boys. Benny Simpson [one of Tony's victims] was one who was receiving money to keep his mouth shut. And this was information that we were eventually receiving from a lot of individuals. Some of the boys were given things, gifts, and then some of them were given money. . . .

"After the investigation was known I would say that there were some additional victims we wanted to interview who didn't want to talk to us and—with what we were told—we very definitely felt that there was payoff money being given to them as well."

Hudson talked of the many frustrations he met with in prosecuting the case: "He [Mark] told me that he was also sexually assaulted by Leyva and Morris in Roanoke City and I tried to get Roanoke City to [file] charges on that, but ... they didn't want to do it ... [t]hey were talking about the length of time that had passed [since it had happened] and they wouldn't deal with that.

"You see, Roanoke City has its own jurisdiction. Everyone else—Salem, Vinton, and the rest of Roanoke County—is under [Roanoke] County jurisdiction. I mean, we could prosecute cases inside Roanoke City if they occurred within three hundred yards of the Roanoke City line. But they had their own courts, their own police department, and their own Commonwealth's Attorney's Office. It's a jurisdictional thing."

The City of Roanoke's Commonwealth's Attorney functions as the district attorney for the city and prosecutes crimes occurring solely within the city which, in turn, is surrounded by Roanoke County. Since 1980 that man has been Don Caldwell, a prosecutor some members of the local law enforcement community describe as cut from a "good old boy" bolt of cloth and one who always plays his cards very close to his chest, especially when he smells the involvement of the media or publicity of any kind.

In a long-distance telephone interview in 1993, I attempted to elicit information from Mr. Caldwell about his knowledge of criminal activity within his jurisdiction by Tony Leyva, Ed Morris, and Freddie Herring, but he was not forthcoming.

Echols: "Did you have any involvement in the Tony Leyva case?"

"Who?" Caldwell asked.

I patiently explained: "Tony Leyva. You remember the evangelist who was convicted of child sexual assault in Roanoke County and pled guilty to child prostitution charges in federal court there in 1988?"

Caldwell: "Yeah, I guess. I mean, just what I read in the paper."

Echols: "Okay. Was your office ever contacted about charging him with any crimes in Roanoke City?"

Caldwell: "No, we were not."

Echols: "Or Edward Morris, one of the evangelists who pled guilty in federal [court] along with him?"

Caldwell: "No."

Brother Tony Leyva with (left to right) Macalynn Embert's sons, Jason (11) and Kenny (14), at Disney World, Orlando, Florida, in 1986. (Photo by Macalynn Embert)

Macalynn Embert and Brother Tony together at Disney World, Orlando, Florida, in 1986. (Photo by Jason Embert)

Newly ordained preacher Jimmy Wayne Plunkett and Brother Tony at the Roanoke Civic Center in 1984. Plunkett was the stepfather to two of Leyva's teenage victims and had just been ordained a minister by Leyva in response to his questioning of the evangelist about his sexual habits. (Photo by Susan Plunkett)

Brother Tony speaking informally in the church at his headquarters, the "Tony Leyva Evangelistic Association," in Columbus, Georgia, in early 1988, just prior to his arrest on State of Virginia and federal charges. (Photo by Macalynn Embert)

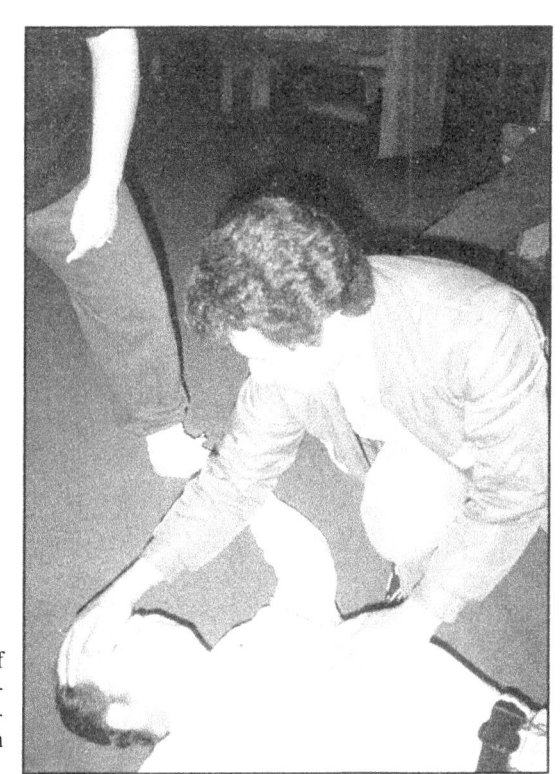

A young Nicaraguan Bible student of Brother Tony's practices "healing" preacher Edward Rias Morris at Leyva's headquarters in Columbus. (Photo by Macalynn Embert)

Macalynn Embert overseeing the setup of a "Happy Birthday, Jesus" revival party under Brother Tony's "big blue top" revival tent somewhere in the southeastern U.S. (Photo by Macalynn Embert)

Thirteen-year-old Jason Embert modeling a nightshirt at Brother Tony's headquarters in Columbus, Georgia, in early 1988. (Photo by Macalynn Embert)

(Left to right) Brother Tony, two unidentified little girls, Macalynn Embert, and a Nicaraguan orphan clown around during dinner one night in early 1988 at Leyva's Columbus headquarters. (Photo by Macalynn Embert)

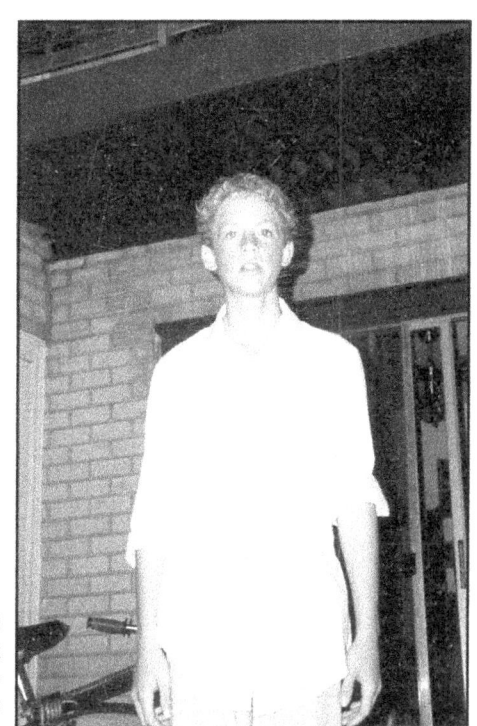

Jason Embert as he looked that night in May 1988 when he, his mother, and his brother had just arrived home in Newark after escaping the horrors of living with Brother Tony at his Columbus headquarters. (Photo by Macalynn Embert)

Jason Embert on his fifteenth birthday July 8, 1989—his first after four years of sexual abuse by Brother Tony—enjoying his birthday glft of a Nintendo game. (Photo by Mike Echols)

(At microphone) Assistant U.S. Attorney Jenny Montgomery is interviewed following the open court confession and plea bargain agreement by Tony Leyva and his fellow defendants, Edward Rias Morris and Freddie M. Herring, on October 11, 1988. (Photo by Mike Echols)

Freddie Herring (left), Mario Ivan "Tony" Leyva (center), and Edward Rias Morris (right) in the foyer outside Senior Federal District Judge John C. Turk's courtroom in the Poff Federal Building in Roanoke, Virginia, the morning of October 11, 1988. (With permission of Time World Corp.)

Tony Leyva leaves the Roanoke County Courthouse during his criminal trial on sex charges, September 1988. (With permission of Time World Corp.)

Tony Leyva is taken away after receiving twenty years in prison for using his ministry to recruit young boys for sex. (With permission of Time World Corp.)

Echols: "What about Freddie Herring, the other evangelist who pled guilty along with Leyva?"

Caldwell: "No. All those cases were tried in the county."

Echols: "Right, Leyva was. And they all pled guilty in federal court there in Roanoke. But I was just curious if there had been any investigation or any information brought to your office about them?"

Caldwell: "Well, I'm not saying that there wasn't, but I'm saying that I don't recollect anything at this time."

Echols: "Could you ask around in your office about that and I'll call you back?"

"Sure," the Commonwealth's Attorney responded.

Ann Martin also confirmed Caldwell's intransigency: "Now, on the Leyva case we also had victims who were sexually assaulted in the City of Roanoke's jurisdiction, but we could not convince them to go with the case. They just didn't want to deal with it.

"I talked to Don Caldwell right in his office about this and he was pretty much of the opinion, well, because of the length of time, because the federal government was involved in it . . . he just basically didn't want to do anything. In fact, he even referred to the victims as 'poor white trash' and suggested that they might have asked for it!

"And I went back and talked to Caldwell more than once, but I never got anywhere with him. So, basically, we were on our own."

When told of Caldwell's difficulty in even recalling who Tony Leyva was, Roanoke County Assistant Commonwealth's Attorney Randy Leach chuckled before responding. "I've never had that experience with Don. He's usually pretty straightforward with me."

Said an incredulous, angry Ann Martin: "He's playing the fool!"

After speaking with Martin, I phoned Don Caldwell two weeks later and told him that Ann Martin was certain that she had spoken to him in person on more than one occasion about prosecuting Tony Leyva in his jurisdiction. Responded Caldwell: "Uh, I don't have any independent recollection of that, but, I mean, that might well be true."

Echols: "Well, Ms. Martin, as she explained it to me, went to you and detailed Mr. Leyva's sexual assaults on boys within the City of Roanoke and you declined to prosecute Mr. Leyva. It had been investigated by her and your office—in fact, you yourself, is what she told me—declined to prosecute him. And when she learned of this, she went and saw you personally and discussed with you what she had found in terms of Mr. Leyva's sexual assaults on boys in your jurisdiction and tried to convince you to prosecute him."

Caldwell: "Well, I mean, like I say, Mike, I'm not . . . you know . . . I don't have an independent recollection of that conversation, but all I can do is rely on my, I guess, prosecutorial experience and prosecute those cases that I think we can prove and we don't prosecute those cases I don't think we can prove."

Echols: "Do you recall making a reference to these youngsters as being 'poor white trash'?"

Caldwell: "No, mam' . . . er, sir."

Echols: "Do you recall any reference to them as 'asking for it' "?

Caldwell then got very agitated and shot back: "I don't recall the conversation, period!"

Echols: "Okay. Okay. What is your position as far as—you yourself—your concern in your official capacity about the sexual abuse of children if they are, say, teenagers . . . sexual assault of teenagers?"

Caldwell: "I don't understand the question."

Echols: "Well, is there a difference in your concern about sexual assault cases involving children after they have reached a certain age? In other words, is there greater concern, for instance, say, for six, seven, eight-year-olds than there would be for thirteen-, fourteen-, and fifteen-year-olds?"

Caldwell: "My concerns are based on what the law is and what the facts are. If we can prove a case, we prosecute. If we can't, we don't."

When I read the foregoing interview transcript to Ann Martin, she laughed sharply and stated adamantly: "I was there in his office and spoke directly to him and on *more* than one occasion!

"The problem with the City of Roanoke has always been their policy that if cases were older than three years they had to have special permission—I would assume from Don Caldwell—to go forward with them.

"When I couldn't get anywhere with Caldwell, I went and talked to his assistant, Betty Jo Anthony. But they were all pretty much like, 'Well, everybody else is already involved. We don't need to get involved, too!'

"I mean, we were prepared to hand them the case and they wouldn't have had to do a lot of work. . . . But the big thing was they just weren't interested and they weren't going to prosecute Leyva and the others. And then when Caldwell felt the way he did about who the victims were and all . . . well, I just couldn't understand him," Ann exclaimed.

"But we had had cases we were working with them, when they should have been doing the actual prosecution of the perpetrator, where they said that the child is over a certain age or the case is older than this many years, and then they'd tell us, 'We're not going to do it.'

"Oh, I didn't like it! Because, see, when Hud [Detective Hudson] and

I worked together we worked child sex abuse cases that were ten, fifteen years old that we took to court and got convictions on. In Virginia there is no statute of limitations on sexual abuse of a child, so Hud and I had cases that we took to court when the victim was six years old [at the time of assault] and now they were an adult, and we got convictions."

A dedicated professional who feels quite strongly about prosecuting child molesters and who is not afraid to voice these feelings, Ann Martin described her and her partner's approach to dealing with crimes against children: "Hud felt the same way as I did in that . . . we knew that what the victim was telling us was true and we felt we really had a case, if nothing else we were going to take that case to court. Whether we won the case or not, for the victim's sake we were going to go to court with it.

"We were somebody believing in the victim. It was a roll of the dice, but in my mind doing that meant that we were at least giving the victim something. And we just might stop the perpetrator from doing it again . . . because that's what they usually do, you know.

"In the eyes of the law children are very poor as individuals when it comes to [their dealing with] physical abuse and sexual abuse and until the courts start treating children as individuals and not as [the] property of their parents, then the problem is not really being taken care of.

"I worked a whole lot of child sex abuse cases where they could lead to death. There is a lot going on out there that is frustrating to deal with, but Hud and I were very, very gung-ho and went after every case and tried many, many sexual perverts . . . and I *always* felt like court action was necessary. If nothing else, to validate for the victims that what had happened to them was wrong . . . at least give them the sense of someone believing them and trying to help them.

"But dealing with the court system was the part that I found the most frustrating because of what was available and what you could do for the victim. The best we could do was to do a good investigation."

But the real credit for finally forcing federal agents to get involved in the case goes to Detective Hudson: "We had a very hard time just trying to get the FBI to investigate Leyva and get involved in it. I had to call and call . . . I got kind of pissed off about it!

"But toward the end of trying—after repeated attempts to get someone at the FBI to help me—because this was interstate stuff and I was a local jurisdiction and I needed interstate help—I finally just called over to the Roanoke office and said, 'Well, okay, while you boys are sitting on your asses, my boys—these kids—are getting it up their asses!'

"The FBI took a long time getting somebody to help me. It took a couple of months . . . but when they finally did get somebody to help me, he did very, very well. They got [FBI agent] John Terry . . . and he did great! I only have good things to say about John!"

Roanoke County Assistant Commonwealth's Attorney Randy Leach also praised FBI Agent John Terry's cooperation once the FBI did get involved: "I worked with Jenny Montgomery [Assistant U.S. Attorney in Roanoke] and John Terry and they were helping me locate victims and interviewing people and that kind of thing. They did help bring in some people who knew some things. They were real cooperative on that.

"We had several victims here in the county—a couple of victims are all we charged Tony Leyva with—and the FBI guys were more than willing to interview people all over the place and provide us with statements so that we could use them and I put on a number of those people in rebuttal when Leyva said he never did anything like that. And that was all the feds getting those people and helping me get those people lined up."

Leach said that even though people in his office had not done much joint work with the FBI prior to the Leyva case, what joint work there had been had been cooperative.

But Detective Hudson stated that because of his difficulty in getting the FBI involved, it took him until early 1988 to get the Roanoke County case against Tony Leyva together. In fact, in an attempt to gather necessary information in other states on his own, he called law enforcement in small towns in Georgia, Louisiana, Mississippi, and several other states. Many told him of similar FBI disinterest when they had contacted the bureau regarding Tony Leyva and his fellow evangelists.

"When I interviewed two or three of the Roanoke boys who were victims," Hudson said, "they told me about the other localities where Leyva had sexually assaulted them. . . . I called the police there and what I kept getting everywhere I called was that a couple of years before Leyva had come through and sexually assaulted a boy and the parent or the boy told the police . . . in many cases the police response to Leyva was, 'Okay, get out of town before sundown. Pack up your tent and get out of here.'

"And that's what . . . Detective Dennis Murphy [Salem, Virginia, Police Department] did right here in Salem! You see, in '86 Leyva had been to the Salem Civic Center and stayed in that motel over on Melrose, and Murphy had been told about [Leyva] sexually assaulting boys . . . but he had just told Leyva to get out of town. I mean, it was right in our own back yard that a detective with our local police department had told Leyva and them to just leave!

"I talked to Murphy trying to get him to investigate and prosecute Leyva in Salem because it had happened in their jurisdiction, but he never did do anything about it. These kids were telling me all about the sex assaults by Leyva . . . that it happened here and it happened there and I was trying to get these other jurisdictions to prosecute Leyva . . . because it was just everywhere that these kids had been molested.

"As to Slidell [Louisiana], I called the [St. Tammany Parish] sheriff's office down there and told them what had happened and tried to get them to get an investigation started and they said that they would look into it. But . . . I wasn't convinced that they would really do anything. They didn't seem too interested. They should have a record that I called them, though, because if they're like our dispatchers, they make a card on everything that comes in.

"But, in some of these rural departments, my gosh, somebody could commit a murder and you'd get maybe a one-page report on it if you were lucky. But here in Roanoke we really document things . . . but it's not that way in other places.

"You know, it would probably blow peoples' minds to find out just how many places Tony Leyva was run out of!"

✝ ✝ ✝

Down in Slidell, St. Tammany Parish, Louisiana, Deputy Sheriff Emily Holden had heard nothing more about Tony Leyva since he skipped town and her state back in 1985, until she got a telephone call one day from Detective Hudson and was subsequently contacted by the FBI. I interviewed her in 1989 and again in 1993.

"Well, you see, we had a warrant on [Leyva] but I did not get a physical arrest on the man and had a 'walk'* on him and that's why the FBI found out about me down here when they got him up in Georgia.

"I talked to the feds [about Leyva], but it was the northern feds [in Roanoke], not down here. They told me that they had almost a hundred and some odd counts of him doing this sort of stuff.

"Well, now, that young [FBI] man . . . that had worked on this case . . . John Terry . . . had taken such an active interest in the whole thing because it had been shuffled around back and forth to the FBI in about three different states before it got there."

---

*A walk is when a suspect named in an arrest warrant flees before he or she can be arrested.

"But," continued Detective Hudson, "what really blew me away was when we discovered that one witness [Anthony Grooms] that it happened to down in North Carolina in '67 . . . over twenty years ago! And he told me how this all started . . . when Leyva sexually assaulted him in the church in Fletcher!"

Said Ann Martin: "When we first turned it in [to the FBI], we had to wait for quite a while for them to get back to us. When Hud made the original phone call to the FBI it took them two and a half months to call us back. We just felt that they didn't really care a whole lot.

"But when they did eventually get back to us we gave them everything we had and talked with them about it. Then they developed a lot from the information that we had given them and it led to all of these other places that [Leyva, Morris, and Herring] were going to for their revivals and then sexually assaulting boys."

And all this time Hudson and Martin continued their own dogged investigation. As they did so Mark Crump led them to more and more young victims in the Roanoke area and elsewhere.

✝ ✝ ✝

Patti Casey recalled: "When Detective Hudson and I got Mark back in August of 1987, Mark admitted it all to me and I told him, 'I want you to tell Harriet Myers—that was Larry's mother; Larry was supposed to go down there to Georgia. I says, 'Tell her don't let Larry go back down there with Tony Leyva.' I said, 'Please do what the Lord would have you to do!'

"And so I called Harriet from work and had her come by here to my home and I told her what the Lord had shown me and what Mark had said and then she said, 'Well, I'm not letting Larry go back. I'll talk to Mark.'

"But instead of getting Mark to himself where he would have been able to talk to her openly about it, she got him on the phone with Ed Morris and Mark got panicky and he denied it.

"Then I felt alone. All of Tony's followers up here [in Roanoke] attacked me. They really did!

"They said, 'You're lying on him! He's God's prophet! You're touching God's anointed!' And so I felt crowded in on. Everything just fell apart. Mark had denied it to them, but I knew what God had said and I knew that what Mark had told me was true and I was going to go alone with it, you know.

"And by then Detective Hudson hadn't had enough time to arrest nobody, so I said, 'God, you showed this to me; now you know what situation I'm in. Help me! Please, God!' "

The attendant ruckus brought Ed Morris to Roanoke on the double, apparently to try and find out what was going on, as much for himself as for Tony and Freddie. And, Patti continued, "Even my husband got after me, although he did go get Ed Morris's license plate number at my insistence 'cause Mark was not going to leave with him and go back down to Georgia . . . no matter what!

"Ed Morris called and got on the phone to Mark and I had to speak to him, too. I said, 'Don't you dare take my son out of state! If you try . . . I'll have the law stop you! My husband's got your license number!'

"And he says, 'With his daddy's permission, I can take him anywhere I want to.'

"I said, 'You ain't got no such permission, so don't even try to! If you do, you're in big trouble!'

"And he said, 'Sister, why are you doing this?' and that did it! That made me mad!

"I said, 'I'm not your sister and you're not my brother!'

"And he said, 'Why? Why are you saying this?'

"And I said, 'Because I've been on my knees and God revealed to me that you're a homosexual [pedophile] and my son has told me what you did to him.'

"Then he got real smart and he said, 'God revealed to me you're a lesbian!'

"And I said, 'Your God and my God are not the same. Your God is a liar and mine is true!'

"We had quite a few words there with my husband listening in on the phone and Jimmy [Casey] got very upset with me. He said, 'You didn't handle that right, Patti. You didn't do it the right way!'

"But after that a friend of mine named Judy Cooley called. Her boy, Ronald Paul, had been travelin' with Tony and them, too. And when she called she asked, 'What's wrong?' and I told her what had happened.

"Well, she said, 'Patti, I can't believe all that! If God shows me, personally, I've got to go with what God shows me. But unless He shows me Himself, I can't believe it.'

"I said, 'Okay, I pray God will show you.'

A little after that conversation Judy called back and she said, 'I've got something to talk to you about. Can you talk?'

"I said, 'Yes.'

"Then she said, 'I mentioned to Ronald Paul about what Mark told you and he said, 'Mama, don't say what you're sayin'! Mark might lie.'

"But then she said, 'Then after a bit Ronald Paul told me that it was all true' . . . that it had happened to him, too. He said, 'Tony and them done the same things to me, too.'

"So, that was a confirmation! God, that was wonderful! So, I'm not in it alone after all!

"Then Mark called me from a friend's here in Roanoke. He was in a private place where he could talk. I asked him why he had denied it to Ed Morris and he said he was scared. And I asked him why he went down to Georgia after it had happened in the first place and he said, 'Because I didn't have no place to stay.'

"I said, 'Mark, you could've come home. You could've come home and stayed here with me!'

"But he said, 'No, I wasn't gonna come home because of Jimmy. I'm not never staying there with Jimmy Casey again!'

"But still . . ." Patti's voice trailed off as she sadly shook her head and began to cry. "I would actually take the Bible in my hands and would explain it to my brothers and Mark. And I said, 'If Tony Leyva is doing any of this' . . . well, I did. I tried. And even Jimmy would talk to them about homosexuals and the sin of it all . . . the wrong things in it."

Regaining her composure, she continued slowly: "I would tell the boys these things and tell them that God's not pleased about this, that if Tony was doing this type of thing, he was not a man of God, that he was being used by Satan and not by the Lord.

"But still, I guess, I really wanted to believe that Tony Leyva was a man of God. Also, I believed in the man because at the first, none of my brothers would tell me about what was happening. Like I said, I didn't have no grounds. The boys wouldn't tell me nothing. They wouldn't admit it . . . that something was happening to them."

After reflecting a few moments on all that had happened Patti softly said, "Maybe I didn't approach it right. I tried to, you know. I really tried. But I feel bad, very bad about it! I should have protected the boys. I really blame myself for what happened to them!"

13

"I told [the FBI] how from the time I was twelve till I was about sixteen, Tony Leyva and the other ministers did sex with me . . . so many times I kinda lost count."

During the fall of 1987, Detective Garrick Hudson of the Roanoke County (Virginia) Sheriff's Department began his investigation of Tony Leyva; and thanks to Hudson's persistence, during this same time, the FBI in Roanoke finally inaugurated its own investigation, an effort which eventually involved agents in field offices in a dozen different states. As the agency tracked down and talked to the young victims one at a time, each boy told the FBI about still more towns, churches, and buildings where Brother Tony held his Miracle Restoration Revivals, and each of these yielded still more victims.

Meanwhile, down in Georgia, Leyva and his cohorts had left the Moonraker Apartments in Marietta for Columbus where the North Highlands Assembly of God Church, which had moved into their new plant on the north edge of town, wanted to sell their old facilities on 38th Street, a couple of miles north of downtown. Earlier that year, in the wake of Tony's failure to inveigle people to give him enough money to purchase Soulé College, the trio of pederasts had been discussing potential locations for their ministry's headquarters and planned Bible college for teenage boys when Freddie Herring remarked that the old North Highlands Assembly Church was on the market. It was an area Freddie knew well, he confided; one where he had often found it exceptionally easy to pick up willing male teenage sex partners, so much so that he kept a small apartment in Columbus.

Quickly Tony arranged a business trip to Columbus, a city of 166,000 located next door to the U.S. Army's Fort Benning. He liked what he saw of the old church and especially enjoyed the pair of sixteen-year-old boys he bedded while in Columbus. Before he left, he completed negotiations with the board of North Highlands for a lease-purchase on the sprawling, old red brick church. Tony happily noted that the place took up the better part of a city block, had a church seating over five hundred, two dozen Sunday school classrooms, a kitchen, dining and meeting hall combination, and a parking area—all in all sufficient space to finally establish his long-dreamed of boarding school to teach the Bible to the teenage boys he constantly recruited, along, of course, with other required subjects. And he promptly began grandly referring to his new facility as the Tony Leyva Evangelistic Association Bible College.

Columbus had already been an occasional stop for the Tony Leyva Evangelistic Association. During one recent revival service there, Brother Tony had landed a huge catch in *nouveau* millionaire Gary Thompson of Phenix City, Alabama, just across the Chattahoochee River from Columbus. In the late 1940s this small city was extremely corrupt and would have made early Las Vegas underworld types jealous. Thompson's money came from the tremendous fortune left him by his father who for years controlled Phenix City's bars, gambling, and prostitution rings which served the soldiers from Fort Benning on the other side of the river. But there was a major crackdown in the early 1950s following the release of Hollywood's documentary-style feature *The Phenix City Story*.

To hear this singular scion tell it, after meeting Brother Tony he thought that he had met God himself, or someone with a direct line of communication with Him. Immediately he fell under Leyva's charismatic religious spell, began attending most, if not all, of the evangelist's services, and was soon unwittingly underwriting corruption far darker than his father ever had.

Though Thompson's moods were unpredictable, Tony realized that this man's relatively unlimited funds gave him the wherewithal to compensate for his rapidly diminishing collections to supply funds to cover the expenses of his ever-growing stable of young adolescent boys. In short order Tony, Ed, Freddie, Tony's young catamite Danny Perez, several other boys—at Leyva's personal invitation—and soon Macalynn Embert and her sons, Jason and Kenny, all took up residence in the facility. Several of the classrooms were turned into bedrooms for the growing number of inhabitants. And with a master suite from which he could use the intercom to page his choice of several resident lads to spend the night with him, Tony thought that he had it made.

Also on her return to Tony Leyva's fold, Macalynn found an interesting change: Mike Page, a menacing-looking man in his late thirties who had been a union enforcer along the Gulf Coast, had joined Tony's revival operation as a business associate. Unofficially, Page also functioned as Tony's bodyguard and truly looked the part.

However, Brother Tony had not counted on the twin persistence of Mark Crump and his mother, Patti Casey, in detailing the evangelist's criminal sexual assaults to local law enforcement back in Roanoke; the increasing anger and moral and professional dedication Garrick Hudson and Ann Martin and the dutiful involvement of FBI Agent John Terry in locating Leyva's victims all across the United States; or the domino effect Mark's disclosures were having on other victims.

Robert Earls said that at the time it was happening, he didn't deeply question what Tony Leyva was doing to him and his brother. But when he was about seventeen "and I started being around people my age and told them . . . I found out that nobody else had that sort of thing happening to them. Never even heard of it! And before, I guess that I had thought it was wrong, but I didn't say anything to anybody about it. And then when I found out, I was afraid to say anything because of what people'd think about me. And so I just held it in till after Mark had come forward.

And so the events of late 1987 led, in early 1988, to an obvious emotional catharsis for Robert Earls. He finally began talking about what Tony Leyva had forced him to do and keep secret for years. He went to lead FBI agent John Terry and told him everything.

"You see, I'd heard about Tony Leyva getting in sex trouble with an orphan and I knew what happened with me. So, I decided to call and tell [the FBI] about me. I went straight to John Terry. I'd heard that he'd been trying to call me and I was trying to avoid him. I didn't want to talk about it at first, but I finally came in to talk to him.

"[John Terry] explained to me what was going on with the other guys that Leyva had done sex with, what was involved, and he told me that I didn't need to be afraid to talk to him about it. That he was on our side instead of against us."

And once Robert Earls began to talk about what had happened, he didn't hold anything back. It was as if he had finally learned that he could talk about the most despicable aspects of his terrible history with Tony Leyva and that he wouldn't be blamed for what the evangelist had done to him in the name of God.

"I told John Terry how from the time I was twelve till I was about sixteen Tony Leyva and the other ministers did sex with me by mouth and by masturbating me with their hands about two hundred times . . . so many times I kinda lost count.

"And I told him how Tony also took pictures of James Cash and me laying on our backs on the bed. First he took a few pictures with our things regular, then he got us excited and took some more pictures with 'em that way.

"And I said how [Tony Leyva] did it in the shower. Lots of times I showered with him. He forced me to. And when he got me in the shower he got down on his knees with a bar of soap in his hand rubbin' on me at the same time he'd do oral sex on me.

"Then there were them pictures. He got . . . James to go in the bathroom and stand there unclothed while he took pictures of him using the bathroom, standin' up. But James wouldn't get involved in talking to the FBI."

✝ ✝ ✝

"In February of '87, I was upset to have to leave because I loved the ministry," Macalynn Embert said most enthusiastically. "I loved what I was doing! I was the one that got the tent set up for Tony's ministry! Even though he had treated me like shit when he couldn't get the insurance to keep preaching under the tent. In fact, he walked off and left me without a penny, owing me over two months of paychecks and me with two boys to feed!

"Then, Christmas 1987, I was living back in Newark, Delaware, at the Wellington Arms and Tony called me and asked me if I would be willing to come down and run his twenty-four-hour day care center. And he told me when I came to bring [Jason]. He didn't even mention Ken. . . . But anyway, I packed up and went."

Much to Jason's and Kenny's chagrin, she pulled both boys out of school in Delaware in mid-January of 1988 and headed south for Columbus, Georgia. "After we were already down there," Macalynn continued, "Tony told me that he didn't want Kenny there. He said that Kenny was lazy and that he wouldn't work, and that he caused trouble with everybody. But I never seen any of that!

"Kenny did, however, refuse to go to Tony's services. And when I asked him why, the only thing Kenny would say is, 'Tony is a hypocrite.'

"I asked Ken, 'What is it that makes Tony a hypocrite? You tell me what it is that makes Tony a hypocrite and then I'll side with you.'

"But Kenny would not tell me. He'd just say, 'Never mind. You wouldn't believe me.' Then he'd walk away. But he knew what was going on. I didn't know it then, but later Tony told me that he was afraid that Kenny would tell about the sexual abuse. But at the time all Tony would say is that he couldn't understand why Kenny didn't like him."

At this point in her story Macalynn sat back and reflectively asked herself, 'Why did I go back?' Then she as much explained her reasons to me as to herself: "I guess because I wanted back in the full-time ministry. I was thrilled to come back! He gave me a chance to be a minister! I loved the ministry and I loved him! I really did! . . . I loved being able to go from place to place, and I loved seeing what God was doing with the people!

"I guess, too, because I'm just as impressionable as any other woman . . . a single parent that was looked up to and wanted to be with Tony and have the honor, and the kids would have the ideal world: They would be growing up with a full-time father. What better way to bring your kids up? They would have private schooling there at the Bible College. They wouldn't have to put up with all the garbage all the other kids were subject to in public schools. And I would have my position back with Tony. To me, Tony was the answer to my prayers!"

As she herself recognizes, at the time Macalynn was blinded and mesmerized by a combination of Tony Leyva's inherent charm and her own insatiable desire to be a part of what she viewed as a godly ministry. Therefore, she was only too happy to accept Brother Tony's offer to return to his "holy work" and to offer him—although Macalynn didn't know it at the time—base carnal knowledge of her younger son.

✝ ✝ ✝

In the winter of 1988 Tony was grandly making plans to expand his revival ministry while at the same time moving into mainstream fundamental Christian acceptance. If the Louisiana evangelist he had tried to befriend wouldn't have anything more to do with him, maybe another well-known evangelist would, so he charted a brief, ill-fated course to try and convince televangelist Oral Roberts that he should join Brother Tony's efforts at the Bible College and make it a joint venture by investing some of his millions in it. But after a couple of letters back and forth—those from Roberts being totally noncommittal—Roberts's operatives briefed him on the true agenda for this social-climbing evangelist in Columbus, Georgia, and the televangelist dropped Leyva even from his ordinary mailing lists.

But Brother Tony was not so easily dissuaded. In short order he established his own television show* every Sunday on the Columbus area's local independent television station, complete with appearances by the Gospel Trio singing old-time gospel songs and what Tony considered to be the appealing appearance of his "family": Macalynn Embert and her sons, Jason and Kenny.

On camera Brother Tony paraded "my son, Jason" in a false fatherly fashion, but the handsome thirteen-year-old was increasingly torn emotionally over the deep, dark secrets Tony forced him to keep. In particular, it grated mightily against what Jason genuinely knew was godly and right when the preacher required him to submit to fellatio immediately prior to Tony's taking to the pulpit to preach. The evangelist slyly, pathetically, and diabolically insisted on this so that—he said—he could taste and swallow the lad's sperm, "so I can be filled with the Holy Spirit to preach." Although still being forced into these despicable acts on a fairly regular basis, Jason wasn't buying any part of it; he himself knew that it was only a matter of time before he would rebel.

During the days after her arrival, Macalynn busied herself getting Tony's new twenty-four-hour Christian day care center ready to open. Most nights she read and studied the Bible while at the same time, not far away, her son Jason was fighting a battle of wits and will against Tony Leyva's lecherous desire. Macalynn deluded herself by thinking that her exile to a solitary bedroom was befitting of the spiritual partner of such a godly man to whom she would one day be married.

But in more ways than one things had changed since the good old days of 1985 to early 1987, when Macalynn had been on top of the world as a minister and preacher in Tony Leyva's ministry and organization, frequently allowed and even encouraged to preach sermons herself as they traveled the revival circuit together. Immediately on her return, Macalynn threw herself into a frenzy of work for Tony at the Bible College: "Within a couple of weeks after I'd got back I had gotten almost everything done to open the day care center. The lady from the fire department said she would have to come back and check everything. I had it all painted and everything and ready to go. I worked real hard to get it all set up for Tony."

However, Macalynn Embert quickly noted that the money the ministry

---

*Interestingly, Tony got his thirty-minute slot on the station on Sunday mornings when televangelist Jimmy Swaggart's syndicated program was pulled due to the latter's well-publicized involvement with prostitutes and his tearful public apology to his flock.

had had before—prior to February 1987 when Tony had let her go—had continued to shrink. She had thought that Tony's move to such a large facility must have meant a considerably improved cash flow. Macalynn recalled: "When he had the tent up he could get about $30,000 a month in his collections. A lousy night under the tent would be around $500; a good night about $3,000. Of course, the tent wouldn't hold as many people as the halls and other buildings."

But the most lucrative revival venues came from the permanent facilities like auditoriums and community civic centers. And when he rented these facilities, he didn't have to split his take with a local church pastor. It was all his. Said Macalynn: "When Tony preached his own revivals at the Longshoreman's Hall and other big places like the Salem Civic Center, he would really wipe up! He would get $8,000, $9,000, even $10,000 a night on Friday, Saturday, and Sunday nights. I know, 'cause I counted it! I remember lots of nights like that . . . particularly in Ft. Lauderdale. And one night he got so much that it took a whole bunch of us half the night to count it all! And I never did know how much it was. He kept them figures to himself.

"Back then, if it was just him and me, if we would go to a small church somewhere in Florida, it would just be seven or eight hundred dollars. But if it was a big meeting, I wouldn't know for sure how much he brought in 'cause he'd take it out of the buckets real quick, dump it in his bank bags or briefcase or suit cases, and then close 'em and lock 'em and count it later by himself."

"All I know is that he did a lot of stuff . . . said a lot of stuff to get the people to give him money and . . . when I asked him about that, he just smiled and made a comment to me that 'You have to do what you have to do to bring the money in.'

"See, he had people like that woman in Okeechobee [Florida] who came to his Wednesday afternoon service regularly when he had it down there and she always gave him five hundred dollars. There wouldn't be but four or five people there at the service, but then Tony'd make her feel special and she'd give him that money every Wednesday afternoon . . . just like she was playing the lottery!"

But looking back to the way things had begun to change so dramatically for Brother Tony's ministry beginning in the fall of 1986, Macalynn said: "I was Tony's tent manager up until February 1987 and I left then since he couldn't go back on the road with the tent due to the insurance costs. He couldn't pay for the insurance 'cause he didn't have as much money as he had before."

"Why?" Macalynn shook her head and said that she just didn't know. She did note that once she returned fewer people attended his revivals in towns where there had previously been huge crowds; that he avoided holding revivals in other locations where in prior years he had done well; and that much of the money he did take in these days seemed to disappear.

Had rumors about Tony's pederasty reached so many of the faithful as to drastically affect the size of his audiences, the areas in which he appeared, as well as the amounts given to him? And had he gotten so desperate to try and circumvent rumored law enforcement investigations as to brazenly pimp some of "Tony's boys" to "government men" with a predilection similar to his . . . as well as to make more payoffs to other boys?

It did seem plausible, given the many people involved and Tony Leyva's longevity on the revival circuit in spite of his criminal activity.

† † †

But it didn't take long before Macalynn saw shades of the old, tricky Brother Tony coming back as he connived to milk his congregations for money: "One Wednesday night in Columbus the people had just gotten paid—Tony would check up on that sort of thing—and he preached and begged so good that he got over $12,000! That was the night that Freddie Herring stole [skimmed] $1,200 and that wasn't nothin' out of what Tony had took in that night, so Tony wasn't even worried!"

By early March of 1988, Tony Leyva had heard about the investigations back in Virginia, as well as, (thanks to the FBI's involvement), the growing investigations in nearly twenty other states, but he kept it to himself, telling Macalynn duplicitously that his worry came from his "preaching so much."

Macalynn didn't really understand what was wrong but she did know that "he was hollering that he was gonna have a nervous breakdown and that he might have to kill himself because he couldn't handle all the problems with the ministry. So," she sighed, "I went and rented him a little cottage for a retreat about fifteen minutes away from the college there in Columbus. And nobody knew about it. Mike [Page] didn't even know about it. I got a woman supporter of his to pay for it, right down to a disposable toothbrush and his Benzedrine for his hives . . . the whole kit and caboodle!

"And we'd go out there after his services and we'd sit there and we'd talk. He'd tell me how he felt, who he was leery of, about how he was gonna get more money out of Gary [Thompson], and how Mike was givin' him a lot of problems by budgetin' his money without his approval and how he was worried about that. Then he'd talk about how he had a special love for me and how it was like God sent me there to keep him safe from the other women. He knew that as long as I was there he would be able to be aware of which women was serious and which women had designs on him, as far as getting too close to them.

"I'd just sit there between his legs and we would just talk and hug and kiss, hold hands, stuff like that. I almost had him in the bed there one night. God, one time I had an erection on him. But he never did actually go to bed with me. But, if he would have, boy, it would've screwed me up even worse.

"But Tony would have me lay on the floor with my shirt unbuttoned. Or he'd have me sit in a certain position in the chair so he could look up my skirt. Like the last service I preached, he almost fell over out of the pew trying to look up my skirt. I thought, you know, well God, he is mad! But I never did get nowhere with Tony, and I wondered; if I had been better looking or had had a better body, maybe I could have succeeded with him."

By the time of her return, Macalynn said that Tony was depending on $100 pledge envelopes. At his services he would pass out envelopes for people to put $100 cash in and then sign a pledge to keep giving him $100 on a regular basis. Then he warned them, "If you fail to keep your pledge to God, he'll know!"

Macalynn said, "Everybody was giving him $100 pledges so he could put the down payment on that place and then he had to pay $5,500, and that's when he got Gary Thompson to foot the bills and make the payments to the North Highlands Assembly of God Church.

"When I got down there in January of '88, Tony had just gotten $20,000 from Gary Thompson. Tony had convinced Gary to bankroll him and then Tony came to me and said, 'Now Macalynn, do whatever you gotta do for Gary. Fix up a room for him, give him the best that you can, wait on him. We have to keep him thinking he's important, because without his money, we're down and out. Cater to him, give him the best of the food, you know . . . do whatever you gotta do, Macalynn!' So, that's what I did.

"But Gary was on so much medication that for his own personal expenses he was gettin' just $7,000 a month from his accountant—from a trust fund—and even on that he was tithing $700 to Tony.

"But Tony got so cheap sometimes toward the end that when he wasn't payin' us regular he'd keep the bills and I'd keep all the change [from the collections] and do my grocery shopping with it. That always profited up to a pretty sum, at least fifty to sixty dollars a night three, four nights a week just in coins."

And Macalynn told about a light-fingered Mike Page allegedly taking advantage of Tony: "He was skimming money off of Tony and Tony confided in me about it one night when I was with him in his room there at the college. But Tony said that he didn't do nothin' about it 'cause Mike had some sort of information on him. But Tony never did tell me what. But now I think I know what it was!"

During Tony's own version of "the last days," he got a new Cadillac to drive. One of his supporters bought it and gave it to him. But he hadn't had it very long when it was wrecked. Laughed Macalynn, "A guy hit it. Tony was sitting in it and a drunk guy hit it and totaled it. Just shook up Tony, though. But Tony made a big point in his revival testimony about it being given to him and that it was a drunk that totaled it. But, of course, Tony was a drunk, too. He was drinking NyQuil constantly and he tried to tell me that he wasn't an alcoholic. But I knew better!"

Macalynn also soon knew better about one of the other three evangelists with whom she had cast her lot and that of her sons: "One time when we were out on the road from Columbus we didn't have food in the camper that night, and Freddie was havin' a fit about it and 'cause it was cold. See, Tony didn't care how you lived or whether you had food or anything else you needed. As long as you was doing for him what he wanted done, that's all he cared about. But, with Freddie it was different and I appreciated that. He cared about me and the boys.

"But all that changed the day Freddie left his briefcase with me and asked me to count his collection money while he went in and changed clothes. And when I opened the top of his briefcase where it was divided off, I took out this big brown envelope that I thought had his money in it but there was this . . . magazine just full of naked kids and men. It had been sent to him with his name and address on it from a P.O. Box somewhere. So, that changed the way I felt about Freddie!"

✝ ✝ ✝

For Mario Ivan "Tony" Leyva the beginning of the end came on April 20, 1988. He had told Macalynn and others at the Bible College that he had gone to Roanoke to preach a revival, but in reality he went to appear before a federal grand jury in response to a subpoena. The panel had begun an extensive hearing of evidence presented to them by Assistant U.S. Attorneys Jenny Montgomery and Morgan Scott—and assisted by FBI Agent John Terry—who were seeking multiple charges against the evangelist and his cohorts for violations of federal laws, alleging "interstate transportation of teenage boys with intent to engage such minors in criminal sexual activity and prostitution." Brother Tony also had to appear before the Roanoke County grand jury investigating his sexual assaults on several local boys.

Accompanying Tony to Roanoke were Ed Morris and Freddie Herring. When Tony got there, he hired Salem criminal attorney Harry F. Bosen, Jr., to represent him and Ed retained Roanoke Baptist layman and criminal attorney Daniel L. Crandall. Freddie had brought along from Columbus criminal lawyer John C. Swearingen, a counselor well versed in the ways of political maneuvering in the courts of Georgia, but like the proverbial fish out of water this far north.

Accompanied by Bosen, Tony testified before both the state and federal grand juries that the boys alleging sexual abuse were in fact drug addicts and delinquents who were attempting to blackmail him. While in Roanoke, Tony agreed to take a polygraph test for federal authorities, the results of which he then felt would exonerate him. However—as Tony did not learn for several months—the polygraph test proved quite the opposite. Indeed, agreeing to take it was a decision which he would live to regret.

Feeling vastly overconfident, Brother Tony returned to Columbus to resume his revival schedule; but less than a month later, Roanoke County (Virginia) authorities issued a warrant for his arrest and Columbus (Georgia) police showed up at Tony's headquarters on 38th Street to serve it. Tony went with them quietly, and was returned to Roanoke where he was jailed while Harry Bosen arranged with a bondsman for him to be released.

Although she didn't know this until later, Macalynn admitted: "In fact, Gary Thompson's the one [who] paid for Tony's bond, Tony's attorney, and Freddie's and Ed's attorneys and bonds, too! Not only did Tony tell me that, [but] the federal officers in Roanoke told me. . . . Tony had Gary so snowed it was ridiculous!"

However, before Tony returned to Columbus, Macalynn spoke briefly with him by phone during his stopover at his mother's home in North Carolina. "I talked to him and I asked him point blank, 'Were these charges to do with boys?'

"And he said, 'Yes.'"

"I asked, 'Are they sexual charges?'"

"And his voice got real low and he said, 'Yes.' Then he said, 'I'll talk to you about it when I get back.'"

"I started pushing him then because I wanted to know what was going on, were my boys involved, but then Mike [Page] got me off the phone and he talked to Tony privately.

"Well, I know how to get my information. I know what I gotta say and who I gotta talk to to get what I want to know. So I called the police up there. I knew how to ask the cops what the charges were, but I knew the cops wouldn't just pick up the phone to talk to anybody and tell them what was going on. But after I explained who I was I did get them to tell me what was going on, what the charges were, and so then I knew. And even though I didn't know then about Jay [Jason] and Kenny, I was afraid for them.

"But when I talked to Tony on the phone, I think he knew then that I knew in my heart about what he had done to my boys."

As she struggled to come to grips with the knowledge that her sons had been sexually molested, Macalynn said that it struck her especially hard because she had been sexually assaulted herself as a small child, something she said she never dreamed would happen to her own children "since they were boys."

"When I was three years old, the farm hand that worked for my grandfather sexually molested me. But the only time I remember it myself is sometimes when I read about it [other cases] or something like that. But it fades and you deal with it. But I never did think it would happen to my own children!"

Tony immediately was bonded out of the Roanoke County Jail and quickly and quietly returned to Columbus. However, he did not know that he had gotten out of Roanoke just ahead of FBI Agent John Terry who had an arrest warrant charging Tony and his associates, Edward Rias Morris and Freddie M. Herring, with multiple counts of interstate transportation of juveniles for purposes of prostitution.

Following his return to Columbus, Tony posted a note on the front door of the college. The note, given to me by Macalynn, reads:

PLEASE! PLEASE! PLEASE!
   I will make myself available as soon as I am ready
   —But I sure do need some *extra rest*. I hope you'll understand. It's been a very trying couple of days—just got in at 5:00 A.M.

I will be in the *Prayer Room* 6-7 P.M. tonite and every nite before service. Please join me if you can.

I love and appreciate you—

[Signed] Bro. Tony

P.S. Please help make sure *all doors* in this building are closed, and locked—all doors—it's more important than you can imagine—

But before Tony went to bed he went out behind the Bible College and in the gray dawn light used the trash drums there to burn his entire collection of child pornography: his personal collection of thousands of Polaroid pictures; his relatively small collection of commercial "kiddie porn" magazines; and *Mikey Likes It*, the video featuring a pair of naked fifteen-year-old boys riding motorcycles and engaging repeatedly in oral and anal sex, which he always screened for new members of "Tony's boys."

Tony was still sequestered in his master suite at the Bible College when the FBI arrived late that Saturday morning. Said Macalynn, "I went up to his door and told him that the FBI was there to see him and he told me he was tired. But when I repeated that it was the FBI he opened the door and was taking off his Rolex watch and sterling silver praying hands necklace and emptying out his pockets. Then the FBI men came and handcuffed him and took him away . . . arrested him and took him back to Roanoke."

✝ ✝ ✝

After Macalynn first learned of Tony's sexual abuse of the boys up in Roanoke—she still did not know about Jason and Kenny—she confronted him, but he enigmatically responded with: "The only thing I can do is to throw myself at your mercy."

As Tony had expected, this drew a sympathetic response from Macalynn: "That's unfair. After everything you've done to me and the boys, we still love you."

Macalynn tried to explain why she wasn't harsh with him: "At that time there was an awful lot of pushing from Mike Page and his wife, [from] Rose in the trio, and [from] all of them that you didn't do anything to harm your prophet, and Tony was our prophet, they said. They were all real good at quoting scripture when it served their purpose, like, 'Listen to your prophet and you shall prosper.'

"I was told that if I did not immediately forgive him everything he had done, that God wouldn't ever forgive me for anything. And I was afraid. I was in such a turmoil that night when he apologized to me and asked for my mercy there in the hallway at the college. He had locked his door and started crying. He said, 'Macalynn, I'm so sorry that I brought you down here and got you into this garbage.' And at that point I did not know that he had done anything to Jason and Kenny . . . just what he had done to the other boys up in Roanoke.

"And at that time Jason was on a trip to Oklahoma. One of the ladies in Tony's gospel trio, Jackie Barstow, had family in Oklahoma and she took her daughter . . . and Jason with her on a trip to see them. That was in May and it was while they were gone that all hell started to break loose about Tony."

After Tony's arrest and just before he was bonded out of the Roanoke County Jail—and before she had the chance to know the scope of her sons' sexual abuse—Macalynn suffered a harsh preemptive strike by Mike Page: "Before I knew how deep Jason and Kenny had been involved with him, Tony's lawyer [Bosen] told Mike Page to get Jason and Kenny out of the Bible College so that Tony would look good. Bosen said, 'We need to get Kenny and Jason out of here because they are the only two minors there'—which was garbage; there were other boys there. But he said that it wouldn't look good for Tony for them to stay there.

"So then Mike Page told me, 'Get out of here!' Then I started bucking it and I said, 'Why should we leave? You've got this trio lady's little boy here. You've got other boys here! Where am I supposed to go? Put the kids out and go live in my car?'

"He told me that if I testified against Tony, he'd find me if it took him the rest of his life to do it. Mike knew that with Tony he could get plenty of money and he told me that he would do *anything* he had to to keep Tony out of any kind of trouble. Mike said he would do anything he had to to stop me from testifying against Tony . . . take my kids away from me, whatever he had to do to shut me up. And I asked him, 'What do you mean by that?'

"And he said, 'You're not dumb! You know what I mean! Get out of here!' Then he went and got a U-Haul, and I got as much of my stuff as I could and got out. Mike Page literally kicked me and my boys and Bubba Gordon out that night!

"That night when I got thrown out, Tony was out on the road preaching a one-night stand. He got out on bond for committing oral sodomy on those two boys up in Roanoke and when he came back to Columbus he went right out on the road preaching!

"But, throwing me out . . . I didn't believe that Tony would let Mike and them do that! I really didn't! I kept wishing Tony would have been there because I knew no matter what had happened he would not let them take my kids away from me and put me in jail . . . no matter what had happened."

Macalynn was asked how on earth she would even consider staying at the Bible College after she had found out that Tony had molested boys, even if she did not yet know about her sons' abuse. Said she, "Well, number one, Bubba and Kenny had me under the assumption that Tony hadn't touched either one of 'em, even though Kenny had told me that Tony had tried and that he had put a halt to it and that was it. Plus, I didn't have a penny to my name and didn't know what to do. Where was I going to go? Put the kids in the car and go sleep in the park?

"But right after Jason got back, I found out that Tony had done it to both boys. I just didn't know how bad then. You see, Bubba come to me when we were all sitting in a restaurant right after we all got kicked out that night and he told me that Tony had had sex with both of them . . . Jay and Ken. And I said to Ken, 'My God! My God! What has he done to both of you boys?'

"Kenny and Bubba both told me that Tony didn't touch Jason. And then Bubba was quick to say, 'Oh, no! Oh, no! It was just me.' 'Cause he saw what it had done to me.

"Two days after I got kicked out and into this lady's house [i.e., a woman in the church who had offered her house to stay in] Jackie got back with Jay [who had been on a trip to Oklahoma]. I . . . picked Jay up, went and got a pizza, and then brought him straight back to this lady's house, and then that's when everything came out that night. That's [when] I called Tony at his mother's—he'd gone up to Hendersonville—and I confronted him about what he'd done."

A few nights later—knowing that the college was deserted because Tony was out on the road with the remaining revival members—Macalynn gathered up her sons and young Bubba Gordon and drove them all back over to the Bible College to try to recover the things Mike Page had forced them to leave behind. "I wasn't a total fool," said Macalynn. "I knew that I shouldn't go in there. The boys were all minors and I knew if they went into the college that they would get away with it.

"And then, too, the kids went in through my own bedroom window. Well, what *used* to be my bedroom window."

Angry about what Tony had done to her and her boys—although she had yet to hear the worst from Jason —Macalynn returned to the college with the boys late one night, broke in, and took what was rightfully theirs—as well as some things that were not. "They pinned a lot of garbage on me when we ransacked [Tony's] room," Macalynn said, "you know, immediately everything that was missing was [my fault], like the cross and chain that Tony had bought for me and an anklet that I bought myself. I took it and I pawned that stuff to get groceries to feed my boys because I didn't have any money.

"While I was getting my stuff, Bubba took a television and a VCR and some other stuff. He had it wrapped up in a bedspread and I said, 'What have you got there?'

"And all he said was, 'I just threw everything in here that Tony gave me.'

"And," Macalynn said with considerable pride, "I went into Tony's office and took two boxes of his files and stuff."*

After Tony's arrest Macalynn said that things didn't change that much for the ministry because "after he got bonded out on the federal charges, Tony went back out on the road preaching revivals regularly. He had apparently decided that as long as he was gonna plead innocent—that he hadn't done this—naturally he was gonna stand up in the pulpit and say that this is a satanic attack. . . . He began hitting people up for more and more money to fight Satan!

"Tony started prophesying that God was gonna strike dead everybody who testified against him. It was mostly the mothers of these boys—like myself—who spoke out against him and his ministry and what he'd done to our boys. . . . I never learned what Tony had done to Jason until after he got back from Oklahoma. The night he got back . . . I lied to Jason and told him that I already knew what had happened between him and Tony in order to get him to tell me the truth. I told him, 'I just want to hear it direct from your mouth.' And when I did that, Jason went ahead and told me all about it."

---

*As noted in the Preface, the FBI took one box of this evidence and declined the other one; and later that year Macalynn gave this remaining box to me.

14

"I've been in full-time ministry since the night of my twelfth birthday!"

The summer of 1988 was a period of readjustment for Jason and Kenny Embert and their mother. They moved back to their home town of Newark, Delaware, and tried to readjust to friends and family there as well as to rid their minds of the three pederasts masquerading as men of God. But on numerous occasions they had to travel to Roanoke as Virginia and federal authorities progressed with their plans to try Tony, Ed, and Freddie.

Delaware did not have an overabundance of Pentecostals: Here there were many more Roman Catholics as well as mainstream Protestant denominations including the Methodists, Presbyterians, Congregationalists, and Episcopalians. At one Episcopal church in Newark Macalynn found a staff regularly and honestly willing to help her and her sons, then fourteen and seventeen, get on their feet even though they were not members and had no intention of regularly attending or joining.

But when the boys' mother tried to arrange free or affordable counseling for them, since she had no steady job, she was unsuccessful. And by late August the boys, still suffering from the trauma of their sexual assaults, faced returning to school after having missed so much of it during their four years living and traveling with Brother Tony.

When school finally began, Kenny refused to go. He felt too embarrassed and daunted by the prospect of trying to catch up, and started instead to look for a job.

However, Jason—an exceptionally bright young man—took entrance tests at Newark High School and scored so high that he was allowed to skip the ninth grade completely and go straight into the tenth. Indeed, life was just beginning to settle down for Macalynn and her sons when in August they were all subpoenaed to be witnesses at Tony's Commonwealth of Virginia trial in Salem and the federal government's trial of all three evangelists in federal court in Roanoke.

✝ ✝ ✝

As the scheduled late September 1988 date for his trial in Salem approached, Tony Leyva made one last revival circuit around the Southeast. He had sent out a postcard announcing the locations, dates, and times. The front of the card read, "Special One Night Only Miracle Rallies Under Gods [sic] End-Time Prophet, Tony Leyva" and gave the cities and dates. On the reverse of the card Brother Tony stated: "I will be in the following cities [listed] on the following dates [also listed] with what the Holy Spirit has prompted me to call 'END-TIME TRUTHS SEMINARS.' Four three-hour sessions. The opening night 7:00 P.M. only with a fifty-five minute video 'AMERICA YOU'RE TOO YOUNG TO DIE.' Three three-hour sessions the second day . . ." followed by the session times. Brother Tony noted the content of the sessions: "Using tabernacle schematics tracing the sleeping Adam to the waking Adam—the Elijah anointing of the 1990s. Bring a pen, and lots of paper. All sessions professionally recorded."

Several appearances were listed for cities and towns in Mississippi, Tennessee, Ohio, Virginia, North Carolina, Florida, and Alabama, including two "Tent Revival Specials," apparently for old-time's sake. Brother Tony made certain that were he convicted and sent to prison he would have spent his last free days out preaching God's Word as he interpreted it "with what the Holy Spirit has prompted me."

✝ ✝ ✝

On September 20, 1988—and with considerable trepidation— Macalynn, Kenny, and Jason Embert set out in Macalynn's old red Toyota for the daylong drive to Salem. The next day Tony Leyva would stand trial for incidents alleging his sexual assaults of young teenage boys, dating as far back as 1984; charges that he orally sodomized Mark Crump, Ronald Paul Cooley, and Darrell Wayne Sharp after he had preached revivals at the Salem Civic Center.

The day before the trial, Leyva did his best to garner favorable news coverage: He disingenuously told a gathering of reporters that the complaining witnesses—former tent crew members—had made up stories about his "homosexual activity" because he had fired them for using drugs, adding that one of the boys had even tried to blackmail him by demanding a large cash payoff.

But on the morning of Wednesday, September 21, 1988, Leyva's first criminal trial began in the circuit court of Judge Kenneth E. Trabue before a jury of eight men and four women, several of them Pentecostals. When the charges were read, the self-proclaimed "Super Christian" placed his faith in his God and his high-strung, voluble criminal attorney, Harry F. Bosen, Jr., who he trusted would prove that he had not used his revival ministry to recruit, seduce, and sexually assault these boys.

The courtroom was packed with Leyva's victimized former tent crew members and their parents, anxious to see the evangelist convicted; there was also an assortment of Tony's remaining supporters, ranging from Danny Perez and other former "Tony's boys" to volatile septuagenarian and Leyva fanatic, Margaret Weiss.

And even though several of the young supporters present such as Benny Simpson, Matthew Grisham, and Jimmy Myers had themselves been sexually victimized by Tony Leyva, the Pentecostal scriptural mantra of "touch not mine anointed," and "do my prophets no harm" had convinced them not to tempt fate by testifying against this man of God. Indeed, late in the trial some of them briefly took the stand for the defense to disingenuously proclaim that they had never known Brother Tony to do anything wicked.

Several of Leyva's victims (including Mark Crump and Jason Embert) had given statements to federal authorities that they had repeatedly witnessed Tony Leyva in bed with Danny Perez. Further, they attested that Danny had repeatedly disclosed details of these acts; but when the boy was questioned by the FBI he swore that this never had happened. Remarked Mark Crump, "I couldn't believe it when Danny came in to court over in Salem to support [Leyva]."

Assistant Commonwealth's Attorney Randy Leach called victim Ronald Paul Cooley who testified that when he was just twelve, Brother Tony lured him to the Econo Lodge in northwest Roanoke and, once in the room, had the boy undress down to his underpants and then coerced him into sleeping in the same bed with the preacher. Ronald testified how Leyva "asked me if he could put his arm around me . . . he started fondling my chest . . . he just kept on fondling me . . . and he moved down to my underwear."

Carefully Randy Leach led the teenager through his testimony: "He just kept fondling me and he rolled me over and asked me to take off my shorts. I was scared and I did. He began kissing on me . . . on my neck and he worked his way down . . . and he started sucking on my penis." Afterward, Ronald said, "I told him that this was wrong, this was very wrong. He went on to say he knew it was wrong. So we got down beside the bed and he prayed with me." Asked for an explanation of why Tony did it, "He said he loved me."

The testimony was electrifying to the people in this Bible Belt courtroom, only a little of the tension being inadvertently broken a few minutes later during Bosen's cross examination of Ronald when he kept referring to Detective Garrick Hudson as "she" and "her" and he pounded the lad with yet another question: "Do you remember telling her when she asked you, Ronald, . . . ?"

Ronald shot back, "Detective Hudson is a guy!"

Bosen: "Excuse me?"

Ronald: "Detective Hudson is a guy! And, yes I do!"

However, for some reason this wasn't getting through to Bosen and a minute later he asked Ronald, "It was only later after the detective's questioning that she put the words in your mouth . . . is that correct?"

Ronald: "*He!* [then] No, that's not."

Next a long-forgotten skeleton fell out of Tony Leyva's closet. Randy's carefully laid plans for the State's rebuttal testimony were sprung on the defense when Tony's first known, documented victim, Anthony Grooms from North Carolina, whom Tony had seduced as a twelve-year-old in his church office in Fletcher in 1967, was called to the stand.

Judge Trabue excused the jury so that he could consider the admissibility of Anthony's testimony; but after hearing it, he later allowed the jury to hear Anthony. Now a grown man, Anthony recounted exactly and convincingly how Tony seduced him, removed his pants and underwear, and performed oral sex on him. All the while Tony squirmed uncomfortably in his chair beside Harry Bosen.

Following this, Leach elicited direct testimony for the State from victims Mark Crump and Darrell Wayne Sharp, about whom Detective Hudson remarked, "Darrell Wayne was real good helping me on my investigation. He's a little go-getter. He is really somebody that you can count on."

At times staring directly at Tony Leyva, Darrell Wayne very clearly stated his name, date of birth, occupation, and then told how he first met the evangelist when he was "approximately around seven, eight years old."

Randy Leach then led Darrell Wayne through the particulars of his growing acquaintance with the preacher who seduced and sexually assaulted him at the Embassy Motor Lodge on Melrose Avenue in Salem. "Next as I can remember in my mind is he started putting his hands on me," Darrell Wayne recounted firmly. "He started softly touching me on the shoulders. Wanted to start kissing on me . . . my mouth . . . he was putting his tongue in my ear, my neck area. The next thing I know, he starts putting his hands on my underwear, down in my privates."

Asked Randy Leach: "Did you say anything to him at that time?"
Darrell Wayne: "No, sir."
Leach: "Why not?"
Darrell Wayne: "I was . . . uh . . . frightened, sir."
Leach: "Did you become sexually aroused?"
Darrell Wayne: "Yes, sir."
Leach: "Did he touch your private parts?"
Darrell Wayne: "Yes, sir, he sure did. After that, he proceeded on. He took my underwear off and next thing comes to mind, he places his mouth on my penis."

Darrell Wayne spent a very uncomfortable night in the motel room with the pederast preacher: "I rolled over to the edge of the bed far as I could and I was shaking so much, I just went ahead and went to sleep."

Leach asked Darrell Wayne, "Did [Leyva] speak with you about the incident for the rest of the time?"

"Yes, sir, he sure did," Darrell Wayne responded.
Leach: "What did he have to say to you about it?"
Darrell Wayne: "He told me [not to] tell anyone about this incident, keep it between ourselves . . . and don't let it hurt my faith."

✝ ✝ ✝

That afternoon the local paper, the *Roanoke Times & World News,* carried an interesting story about Tony Leyva:

> In an effort to counter reports about flunking the FBI test [Mike Page, one of Leyva's employees,] said Leyva took his own lie detector test last week and claims to have passed. [Page] delivered the test results to var-

ious news reporters Tuesday, saying he wanted to make sure the jurors who try Leyva know that the minister also passed a lie detector test.

"I think it's only fair that Leyva gets to have his side out," Page said.

[Judge] Trabue said today before the trial began that he was concerned that Leyva was seeking a change of venue at the same time he was seeking publicity.

"I thought this fairness was a two-way street," Trabue told Bosen. Bosen said Page had contacted reporters "contrary to my advice."

Page said Leyva was given the lie detector test September 13 by John Papis, a polygraph operator with Accredited Polygraph Services of Mobile, Alabama. According to Papis's report, Leyva was questioned about the sex allegations against him.

Leyva denied any homosexual activity with any boys, according to a letter from Papis, and Leyva maintained that one of the boys who has accused him tried to blackmail him on several occasions.

Papis wrote that based on the tests he gave Leyva, "it is the opinion of this examiner that the subject was completely truthful on all relevant questions."

In a telephone interview from Mobile Wednesday, Papis said he could not account for the different results between his test and the FBI exam.

"I stand by my opinion and my results," said Papis, a former Mobile police officer who says he has thirteen years of experience giving polygraph exams.

When I interviewed Harry Bosen, he had some most interesting details to add to this story:

"Now let me give you an example of Mike Page. Page controlled Tony Leyva. Page is the one who set up that false polygraph or whatever polygraph was taken. I said, 'Do it here locally.' He said he knew an examiner who would do it for free.

"I don't know who took the polygraph examination. It was reportedly Tony, but I don't know who took it or what's going on on that. I don't know whether it was false or not. The prosecutors called it false. I saw the report but I didn't know anything about [the examiner] except that he had a good reputation in the state of Alabama.

"But, based on what I heard Tony confess to later, I wonder who took the test. Was it somebody saying he was Tony Leyva who took the test? Because I believe the polygraph examiner tested somebody. But did he know who he was testing?

"A pathological person who has convinced himself that he's not guilty could pass the test. But I don't know. . . . I had absolutely nothing to do with that . . . except the fact that I sent copies of the papers about the charges down to the polygrapher so that he could question [Leyva] about the charges because they have to have the date of the offense, the offense charged, and that sort of thing.

"Other than that, I didn't know anything about it. It was done in Mobile, Alabama, and I wasn't there, so I don't know who did what. But it was suspicious in my mind when Page, contrary to my advice, turned around and released it to the press. I told them not to release it, it wasn't admissible evidence [in court] anyway."

✝ ✝ ✝

Randy Leach called to the stand bright, blond, handsome fourteen-year-old Jason Embert—about whom Leach remarked, "Every man and woman on that jury would have loved to have him as a son"—to recount his tale of sexual assaults by Leyva, one in many ways identical to those of the others. Only Leyva's last assault on Jason had occurred just six months earlier, in April of 1988, only a week before the evangelist was arrested.

Macalynn Embert commented: "We were victims; we were not criminals. God saw it! And just before Jason went on the stand in the state trial to give the rebuttal testimony, we prayed for ten minutes that God would make Tony admit it out of his own mouth. But he wasn't ready to do it . . . not yet anyway."

Jason told how on only his second night with Brother Tony, the pederast began efforts to sexually excite the then ten-year-old.

Leach: "Whose idea was it that you both sleep in the same bed?"
Jason: "I guess it was his."
Leach: ". . . What happened?"
Jason: "He gave me a massage."
Leach: "Where was he massaging you?"
Jason: "Around my privates and everywhere."
Leach: "Now what happened after he began to touch your private parts?"
Jason: "I guess I just got emotionally or . . ."
Leach: "Did you get sexually excited?"
Jason: "Yes."
Then Randy Leach led Jason through a description of how Tony Leyva

put on a vibrator and began massaging the young boy on his naked penis. And then the questions and answers went through an entire series of other nights and locations where the pederast bedded and assaulted Jason.

The direct examination ended with Leach instructing Jason, "Okay, now I want you to look to the jury . . . and tell them what happened to you that was different."

Jason: "He put me on his stomach and rubbed my back until I got physically excited and then he sucked until I ejaculated . . . He gave me a blow job."

Leach: "Did you stay there with [Leyva] and these same incidents kept happening?"

Jason: "Yes."

A bit later, during redirect examination, Leach asked: "Jason, why did you wait until all of it broke out [Tony's arrest] to tell?"

Jason: "At that point, I liked Tony a lot because he was a father to me."

Harry Bosen then called his client, and with a broad smile on his face, "Mario Ivan Leyva . . . I'm also known as Tony" took the stand. With little prompting from his attorney, Tony grandiosely lied about his ministry: "I am a full-time evangelist and also I'm the college professor at the college in Columbus, the Tony Leyva International School of Evangelism . . . a church building with a hundred Sunday school rooms and we use them for dormitories and classrooms and so on and so forth . . . we have church services on Sundays, periodic crusades from guest ministers coming through . . . our college sessions themselves . . . also, our offices are there.

"We have students from overseas as well as ministers of various denominations and independent churches throughout the United States."

Bosen then asked the preacher, "Do you still go on the road with your ministry?"

Taking a deep breath the grinning evangelist explained, "I'm on the road when I'm not teaching at the college."

Bosen's question "Where do you go?" inaugurated a geographical excess from Tony: "Throughout just about all of the East . . . all states east of the Mississippi from Florida and northward . . . Florida, Louisiana, Alabama, Georgia, Mississippi, Tennessee, South Carolina, Ohio, North Carolina, Pennsylvania, Virginia, Arkansas, New York, Illinois, Indiana, [and] sometimes Texas and California and other states."

At one point during the recitation Bosen remarked to his client, "You're going faster than I can write!" But Tony only smiled yes and kept going.

Asked about his religious background and training, Tony repeated his oft-used remark, "I've been in full-time ministry since the night of my twelfth birthday, May 3rd, 1958!" before assuring the members that he had indeed received a proper education with "I graduated high school, yes."

The words seemed to come far more quickly than Leyva's mental ability to handle them, as in his response to Bosen's question about when he first took his ministry on the road and what that ministry was: "Uh—it was since I was twelve, I would go on the road on weekends and all summer. And then as I graduated I was out full time even when I pastored, which my first pastorate was at the age of seventeen.

"I—no denomination, no"—when Bosen had what his client regarded as the temerity to interrupt him with a question—"I was raised Assemblies of God but I always felt inwardly to be nondenominational, so I could flow nationally and internationally within different circuits, not confined to just one group or movement. . . . We're of a Pentecostal foundation but I preach in Pentecostal, Baptist, Nazarene and just about anybody who'll listen at me.

"We've been on radio since I was eighteen years of age and also in gospel tents. And our radio broadcasts and our taping ministry because of our sermons and messages have been in demand all these years. Our radio ministry was on—this year closing out—half a dozen national stations and then one international station that reached all of South and Central America [and the] Caribbean.

"I was on television up till April this year when these events began to transpire. I had to stop our television operations."

Bosen took a little wind out of Tony's sails by asking, "All right, was this a large television enterprise?"

"No," Tony sighed, "it was just local in Columbus, Georgia . . . at *that* particular time."

But when Bosen asked Brother Tony a question about preaching "outside the United States of America," the witness went on and on:

"About fifty percent of the time my work involves missions [in] Haiti and South and Central America, Jamaica, [the] Dominican Republic, Cuba. My father being a Cuban, I was allowed to go in to visit our family and I went to the [Cuban] Council of Churches and gained permission and I have preached . . . in their local churches. Assembly of God, Nazarene, and Baptist churches. This was in '82 but I've been two more trips since then and preached the first crusades in Cuba."

Bosen then asked Tony, "Did you have many people attend?"

"Uh—that was the problem, we had too many people attend and [it] began to be a problem. Some extremists on our last trip shot at us and kind of—we had a high-speed chase on one particular incident because they didn't like especially gringo preachers in their country preaching."

Next Bosen and Tony tried disingenuously to blame Tony's court appearance for keeping him from preaching: "I'm supposed to be in Cuba this month," Tony lied, "and going from there at the invitation of the Church of God denomination to Nicaragua. I was invited by the national pastors and specifically by the Church of God in Nicaragua. They said I was the only one that would go, all their other preachers were afraid to go at this time."

Tony told how he'd been "in and out of tent ministries for twenty-five years. We've been in and out of tents since I was eighteen years old."

Asked by Bosen what kind of tents these were, Tony said, "Revival tents, like a circus tent. We would travel in a caravan of vehicles. We had a couple of tractor trailers and then a van and an automobile," Tony said before Bosen brought in testimony to try and defuse prosecutor Randy Leach's opening statements concerning Tony traveling around in a limousine.

Said Tony: "After I pastored six and a half years in West Palm Beach, Florida, I was given the gift by a family as a going-away present. They was trading it in on their new model. It was an older used one for them and, uh, they were trading it in and instead they felt to give it to my ministry so I'd be able to have something a little bit nice to travel in," Tony explained, never revealing that it was but one of several limousines he drove through the years.

In response to still more questions from his attorney, Tony detailed how his revival ministry functioned: "I would have a base of operations. I wouldn't always get to be there, but I'd have a rather large apartment some place and I would generally put an individual, sometimes it was couples, and they would run the business secretarial-wise and staffing and take care of our mail . . . our telephone calls and coordinating the ministry. For a long time in West Palm Beach and consequently in Marietta, Georgia, for two years. And then—now Columbus, Georgia.

"We always had understood rules and then back in '83 we began to put them down on paper. As per alcohol; as per drugs; as per any other kind of misconduct that could be imagined; anything that would question Christian character . . . as per representing this ministry."

"Did that include illicit sex?" Bosen sharply inquired.

"Yes, it did. Positively did!" Leyva rose to his lawyer's journeyman-like question as readily as feeding chum to fish.

Tony then talked about having a son and daughter who were young adults, about how he had gotten close to his son in recent years, but that he had not been able to reach either his son or daughter "since all this trouble has broken out," as Bosen put it.

This window dressing out of the way, the moment of truth had arrived. Bosen began: "Mr. Leyva, did you ever have sexual relations of any type with Ronald Paul Cooley?"

"No, sir, I never did," Leyva replied. As to the matter of his having "naked pictures of boys" in his possession at any time, Leyva prevaricated with: "These things would be risky for anybody in my position to even have."

Previously Mike Page had told the press that some of the boys involved in Leyva's ministry had tried to blackmail him with allegations of homosexuality and that one boy demanded five hundred dollars to keep quiet. Therefore, it did not surprise Randy Leach when Bosen asked, "Why do you suppose these boys are making these allegations against you?"

"I don't know all of the reasons," Tony began, "but I believe part of the basic reasons are because of some of the retaliation for the[ir] dismissal on account of conduct and drugs. I do know that there was some, uh, a situation arose back in the fall of '86 concerning some monies that were wanted and I did not have. And it just grew from bad to worse until it's amounted to what it's evolved in[to] today."

Bosen attempted to paint a rosy picture of Brother Tony, the lonely child's savior, with: "You always had a soft heart for the underprivileged and children from repressed backgrounds and this sort of thing?"

Paying close attention, Tony quickly responded, "Positively have. My father comes from a repressed background. In these last years because of our ministries that are supportive of orphanages and so on and so forth, and here in the States I would have an especially heavy heart for abused children, underprivileged children, and would do my best to give them as much attention as I possibly was capable of."

To Bosen's question about accumulating personal wealth, Leyva rose with sermon-like intensity in his response: "I have no wealth. I have no personal items. I live in a Sunday school room at the college. And anything else that I have belongs to the ministry. I do not so much as purchase the clothes on my back. Everything I have is given to me by people in our ministry through gifts, down to the socks and hankies and shoes and anything else that I have to wear, even colognes and deodorants. And, uh, God's always been sufficient in supplying my needs in every way. But as far as wealth, having anything personal, I have nothing. Never have."

Alluding to televangelist Jim Bakker's then current legal problems, Bosen asked: "You don't have any million-dollar dog houses or anything like that?"

"No, sir, don't even have a dog," the preacher replied.

But Randy Leach's cross examination quickly led the defendant back into the deep water skirted by Mr. Bosen.

Leach: "Mr. Leyva, you indicate that you have been warned by preacher friends of yours before about your habits involving young men, is that correct?"

Leyva: "Have not really been warned; it was brought up as a matter of caution in conversation."

Leach: "As a matter of caution and it's been brought up repeatedly, has it not?"

Leyva: "Not repeatedly, just on occasion."

Leach: "And you chose to ignore that and continue putting yourself in situations where you were spending the night alone with young men in your motel room?"

Leyva: "That's true."

Then Randy Leach began asking questions about Leyva's marriage and previous allegations of sexual abuse of boys.

Leach: "Now you've also testified that the reason you and your wife split up was the fact that you were married to your ministry, that you were spending too much time [in it]; that's not exactly the whole picture, is it?"

Leyva: "Yes, it is."

Leach: "There were some other allegations there, were there not?"

Leyva: "They were brought up later, yes."

Leach: "They were brought up later. And indeed in some prior testimony that you have given, you attributed this entire mess to your ex-wife, is that correct?"

Leyva: "Partially, yes."

Leach: "Partially, I see. So she's responsible for it even though you haven't been married to her, at least partially, for thirteen years, is that right?"

Leyva: "She had contacted most of the ministers I was involved in at that particular time to try and persuade them against our ministry."

Leach: "Does she know Ronald Paul Cooley?"

Leyva: "Uh . . . no, she don't know Ronald Paul Cooley."

Leach: "Does she know Mark Crump?"
Leyva: "She doesn't know Mark Crump."
Leach: "Does she know Darrell Wayne Sharp?"
Leyva: "No. She doesn't know Darrell Wayne Sharp."
Leach: "Does she know Matthew Grisham?"
Leyva: "No, sir, she doesn't."
Leach: "Does she know Jason Embert."
Leyva: "No, sir, she doesn't. But she knows most of their mothers and their families."
Leach: "Oh, I see, so she does know their families?"
Leyva: "Um-hmm."
Leach: "And you think she might be partially responsible for this?"
Leyva: "Not for the recent ones, no."
Leach: "Not for the recent ones?"
Leyva: "No, sir."

Next Randy Leach embarked on a short, mostly successful effort to show that the preacher had indeed been involved sexually with the boys. Inquiring about the night Ronald Paul Cooley spent with him, Leach asked: "And he stayed in your room?"

Leyva: "That's correct."
Leach: "And you slept in the same bed?"
Leyva: "That's correct."
Leach: "Why? There were two beds in the room, were there not?"
Leyva: "Yes, he chose to sleep in the bed with me."
Leach: "So it was his choice?"
Leyva: "Yes, it was."
Leach: "So you basically admit all of the incidents occurring except for the actual sex?"
Leyva: "Absolutely."

Randy Leach revisited the issue of sleeping in the same bed with: "And then they would sleep in the same bed with you again, is that right?"

Leyva: "Most often, yes."
Leach: "And every one of these boys chose to do that on their own?"
Leyva: "Yes, they did."

After Tony Leyva left the stand Randy Leach called Jason's mother, Macalynn Embert, as a rebuttal witness, asking her: "What did Tony Leyva tell you specifically about the allegations involving Jason?"

Macalynn: "The first thing he did when he call[ed] me, the first thing I said was, 'Why did you do it, Tony?' "

Leach: "What was his response?"

Macalynn: "I told him that I knew then what he had done and he said, 'I don't know why to Jason out of all the boys . . . I don't know why Jason. I worship[ed] the ground that Jason walked on.' He said, 'I don't know why.' "

Soon thereafter Macalynn said: "I asked him point-blank if he had had oral sex with Jason."

Leach: "What was his response to that?"

Macalynn: "He said that that was what he had done."

Then came Anthony Grooms, this time to give his testimony in front of the jury to show that the sexual assaults which Brother Tony stood accused of were the same crimes which he had been committing on young boys for over twenty years.

After succinct instructions from Judge Trabue, the jury left the courtroom for their deliberations. It took them only two hours.

When they returned, it was very anticlimactic: after two days of testimony, the jury announced that they had found Mario Ivan "Tony" Leyva guilty on both counts of orally sodomizing boys, yet inexplicably they recommended just two and one-half years in prison, several jurors publicly voicing a desire that Brother Tony get his life straightened out so that he could once again function as a preacher of the Gospel. Formal sentencing was set for early 1989, and, given the light sentence, Judge Trabue allowed Leyva to remain free on bond until then.

15

*"He said to me, 'Tony and me got a secret,'
the classic line."*

On Friday, September 23, immediately following the guilty verdicts against Tony, Macalynn and Jason Embert happily telephoned Kenny in Delaware with the good news. Then they drove out of Salem as quickly as they could back home to Newark.

As they traveled north past historic Natural Bridge, Lexington, and Staunton, Jason's lanky body relaxed now that the gut-wrenching testimony he had had to give was over. But every once in awhile, his face reddened and his body briefly tensed as his mind drifted back to his nervous testimony about "it" before the packed courtroom: "He did . . . just . . . you know, put his mouth on me. He just . . . gave me a blow job."

By the time they reached Virginia's fabled Shenandoah Valley, Jason's thoughts had turned to his friends in the tenth grade at Newark High School and his secret about "it" that he continued to keep from them, a numbing pang of fear shooting through the fourteen-year-old as he recalled defense attorney Bosen's pointed question: "When you were first asked if there had been any sex between you and Mr. Leyva, you denied that anything ever happened, didn't you?"

To this Jay had defensively but honestly responded, "Yes. Because I didn't want people to think that I was some yukkie kid that they didn't want to stick around no more." Reflecting on this increased his anxiety so much that he tried hard to think about something else—homework, girls, *anything else*! But his apprehension grew when he remembered that he would have to testify about "it" yet again in federal court in less than three weeks' time, which would surely lead to his being found out by his peers. Try as he might Jason couldn't shove "it" and the attendant numbing fear from his mind that somehow his friends would find out the real reason he had been absent just three weeks into his first full year of school since he, his mother, and his brother had gotten hooked up with Tony's goddamned revivals!

Jason had just discovered girls. He smiled as he also thought how they had just discovered him, and the terrifying realization that they just might learn about his secret was almost more than he could bear. Except for talking about it with his mother and brother, he continually tried to stuff it deep down inside himself.

Macalynn had already confided to Newark High School's vice-principal the true reason for her younger son's need to be absent; she told him about the spring and summer interrogations by FBI Special Agent John Bill, the trips to Roanoke for Jason to testify before state and federal grand juries, and now the trip back again for Jason to testify at Leyva's state trial. And the vice-principal was most understanding and kind; he assured Macalynn and Jason that he would keep the truth to himself, and mark down Jason's absences as "due to illness."

✝ ✝ ✝

Detective Garrick Hudson was full of praise for the Assistant Commonwealth's Attorney's handling of the case: "Randy Leach did an excellent job prosecuting Leyva!

"But our biggest thing—Randy's and mine—was . . . that . . . we wanted Leyva convicted in Roanoke County Court because whatever the feds did, Leyva would then be a convicted child molester. I think that . . . it was so, so important for us to get that conviction. Because then with the feds he ended up confessing a lot of things."

After Tony Leyva was convicted in Salem, Ann Martin said: "In the state trial, we were glad that we got a conviction. We realized that on the jury we had one hold out. She just could not believe that a minister would do that sort of thing and when they read the verdict, she cried. It was a compromise: They would say that he was guilty, but they would recommend only so much time. I would have liked to see him get more time than he did, but we were just thankful for the conviction."

✝ ✝ ✝

Even before April 1988, when Tony had been indicted on the two state counts of orally sodomizing teenage boys, as well as eight federal counts of trafficking in teenage boys for purposes of prostitution, attendance at his revivals had gone down steadily. This had forced Mike Page to relocate many of his boss's Miracle Restoration Revivals from large municipal auditoriums to the homes and small churches of the ministry's dwindling numbers of followers. This greatly decreased the revival contributions, which upset Page to no end.

In the summer of 1988 Page aggressively proclaimed Tony's innocence but became quite upset when Tony felt obliged to make public statements from the pulpit about his "legal problems." Tony attributed these problems to "Satan persecuting me" and efforts by the Evil One's temporal equivalents—his teenage victims, law enforcement officers, and newspaper reporters—who were "spreading lies" about his and his cohorts' "homosexual" involvement's with teenage boys. Indeed, by September Mike Page was troubled at having yet another set of bills to pay: Tony remarked to his closest supporters that Page had laid out "$75,000 trying to keep my ministry going and trying to take care of my attorney."

However, try as he might to coax his ever-shrinking flock to give still more money to his ministry, "to fight God's fight," it was all for naught. On September 17, 1988, Tony Leyva preached his last revival sermon to a handful of the faithful in the Longshoreman Auditorium in Fort Lauderdale, Florida. After passing around his Kentucky Fried Chicken buckets three times, Tony collected less than one hundred dollars—not even enough for rent on the place, but the evangelist was saved from ignominy since Page had made a rent-free arrangement with the union.

The next day Ed Morris and Freddie Herring, along with Page's wife dejectedly drove back to the virtually deserted Tony Leyva International School of Evangelism and Conference Center in Columbus, Georgia, while Page spent two days driving Leyva the eight hundred miles to Salem, Virginia. There Tony met with Harry Bosen, to prepare his defense against what he still claimed to Page and his attorney were false, malicious charges that he had repeatedly orally sodomized two teenaged male members of his tent crew.

Even with his conviction, Leyva's few remaining die-hard believers continued to loudly proclaim that while their beloved Brother Tony may have lost a battle to Satan, he had just begun to fight the war. But the convictions in state court confirmed for thousands of the evangelist's former followers around the United States what they had suspected for years. The day after the sentencing, anyone calling Leyva's twenty-four-hour prayer line in Georgia would have heard a recording of Tony's gravelly voice delivering the following rapid-fire sermonette. Here it is, just as I heard it and transcribed it:

> The Lord has given to every man his work. It is his business to do it and the devil's business to hinder him if he can. So soon as God has given you a work to do, Satan will try to hinder you. He may present other things more promising, he may allure you by worldly prospects, he may insult you with slander, torment you with false accusations, set you to work defending your character, employ pious persons to lie about you, editors to assail you, and excellent men to slander you.
>
> You may have Pilate, Herod, and Anyas, Caiaphas all combined against you, and Judas standing by ready to sell you for thirty pieces of silver, and you may wonder why all those things have come upon you. Can you not see that the whole thing is brought about through the craft of the devil to draw you off, and the work [sic] and hindered your obedience to God. Keep at your work. Do not flinch because the lion roars. Do not stop to stall the devil's dogs. Do not fool away your time chasing the devil's rabbits. Do your work. Let liars lie. Let sectarians quarrel. Let corporations resolve. Let editors publish. Let the devil do his worst. But see to it that nothing hinders you in fulfilling the work that God has given you.
>
> He has not sent you to make money. He has not commanded you to get rich. He has never bidden you to defend character. He has not set you with work to conquer the falsehoods which Satan and his servants may start to peddle. If you do those things you will do nothing else. You will be at work for yourself and not for the Lord. Keep at your work, let your aim be as steady as a star. Let the world boil and bubble.
>
> You may be assaulted, robbed, insulted, slandered, wounded, and rejected, and you may be abused by foes, forsaken by friends, despised and rejected of men, but see to it with steadfast determination, with unfaltering zeal, that you pursue the great purpose of your life and object of your being until at last you can say, "I have finished the work which thou hast paid me to do. Thank you, Lord Jesus!"
>
> This is evangelist Tony Leyva saying, *"Thank you!"* for tuning our direction today. Jesus said, I must be about the Father's business. We're about the Father's business today, in spite of *all-l-l-l* the attacks of the enemies that would come against our ministry! I'm praying for you and I

wondered if you would pray for us. Our ministry is under great attack. We're in need financially into the thousands of dollars so we might stand the course and fight the battle. And I'm askin' God to touch you in your soul! . . . In your mind! . . . In your body! . . . In Jesus' name!

Amen, amen, and *aaamen*! Thank you for calling! God bless you *is* . . . *my* . . . *prayer!*

✝ ✝ ✝

Immediately after the jury found Leyva guilty on September 24, 1988, Bosen announced that his client would "definitely" appeal the verdict. Circuit Court Judge Trabue allowed Leyva to remain free on bond until his formal sentencing in early 1989. The next day, as Macalynn and Jason Embert were heading back home, a still protective yet very disappointed Mike Page drove his boss back to his all but empty Bible College in Columbus, Georgia.

When they arrived, Herring and Morris joined them and with heavy hearts the four suspended the ministry's revival schedule. Over the next few days the evangelists spent many hours closeted and discussing possible defenses for their federal trial. During these sessions Leyva tried unsuccessfully to convince his fellow evangelists to join him in using his already failed defense that drug abuse and thievery "caused me to dismiss the boys that are now accusing me of these wicked things."

In May 1988, soon after the Virginia and federal charges became known, Donald Thorpe, Lowell Thaxton, and other youths who had lived at the red brick Columbus headquarters went to Columbus Police with accusations of sexual assault; however, five months later the police had still not charged the ministers. And they never did. Rather, at Leyva's request they had ordered extra patrols around his facility to help prevent others from entering as Macalynn, her sons, and Bubba Gordon had done.

Early on Saturday, October 1, Morris, Herring, and Page helped Tony load his customized van for the 564-mile drive to Roanoke. They arrived late that night, and since their finances were nearly depleted and Gary Thompson now refused Tony further support from his trust fund, they checked into an inexpensive motel, ironically just a block from the Holiday Inn and Econo Lodge where Tony had committed some of the crimes of which he stood convicted.

The next morning the four arrived at the home of Margaret Weiss, Brother Tony's most fervent remaining supporter, where they met their ministry's now handful of adoring followers for a low-key Sunday service. After scripture readings and prayers, followed by one of Tony's classic "hell fire and brimstone" sermons, they all sat down to a typical Southern after-church dinner of fried chicken, mashed potatoes and gravy, fried okra, biscuits, corn bread, and coconut meringue pie, all washed down with big tumblers of iced tea.

✝ ✝ ✝

On October 5, after several conferences with his attorney, Tony Leyva was still professing total innocence. Harry Bosen wasn't buying it, and later said: "Once I heard the Embert boy testify and once they got that conviction [in state court], I knew in my mind he'd [Tony] been lying to me. I *knew* it!

"So out of the blue one day I called [U.S. Assistant Attorney] Jenny Montgomery and I said, 'I tell you what we're gonna do: Tony Leyva is coming in to my office. I'm gonna use as a pretext to get him in the car alone that I've got to take him to your office to review the federal government's evidence, Okay? Because . . . the only way I can get him away from Page is to say that you will not allow anybody but the defendant and his attorney there.'

"And so when Tony and Page showed up in my office on the appointed day I told Page, 'Tony and I are going to . . . the federal prosecutor's office to review their evidence . . . They will not allow anybody but me and Tony. Let's go, Tony.'

According to Bosen, Page acted as if he hadn't heard a word and responded, "Fine. I'm ready to go. Just let me take a leak first."

But as soon as Page excused himself Bosen jumped up, grabbed Tony by the arm, bounded down the stairs, and dashed to his car. Just as they drove off an agitated Mike Page ran wildly from the building flailing his arms and shouting at them to stop. But Bosen just kept driving while the angry Page ran to his car, jumped in, and followed them in hot pursuit.

"Between [my office] and Roanoke," Bosen continued, "which is about a fifteen-minute ride, Tony confessed. And so when we walked in the prosecutor's office it took me about a half hour of talking to him and telling him what he was up against . . . and they showed me some of their evidence, how many witnesses they had to testify. And he started confessing.

"I had to arrange first, before I let him confess, that the state would not prosecute him for perjury, nor that they would move for a new trial or anything like that. So, Jenny Montgomery called Randy Leach and I got Randy to promise immunity from all other state charges including perjury. I got the government then to work on the plea bargain, [which] we signed. . . . Tony spent eight and one-half hours confessing, until about one o'clock in the morning.

"That's how it happened. If I had not gotten him away from Page he would have never confessed. He would have never owned up to what he had done."

What Bosen didn't say, but what I later learned from Randy Leach, was that Bosen had also painted for Tony a hopeless picture of the upcoming federal trial to begin on October 11. So by the time they had arrived at the Poff Federal Building—Page parking right beside them—Tony had taken a deep breath, prayed silently, and tearfully admitted his extensive guilt to Bosen. He told his attorney that if the charges against him were reduced and he was promised a lesser sentence than the sixty-five years he faced, he would plead guilty to avoid another trial.

Harry Bosen was also thoroughly convinced that Mike Page manipulated Tony Leyva as if he were a marionette: "Page did not allow Tony to be alone with his own attorney unless he was there. Page controlled Tony. And I think it was totally a money tie.

"Page kept pleading poverty [as the reason] they couldn't pay my attorney's fees: 'You know, we're not getting any money. The money's not coming in . . . we can barely make our mortgage payments on the college.' I found out later from the FBI that some millionaire was making them all along.

"What was Page doing with all that money that he wasn't paying either on his attorneys' fees or for the mortgage payments? Tony wasn't getting the money! I'm gonna tell you right now. [At the time of the trial] Tony lived like a pauper. Somebody else benefited. Tony lived hand to mouth. I'm telling you, I could see it! Tony did not benefit financially at all. He was a pawn for somebody else to benefit financially and I think we know who that was . . . Mike Page!

"Tony was not a high spender and a high roller. It was the others around him who were milking him. Tony was Page's cash cow. That's what this case is all about. Tony was delusional enough to let others use him as a charismatic religious leader to bilk other people out of their money. That's my opinion of the situation!"

☩ ☩ ☩

On October 6, Daniel L. Crandall, the Roanoke criminal attorney representing Leyva's associate and organist, Ed Morris, used an approach similar to Bosen's on Leyva to convince his client to accept the federal plea bargain, which offered him fifteen years in prison instead of the twenty-five he had been facing in return for pleading guilty to fewer counts of "transporting minors in interstate commerce with intent to engage such minors in criminal sexual activity and prostitution." As with Leyva the agreement required Morris to "cooperate fully" with the FBI's debriefing about their sexual activity with hundreds of young boys attracted to the Tony Leyva Evangelistic Association's revivals.

✝ ✝ ✝

On Friday, October 7, the Evening Edition of the *Roanoke Times & World News* carried on its front page the bold headline proclaiming "Leyva Bargain Reached," explained below by "Two evangelists expected to plead guilty in sex case."

The article, by Douglas Pardue and Victoria Ratcliff, reported that attorneys Bosen and Crandall had worked out plea bargains with federal prosecutors for their clients. The article also stated that "psychiatric examinations will be conducted at a federal prison in Butner, North Carolina" and that "the two would serve their sentences at that prison, which has a special pedophile unit for those serving time for sex crimes against juveniles." The coda to this piece was a classic understatement: "Attorneys for the two were afraid of what might happen to their clients if they were locked up in a regular prison."

But courtly, grandfatherly Freddie Herring still refused to plead guilty. His Southern, countrified attorney, John Swearingen, of Columbus, Georgia, described his client as "an old, harmless feller" whom he still planned to defend at trial the following week, although he had asked federal authorities to send his client to Butner for a psychiatric exam.

However, by 5:00 P.M. on Friday, October 7, formal plea bargain agreements had not been signed and filed with the Federal District Court Clerk. Assistant U.S. Attorney Montgomery, when asked by reporters if there would be a trial on October 11, issued a "no comment," then added briefly, "Any pleas will be Tuesday morning." And so the long Columbus Day weekend began with all three evangelists still facing trial on October 11 before Federal District Judge James Turk.

Over the weekend, in order to be ready if they indeed went to trial,

Chapter 15

Montgomery and fellow Assistant U.S. Attorney Morgan Scott brought thirty-three witnesses into Roanoke and housed and fed them in local hotels, motels, and restaurants. Thirty were victims of the amoral trio, while the remaining three were parents of these abused boys.

✝ ✝ ✝

A little after eight o'clock on Tuesday morning, October 11, Macalynn, Jason, and Kenny Embert walked from the lobby of the venerable Patrick Henry Hotel in downtown Roanoke and headed for the Poff Federal Building several blocks away. They had driven down on Columbus Day, both Jason and his mother thankful that the holiday reduced by one the days he would miss from school. But now Jason and Kenny were rapidly becoming uneasy at the approaching specter of testifying about Brother Tony's sexual assaults on them. Macalynn marched along with her jaw set in the firm desire to see her former boss convicted yet again—reporter Douglas Pardue described her admiringly as "a tough old bird"—but her sons struggled farther and farther behind. At each intersection she paused and admonished the boys to hurry along so they wouldn't be late. But Jason and Kenny wished desperately they were anyplace other than on their way to court to testify against this depraved preacher of the Gospel whom they had once called "Dad."

By 8:30 the foyer of Judge Turk's courtroom on the fourth floor of the Poff Federal Building resembled the first day of classes at an all-male junior-senior high school, with dozens of young teenage boys and their parents and guardians nervously milling about. Each time the elevator doors opened, the noisy crowd hushed to a chorus of whispers: "Is it them? Is it Leyva?"

Macalynn, Jason, and Kenny, along with Judy Cooley and her son, Ronald Paul, emerged tentatively into the pointed gazes of reporters and the lights of TV news cameramen, plus a small knot of Brother Tony's diehard adherents. But then they spotted their supportive fellow witnesses, many of whom greeted the new arrivals warmly.

Macalynn's smile faded when she saw her archnemesis, the vocal, gray-haired Margaret Weiss trying to shame her and her sons by shouting that they were "messin' with God's anointed." Margaret was so certain of Tony's innocence that she loudly proclaimed her belief in him to reporter Pardue: "I still believe in him. He's being railroaded. I'll fight for him with every drop of blood I have. I believe he's lying [by pleading guilty] because he has to. I'll never believe it until he tells me to my face."

Also in the crowd were diminutive twelve-year-old Eric Owens and his father, Bill, from Delaware, Ohio. As they paced the foyer outside the courtroom awaiting Brother Tony's arrival, they vividly recalled an incident in June 1985.

✝ ✝ ✝

On a summer night three years earlier, Eric, then ten, had been Leyva's overnight guest at a Holiday Inn in Columbus, Ohio, following the evangelist's guest appearance on a TV program hosted by Bill Owens. Owens told me: "We had known Tony by this time for two or three years and there had been no indications that he was a pedophile. . . . Me and Tony went to a meeting in the morning and that night we went to the station. He was on the air on the late program and my two sons were there with us."

After talking with Tony, the boys "asked if they could go with Tony and I asked, 'Two?'"

"Tony said, 'No, just one. I can't have two kids in the hotel room.'"

"So, I said okay. We trusted him. We were told to trust him. We just trusted the guy implicitly!"

Added Owens's extremely candid son, "Well, Brother Tony suggested it, ya know. He said that he wished we could come with him. He kept on saying that."

The charismatic evangelist had told Eric that he would teach him how to study the Bible. But when the two got to Tony's motel room, he persuaded Eric to strip down to his briefs and then climb into the same bed with him, although the boy admitted to having been disconcerted about this.

After they got into bed Leyva began massaging the now alarmed boy's back and buttocks; suddenly, he jerked down Eric's briefs, flipped him over, and orally sodomized the terrified youngster.

"He forced me into it," Eric softly responded as if apologizing. "I kept on trying to, ya know. . . . I didn't go down on him, like, the first three times [Leyva tried]. Then, he just kept on." The boy's voice trailed off as his gaze grew distant. Catching himself, Eric continued, "I kept on kicking him off. I wanted to go home! I wanted my dad! I was thinking what I could do to stop it. I felt scared for the most part. I thought that nobody had gone through this before. I thought that I was the only one!"

Finally, after one final attempt, Eric successfully pulled away from Tony and stopped the assault. Leyva's response was to sit the boy down on the edge of his bed, try to comfort him, and then phone Bill, saying, the father recalled, " 'Your son is very homesick and he's crying. Maybe you could try to talk to him and calm him down, make him feel better.' "

Eric then spoke briefly with his father but, Eric recalled, "I couldn't tell on him on the phone 'cause Tony was there. And after hanging up, I didn't sleep.... Tony fell asleep. But I didn't sleep at all."

Eric's father tenderly wrapped his arms around his son as he recalled the day after the assaults: "My son changed and I knew something was up. Number one, he went to sleep during the service in the morning. That meant he didn't have any sleep. Number two ... just the way he was acting ... I could just feel it. So, I said, 'We're gonna go out and sit down and talk.'

"So, he sat there kinda sheepish, very tired, and I said, 'Okay, you're gonna tell me what's wrong.' He said to me, 'Tony and me got a secret,' the classic line. So, I asked him the normal questions about who's involved in it. He seemed truthful with me. He just said, 'Don't tell anybody.' It wasn't to the point where he needed a medical examination from what I could determine.

"So, we went home and I was trying to determine what to do. I knew Tony was going to be at the station that night. I went back to confront him and two of my friends went with me. That night I wanted to be objective about it, because I had a forty-year-old versus a ten-year-old and it was very hard to deal with. I was angry. I guess I wanted to punch him! But Tony zipped out of the station pretty fast!"

Since that summer, Bill and his son had tried to forget what had happened. "Then," said Bill, "the FBI got a hold of us and told us how extensive Tony's sexual assaults on boys were, and we volunteered to participate in their prosecution of him."

Hugging his son tightly the father concluded by saying, "Coming here helped Eric a lot because he could see that he wasn't the guilty one; that Tony was in the wrong. That's essentially why we came. My wife and I asked Eric, 'What do you want to do to him?'

"And Eric said, 'The biggest thing is that I don't think he should be able to do this thing to anybody else. We should stop him.' "

At this point Eric looked up with his bright, steel-gray eyes and said, "I just want to put him in jail for what he's done."

☦ ☦ ☦

Because of numerous death threats against the evangelists, the foyer outside the courtroom was guarded by several armed U.S. marshals, who searched handbags and briefcases and required everyone to pass through a metal detector before entering.

A few minutes before nine o'clock the elevator doors parted once more. Grim-faced and stooped with embarrassment, out shuffled Morris and Herring closely followed by a boldly strutting Tony Leyva, smiling broadly and waving and greeting supporters and even some of the witnesses, while obviously basking in the TV cameramen's bright lights as if he were a popular political figure. Attorneys Bosen, Crandall, and Swearingen all appeared humiliated by Leyva's brazen behavior and did their best to rush past him into the courtroom before the angry, hissing witnesses could catch up with them, too.

At 9:35 A.M. Federal District Court Judge James C. Turk entered the courtroom and gaveled the court into session. Assistant United States Attorney Jenny Montgomery stood and announced that all three evangelists had finally admitted their guilt and signed formal plea bargain agreements in her office that morning in return for assurances that the U.S. Attorney's Office would ask the Court to do the following:

1. sentence Leyva to serve no more than twenty years in prison;
2. sentence Morris to serve no more than fifteen years in prison;
3. sentence Herring to serve no more than twelve years in prison (all approximately one-third the maximum sentences they could have received);
4. and assess fines of no more than $10,000 each. (Leyva alone could have been fined over half a million dollars.)

Also the U.S. Attorney's Office agreed not to prosecute the evangelists for their perjured testimony before the Federal District Court Grand Jury in April 1988, or charge and try them for any additional crimes arising out of the FBI's investigation.

Tony Leyva's agreement permitted him to plead guilty to just five of the eight original counts of his indictment; Morris pled guilty to four counts of his five-count indictment; and Herring had finally agreed to plead guilty to two of his three-count indictments. In response to a question from Judge Turk, Montgomery disclosed that the signed agreements allowed FBI Special Agent John Terry to debrief the evangelists, and that if those debriefings were deemed incomplete or dishonest, the plea-bargain agreements would be revoked and the accused tried in court. Then she called Agent Terry to testify about his investigation of Leyva, Morris, and

Herring and their collective and individual sexual assaults against hundreds of young boys across the United States.

Guided by Montgomery and a list of victims labeled "Male Minors One through Twelve," Terry began a considerably abridged, at times rather dry, account of the bureau's investigation.

He began by recounting how Detective L. G. Hudson of the Roanoke County Sheriff's Office had telephoned him in August 1987 and "he advised me that he had some information concerning allegations of sexual molestation by traveling evangelists against some male minors that lived in the Roanoke area." Soon thereafter Agent Terry launched into an occasionally hard-to-follow narrative of the three evangelists' sexual assaults on numerous boys, jumping back and forth from "Male Minor Number Ten" to "Male Minor Number Twelve" to "Male Minor Number Eight," all so identified to shield their identities.

"Male Minor Number Eight," Terry reported, told about being "orally sodomized by Mr. Morris and Mr. Leyva while traveling with them through the states of Georgia, Louisiana, Arkansas, Mississippi, and other areas of the southeastern portion of the Unites States."

Then came startling testimony that "Male Minor Number Eight" had told the agent how he had gone to the police in both Roanoke and Salem, Virginia, in 1983 and 1984, and told them about his repeated sexual assaults by Leyva. But no charges were ever filed, no investigations were ever conducted. Agent Terry had talked with Roanoke Police Detective Allen Clark and Salem Police Investigator Dennis Murphy, and "their stories were essentially the same as to what Male Minor Number Eight had said to me. Detective Clark also showed me a letter that the Commonwealth's Attorney for Roanoke, Donald Caldwell, had written to Lieutenant Dean of the Roanoke City Police Department regarding the allegations made by Male Minor Number Eight against Mr. Leyva and others. This letter contained the same information that I also learned from Male Minor Number Eight," Agent Terry testified as witnesses' heads shook in sad disbelief that four years earlier the Roanoke and Salem police departments had both had sufficient information about Tony Leyva and yet had failed to stop his assaults on young boys.

Agent Terry told how in 1978 then-twelve-year-old "Male Minor Number Seven traveled to Evansville, Indiana, with Mr. Leyva and was orally sodomized and masturbated by Mr. Leyva there." The boy had likewise traveled with Leyva to Columbus, Ohio, where the evangelist orally sodomized him before taking him to Georgia, where the lad was "orally sodomized by Mr. Morris on that same trip." Terry also recounted how Leyva's ex-wife, Tammy Sue, had said that Leyva had sexually assaulted several brothers from a family well known to her family, and how on one revival trip, while they were still married, her husband had "made her sleep on the floor while Mr. Leyva shared his bed with another young boy."

He continued by describing the three preachers' appearances before the Roanoke Federal Grand Jury on April 20 and 21, 1988, during which "they denied ever having sex with any boys or men," and that the Grand Jury had indicted all three. The FBI executed a search warrant at Leyva's headquarters in Columbus, Georgia. There, according to Agent Terry, "we retrieved several photographs and an address book. We researched them and I sent out additional requests for more interviews to approximately twenty different divisions of the FBI which resulted in approximately one hundred interviews regarding knowledge of sexual activity with male minors by Leyva, Morris, and Herring. As the results started coming back in, we identified approximately thirty victims of molestation by Mr. Leyva. We identified approximately eleven victims by Mr. Morris, and approximately nine victims by Mr. Herring."

Terry also explained how the three evangelists had enticed and gained the loyalty and silence of many of their victims by providing the boys with the love, attention, and affection that most of them had never received at home, plus money to play video games, new clothes for their more frequent sex partners, and always a nice dinner in a good restaurant prior to having sex.

One of the victims had called Terry after he had "received a letter from Mr. Bosen in which Mr. Bosen had explained to him the dates of the court appearances and asked him to travel here to testify in Mr. Leyva's behalf." But his testimony would not help Tony, the agent said, because "the young man explained that on a regular basis he was rotated sexually between Messrs. Morris, Herring, and Leyva and estimated that he was orally sodomized sixteen times by Mr. Leyva, twenty times by Mr. Morris, twice by Mr. Herring, and masturbated by Mr. Herring and anally sodomized by Mr. Herring."

When he finally got around to recounting his own initial debriefing of Tony Leyva, Terry said that the evangelist had admitted to having had sex with one of his victims as many as 150 times. "Leyva stated that he's aroused by younger boys, not men, and he estimates he's had sex with approximately one hundred boys.*

---

*Based on their debriefings of the three evangelists, and their knowledge of pedophiles and pederasts, FBI sexual assault experts feel that the trio could have assaulted as many as eight hundred to nine hundred boys since Tony Leyva admitted to first doing so as a teenager in 1962.

A startled gasp passed through the packed courtroom when Agent Terry elaborated that "Leyva stated he enjoys orally sodomizing and masturbating minor boys and that he had had sexual relations with minors in almost every city that he traveled to, with either a young man that lived there or who traveled there with him, and Mr. Leyva has been traveling as a minister since approximately the mid-1960s."

According to the agent, Leyva admitted that the tale about his conducting an orgy with three boys and taking nude pictures of them in July 1983 was indeed true and he added other salient details: "They were all in the room together naked. Mr. Leyva took turns orally sodomizing the boys, and then encouraged the boys to do the same to each other while he took pictures. He estimated he took eighty to one hundred pictures of the naked boys in his room at the Embassy Motor Lodge in Salem."

But still more shocks were in store for the spectators when Agent Terry turned to the FBI's debriefing of Ed Morris: "Mr. Morris stated he considers himself promiscuous in that he's willing to engage in sex with anyone, anytime. He estimates he's had sex with twenty to twenty-five boys under the age of eighteen. And Mr. Morris stated that 'Mr. Herring usually wanted to have sex with every boy that either Mr. Leyva or I brought into the ministry.' "

As to the possible reasons why the evangelist had begun sexually assaulting boys in the first place, Agent Terry said that Ed Morris claimed that at the age of seventeen he had been seduced and orally sodomized by a North Carolina evangelist, and that Freddie Herring said he had been anally raped by a neighbor when he was twelve. But Tony denied experiencing any such incidents when he was a boy. Sadly, Agent Terry revealed that the FBI had discovered that one of Tony's very first victims—who had been just twelve when Leyva first orally sodomized him—"is now an adult doing the same type of activity to other young boys."

After Agent Terry's testimony concluded, U.S. Attorney Montgomery called Tony Leyva to the stand. With a slight, incongruous smile pasted on his face, Leyva responded affirmatively, nodding his head as he did so, to every one of the prosecutor's pointed questions:

Have you ever had sexual activity with a boy under the age of eighteen?

On numerous occasions?

Has this activity continued from that time [1965] up until, almost up to the time of the indictment in this case?

Did you find Agent Terry's testimony to be accurate?

Did you take nude photographs of four young boys involved in this case engaged in homosexual activity with you?

Have you, in fact, destroyed those photographs?

Was your testimony under oath to the Federal Grand Jury on April 20, 1988, false?

Are you here today in open court admitting that you have engaged in homosexual activity with the boys named as Male Minors One through Twelve?

Are you here telling us today that the number of boys whom you have engaged in sexual activity might range as high as one hundred?

And is it fair to say that many of the young boys with whom you engaged in sexual activity trusted you implicitly?

Would do whatever you asked them to do?

Did they consider you a father figure?

Did you tell most of these young boys whom you engaged in sexual activity that you loved them?

Close in time to the sexual activity taking place?

When you testified in your own defense at the State of Virginia trial that you had not sexually assaulted those . . . boys, that testimony was false, wasn't it?

And when you testified at that trial that [two] boys conspired to tell lies about you, that was false, too?

Throughout his testimony Leyva maintained a faint, benign smile, his buck teeth protruding noticeably, as he softly yet courteously responded, "Yes, ma'am," to each of Montgomery's queries.

Judge Turk excused Leyva to return to the defense table as Jenny Montgomery turned over the next round of the defendants' testimony to her co-prosecutor, Assistant U.S. Attorney Morgan Scott, and Ed Morris was called to the stand.

After difficulty in hearing the soft-spoken Morris was cleared up, Scott asked him, "What do you do for a living, Mr. Morris?"

Chapter 15

He responded, "I worked as a minister, organist, and office manager for Tony Leyva Evangelistic Association."

This prompted a query from Judge Turk: "Have you had formal training on piano or organ?"

"No, I haven't," Morris answered, "I fasted and prayed three days. I had a minister point at me and say the gift of God is upon me, and I sat down and played that night. A natural, God-given gift. I've never taken music. As I said, he ministered to me and I played in the service that night."

Scott asked Morris to describe his background as a minister. "I was ordained at seventeen by the American Evangelistic Association and also the Freewill Holiness Conference in North Carolina."

Scott: "Have you been a minister yourself?"

Morris: "Yes. My wife and I pastored a church up to this past year, and I also went to two Bible schools, but I did not complete the courses at either one."

Then the quiet, succinct, straightforward Scott hit home: "Sir, just to get things started, have you ever had sex with a male under the age of eighteen?" Morris answered yes to this and each of the following questions the Assistant U.S. Attorney put to him:

> Was the testimony given by Special Agent Terry about your involvement in this case accurate?
>
> On April 20, 1988, did you testify that you had never engaged in any type of sexual activity with any male minor?
>
> Was your testimony before that Federal Grand Jury false?
>
> Did you, on October 5, 1988, come to the U.S. Attorney's Office and meet with myself, Ms. Montgomery, and Agent John Terry of the FBI, along with your attorney, Mr. Crandall?
>
> And at that time did you spend several hours telling us about your involvement with the Tony Leyva Evangelistic Association and your involvement in homosexual activity with male minors?
>
> And did you indicate at that time that you had had oral sex with several male minors under the age of eighteen who had been directly introduced to you by Tony Leyva?
>
> Did you engage Male Minor Number Eight in oral sex?
>
> Did you engage Male Minor Number Twelve in oral sex?

Following his examination, Mr. Scott handed the witness over to his attorney, Crandall, for a few questions which Morris answered weakly in an ineffective bid to discount the scope of his depravity and guilt.

Last of all, the distinguished-looking, silver-maned Freddie Herring was called. Head bowed like Uriah Heap, he slowly shuffled his way to the witness stand.

After Scott got Herring to identify himself as pastor of the Lighthouse Assembly in Douglasville, Georgia, the federal prosecutor thrust sharply ahead: "Have you ever had sex with a male under the age of eighteen?"

"Yes," a subdued Herring almost whispered.

"And," continued Scott, "in that connection, sir, was the summary of the investigation by Special Agent Terry of the FBI in regard to your involvement accurate?"

"Yes," Herring again softly responded.

"And what type of sexual activity did you involve these boys in?" the Assistant U.S. Attorney queried.

Herring unblinkingly answered: "I prefer anal sex with boys."

Then, in a compassionate shift, Morgan Scott recalled Agent Terry's earlier testimony: "I believe you heard, did you not, sir, the testimony of the agent wherein he said you, yourself, had been the victim of a homosexual assault at the age of twelve?"

Herring looked down at his feet and responded, "Yes."

Scott then felt obliged to ask, "Is that accurate, sir?"

Freddie Herring looked up at the prosecutor and replied "Yes."

Judge Turk intervened, "Have you never been able to forget that or put it out of your mind?"

Freddie turned slowly toward the judge and replied "No, sir."

Scott proceeded to ask Herring the same questions put to Leyva and Morris. Like his cohorts, Freddie responded affirmatively to each one and admitted his guilt just as his fellow evangelists had done.

Scott then turned the witness over to his defense attorney, John Swearingen, for a brief cross-examination.

Swearingen: "Reverend Herring, as Mr. Scott asked you, as he called it, the confessional [sic] you entered into yesterday with Mr. Terry and the Assistant U.S. Attorneys, do you feel that you're a better person now?"

Herring: "Yes, I feel like a load is lifted off my shoulders."

Swearingen: "Do you feel that with God's help and the judge's help and the prison authorities, that you can go ahead and lick this problem and come out with your problem resolved?"

Herring: "Absolutely."

Swearingen: "Do you have anything that you would like to say publicly to these young men or the families of these young men here today?"

Herring: "Yes. I'm sorry that this happened and I hope that the hurt will not linger."

Swearingen: "You're asking for their forgiveness?"

Herring: "And I ask for their forgiveness."

Swearingen: "And have you prayed for forgiveness?"

Herring: "Absolutely."

After Judge Turk ascertained that there would be no additional testimony or cross-examination of Mr. Terry or the three defendants, he then announced, "The Government rests."

There being no "evidence concerning the question of guilt" from the three defendants and their attorneys, Judge Turk asked the defendants to rise and pronounced sentence:

> Mr. Leyva, on your pleas of guilty and on the evidence that the Court has heard, the Court finds you guilty as charged in counts one, two, four, seven and eight.
>
> Mr. Morris, on your pleas of guilty and on the evidence that the Court has heard, the Court finds you guilty as charged in counts one, two, four and eight.
>
> Mr. Herring, on your pleas of guilty and on the evidence that the Court has heard, the Court finds you guilty as charged in counts three and eight of the indictment.
>
> I'm going to grant the Government's motion at this time to dismiss all the counts to which these people have not entered pleas of guilty.
>
> Now, Mr. Leyva, on your plea of guilty I'm going to sentence you to forty-five years in federal prison. Mr. Morris, on your plea of guilty I'm going to sentence you to thirty-five years in federal prison. And finally, Mr. Herring, on your plea of guilty I'm going to sentence you to federal prison for twenty years.

As each sentence was announced there were audible swells of approving remarks from the victims and their relatives. But these positive responses would be short lived. Judge Turk continued:

> But I'm doing that so that you can all receive psychological and psychiatric evaluations at the Federal Correctional Institute down in Butner, North Carolina. Then, after this Court has received your evaluations, and if I receive reports that you have all cooperated completely with the

FBI and told them absolutely everything that you can about your despicable sexual molestations of all of these boys, in about 120 days, you'll return to this Court and I'll adjust your sentences as the law requires me to do.

At this most of the assembled witnesses and their family members commented negatively in stage whispers, or hissed, or booed—almost to the point where Judge Turk had to call for order:

Therefore, I'm going to order you, Mr. Leyva; you, Mr. Morris; and you, Mr. Herring, to report to the Federal Correctional Institute at Butner, North Carolina, in two weeks, on October 25. And I'm going to allow you all to remain free on bond until that date.

It took a moment for this to sink in, but soon cries of outrage swelled to the point that Judge Turk had to bang his gavel and demand order so that he could formally bring the hearing to a close.

After the bailiff called for those in the courtroom to rise and the judge had left the bench, many of the courtroom spectators noisily pushed their way out into the foyer. But a number of young victims stood back and stared blankly ahead in silent, stunned disbelief that the repeated promises of U.S. Attorneys Jenny Montgomery and Morgan Scott that they would be allowed to testify in court about the sexual assaults they had suffered had not been kept. In the absence of professional counseling and therapy—which most of the boys and their families could ill afford—many of them had felt that testifying about what had happened to them would help them start to heal.

But now they were hurt beyond words that they had not been able to do so, and, even though the three evangelists would have to report to federal prison in two weeks, many victims voiced a half hope that Tony would commit suicide first. Then, in disbelief, the boys watched as Leyva, Morris, and Herring walked free from the courtroom.

✝ ✝ ✝

Within moments, the foyer on the fourth floor of the Poff Federal Building exploded into a scene of emotional devastation as the young victims came to grips with "being raped a second time, this time by 'the system.'" They looked around vacantly, cursed, or wandered idly about. Along a side corridor I interviewed Macalynn Embert as Jason played with his mother's cigarette lighter: he flicked it on and off as he made angry, barely feigned attempts to set fire to a nearby wall, grinding his teeth and contorting his features as tears streamed down his cheeks and he lamented what Leyva had done to him.

Macalynn angrily recalled her and her sons' relationship with Tony: "He would spend a lot of time with them. Took them to Disney Land. And him and me were as close as a man and woman can be without having sex. And all the time he was molesting Jason!" she spat with fire in her eyes.

The whole time his mother spoke Jason kept his eyes on her lighter, flicking it on and off as he listened intently to her. Then he commented briefly: "He acted like a dad. He'd do things for me. He'd take me places, ya know. But when we'd go to bed at night he would just pull off my underwear and start sucking me and stuff like I owed him. I didn't like it! *Nobody* would!"

✝ ✝ ✝

I interviewed (retired) St. Tammany Parish Deputy Sheriff Emily Holden in 1989 and 1993. When she learned what had happened in Roanoke, she remarked: "Something like this reminds you of all your damn work you've done all of your life. And one of the things that bothered me up in Virginia was that they weren't interested in bringing all of the victims there for a trial because it would cost quite a lot and so that was the reason they let him go ahead and plead."

Then when told that the U.S. attorney's office in Roanoke had paid to bring in a couple dozen of the young witnesses, Mrs. Holden remarked, "Oh, yeah, yeah . . . it was few of 'em but not no hundred-some-odd kids.

"But it was right before my illness and open heart surgery that this thing come up and so I just hoped that somewhere somebody who followed behind me would take care of it. But I guess they didn't. When I left the department [in 1988] I don't know what they did with the warrant here, but I got a feeling they most likely just put it in what we call 'file 13.' It's there but it's not being acted on."

✝ ✝ ✝

At noon the federal employees left for lunch, but the victims and their families continued milling about on the fourth floor, the boys in particular making lunch out of the sweet rolls and juice laid out that morning in the witness assembly room.

Shortly after one o'clock U.S. Attorney's Office Witness Coordinator Betty Fitzgerald began calling witnesses and their parents and guardians into her office one by one and she issued them vouchers and checks to pay for their hotel bills and to reimburse them for their meals and transportation to Roanoke.

Soon word spread that Jenny Montgomery had called a meeting in the witness assembly room. There, along with Jenny and Morgan Scott, were a female psychologist and a male psychiatrist from Roanoke—actually Ms. Montgomery's brother-in-law, William Gray—who had already begun treating one frequently assaulted Roanoke victim for free.

When the meeting began, I along with the victims, their parents and other family members, as well as a number of reporters were present when Ms. Montgomery announced that since the victims had not been able to testify in court that day, "we will bring you all back at government expense to testify just before they are formally sentenced." She then continued to publicly pledge, though without offering any specifics, that the Justice Department would help the victims and their families obtain professional counseling and job training so that they could get on with their lives. Then after quickly introducing the psychologist and psychiatrist, she told those assembled that these mental health professionals' time was limited but that "if any of you need to talk or ask questions, they'll be here for the next thirty minutes." This, in effect, was the extent of the United States Department of Justice's efforts to provide professional therapy and counseling to the young victims.

The boys and their families were stunned. Had they not been promised the opportunity to testify about what the evangelists had done to them? And hadn't they made the emotionally tortuous trip to Roanoke so that they could express the hate and outrage they felt toward the evangelists and thereby start to heal?

At this, through clenched teeth, Kenny Embert sputtered: "It's not fair! It's just not fair!"

Macalynn recalled thinking, "They gotta be joking! Like that's gonna really do something to help!"

✝ ✝ ✝

Before returning to Delaware, later that day Macalynn went into the U.S. Attorney's Office to cash the check given her to cover her expenses, and there she saw Freddie Herring flanked by two women. "He looked right at me and when I first walked in he said to these women with him, 'Yes, that's one of 'em.' Then I sat down and picked up a magazine, but I couldn't read. So, I sat there and looked at him.

"And Freddie looked at me and says to them women, 'Well, these women that persecuted us and tormented us and harassed us so bad and put us through all this hell are gonna be beggin' to hear our ministry but they're not gonna be able to hear it because it's done and it's over with. And they're gonna have to pay for what they've done and we're gonna be able to preach our hearts out in prison!'

"He said, 'We can do what we wanna do. We don't have no phone bills to pay no more. We don't have no rent to pay, we don't have to worry 'bout money no more! Thanks to God, it's all gonna be provided for us so we can live like kings! We can say what we wanna say and God's gonna take care of these terrible women for what they have done to God's prophets!' "

✝ ✝ ✝

Thinking that the story was all over, many readers sighed in disbelief when they picked up their evening *Roanoke Times & World News* and read: "[U.S. Attorney] Montgomery said the government has the names of seven other ministers involved and has passed the names to authorities in other jurisdictions for investigation."

But what would be done to help the hundreds of victims? Concern about this was uppermost in Macalynn Embert's mind as she witnessed her sons' anger continue to build during their long drive home to Delaware. Said Macalynn, "With what happened, the kids felt that they had been robbed! They were gonna testify!"

16

"I believe that Tony Leyva is the Antichrist . . . straight from the very pits of hell!"

Dozens of young men and boys had been subpoenaed to Roanoke federal court to testify in criminal proceedings against the men who had sexually assaulted them. But now they were being told that their abusers had entered guilty pleas and that therefore their testimony would not be needed after all. For many people so subpoenaed to testify in court, this would be a blessing: However, for these young people it quickly became an emotional plunge the likes of which they had never experienced before.

After struggling through having to admit that it had happened to them in the first place, and then being questioned and evaluated and primed to testify repeatedly for a year, it seemed as though the floor had just been pulled out from under them. The young witnesses had been prodded into agreeing to testify by John Terry and other FBI agents; Jenny Montgomery, Morgan Scott, and other federal prosecutors; officers from various local law enforcement agencies; and even a government-provided psychiatrist. Most of these professionals honestly convinced the victims that by appearing in court and testifying against Leyva, Morris, and Herring, they would take their first giant step on their individual roads to healing. They were prepared. They were not afraid. They were no longer ashamed. And then the world they were prepared to face had been turned upside down on them.

As Assistant U.S. Attorney Jenny Montgomery had said, getting the evangelists to plead guilty and thereby avoid a trial and all the attendant possible legal pitfalls that can occur had been a prosecutorial decision and one that, in the abstract, had to be considered honestly. But these boys were straining at the bit to tell the public once and for all what had been done to them. Now they were not going to be allowed to get on the stand and do so. Truly, that would have been the best thing that could have happened to them at that point in their young lives.

However, looking at and listening to this crowd outside Judge Turk's courtroom reminded many of the victims' parents just how much their sons' lives had been destroyed by Tony Leyva and his ilk. Later, Patti Casey painfully reminisced about what Tony Leyva had done to her brother Stephen Cash, saying softly: "He's . . . a very troubled boy. Even today you can look into Stephen's eyes and, I tell you, there's nothing but pain, sorrow, and misery.

"Now he's in the James River Correctional Center [prison] for drugs, and I guess it's a blessing he's not here to see all this. You see, he got involved in drugs and alcohol which he said was to help him forget the instances that happened with him and Tony Leyva. His dad won't even talk to him.

"Tony Leyva hurt Stephen bad. He doesn't talk about it unless you really talk to him, you know. He's very quiet. Very withdrawn. Very sad. But he's got a very tender heart. . . . All of my brothers have. . . . But with what both Tony Leyva and [my husband] Jimmy Casey done to them, I don't know. All of that changed them all an awful lot. They'll never be the same, they won't. . . ." Her voice trailed off.

On the evening of October 12, 1988, I interviewed Patti Casey's son Mark, as well as Robert and Timothy Earls who, among them, had suffered over four hundred sexual assaults by Leyva, Morris, and Herring. It was with bitterness that Mark detailed his and his uncles' slide into sexual assaults by Tony Leyva. But Mark took great strength in his uncles, remarking after the plea bargains were entered: "Jonathan, James, and Stephen are three of the best uncles! . . . And now we're all talking about what happened to us with Tony Leyva."

Asked if they knew why Tony Leyva hadn't been charged in state court for the sexual assaults on Mark's uncles and the others, James Earls said: "See, there was some of 'em like Stephen and Jonathan that Tony done things to that they was supposed to bring charges up on him for, but by the time they learned about them, it was already too far into the case to bring up more charges, so they just used them—the guys like Jonathan—as witnesses."

All three young men were very candid in answering the question almost everyone asks when first hearing about the case: "How on earth could Tony Leyva get away with sexually molesting so many boys for twenty-one years?"

Remarked Robert Earls, "Due to a lot of things. First off, an awful lot of people loved and admired and respected Tony Leyva. He was like God to 'em. Ya know, 'Touch not mine anointed' and all that crap."

Mark added, "People said things about what he was doin', but nobody felt strongly that a man of God like him would do things like that to the point that they would even check up on it."

And Timothy remarked, "Everybody believed in Brother Tony . . . believed he was a man of God. And when bad things were said about what he was doing, they said it was Satan talking and they just dropped it. Nobody really cared to find out the truth.

"At first, they didn't think that it was a big enough case to get concerned about [because] it was just kids saying things about somebody as big and important as Tony was. They didn't want to touch him. Couldn't believe it was really happening."

"Nobody'd touch him," said Robert Earls, "not even the police or the sheriffs."

"In Roanoke City in 1983," Timothy added, commenting on the data that had been compiled, "they said they was gonna turn it over to the FBI. But the FBI never did anything about it till somebody from the sheriff's office in Salem reported it again last year [1987] and finally got the FBI to do somethin' about it. Me personally, I was always confused by it, why nobody wanted to believe it and why they didn't do nothin' about it for so long."

When the boys were asked how their abuse by the preachers had affected their spiritual life, Mark Crump took off running with great anger spilling in every direction: "Screwed that up! Since it all happened, I ain't picked up a Bible yet!

"I talked to Tony after he confessed, the day he confessed and he told me that he was sorry. Morris and Herring never did, though. He told me he was sorry, that he didn't understand how he was hurting anybody, that he really didn't understand that. But that's bullshit!

"I mean, he had to do it knowingly, and if he did it, he knew that . . . it was wrong 'cause he knows the Bible. He knew it was wrong but he kept on doing it over and over and over. All the time I was with him and he was doing that stuff to me and the other boys he'd work all the time. Monday through Sunday he'd be holding them revivals all around Georgia, Alabama, Mississippi, wherever, then at night he'd be doing sex with us.

"I think myself, they should castrate him and give him life 'cause with parole or something like that he'll get out and do it again. And I think they ought to have done the same thing with Ed Morris. Freddie Herring, too. And anybody else who claimed that they were Christians and believed in God and then went out and messed with kids 'cause they ain't gonna have to pay for it down here, they're gonna have to pay for it up there!

"I'm not really against God or anything like that, but I doubt I ever will go to church again. I think it's all a bunch of hogwash because if a Christian is supposed to be Christ-like, and if that's Christ-like then I . . ." At this point, tears came into Mark's eyes and he began to sob.

After regaining some of his composure, Mark continued: "If some man came up to me now and says 'I love you and I care about you,' I'd probably blow their head off! Fuck 'em! I mean, I looked up to Tony Leyva as a father like most everybody else did. He was somebody who really acted like he cared. Most of us didn't have a father and I believe that if I would have had parents there, with me, that I could count on, then it never woulda' happened.

"It wasn't just bad . . . it was worse than bad! I mean, it was . . . terrible! It's messed me up pretty well, mentally. It messed up everybody!" (Mark at this point admitted that he was taking antidepressants.)

"Anybody that has the guts to go out and molest children has the guts to spend the rest of their lives in prison. Even if they're not professing to be a Christian or anything like that, they're still hurting somebody and they deserve the same punishment.

"I mean, it worries me something terrible that I may turn out the same way. I mean, here I am, I had this whole thing going with Tony Leyva and them and then what if I turn around years later and molest other kids myself? It weighs heavy on my mind! I really doubt that I would do anything like that, but I can't tell you I'm not gonna do that. I wouldn't want to have kids and then molest them or sexually molest anybody else's kids 'cause it's been done to me! I couldn't live with it! I just couldn't! . . .

"But I can honestly say I hate all three of 'em 'cause, honestly, they messed up my life . . . and I can probably never forgive them for that. I mean, I may say it from my mouth, yeah . . . 'I forgive them.' But from my heart I know that I can't . . . It's something I guess that I will probably never forget. I can't get the details of what happened out of my head.

"But . . . what if nobody had said anything and I didn't say nothing? I know if I had a kid and Tony Leyva molested him and then my kid had to be in the same shape as me, I couldn't live with that. That's why I had to speak my piece about what they done, so people would know and try to protect their kids.

"I mean, I can relax with myself some now 'cause I talked about it . . . told people about it and showed that I didn't want it to happen to anybody else."

With Tony Leyva having been convicted in state court and having entered a guilty plea in federal court, Patti Casey said: "I have forgiven him. That doesn't mean that I set him free, but it means that I've set myself free.

"While the state trial was going on, on the last day, it looked pretty much in favor of Tony Leyva getting off. . . . Witnesses had actually gotten up there and lied on his behalf and denied for him . . . knowing what they knew—supposedly Christians themselves—then they lied.

"I'm just saying, the lies and stuff . . . it really looked bad on all of those who were innocently involved. When I was taking Mark to lunch that day he was very sincere. He looked at me and said, 'Mama, I got down on my knees last night and prayed for the first time since this thing started.'

"I said, 'Well, Mark, I think that's wonderful!'

"Then he looked at me and said, 'How could I ever believe in God again if he gets off of this? If he's found innocent, where's God?'

"And I see his point. What Tony Leyva and them did to Mark and the others physically is bad enough; but what they did to all of these boys spiritually and mentally, they actually destroyed these boys in those ways! They took away from them everything that was good!

"But I don't understand how it all continued for so many years. I wish I knew the answer! It also leaves a question in the mind of the children and I'll even say it for myself: Why did God permit this to go on for so many years?

Patti laid much of the blame for what happened on herself, for having married a man who gave her brothers and her own son no affection, which left them vulnerable to Brother Tony's advances. And she ended with a warning to other parents: "Regardless of who the person is, if anyone shows any unusual affection for your children like giving them money, wanting them to spend nights with them, staying with them, hugging them all the time, and especially wanting to be alone with them and anything else like that that sounds suspicious or unusual, then they should be very cautious and concerned about that.

"Parents should check out people who want to be around their children very, very carefully because I don't believe that a normal man would take a young child or a teenager and always be kissing and hugging them and buying things for them . . . taking them and spending money on them all the time for no real reason.

"I think parents should be very, very careful if they see anything like that because people don't usually take such an interest in children, and if they do, they usually do it in a way that helps the child and not in a way that does not look right. Here in Virginia it is very, very suspicious for a man to take a young boy that's not his and hug and kiss him like Tony Leyva did.

"However, after his services the people would all come up to him and he would hug everybody. It's just that he apparently got more out of hugging the boys than he did the others that attended. In fact, he made a comment to Jenny Montgomery that while he was preaching he would look out over the audience and spot boys and have a sexual desire for them. I mean, it's sick! It really is!

"If a Big Brother wants to help a boy to learn how to play baseball or something like, a friendly slap on the shoulder or a smile, a fun-type of thing to get them interested in it is okay. But all this hugging, this unusual extra closeness, I'd be very leery about it. I would be very, *very* suspicious if I saw that!"

† † †

After the federal plea bargain hearing, Mark Crump attempted suicide by overdosing on the Prozac that his doctor had prescribed for him. Strange, however, was the quantity of antidepressant pills he had on him.

Said Mark, "There was a bottle of two hundred and I took them all. . . . I was in the hospital for two days and then I went to Roanoke Memorial Rehab."

† † †

The oldest of Tony Leyva's identified victims who came forward to testify, Anthony Grooms, from North Carolina, had some interesting views of his perpetrator's conviction in Virginia state court: "Knowing the judicial system as I've come to know it . . . , I was surprised that he got as much as he did on the state level because some of the witnesses' testimony was credible and some of it was questionable. But I would have loved to see him get more time there in Salem!

"Randy Leach did a real good job. Randy told me that he had some of those kids that had been in trouble and that it was gonna be hard to convey it to the jury because Leyva had a good lawyer. And Harry Bosen was a good lawyer for Leyva, but then he referred to me in the closing arguments as the 'ghost of Christmas past.' . . . Randy just very quickly picked up on that and said, 'Well, I'm sure that Mr. Grooms would appreciate that title if Mr. Bosen wants to give that to him because the 'ghost of Christmas past' had a mission and that mission was to bring out the truth, and that is exactly what Anthony Grooms did!'

"You know, Bosen stuck his foot in his mouth on that one and Randy Leach shoved it right on down his own throat! Randy was very sharp and quick to use it for his own advantage . . . and that of those Leyva abused, too."

Even though he had to struggle to dredge up his own painful memories of childhood sexual abuse, Anthony acknowledged that he wanted to testify: "I wanted to believe that I had a hand in [Tony's] being convicted for what he done to all them boys."

And it is to his credit that he did so in spite of threats. Before he testified David said that he received an anonymous, threatening phone call: "It was a male. He said that I shouldn't go to Salem to testify. It was just that for my own safety he didn't think that I should go. I'm sure that he was tryin' to be disguised. It was a coarse, man's voice."*

☩ ☩ ☩

At her home in October 1988, Patti Casey described for me the frightening, threatening letter which she had received that August from Tony Leyva, just before his state trial. It was very similar to the letter which had been received by Martha Sharp.

"The letter came and my husband [Jimmy Casey] was sitting here on the couch reading it with me and I said, 'This is strange, Jimmy. He has not sent us any mail since this thing started happening over a year ago.' You see, we were put off his list when Mark come back and all that stuff started last fall.

"And he read it again and then he handed it to me and I read it again.

"Then he said, 'What's circled?'

"Then I looked again and I saw that Tony had circled 'I'll kill you.'

---

*Prior to the state court trial in Salem, Virginia, similar anonymous, threatening phone calls from a man with a similarly described voice were received by witnesses Darrell Wayne Sharp, Macalynn Embert, Mark Crump, and his mother, Patti Casey. And in 1989, after making known my intention to write this book, I received such a call as well.

And again later in another sentence he had circled, 'kill you.' Then on down further he had underlined 'right now.' And . . . it just loomed out at me . . . so then I called John Terry."

"The FBI got the letter," Patti told me. John Terry came over here and got it from me himself. The threats were all circled very boldly and [the FBI] had copies of it. It was written to 'My Beloved Enemy' and it was a form letter. But the envelope was addressed to me. And it had his signature on it: 'Brother Tony.'

But even though Patti gave the letter to the FBI, nowhere in the federal court records is there mention of it or its contents.

✝ ✝ ✝

During 1987 and the first half of 1988, as his ministry was collapsing, Brother Tony's friend and fellow preacher was the Rev. James R. Carter who, along with his wife, the Rev. Eunice Carter, pastored a small flock in Roanoke. Still unaware of Leyva's activities, both remained faithful supporters. During this time their small church became Brother Tony's occasional Roanoke venue during his "last days" out on the revival circuit before his State of Virginia and federal trials.

The Carters had known Tony Leyva for many years; however, Rev. James Carter had difficulty recalling exactly when he had first become acquainted with Brother Tony when I interviewed him in July 1993: "I heard about him prior to my ever seeing him and I just thought that he was a good, all around, Pentecostal-type person . . . a spirit-filled person that was trying to be as deep in the knowledge and Word of God as he could be and he was trying to explain to his generation of people and trying to get them toward the Lord as far as he could."

Regarding the end of Tony's ministry, James Carter said: "It got down to where the following wasn't all that great, as far as I was concerned. There wasn't half the people that was coming that originally come in years past. But there was always skeptics here. There are always people who come to pick up something to run their clapper about because this 'yak-yak' business had done got to where people began to get skeptical about Tony."

Then Rev. Carter said enigmatically, "With Tony, it's always been hard to get at the truth." But when asked what he meant by that, he would only respond, "You go figure it out!"

Rev. Carter blamed what he repeatedly called Tony Leyva's "problems" on what he considered to be the troubled teenage boys who followed his ministry around. "I think that maybe Tony wanted to be good to everybody and to all the people, but you can't do that all the time. So many of the kids [around Tony], their parents had married and remarried and you got your kids, my kids, and our kids. [laughs] And everybody else's!

"[And] especially if it's some [boys] that's got to have some type of alcohol or drugs, too many people have tried to be nice to them and have got hurt because they give 'em love. So many times these kids that are poor are young folks that run in gangs like wolves, and I didn't want to know nothing about 'em because they didn't seem like somebody that had any goodness or ability about them or wanted to do anything other than get something out of you for nothing. I don't have much time for people like that!

"I've *always* respected Tony's ministry and Tony and what he tried to do! But the things that come about here and other places, like down in Georgia someplace, a lot of people have apparently told stories about Tony.

"The things that come up about him seemed like they might have been drummed up, like some sort of conspiracy to kill his ministry . . . a bunch of people got together to do and say things to get him out of circulation. But I don't believe a word of what was said! I did not see anything in him to lead me to believe that Tony is anything other that what he said he was!"

When Tony was charged, Rev. Carter said, "I never did ask him anything about it because I didn't want him to think there was even the slightest doubt in my mind about the type of person he was. I didn't see any reason to believe that he did anything bad to them boys, although I do know that just like other ministers there were always a bunch of deadbeats that would follow them around just like they did Christ. There's always been that bunch waiting to get at the fishes and loaves and there always will be."

But by the time the state court jury went out to begin their deliberations Rev. Carter was fairly certain that Brother Tony would be convicted: "Well, sure, we done all we could [to help Tony], but then people can be very skeptic[al], they can be rude, they can be very hateful, they can be everything!"

And when the jury came back in with its guilty verdict, Carter said: "Some of his people didn't think he'd ever be convicted, [but] when it did happen they were in total shock from it happening and just at a dead end, so to speak.... The people that were supporters of his didn't have no money to go out and hire no big-time lawyers or nothin' and that case didn't run into no appeals or nothin'. The money wasn't there to do it with. These poor people don't have no money to hire no lawyers!"

When the subject of Tony's attorney, Harry F. Bosen, Jr., advising Tony to plead guilty on the federal charges came up, the Rev. Smith became extremely agitated: "Tony called me and told me he was gonna plead guilty 'cause that's what [Bosen] told him to do, and I wouldn't agree with him on it. . . .

"I think Mr. Bosen got his $20,000 [fee] too cheap! He turned faces on Tony in the end! I don't know whether Tony gave him all the money or not, but Bosen probably got teed off because he didn't get all his money, so then he turned around and, in other words, bit Tony in the backside and got him to plead guilty. If he didn't get it, I hope he don't ever get it!

"And those kids . . . I wouldn't believe a one of 'em! I don't want to blame the courts for it, but I think they tried to go too far toward those little criminals rather than toward the innocent Tony Leyva to try and drum up some kind of case against him. It was just this same ol' information about this child sexual abuse stuff and they just ran it in the ground!

"But I remember when Tony would go out to eat, he would always buy them kids food because he thought they were poor. He was just more or less trying to be a good Samaritan. But, like I say, the younger generation can be a bunch of little crooks! They get pretty well educated at it!

"Many a time I told [Tony] to get away from them kids, but I'm sure he had a lot of people giving him advice. And I guess a person in that position comes to the conclusion that everybody is trying to tell me what to do, and so I'll just have to play it by ear. And maybe again Tony just couldn't hear too well!"

Perhaps, the Rev. Carter felt, some of the blame should also be assigned to Freddie Herring and Ed Morris: "I had seen both of 'em, but as far as knowing anything about them, I don't know the lives they led or what kind of preachers they were. But I know that you can get around people like that and if they get into things, sometimes you get branded with the same iron. And that might have been what happened to Tony."

When Carter was told about Tony Leyva's brief flirtation with other questionable evangelists, he shot back: "That don't make him no outlaw!" Then he put an interesting spin on Leyva's contacts with them: "Well if back there in the '80s [Tony] even knew that they were in some trouble it was [Tony's] duty to go to them and try to straighten them out. . . . I know that if somebody saw Tony with them and put two and two together, then they'd come up with four. [laughs] But you can hear anything! And so, I don't put any stock in that. If I don't see something myself, then forget it!"

✝ ✝ ✝

There was, however, something still gnawing on Patti Casey, something that she felt had not been resolved: "They asked Tony Leyva about his pornographic pictures in court and he said that he destroyed them because he didn't want to hurt anybody of Christ anymore. Well, all I know is that my brother Jonathan was extremely disturbed when he saw them [when he discovered Leyva's cache of child pornography].

"Jonathan wouldn't tell me all the contents of that box, but he did say that if someone would have seen them that Tony Leyva could have gone to the electric chair. And that made me believe that Tony could have killed someone . . . could have killed a boy!

"In the Bible it says that the Antichrist will display his love and there will be such a flowing of love that you will be deceived into thinking that this has got to be God. Well, I believe that Tony Leyva *is* the Antichrist! I believe he is straight from the very pits of hell! I really do! I believe he has the power of Satan to give a counterfeit love, to show that people would really feel this and sense this because he has it in him that he is a god. A false god if ever there was one!

"I believe that Tony Leyva has blasphemed the Holy Ghost over and over and I don't think that he can ever be redeemed and used again. For one thing, he said that the Devil brought this whole thing upon him. And he said that God caused it all to happen for his glory. Well, I know God and God doesn't work that way. Not my God. In fact, in my opinion, I don't believe that Tony Leyva has *ever* been with God!"

17

*"He probably asked for it . . .
most of those boys did."*

On Sunday, January 29, 1989, Mark Crump was still struggling mightily to deal with the emotional turmoil of the repeated sexual assaults by Tony Leyva as well as the deep anxiety that coming forward and testifying about them caused him. Frequently going from pillar to post and back again, by the time that night rolled around Mark had been staying with his mother for a couple of weeks. Patti Casey had moved out of the house she shared with Jimmy Casey after Jimmy refused to let Mark come back home to live with them. She was now living in an apartment in Vinton, Virginia. "I come home that night so tired out that I just went to bed and went to sleep," Mark recalled through several beers. "I woke up the next morning when I heard three gun shots and I jumped out of my bed and ran towards the living room 'cause that's where it sounded like it was coming from. At first I didn't know what was happening, but pretty quick I thought of Jimmy 'cause he'd been calling Mama and saying he was gonna kill her. Mama had told me this and we'd all heard it. . . . Stephen, Jonathan, me.

"We knew that he could do it, too, 'cause he always went around with a gun. So I was careful when I heard them shots, okay, 'cause I thought of Jimmy and that he might be in Mama's apartment.

"I was real careful going through the kitchen and hid behind the counter so nobody would see me. But when I peeked in the mirror I seen Jimmy Casey going out the front door. And there was my mama lyin' on the floor. Jimmy had killed Mama . . . shot her dead with this big pistol that he carried with him."

The next day, January 31, the *Roanoke Times & World News* ran an article on the murder, which began: "Vinton police still are searching for the estranged husband of a thirty-five-year-old woman who was shot to death in her Mansard Square apartment early Monday morning.

"Patricia L. Casey died of multiple gunshot wounds, said Dr. David Oxley, deputy chief medical examiner for Western Virginia. Casey was shot twice in the head and once in the chest, Oxley said.

"Police are looking for Casey's estranged husband, Jimmy F. Casey, forty-one, of Roanoke County. Casey, who will be charged with murder and using a firearm in the commission of murder, is believed to be driving a rose-color Chevrolet that he rented Monday morning before Patricia Casey was killed."

Continuing his own account of his mother's death, Mark said: "See, Jimmy'd been saying he was gonna kill Mama for a long time 'cause she left him. But then Tony Leyva wrote these letters to him from prison and told him to 'take care of Patti.'

"When [the Vinton police] took me down to the . . . station a policeman said that Tony Leyva wrote to Mama and to Jimmy about 'touch not mine anointed and do my prophets no harm' and they thought that Tony Leyva might've had something to do with getting Jimmy riled up at her enough to go and kill her. . . .

"He didn't show the letter to me, but they showed it to my uncle Stephen. . . . Tony Leyva had sent it to Jimmy from prison down in North Carolina where they had him locked up. Stephen said that Tony Leyva had wrote to Jimmy saying that he wanted Jimmy to 'do something about Patti' . . . that he ought to kill her . . . because she 'destroyed my ministry.' And Stephen said that Tony Leyva wrote how he was real upset that my mother was the cause of all this stuff coming down on him . . . her getting behind all these detectives and the FBI and causing him to go to prison."

Detective Hudson recalls having taken those letters as evidence during his execution of a search warrant at Jimmy's house on Burlington Drive in northwest Roanoke following the murder. He said that he does not know what happened to them after he turned them over to Vinton Police, in whose jurisdiction the crime had occurred.

On February 4, 1989, Jimmy Casey was arrested by the FBI at a motel in Randolph County, North Carolina. He voluntarily confessed to the agents who arrested him that he murdered his wife, waived extradition, and was returned to Roanoke and housed in the Roanoke County Jail.

Chapter 17

When Mark was interviewed on March 27, 1989, he said that Jimmy had already had his court appearance. "Me and my uncles were there. If we could've got to him then, we'd have killed him then and there! He's done pled guilty. He told the FBI that he killed Mama when they arrested him down in North Carolina. Some of his people called the cops and told them where he was.

"He had a whole bunch of money on him when they arrested him. I heard it was something like ten thousand dollars in cash. I don't know for sure, but I think, maybe Mike Page gave it to him for killing my mama for Tony Leyva. That's what me and my brothers think, 'cause of all them letters Tony Leyva sent to Jimmy saying 'You got to do something about Patti . . . she destroyed my ministry.' And I heard he'd gone to Mexico, too. The Vinton Police told me all about it."

Assistant Attorney Randy Leach, who asked to be assigned to the Casey case, remarked, "As I recall, . . . the FBI people actually obtained a confession from him in North Carolina when he was arrested and that was part of the evidence that we used against him."

After Jimmy shot Patti, Detective Hudson indicated that the Roanoke County Sheriff's Department was looking for Mike Page: "We were hot on him because he was . . . Jimmy's only friend in the world. So, with what Mark is saying about Mike Page, let me put it this way: It would not surprise me one iota! Number one, it wouldn't have taken much to put Jimmy over the edge anyway. He was already supremely pissed off at Patti, so all he needed was another little push. And I'm sure Tony Leyva knew that Patti had left Jimmy. I'm sure he knew that! So, I'm sure another little wedge stuck in there would have pushed him over the edge. No problem!"

When Hudson was asked why Randy Leach would not give credence to this scenario, Hudson replied: "I know that we were looking at it at the time . . . looking at that connection. See, I didn't investigate that, but I know the homicide investigators at that time thought about that. I'm sure they interviewed Jimmy at length. I definitely wanted to talk with him, but I thought better of it because it wouldn't have been real nice since it wasn't my case. It was homicide's case and investigating homicides was not my job.

"So, I'm certainly not going to sit here and discount that [scenario] or even the possibility of it. I'm not saying I know any connection as absolute fact, but it certainly went through my head!"

The Reverend James R. Carter, was also acquainted with Mark Crump, as well as Patti and Jimmy Casey, about whom he said: "Well, I knew

Jimmy for a brief period of time . . . maybe for a couple of years off and on. He was one of these type people that in public wanted to be seen. He wanted to try and impress people. And what I'm trying to say is, much of the time he pushed it too far. He would get out on a limb as far as his intellect was concerned. [laughs] And he would fall on his face because anybody that knew him could see through him just like a screen door.

"His wife was a very sweet woman. She was a very, very nice girl. And it was a pity that he got so bent out of shape with his thinking and all that he did such a cruel thing. . . . It was just stupidity in the first degree!"

After Jimmy Casey had been jailed, Mark and his uncles began the sad task of cleaning out Patti's home. It was there where, in addition to the letters from Tony, Garrick Hudson found a collection of greeting cards—"one for each day for Jimmy to send to Patti right up through Valentine's Day."

As they worked, they discovered a grim reminder of the never fully understood—even to this day—relationship between Brother Tony Leyva and Jimmy Casey, the certificate making Jimmy a minister in Tony's church:

> This is to certify that Jimmy Casey of Roanoke, State of Virginia, upon the recommendation of ministers, is hereby recognized as an ordained minister in good standing with the Tony Leyva, Evangelistic Association, Inc., Ministerial Fellowship, with full authority to perform all ordinances of the church, with the approval of the Board of Directors of said Ministerial Fellowship.
>
> PRESIDENT [signed] Rev. Tony Leyva

Mark recalled, ". . . After he got locked up Tony Leyva even sent Jimmy his sterling silver praying hands that he wore on a chain around his neck . . . I seen Jimmy wearing 'em at my grandpa's funeral soon after Tony Leyva and them went into prison.

"I know they were the same ones that Brother Tony used to wear 'cause I know what they looked like. I seen them around Tony Leyva's neck lots of times: At his revival services, when I traveled with him, and when I stayed with him and he had sex with me in bed. Tony *always* wore them!"

This was solidly confirmed by Detective Hudson: "Yeah, I remember all of that quite well and I'm not gonna cover things up because I think that the facts should be out there for people to know."

"When Jimmy Casey was still on the run, . . ." Hudson continued, "Mark stayed with me for a good while. I got him a bullet-proof vest from the SWAT team out here. It was a pretty scary time! I know that Jimmy Casey was obsessed with Patti, period. Then you add to that the fact that Jimmy never accepted the fact that Tony Leyva sexually abused Mark . . . never did really believe that that had happened. And then the fact that he was a pervert himself. Jimmy Casey had sexually molested children and been convicted of sexually assaulting one little girl and—maybe I'm just going out in left field—but maybe he had participated in that sort of thing himself with Leyva. Just to talk to him, Jimmy Casey was a weird, weird person!"

✝ ✝ ✝

Leyva's attorney, Harry Bosen, was asked about Jimmy Casey's murdering his wife, perhaps at the request of his client. Bosen acknowledged having heard about Tony sending Jimmy Casey his praying hands from prison, writing letters to Jimmy suggesting that he "take care of" Patti, Jimmy's brief flight to Mexico, and his having thousands of dollars in cash on him when he was arrested, but with this proviso: "I think you ought to talk to Page about all that. He was the one [that] controlled Tony!*

"Let me tell you something. There was a follower of Tony Leyva's in Franklin County, a schoolteacher. . . . She even contributed some money towards Tony's foundation or church or whatever it is. She had attended all of his local meetings. She supported him right up to the end of his trials. . . . A very nice lady in her early thirties.

"After Tony's convictions she inherited something in the order of half a million to three-quarters of a million dollars. Guess who divorced his wife and married her and now lives with her in Franklin County, Virginia? Mr. Page!

"Financially, Page was the culprit in this whole thing."

✝ ✝ ✝

Randy Leach knew nothing about Tony Leyva's letter to Jimmy Casey or the praying hands: "If it happens after he's in jail, I'm not entitled to know what he sends or gets in the mail and all that. I wasn't aware of all that stuff.

"I mean, we had Jimmy Casey. Basically, we had every bit of evidence we needed [to convict him of murder] forty-five minutes after the crime was committed. I never heard that he and Leyva were communicating in any way.

---

*Numerous, unsuccessful attempts were made to speak with Mike Page. He refused to make any comments or statements one way or the other.

"I do know when he came and sat at his sentencing and all that stuff that he was wearing a T-shirt saying that 'Jesus saves' or 'Jesus loves' or something like that. But I never knew that there was a connection [between Leyva and Casey].

"We pretty much were able to determine the motive was that Jimmy Casey was pretty upset that Patti Casey had left him and she was not gonna take him back . . . he was very upset with that and had told several people that. That was as far as we could determine the motive.

"Once we had got him he had already made a couple of statements, one to the FBI and one to the Vinton Police Department talking about what he had done. But, you know, other than 'she left me, I wanted her back,' . . . he never did discuss anything else. The investigation was open and shut. He was guilty.

"What we heard from the people at Jimmy's place of work was that he . . . worked the third shift and he took the morning off, or left early. He just made comments that he was gonna go take care of things. There was never any comment about Leyva or any connections that we knew of. I mean, it never came up."

Concerning the rumors that Jimmy fled to Mexico immediately after the murder, Randy said: "Well, there was a lot of speculation of that. We think that he did, but we don't know. . . . There were an awful lot of miles on the rental car that he had . . . we think that's where he went, but we can't swear to it.

"By the time we got him he was back in North Carolina and had gone back to some family's house—a sister or a brother or somebody like that—they called the FBI, and said, 'He's here. Come get him.'"

Roanoke attorney Neil McNally was appointed to defend Casey by Kenneth Trabue, the same judge who had presided over Tony Leyva's Virginia case, and who heard the case against Jimmy. Remarked McNally, "You know, in spite of his confessions, I had taken the approach that we were going to go ahead and go to trial, like I would in any case. I had gone forward with my discoveries and everything else, and none of those particular items about letters and cash came up.

"That would have stuck in my mind, but I don't specifically remember anything because it was the FBI that picked him up. But I just don't remember anything about the cash. All I know is that Jimmy had said that he had had trouble with the boys and that they were tied in with Leyva. And that was really about all that we got into on the Leyva side of the thing."

McNally confirmed that Jimmy did indeed flee to Mexico, "I don't remember where he went in Mexico, but I think that he just kept driving, and he got into Mexico and got scared and came back...."

And even though there are today various conjectures about why Jimmy fled to Mexico and where he got the money, McNally feels that, "You have to understand that the perspective at the time was more of a murderer on the run as opposed to anything else or involving anyone else. The other stuff didn't come out until later.

"[At the time] it was an inexperienced person who is not a world traveler or anything else and he's gonna get scared in another country. In essence he sneaks across the border without passports or any other kind of papers, and he's in a country where your driver's license just doesn't cut it and he gets out. And I think that's what got him scared and so he got back into Texas."

✝ ✝ ✝

On Tuesday, March 21, 1989, FBI Agent John Terry told the *Roanoke Times & World News* staff writer Doug Pardue that the search for additional preachers in Georgia, Florida, and a couple of other Southern states, with whom Leyva, Morris, and Herring had shared boys sexually, was at an end. "It's pretty much all over ... except for the sentencing," is the way Terry—"a federal investigator involved in the case"—put it. When Pardue's article appeared the next day, its content was pretty well summed up with the succinct headline "Boy-Sex Probe Halted." According to Pardue, the federal investigator "said agents were unable to get enough information, other than initials or partial names, to identify the other ministers linked to the three Georgia preachers' interstate homosexual ring."

But more than a dozen of the over thirty boys who had been victimized and were on the federal witness list—not to mention several of their parents—pointedly told me a different story, including giving me full names and home towns of preachers with whom they had been coerced into having sex.

Although he was only one of many to tell similar stories, Mark Crump said: "One of the preachers involved sexually with me and some of the other boys was Bobby Ray Hopkins. He traveled with Tony Leyva some and Tony introduced me to him. He started feelin' around on me just like Tony Leyva done [then] he had sex with me a couple of times ... went down on me, did blow jobs on me, just like Tony Leyva done. It was at Tony Leyva's and Ed Morris's apartment in Marietta, Georgia. I told John Terry all about it."

Several of the boys felt that they were dealt a major blow when authorities in other states decided not to bring additional charges against Leyva, Morris, and Herring.

I am particularly aware of this, for when I was in Columbus, Georgia, with Jason Embert researching this book I took Jason with me to meet a Columbus police detective. The man interviewed Jason privately and then went to see his chief to try and get him to authorize an investigation into not only repeated sexual assaults on Jason by Tony Leyva, but the assaults on other boys by Leyva, Herring, Morris, and any other ministers against whom supporting evidence could be gathered. However, this angered the chief, and when the detective got back to me he said that his efforts almost got him fired.

When Ann Martin was asked her view of the FBI's refusal to further investigate additional preachers, she flatly stated: "They should have gone further. They should have worked the case completely. I never thought that they had done everything they could do. We were well aware that there were other preachers who had abused the boys since our victims had given that to us and we had given it to the FBI . . . everything we knew including information on the other victims and abusers and jurisdictions we gave to them. They talked about having other agents go out in other places and interview, but they never told us the results.

"They never made any indication that they were going to take care of it completely. Our particular take was that we were aware of other information about other perpetrators and other places in other states, but that was up to the FBI. We just did the basic group [of victims] here in Roanoke."

According to Darrell Wayne Sharp, "Tony knew a lot of people. I mean he knew a *lot* of people! And I'm talking about it didn't matter where he went. It all got to me because it was like just every person I ran into when I was with Tony was Tony's friend. [A]fter about a half hour talking to them—they got to talking about sex with men and boys and stuff and they always knew where the gay places were.

"Besides the basic three [Leyva, Morris, and Herring] doing stuff with the boys, there were others: There was another guy in Georgia. The guy was a preacher. He used to bring us boys hundreds of these coins to play his [video] games and he would take whoever was off that day to play his video games.

"And I can remember that when I was down with the tent there were two other people, one a minister by the name of Bobby Ray Hopkins. He was involved sexually with some of the boys, that crooked S.O.B. Excuse me.

"Others of the boys told me that he had sex with them. And one time he told me he was gonna get me, too, but I just said, 'You're fuckin' crazy!' and kept him from doing it to me, but he tried. And he done it to others that I know. They told me!"

✝ ✝ ✝

Compared with October 11, 1988, when guilty pleas were accepted from Tony Leyva, Ed Morris, and Freddie Herring, the trio's formal sentencing on March 27, 1989, proved anticlimactic. Due to federal prosecutors' failure to keep their word and bring back the victims to testify at last, only a handful of the witnesses were present. And this time the three pederasts did not enter the courtroom through the front door. They were led handcuffed and dressed in jail uniforms through the back entrance.

Once the proceedings began it was an uncharacteristically seething Judge James C. Turk who presided. As one by one the evangelists took the stand and reprised their October 1988 confessions, Judge Turk—a Baptist Sunday school teacher—repeatedly interrupted them with scathing comments.

For the record, on the stand Tony Leyva admitted sexually assaulting "at least one hundred boys" and sharing many of the boys with other pederast preachers during his more than twenty years of traveling with his tent revivals throughout the Southeast and Midwest.

At one point Turk said to Tony Leyva, "What troubles me is you had such power over certain groups of people who still are backing you. I think while you're in prison you ought to write to those people and tell them you have sinned!" Turk additionally remarked that he had received "dozens of letters and petitions" from Leyva's supporters saying that they still considered him innocent.*

And at still another point during Leyva's testimony, Turk angrily remarked, "I don't believe there's any remorse in you! Anybody who's ever heard you ought to get up here and kick you good!" At that the small group of Leyva's victims, victims' family members, and their friends erupted in cheers and applause.

Three psychologists who had examined them at the Federal Correctional Institute (FCI) in Butner, North Carolina, during the five months prior to their formal sentencing, said there was little chance that the three

---

*Indeed, ubiquitous supporter Margaret Weiss (who attended virtually all of the court proceedings) shouted after the sentencing "Yes, he's innocent! Yes!" as she pushed television cameras out of her and Leyva's mother's way.

evangelists could be rehabilitated and that they would pose a risk to society if released.

According to the court testimony of one of the three psychologists, Edward Landis, Tony Leyva was not only a pedophile, but suffered from narcissistic personality disorder. This, he went on to explain, contributed to Leyva's need for adulation and admiration from others and made it difficult for him to accept responsibility for his own behavior. Leyva believed he was "very special, uniquely important," Landis said.

Landis further reported that Tony Leyva felt sorry for sexually assaulting only about half of his victims and in those cases only because they looked up to him as a minister and father figure. The other half he held responsible for what he had done to them and considered *himself* to have been their victim.

Indeed, during the proceedings U.S. Attorney Jenny Montgomery introduced a letter Tony Leyva had written from prison in North Carolina on March 13, in which he continued to hold himself up as "God's anointed prophet" and had this to say about Patti Casey's murder: "The woman responsible for all these allegations and charges against me was shot and killed by her husband the other day." Leyva then went on to express his feeling that Patti's death was God's punishment for her because she was the one who caused the first charges to be brought against him, reminding the letter's recipient of his favorite Bible verse, "Touch not mine anointed."

When Leyva testified about the letter he said that he did not mean to imply that Patti Casey had been punished, but rather that "I felt there was a danger of anybody coming against God's anointed." When asked if he still believed he was one of God's chosen, he replied, "I feel I am, even though I have made my mistakes."

When Ed Morris testified he pled for mercy, saying his homosexual desire had destroyed his life. "For a few moments of sexual pleasure, I don't think it is worth the things I've lost."

"We're not punishing you for being a homosexual," Turk interrupted. He told Morris he was being sentenced for sexually molesting children. "Don't you understand the difference between a pedophile and a homosexual?" Turk asked him.

Morris responded with, "I don't know that I've ever molested a child that was under fourteen or fifteen."

Then when Freddie Herring took the stand to testify about his oral and anal sexual assaults on the teenage boys who flocked to Tony Leyva's ministry, his attorney, John Swearingen, asked him, "Reverend Herring, have you licked your problem?"

Without pause but with a straight face Herring replied, "Yes, sir, I have. I'm sure that I really have."

And during his statement to the court on his client's behalf, Swearingen pointed to his twelve-year-old son sitting in the front row. The reason he had brought the boy with him from Columbus, Georgia, now became apparent. Said Swearingen: "Why, I'd even trust my own little boy here with Reverend Herring!"

When Judge Turk asked Tony Leyva if he had anything further to say before he passed sentence, the evangelist replied: "I'd like to reiterate that I'm truly sorry. I'm sorry for the people I hurt. I'm sorry for the God I hurt." Then he added disingenuously, "I hope the Lord will give me the opportunity to vindicate my ministry."

But Judge Turk refused to buy any of it: "All of you, you're con artists, liars, cheats, frauds . . . you're just everything bad . . . bad to the core!" He sentenced self-described "Super Christian" Mario Ivan "Tony" Leyva (then forty-two) to twenty years in federal prison; Rias Edward Morris (then forty-seven) received fifteen years in federal prison; and Freddie M. Herring (then fifty) received twelve years in federal prison. Each of the three ministers was also ordered to pay a fine of ten thousand dollars.

After Turk had finished sentencing the trio he told them, "You've blackened the eye of religion and I pray that you never get to use it again!"

But federal prison officials from the FCI reported that all three ministers had continued their preaching almost from the day they had arrived.

The May 28, 1989 *Roanoke Times & World News* article's spin on the sentencing read: "Turk customarily steps down from the bench after sentencing criminals, shakes their hands and wishes them good luck. This time, he waited for Leyva, Morris and Herring to be led off to jail before leaving the bench to shake the attorneys' hands."

Many victims found some solace in the fact that the trio were going to prison, but at the same time they were as upset as was Judge Turk that the plea bargains worked out with Assistant U.S. Attorneys Jenny Montgomery and Scott Morgan the previous October had not allowed him to sentence them to yet more time in prison. But Judge Turk did take the unusual step of recommending to the U.S. Bureau of Prisons that all three be required to serve their full sentences without the opportunity of parole.

In Leyva's case, if he were to be paroled when he first became eligible he would have to serve just five years. If parole were denied, and—as do most pedophiles in prison—he received full credit for good behavior, he would serve eleven years before being released to serve his two and one-half year Virginia prison sentence (which he could not serve concurrently). Morris and Herring would have to serve a little over three years each before being eligible for parole, if it were granted.

"But," reported the *Roanoke Times & World News*, "Mike Duncan, the federal probation officer in Roanoke handling the Leyva case, said Turk's recommendation, combined with the tendency of child molesters to repeat their crimes, could add a few years to the time the three men have to serve.

"He said he wants the three to serve their full sentences because child molesters have a high rate of repeat crime. The rate is so high, in fact, that one psychiatrist testified that the best way to protect society from child molesters is through chemical or surgical castration.

"Dr. William G. Gray said that counseling doesn't work for child molesters. He said he has treated about one hundred pedophiles and never been successful."

✝ ✝ ✝

After the federal case was closed "Brad"—the boy who first revealed Tony Leyva's pimping of him and other boys to "government men"—was pointedly questioned by me in April 1993, about these incredible incidents. Why had he never told John Terry or Garrick Hudson about these events? He responded: " 'Cause I thought they'd get mad at me, them being government men, too."

Brad was asked why—especially when he didn't even know them—he had had sex with these "government men" at Tony's request. "Well, they was friends of Tony Leyva's and he said that they were okay and that we needed to go with them to help protect his ministry.

"Back then Tony had me thinking that what he was doing was okay. You know, he was a preacher and a prophet of God and all. And I thought that I needed to do this for him. But I know now that it was wrong . . . it was *all* wrong."

Lastly, when asked if he didn't find these episodes very, very strange, Brad responded, "Yeah, but everything about Tony Leyva is strange!"

When Hudson was told about Brad and the other boys' virtually identical stories about being required to engage in sex with "government men," he was surprised neither by the boys' stories nor by federal authorities' failure to investigate them: "Well, they're [the 'government men'] definitely going to cover for themselves."

✝ ✝ ✝

Asked her opinion about the length of the sentences that the evangelists received, Ann Martin replied: "On the federal level, in my opinion they didn't get enough time! No!" When asked if the trio should have been taken to trial rather than having their guilty pleas accepted, Ann said, "Well, that's hard to say because of my knowledge of the system, now that I work for the federal government [as a parole officer since 1991]. I do know that what they got was pretty standard. And the way they handled the plea bargain, that was not unusual. But if they had gone before Judge Turk in a trial, you know, you beat or abuse your mother, your wife, or children, Judge Turk does not care for that at all!"

† † †

At the time of the formal sentencing of Leyva, Morris, and Herring, Mark Crump was still very visibly mourning his mother's murder. He had been kicked out of his living accommodations and refused outpatient services by Dr. Gray. However, Mark said that he still had plenty of Elavil [antidepressant pills] left and that he was continuing to take them.

Mark washed down his pills with cans of beer from his daily six-pack allocation. "I know I got to calm down," he agitatedly said as he nursed a fresh can, " 'cause that's what my psychiatrist told me. He gave me some pills that are supposed to calm me down. But Jimmy's in jail now and if me and my uncles ever get ahold of him, we're gonna kill him! He shot my mother to death in cold blood! I just want to take his head off his shoulders."

When he was admonished about mixing the beer and pills he sighed and said, "I know, I know, but with all that's been happening to me, I can't help it.

"I know I need help, but I can't go back to my psychiatrist 'cause he kicked me out. I was living with him after I got out of Roanoke Memorial Rehab for trying to kill myself when I OD'ed on them pills. He [Gray] took me off the Prozac and put me on this Elavil, but I can still get high with 'em if I want to. Nowadays, I talk to my girlfriend. She knows what's going on. I told her everything. If it wasn't for her, I don't know what would've happened to me."*

---

*Sadly, the relationship did not last for long. According to Garrick Hudson: "Poor thing, soon after [Mark's] mother was killed, his natural father killed his wife and was locked up, so, you know, there wasn't a whole lot of family members left to try and help him keep it together."

✝ ✝ ✝

On May 9, 1989, an extremely emotional, constantly sobbing Jimmy Casey appeared before Judge Trabue to plead guilty to killing his estranged wife, Patti Casey. According to the *Roanoke Times & World News*, when Jimmy was sentenced for the murder on July 11 he sobbed and told the judge, "that he didn't want to live with himself because of what he had done. 'It's like anguish, torture inside. It hurts so bad . . . I'm not worthy to receive what I'm going to ask, but if I have to live with this torture and remorse, please have mercy on me." Judge Trabue then sentenced Jimmy Casey to a prison term of life plus two years.

On Sunday night, September 17, 1989, Jimmy Casey used a torn bed sheet to hang himself in his cell at the Roanoke County Jail in Salem, Virginia. According to County Sheriff Mike Kavanaugh, Casey left a suicide note saying that he had passed sentence on himself and imposed the death penalty.

In a September 18 *Roanoke Times & World News* article on Jimmy Casey's suicide, Sheriff Kavanaugh said, "Casey had written to quite a few of the national evangelists asking if he committed suicide would Jesus accept him into heaven." But the sheriff wasn't sure if he had received any responses.

Commented prosecutor Randy Leach: "Jimmy just came in, pled guilty, and got life plus two years. He probably would have been eligible [for parole] after about fifteen years, but he hung himself in the jail."

As Leach summed up the murder case against Jimmy Casey: "Jimmy kind of weirded out on us at the end in the courtroom. He had his hands over his ears. Sitting there in the courtroom at his guilty plea he wouldn't take his hands off of his ears. He was wearing that T-shirt that said 'Jesus Loves Me' or 'Jesus Saves' . . . whatever. And he wouldn't listen to my summary of the evidence and that kind of pissed me off.

"I really felt like that if you've got the guts to kill somebody you ought to a least listen to what you did! And the judge couldn't say anything to him. He's just sitting there. He wasn't doing anything out of the ordinary, he just wouldn't listen!"

✝ ✝ ✝

During the week following the formal federal sentencing of Leyva, Morris, and Herring in Roanoke, Virginia, Jason Embert traveled with me to

Columbus, Georgia. There we toured Leyva's former Bible College, spoke with local police about what had gone on there, and went to the new facility of the North Highlands Assembly of God Church to speak with one of the ministers there. Indignantly, this man made the following comments:

"I don't trust *any* writers! I don't know what your credentials are, but Tony Leyva has been reported in the press to be associated with the Assemblies of God and he is not!" I offered to show my credentials, but looking at them he spat, "I don't know whether they're forged or not!"

When I brought up the subject of healing for Jason and the other boys who had been assaulted, the minister had this response, "I don't care whether he gets healed or not! It's not my concern that this young man get's healed, Mr. Echols. He probably asked for it . . . most of those boys did!"

18

"I think he's where he belongs now 'cause he's hurt so many people in the name of God."

The only one-on-one interview Tony Leyva ever permitted me took place in the Roanoke City Jail the morning of Tuesday, March 28, 1989, the day after Judge Turk formally sentenced him to twenty years in federal prison. In this extremely strange exchange, Brother Tony claimed that it had not been he who had sexually assaulted the boys but, rather, "Satan, entered my body and did it! It wasn't really me doing it! It was Satan that used me to do it! But God came to me in my cell last night and told me that He is going to turn this whole thing around. God said He's gonna send me back out to preach and use my life as an example to people about how Satan can mess up your life and how God can come in then and straighten it out!"

When asked why he pled guilty in open court, Tony responded: "Well, it was probably just God talking at the time and I don't understand it myself. Whatever I said then, it must have been God talking 'cause last night I turned my whole life over to God and any utterances that come out of my mouth in court come from God. He said them, not me!"

When Tony's friend the Reverend James R. Carter heard this disingenuous alibi for having sexually assaulted the boys, he sputtered: "This is getting rotten to the core! Jesus! I'll tell Tony to his face that that don't make no sense! . . . That's all double talk! It sounds like he turned his story around! That don't say nothin' about obeying the Word of God! . . . God don't do that kind of badness! No way!"

Chapter 18

✝ ✝ ✝

Since that day Tony Leyva has failed to respond to more than a dozen of my requests for an interview. Likewise Leyva's mother, Ada; Ed Morris; and Freddie Herring have steadfastly refused all of my interview requests.*

I did learn that in 1992, under her son's direction, Ada Leyva had begun managing and operating from her home in Hendersonville, North Carolina, a reincarnation of her son's "free world" ministry, renaming it the Miracle Revival Fellowship, International.

Filled with a combination of sermons, Bible study, and teachings written by "M. I. Leyva"—as Brother Tony now calls himself, using the initials of his real name, Mario Ivan—the ministry's newsletter, *Eschatology Digest*† is written by Tony from prison. He then mails it to Ada who claims to make several thousand copies—adding a prominent request "to help keep this ministry up by sending in money"—and then mails them to his remaining followers as well as to new believers who have just learned about—as Ada represents her son—this "ambassador for Christ who is held in bondage by the government."

With this knowledge I could not resist attempting to draw both Ada and Brother Tony out by using the guise of a fictitious "concerned Pentecostal preacher" at the other end of the country, a brother who had just learned about Tony Leyva's "sad, terrible travail in prison." Mother and son bought this hook, line, and sinker.

On the morning of July 20, 1992, assuming the carefully arranged guise of one "Brother Jimmy Ray Martin," a "Pentecostal preacher with a small church near Portland, Oregon," phoned Ada at her Leyva's Uniform Shop in the Four Seasons Mall in Hendersonville and spent over an hour talking with her on the phone.

Ada was thrilled to learn of Brother Martin's "concern and genuine interest" in her son's situation. She promised to send him some of Tony's religious writings and even encouraged this new-found supporter to write to her son in prison. I did. And then, I wrote to Ada. And both of them wrote

---

*Following his federal plea bargain hearing on October 11, 1988, Freddie Herring spoke briefly with me in the outer office of the U.S. Attorney's office in Roanoke. He agreed to an interview, "once I get to Butner [federal prison]." But a short time later he wrote that his attorney had told him to decline all interview requests.

†*American Heritage Dictionary* defines "eschatology" as "the branch of theology that is concerned with the ultimate or last things, such as death, judgment, heaven, and hell."

back. Ada sent Brother Martin one of the monthly issues of their ministry's publication.

Ada's first letter was a charmer and very enlightening.

July 24, 1992

Dear Brother Martin,

Trust things are going well with you. By faith all is well here.

Referring to our discussion Monday, I decided due to the fact that you really do not *know* my son that it would not be right to expect you to write concerning him. But you and your congregation please *pray* for him. *God* knows his love for *Him* and his dedication. He (*God*) knows all the details and can direct you all just how to pray—His one desire is to get on with his life and ministry.

Please pray too that the author who wuld [sic] put finances above the dignity and welfare of someone who only wants to do good would be stopped and realize he could cause a death—or miserable life not only of my precious son—but a great hurt to a family of parents, sisters, and a brother—not to speak of the hundreds—even thousands who have known him for thirty-odd years—and love & respect him very much. I often get letters from people who long to have him out, ministering to them in the power & anointing of the Holy Ghost. And that is his number-one desire. He has preached since he was twelve years old.

It is always good to know that there is a people (God's people) who truly know what real godly love is and will hold you up in prayer. I believe in *PRAYER* and feel not enough is known about the subject and therefore [people] cannot—*do not*—pray effectively. This has been a great concern of mine for years and God has given me a real burden to teach on this marvelous subject.

Thank you so very much—and thank your people for their prayers & love.

Sincerely,
and God bless you
[signed] A. E. Leyva

Four days later I received my first and only letter from Brother Tony himself, then serving his sentence at the Texarkana Federal Correctional Facility.

7/27/92

God Bless you, Bro. Martin:

Greetings, blessings and peace to you and yours in the matchless name of our Lord and Savior, Jesus Christ. I trust this letter finds all well and happy in Him.

As for me, by faith, "... it is well." (II Kings 4:26B)

I received your kind and warm letter of encouragement today. Thanks for writing and for caring. Sounds like you are on the threshold of great "new beginnings" there in the Portland area. Keep up the great work.

As to the matter of special letters being written; Mom, Dad, and a few of our "inner circle" brethren have been working on things that I'm not fully enlightened to—my attorney and family are so paranoid of telephone and mail censure that little is spoken, and sometimes I have to try and read between the lines or pray for discernment. [Here Tony drew a "smiley face."]

Mother once wrote a letter to the federal judge in my case "TO MY DEFENCE" [sic]—and the *headlines* of the Roanoke newspaper read that she told the judge that I deserved to be in prison, and never to be released. Mother almost had a nervous breakdown over that one—it took her six months to get it out of her system—weeping hysterically—I told her repeatedly of my words being twisted, etc.—my family and hundreds of friends have learned what this "government/media" system really is now. I weep for my precious America! Mom, Dad and my family, wisened [sic] and [are] now seasoned veterans in the "political" escapade, are troopers, standing behind me with their love and prayers. I am a blessed man.

I'm glad she's sending tapes and literature to you. I hope and pray you all enjoy them emensely [sic].

Please do pray for Mom, Dad, and the "family." You may find them a little paranoid at present, and with reason. There is an intent to write a book and produce a movie based on the prevarications of the case; and everyone is fasting and praying, binding the powers of darkness against it, in Jesus' Name. Some "crank" telephone calls have "spooked" them not a little. God bless them—they've been through four years of hurt and humiliation—a man never suffers alone, does he?

I'd love to know more about your new work—What is the name of it? Keep me informed as to its progress, okay? I haven't heard from Sis. Margaret Weiss in about a year. I guess Mother does; in fact she talked to her, I understand, only yesterday.

Please do keep me in your prayers. God had given me over 120 +

saved since being down [in prison], and several dozen baptized in the Holy Ghost. I occasionally am called upon to teach a series of studies, or preach here. The Lord did move me to write a 3-year Bible College Avuncular [sic]. It took some 2¾ year, with a minimum 45–50 hours per week. It's being edited—and I'll complete the compelation [sic] and the "Student syllabus" upon completion. God has blessed us with translators who will compile the avuncular and other material into Spanish, French, etc. It's beautiful to see people moved upon by God to do things even beyond our thoughts and planning. Praise God! His ways and planning are always beyond our comprehension—and when we are *His,* He sees to it things are accomplished—Amen?

Well—"Chin up" and "knees down"—God Bless you real real good—do write again when you can—thanks again my dear Brother—God bless you—in Jesus' Name.—

[signed] Bro Tony

PS—Please thank the church for praying for us—God Bless Them All!

Once again my effort to write this book is mentioned; however, I assure my readers that I did not have to resort to "prevarications of the case" against Tony Leyva to tell this story.

During my two telephone conversations with Ada she told "Brother Jimmy Ray Martin" her version of an incident between Tony and a "young black boy" serving time with him in the Federal Correctional Facility in Ashland, Kentucky:

> There in prison in Ashland, Kentucky, my son was dealing with teenagers and there was a lot of Moslems in there and there was this young black boy who was Moslem but didn't have a Moslem accent. But the boy had a Pentecostal background and Tony was talking to him about the Lord.
>
> So, one night my son was sleeping and it was on a weekend when they leave the cells unlocked. They usually lock 'em at eleven, but that weekend they didn't till three o'clock in the morning. And my son and his roommate, too, in the upper bunk, were asleep and this man he come in there and poured hot scalding water over my son. So, my son he believes that it was all due to the Moslems because he was spending all that time with that young colored boy trying to persuade him to come back to the Lord. And my son got terribly scalded.
>
> Oh, I tell you, I can't talk about it yet. He's terribly scarred—his body is—but he's doing fine now. But, oh, he went through it there for a while. And so they transferred him out to Texarkana. . . . In Ashland

there was this man who wanted to kill him and that's part of the reason that they transferred him to Texarkana.

There's been different attempts on his life since he's been in prison. There's been different people that's wanted to kill him since he's been in jail. And they found him a hangman's noose in under the garbage bag in the container next to his cell one time.

My son is safe for now, but there are some problems again because some [other prisoners] come from Ashland to Texarkana, and they just spread rumors about my son as fast as they can, and it's really dangerous for him in the prison. But God is with him. I know He is. If I didn't know that I don't know what would happen to him. I don't believe that I could take it. But God's with him!

I think that they are taking precautions for him there in prison because the warden said to him the other day that they was doing this. Some rumors got out and [Tony] couldn't tell me . . . he really couldn't tell me all about it. He said, 'Mama, I can't talk about it on the phone.' He says that the warden's been taking care of it.

It's a miracle that old Satan hasn't destroyed him. It's a real miracle! I know that God has been protecting him . . . just real protection from the Lord!

But an official with the U.S. Bureau of Prisons gave the lie to Tony's story to his mother when he told me in a confidential telephone interview that what allegedly happened was that Tony attempted to perform fellatio on this "this young black boy who was Moslem," and that friends of the boy retaliated against Tony. My attempts to question Tony himself about this by mail or phone—like all my other attempts to communicate, using my real name—have been met with total silence.

However, according to Ada Leyva, Tony enjoys an active life in prison—ever the "preacher," "prophet of God," and center of attention as he fulfills his omnipresent narcissistic needs. Here follows an excerpt from my July 20, 1992, phone conversation with Ada:

And Tony has written to me, he said, "Mother, one thing about being in here, I would never settle down when I was outside." And [in prison] he is writing and writing and writing now and he took six months to write a verse-by-verse commentary on Revelations. And one Brother in Mississippi—I believe he is—called me and said he was a minister, a Bible teacher, as well as a schoolteacher, and he said that he got [Tony's] book and he said, 'It is a classic. A real classic!' And that just thrilled me!

When he gets out he wants to have a Bible school for young people

and that's what he plans to do and he's been preparing all of those steps for his Bible school. He's written a whole, I guess you call it a curriculum on Bible studies, and when he gets out he's gonna use it to start up his Bible School again like he did in Columbus, Georgia. He wants to do that so bad. And he says, 'If it can't be down there, maybe it can be over in the islands... wherever God would have me. Maybe in the Bahamas.'
... This is his desire.

Surreptitiously "Brother Martin" tried to elicit some comment from Ada about her understanding of what it was specifically that her son had been found guilty of in federal court in Roanoke, asking: "I heard that there had been a problem when your son tried to reach out and convert the children of some people who didn't want them converted."
Silence.
"What was that all about?"
Silence again.
Then I prompted her with, "I hear that there were a lot of teenagers that he was preaching to and bringing to the Lord." Ada fumbled a bit and then prevaricated.

> I...I... now, well, there's been so many things that I don't know all of 'em. I don't know how that was. I couldn't tell you as much. There was a lot of people trying to cause problems with his ministry. But, I'm sure that he's run into things like that, too.
>
> But I want to tell you another thing in the prison is revivals. [And with that she hurriedly changed the subject.] Since my son has been in there God has used him to win over a hundred souls.
>
> They made him pastor there for a while over the Spanish and they have let him preach some. Not much, though. And he teaches. Not because he is my son, but he is anointed and he can teach against sin. He really teaches against sin. And he is really inspired by sin! And he plays some music. God give him the ability to play all the complicated fingers on the organ. But he's never had a lesson on the piano or organ... he fasted and prayed and sit down to the piano and the Lord gave him this gift. He plays and sings everywhere he's gone, up in Ashland and over to Texarkana....
>
> Then there in prison he writes his *Eschatology* every month. It's a Bible study that I send out in the mail to the people on his mailing list.

Ada sent an issue of "M. I. Leyva's" *Eschatology Digest* to "Brother Jimmy Ray Martin." It amounts to nothing more than a long, rambling, confusing sermon—twelve single-spaced, legal-length pages—referencing Bible scripture after interminable Bible scripture for a total of 128 separate references from thirty-seven of the Bible's sixty-six books.

The *Digest* is an excellent example of Leyva's continuing narcissistic self-aggrandizement, even as he languishes in federal prison. And even the masthead of the *Eschatology Digest* weaves a strange mixture of story telling, scripture, and pomposity:

ESCHATOLOGY DIGEST

Miracle Revival Fellowship, International

PO Box 2120

Hendersonville, North Carolina, USA 28793–2120

VOLUME XVI

"STRANGERS IN EGYPT / STRANGERS IN PENTECOST"

PART II

—"THE BIBLE MANDATE AND DEFINITION OF HOLINESS"—

by

M. I. LEYVA

Anyone familiar with M. I. Leyva's background traveling through the Southeast and Midwest as "Super Christian, Brother Tony," using fasts as a cover for outings with his "boys," is struck by his brief digressions into his so-called personal experiences in this issue of his *Eschatology Digest*:

> In a SUPERNATURAL VISITATION during the 70s (on one of the 40-DAY FASTS, and one of the four visits into heaven) a black tattered and torn robe was ripped off of me in the very presence of Jesus. I stood naked and afraid as He came direct up to me, reached around Himself as if to give me a cloak of covering from Himself; what I saw and felt amazed me—His cloak, or covering, I realized at that point, was of the purest light. . . .

On the subject of sacrifice, Brother Tony spoke with perhaps greater personal conviction than he intended when he wrote:

...OUR ETERNAL REWARDS are of far greater value than TEMPORARY PLEASURES. If God had not 'hounded' me with these matters as His concern for the 'END-TIME CHURCH,' and the great 'RESTORATION REVIVAL' just ahead, I would not open myself to further ridicule; but when a ministry has been brought *down* as low as mine has—there is nothing to lose—and nowhere left to go, but UP!

A knowledge of Brother Tony's twenty-one years living a dual life as a self-proclaimed evangelist-preacher-prophet and pederast sexually assaulting boys, and bilking their parents out of their hard-earned money with his sham "Miracle Restoration Revivals" makes one gasp at the way Leyva ends this printed sermon:

... Other Christians and ministers who seem very religious and useful may push themselves, pull wires, and work schemes to carry out their plans, but you cannot do it; and if you attempt it, you will meet with such failure and rebuke from the Lord as to make you sorely penitent.

Others can brag on themselves, on their work, on their success, on their writings, but the Holy Ghost will not allow you to do any such thing, and if you begin it, He will lead you into some deep mortification that will make you despise yourself and all your good works....

This issue of the *Digest* concluded with:

DON'T MISS IT—NEXT ISSUE—VOLUME XVII—A HEART-TO-HEART TALK FROM "AN AMBASSADOR IN BONDS—(DEDICATED TO PRISONERS AROUND THE WORLD)—INNOCENT OR GUILTY....

The average American has little or no concern about those that are incarcerated. Simply put, unless it affects them directly they don't care. But when their son or daughter, brother or sister, or even themselves are arrested, tried, and convicted (and their crime may be insignificant or serious; and they may be innocent or guilty), it is then and only then that they become concerned. But by then it may be too late and there is no one left around to speak up for them. Jesus said, in (Matt. 25:43): "I was ... in prison, and ye visited me not."

At the very bottom of the last page of this lengthy issue of *Eschatology Digest* it was noted:

These are sent free to anyone upon request. God's word is always free to all. God's way is "Freely ye have received, Freely give." (Matt. 10:8) We trust God to lay it upon the hearts of those He chooses to provide the means for publishing and sending out these studies.

Attached was a convenient, self-addressed return envelope for "those He chooses to provide the means for publishing and sending out these studies" to send in their hard-earned money.

✝ ✝ ✝

During my two telephone interviews with Ada she detailed her efforts to get her son out of prison and back on the revival circuit, where he could preach to "a people who long to have him out, ministering to them in the power and anointing of the Holy Ghost."

> We're really working on it and I've got a good Christian lawyer* and he's God's minister as well. And he's gonna help my son. He is working on the parole for the federal, but . . . he still has two and one-half years with the state [Virginia] and they have a detainer on him and he can't get them to lift that detainer so [his state sentence] will run concurrent.
> . . . See, if he got him out of the federal he'd have to go right into Virginia there and my son *does not* want to go back to Virginia. . . . There's people there that want to kill him! So maybe your people could help us pray about this.
> And he wants to get on with his ministry. He told me he'd be willing to go wherever they would let him go, like to Havana, Cuba. He's been to the Dominican Republic three times. And he has a real burden for those people. He preached there three times. He speaks Spanish. He was born and raised there in Miami. He's gone over there different times and, oh, they love him.

Also according to Ada, there have been a number of letters written on her son's behalf asking that he be released from prison. Indeed, there was one about which she was particularly pleased:

> Just lately more than ever I'm getting calls from the finest people that's really wanting to help my son. And he really needs to be out of there so he can go to preaching and telling the people about the Lord again.

---

*Ada hired Daniel L. Crandall of Roanoke, Virginia, who was Ed Morris's defense attorney on his federal plea bargain.

> And I got the most beautiful letter from a evangelist down in Louisiana the other day, a copy of a letter that he wrote to the President of the United States on my son's behalf . . . he just travels around preaching God's word. And I said, oh, if we could just get a lot more letters like that sent to the president and governor we could get him pardoned or get him released without any strings attached!
>
> This evangelist wrote: "He has been in prison for several years and I would like to seek your help in obtaining an early release or parole for him. I've known him for a good many years and I have the highest respect and regard for him as a man and as a minister and also as a man of God. He is not in prison for any act of violence. My personal opinion is that he would make a great asset to the community to which he would be released to. Because I have known him so long I can say that he has integrity and a wonderful love for God and his fellow man and is one of the finest evangelists that I have ever known."
>
> Now, I thought, my, my, my! I just couldn't improve on that letter at all. I felt like it was God writing and working something out for Tony's release!
>
> I've just got to get the address to the governor of Virginia also so I can send him a copy of that letter. And I thought that I'd send it to both the president and him to make sure they both got it. 'Cause we've got to go above them there in Roanoke because they're just not listening to us at all and the media is making it all a horror story.
>
> I read so many things that they wrote that was so untrue in those newspapers up there in Roanoke that it really just turned me off to the media, 'cause they're just hurting our country bad in every way because they just write what they think is safe and they make something out of nothing.

This brought to Ada's mind my work on this book which she roundly denounced:

> And my son is horrified 'cause there's this man who for the last four years he's been trying to write a book . . . out investigating and buying up material from up the road in Roanoke and all. And my son told me that this man, if he wrote this book and put it on TV, that it would be his death sentence and it would destroy his ministry completely! But God is greater than that man or all of our problems and I just have to keep my faith in Him. I'm just really committed to the Lord when I really think about it.

When "Brother Martin" asked Ada to tell him about Brother Tony's ministry before he went to prison, it quickly became apparent that her own considerably sanitized version of it was a favorite subject:

Everywhere he's gone—and he's gone all up and down the East Coast and he's gone some in the Middle West—he's a favorite of the people and they all love him. And now with him in prison I send out these newsletters a lot, several hundred a month. He had thousands on his mailing list when he was out and preaching, and once he got sent to prison there were several hundred that sent back this little yellow card we sent out saying that they wanted to get his newsletter. And it's really about all I can handle by myself.

Tony writes me and says, "Mama, one thing the Lord has really been pressing on me is the writing that I've been doing I would not have done if I had been out and preaching." Because he was preaching two or three times a day at least five or six times a week. He'd have morning services, afternoon services, and night services that he was working in.

I've been through Shreveport, Louisiana, with my son several times. I was there ten years ago and ministered with Tony at one of his Miracle Restoration Revivals in New Orleans. You remember when they had that World's Fair down there in New Orleans? Well, he had a tent set up in, just right there next to New Orleans, in Slidell, Louisiana, out to the east side. And he saved hundreds of souls down there, too.

And he had a work for a while down on Magazine Street right downtown in New Orleans. He was preaching at an old theater down there.

Wherever he goes he makes his headquarters. But most of the time he'd be down in Florida . . . he goes down that way a lot. And he's gone overseas to the specific Latin countries a lot. He went over there to Communist Cuba three times, and the last two times he got the permission. The ministers there got together and got permission for him to come and God really sent a revival to them. Those churches were packed there.

And he was on Beacon, it's called, a big Christian radio station that's down that way [southern Florida] that has a lot of evangelists on it. My in-laws there about a hundred miles southeast of Havana, they used to listen to him. He come on at twelve at night and some of the Cuban ministers said that they would get their little groups together at twelve and they would have their prayer meeting at 12 o'clock in the middle of the night.

He's gone into churches, had tents, auditoriums, he's gone into Holiday Inns . . . he's always been busy-busy and never a letup. He had a couple of burnouts. He's had heart disease. He's always traveled. He's been on the move preaching since, since he was twelve. And he's forty-six now [in 1992]. So you see, God has used him mightily and the Devil surely would love to put him down.

Satan has really attacked him in so many ways that we just feel that his being in prison is just another way that Satan is trying to destroy his ministry.

So, it's up to God to bring him out of prison and put him back on the field. I get so many letters saying, "Oh, how we miss him." . . . He is so desperate to get out of there!

When "Brother Martin" inquired about Ed Morris and Freddie Herring, Ada was only too happy to explain:

They're in prison, too. They're not in with him. I don't really know what city they're in. They've moved them around and I haven't been able to keep up with them.

And this man, Ed Morris, that was working for Tony was a homosexual. And this other man [Herring] that he traveled with continually, his church was being broke up there in Douglasville, Georgia, and he saw that when Tony come that people really flocked back to his church.

Well, he continually had Tony coming there to his church every chance he could get him to minister and preach there. And I kept warning my son about these men, and he'd say, "Everybody's good." Tony never would criticize anybody, except very rare. And, so, they're the ones who really belong in prison. Not Tony.

Since Tony was the minister, the head of the ministry, that's why he's in federal prison there in Texarkana. They have him for conspiracy for, uh, a prostitution ring for young boys. But it ain't true!

And they pulled them other two preachers in, too. And the boys that was with them talked about them [Morris and Herring], too. And I found out who them boys that talked were.

Now, Ed Morris was very seriously involved traveling with them. He was a great musician and Tony needed somebody to help and he had Ed and he went on the road with Tony.

But the other day Ed wrote me the most pathetic letter . . . *pathetic* . . . and he was telling how he didn't care what people thought of him anymore, all he cared was that God loved him. He said, "I know I've ruined myself, but I have made everything right with God no matter what happens." And he wanted us to know he really made things right with God and he was going on with God as best he says he possibly could with AIDS.

It was a real touching letter. It was the first time I'd heard from him. . . . He said that now he is really sold out to God.

When "Jimmy Ray Martin" told Ada that he, his wife, and the people in his "little Pentecostal church here in Portland" were really praying for Brother Tony and "trying to spread the Lord's word and the fire of the Holy

Ghost," she kindly assured him and also supplied her own version of the drug-crazed boys who were allegedly victimized by her son, including Mark Crump:

> I'll be praying for you, too, Brother Martin. My heart goes out to people who are out there trying to do something for the Lord to get the Lord's works started. I know how exciting it is! After forty-something years I'm well acquainted.
>
> I tell you, we're in a warfare, a real warfare against the Devil in this country today. And I believe the media is working with the Devil. I really do!
>
> There in court [in Roanoke] the newspaper asked my son how many young men had traveled with him in the tent and helped him. See, he used a lot of teenagers in his tent working 'cause they were the ones was free to help set 'em up. And he told the paper he used four hundred and so next morning the headlines in the Roanoke paper said, "four hundred boys molested by Tony Leyva."
>
> And my son said, "Mom, all I told them was the ones that were working on the tent." And that's the way the media twist things. It was just so much that has gone on. It was talked about there in Columbus [Georgia] that there would be deaths over this whole thing.
>
> Right after that, in Roanoke there was this boy whose mother went with him to the law and told lies about my son. And this boy was a dope addict and he kept trying to get money out of my son. He'd known Tony since he was a little boy 'cause Tony went up to Roanoke and Salem a lot. And he said to Tony, "If you don't give me five hundred dollars"—money he needed to get out of trouble over his dope—"I'm gonna tell 'em that you molested me and they will believe me." But Tony wouldn't give him the money.
>
> Well, later the boy was living under a bridge 'cause his stepfather had throwed him out of the house. This boy's brother wrote to Tony or called him and told him and Tony felt sorry for him so Tony give him the money to come down there to help 'em and he went down there and he stole money and jewels and went back home and he still couldn't get the money out of Tony he was trying to get so he told his mother lies on Tony. And his mother had known Tony for many, many years, and she had been to lots and lots of his services. Well, she went to the authorities and told them lies.
>
> Well . . . she and her husband broke up right after Tony was in prison. And she started going with somebody else and her husband killed her. Then he was arrested and he hung himself in jail. . . . His stepson was a boy that Tony trusted and called to guard his tent . . . the same boy that was on dope.

So, it's all so heart-breaking, you know. Tony did get mixed up with some bad people. But he loves everybody and don't consider nobody as being bad."

By August 8, 1992, Ada had checked up on Brother Jimmy Ray Martin, his church, and his home town of Cheerio, Oregon, and did not like what she had found. She wrote a guarded and wary letter:

Dear Mr. Martin,
    It is with sadness that I write this letter, as I have no desire to insult or offend no one.
    But if you had a son in prison and you knew that there is a people out to exploit his (and our) hurt and trouble, and someone keeps trying to get information out of you & only a post office number—*no telephone* or *street address,* just a nice voice on the telephone, Wouldn't you be wary? I could be paranoid—But this has been such a tragedy and very hurtful to my health. I developed some serious nerve problems since it all begun—so has my son.
    Margaret Weiss declares she never heard of Ethel Fisher [a fictitious person] and a brother in Portland has never heard of Cheerio, Oregon.
    Please don't be angry with me, if you are for real you will be understanding & forgiving. But I would need much more proof & references than I have. Do you blame me?

                                                        Sincerely,
                                                        [signed] A. E. Leyva

With this my communication with Ada and her son ended.

✝ ✝ ✝

On Saturday, November 14, 1992, the Reverend Gary Marrone of the Church on the Rock married a couple in the parole hearing room at the Federal Correctional Institution (prison) at Texarkana, Texas. The ceremony took barely fifteen minutes, and when it ended Federal Inmate #82355-020 (Mario Ivan "Tony" Leyva) and Sherry Lynn Turner (formerly Barstow) of Oklahoma were man and wife.

Tony's best man was his father, Mario Leyva, who attended with Tony's mother, Ada. The bride was attended by her mother, fellow Tony Leyva Evangelistic Association gospel trio member Carleen Waddell, and her sister, Jacalyn Faye Morison.

In December 1992, those on the mailing list of the association's *Es-*

chatology Digest received a Christmas card "From Tony & Sherry Lynn Leyva and all the family and staff of MIRACLE REVIVAL FELLOWSHIP, INTERNATIONAL" featuring a photograph of the couple in the prison chapel on "our wedding day."

But as of early 1996, the couple has not had the opportunity to enjoy a conjugal night together, since Tony's statutory federal parole hearing will not be until October 20, 1998.

But whenever he does get out of prison and becomes a free man, it is highly probable that Brother Tony will return to seducing and sexually assaulting boys. When asked if she felt Tony could make a change and become a straightforward, truthful, nonabusing preacher upon his release from prison, his first wife, Tammy Sue, said: "Knowing him as I do, he can paint his stories to sound the way he wants it to sound. I'm sure—being the person that he is—he paints his picture to make it stand out and sound like he wants it to sound, that he's innocent and you're guilty. But, no, I don't see him becoming a real preacher if he gets out. Really, I think he's where he belongs now 'cause he's hurt so many people in the name of God."

19

"The boys Gray sexually assaulted he came to know [when they were] thirteen to fifteen years of age."

When she first began putting together a case against evangelists Tony Leyva, Ed Morris, and Freddie Herring, Assistant United States Attorney Jenny Montgomery knew that before using as witnesses any of the teenage boys the pederasts had abused she would have to have them professionally evaluated to assure their reliability. Almost all the boys came from broken homes, many had been emotionally and physically abused, and—she was certain—some had even been sexually abused long before they met the trio she was prosecuting.

Therefore, to assist her in picking the most convincing young victims to testify as witnesses, Jenny Montgomery turned to her brother-in-law, child and adolescent psychiatrist William G. Gray, who in 1983 had moved his practice from San Diego, California, to Roanoke. Indeed, he was one of only three child or adolescent psychiatrists in southwestern Virginia, and one who almost always agreed to evaluate and treat youngsters for government agencies and accept the low fees paid by most governmental entities.

However, had Ms. Montgomery asked individuals in the Roanoke law enforcement community—and had they been honest with her—she would have heard some rather unsavory stories about her brother-in-law's practice. Dr. Gray practiced child and adolescent psychiatry in a large old home he owned in downtown Roanoke and, when convenient, he housed some of his young teenage male patients there. But of particular interest to Jenny Montgomery, perhaps, would have been the stories that frequently surfaced through local police, sheriff's deputies, children's protective service workers, and others that his young patients occasionally made allegations that Dr. Gray had coerced them into oral sex.

Interestingly, similar allegations were said to lie behind Gray's leaving his California practice.

Gray received his education at Wake Forest University, the Medical College of Virginia, and Duke University. He was licensed to practice medicine in Virginia in 1966 and obtained his California license in 1968. However, in San Diego, California, in 1978, after these allegations arose of improprieties with boys, Dr. Gray moved his practice to Roanoke, Virginia.

In 1983 Gray opened his practice in Roanoke and within two years similar rumors about his sexual involvement with juvenile male clients began creeping through the southeastern Virginia law enforcement community. But Jenny Montgomery was a federal prosecutor, had few local law enforcement contacts, and apparently never learned about her brother-in-law's background as a pederast. Regarding Gray's being used by Jenny Montgomery to evaluate some of her witnesses against Leyva, Morris, and Herring, who were also witnesses for Randy Leach in his case against Leyva in Roanoke County's Circuit Court, Leach said: "Well, the federal people may have done that. [laughs] I didn't send them to Dr. Gray! I know we've never used Dr. Gray!

"Everybody thought that Dr. Gray was weird. His fooling around with kids was always kind of common knowledge around here . . . probably for me ever since '88. I heard that Dr. Gray was fooling with some of his juvenile male clients and once we got on to it, . . . we heard that there had been complaints to Roanoke City before.

"But I just went down and saw the sentencing in the federal case and when Dr. Gray got on the stand, that was the first time that I recall having known that he was connected with the thing. Until then I had no earthly idea that he was going to testify! Jenny said to me in passing that Dr. Gray was her brother-in-law.

"And I don't think any of the victims told me that they were seeing Dr. Gray specifically. I do not recall being made aware that the witnesses had been sent to see Dr. Gray."

After Gray's sexual assaults on his young male patients became public knowledge on the front pages of edition after edition of the *Roanoke Times & World News* in 1992, Detective Garrick Hudson remarked with satisfaction: "Dr. Gray has gotten himself into a world of doo doo. I worked on him for the longest time trying to build a case against him for sexually assaulting some of the boys he treated, but I never could get the witnesses in order. For a number of years we kept getting hints of something going on with Dr. Gray. I remember going down there to his mansion office in downtown Roanoke and interviewing. He was a real smooth character!"

According to Ann Martin, of Roanoke County's Children's Protection Service (CPS), "It would have been around '85 or '86 that the people in the local professional community were commenting that Dr. Gray liked children sexually. There weren't any formal allegations at that point, but it was more like people in the professional community would say that he would do that sort of thing. And, because of that, I did not ever refer anybody to him.

"Also, in the opinion of most professional people he overmedicated children . . . especially young children. So, if anybody would have asked my advice, I would not have recommended him as a counselor for any child due to what I knew about him.

"I did, however, have children that I worked with that saw him . . . a couple of kids coming out of State care or that had been with Corrections that were coming back with short [prison] time and they were seeing him. These were all males that I had [and] they ranged from age eight to about thirteen.

"As a whole, there were not a great many child psychiatrists or psychologists that were available in the Roanoke area, especially given the limited government money for such, so if the children were coming through an agency such as social services or the courts . . . there were only a few that would take clients like that and he was one of them."

When Ms. Martin was asked if she ever discussed Dr. Gray and her suspicions about him with people in the City of Roanoke CPS unit, she replied, "Discussed? [laughs] I don't think that there was any coordination of anything official or any kind of investigation, but from our working relationships everyone over there had the same opinion about Dr. Gray as I did. Everybody pretty much knew about that . . . it was a well-known situation."

I asked Ms. Martin if she thought Jenny Montgomery would have known anything about the serious rumors concerning Dr. Gray's sexual attraction to children: "I know she used Dr. Gray to testify in the Leyva case, but I don't know that I would have said anything about his reputation to her because of the relationship. . . .

"I can say that since I have been with the federal government I don't have the kind of access to knowing those kinds of things like I did when I worked for CPS because there is such a separation between the federal government and state agencies.

"In other words, what I'm trying to say is that I don't believe that Jenny would have had exposure to the real working professionals who heard those kinds of things."

"But," Ms. Martin continued, "I knew that Dr. Gray was going to be the government's expert witness in the Leyva case and his testifying should have raised anybody's eyebrows! Actually, what he said on the stand about understanding pedophiles, you know . . . they couldn't be cured. Well, he ought to know! But I really think that Jenny was using him to testify in her case because he was going to say what the government wanted said. . . .

"I don't have personal knowledge as to whether Jenny knew [about Gray's pedophilia] or not . . . some people here may have known about his problems in California. But, had Jenny known that at that point, knowing her the way I know her, I do not think that she would have used him."

She then added reflectively: "I think in any kind of public service that it doesn't take much to look like a conflict of interest, so, you know. I would think that you would try to avoid anything looking like that. I mean, I think it's much more so in public service, it's so much easier. People look at these kinds of things, you know, keeping nepotism out and all of that kind of thing. I would say that that might raise an eyebrow or two with her brother-in-law being an expert witness and the professional treatment person for the witnesses."

Asked if in her opinion Dr. Gray's problems in California would have served to impeach him as a witness, Ann did not hesitate before responding, "I would definitely say that would have! I think any defense attorney would have grabbed a hold of that fact and challenged him as an expert witness and gotten him dismissed then and there."

But unfortunately for Tony Leyva, his attorney, Harry Bosen, was no better informed than the general public and thus knew nothing of Dr. Gray's history of numerous sexual liaisons with some of his male teenage clients until years later.

It was early 1992 before Dr. Gray's barely kept secret went from being insider information among local law enforcement to public knowledge in Roanoke, when the Virginia Board of Medicine suspended his license for a number of alleged violations, including having sexual relations with both juvenile and adult male patients and overmedicating patients. In short order it became known that he was also under investigation for sexually molesting a sixteen-year-old boy in Roanoke County as well as in adjacent Franklin County.

Some of the incidents allegedly occurred at Gray's downtown office, well within the City of Roanoke jurisdiction of Commonwealth's Attorney Don Caldwell, and all had occurred since at least 1983.

But in the first of two telephone interviews with Don Caldwell in the spring of 1993, my efforts to elicit information ran into considerable verbal block-and-parry attempts by him.

Echols: "I am following up on the Dr. William Gray case and I was wondering if you could tell me if your office has had some involvement there and, if so, to what extent?"

Caldwell: "We have not been involved in Dr. Gray's case. There's nothing that comes to mind that I would feel comfortable in commenting on because . . . to my recollection we've not charged Gray with anything that stands out in my mind. I'm not saying that he hasn't been charged here in the city, but nothing that I can discuss with you."

I then asked which it was: Had Dr. Gray been charged or did Mr. Caldwell feel uncomfortable discussing such charges with me?

Caldwell responded ambiguously: "Well, you know, we handle 1,500 felony cases a year. I've been here for fourteen years and 60,000 misdemeanor cases and I'm generally familiar with Gray, but there's nothing specific. I've never been involved in the prosecution of a case that made any impression on me."

Echols: "You personally or your office?"

"Me personally," was his short reply before he elaborated with: "You know, I mean, what I would need from you is something specific. If you ask me a specific question then I might be able to answer it."

Echols: "Okay. I'll try to get a little more specific. Have you been aware through your office of any investigations or any arrests of Dr. Gray in connection with sexual assaults?"

Caldwell: "Not that I can recollect at this time. I don't know. You're probably aware if you've worked with Randy [Leach] that we don't have internal investigators in the Commonwealth Attorneys offices in Virginia. The police may have investigated him on things that never led to a charge."

Echols: "But I know that there is some communication back and forth."

Caldwell: "Yeah, but I can't remember whether they come to us and said they're investigating Gray for this or for that. I just can't. As I sit here at my desk I can't bring up any case where that happened."

Echols: "Are you aware of the investigation of Dr. Gray that took place in California?"

Caldwell: "Just what I've read in the paper that there was one done there."

Echols: "Well, the investigator in San Diego said that the boy who complained was 'a credible witness and appeared truthful.' "

Caldwell: "That's fine, I mean, that's the way he chooses to put it. I'm just saying that my upbringing and my training and my position today. . . . I'm not inclined to comment on things that I cannot corroborate.

"I've been here for a while and I turned down my opportunity to go on

'Unsolved Mysteries' because criminal matters are not easily explained and the only request I made of [the producer] was that I'll go on if you'll agree to air your question and then my response in its entirety. And they wouldn't agree to do that. And, so, it's the same thing in a book. I don't want things attributed to me unless they're put it in the complete context of the question and answer that was given."

Trying a different tack, I asked: " Now, Dr. Gray's office in Roanoke was in your jurisdiction, was it not?"

Caldwell hesitated briefly and then responded, "Yes."

Echols: "And no one came to you or your office within the past year or eighteen months in connection with anything occurring at Dr. Gray's office?"

Caldwell started out "Not of a significant . . ." then changed course with, "Not that I can remember. We have ten assistants here, too, so it is possible that the detectives could have come to somebody else, but I think that if it was anything of any real merit it would have ultimately found its way to me."

Echols: "I have a Roanoke deputy sheriff as well as Randy Leach telling me that it was common knowledge in law enforcement as far back as 1985 that Dr. Gray was apparently involved sexually with some of his minor male clients and I was wondering if you could tell me about hearing about any of this yourself?"

Caldwell: "No. And to be flat out honest with you, even if I had, I would not be willing to say that publicly and have my name associated with that because I think that unless you can prove it—which nobody has been able to do successfully—I think you better be willing to back up what you say with, uh . . . I'm not willing to, like I say, even if I thought it I wouldn't say it."

Since I could not get a definitive response about the involvement of Mr. Caldwell's office concerning Dr. Gray, I asked if Caldwell would check and then I would call him back. Caldwell answered affirmatively: "Sure, I could check on that to see whether anybody recollects anything that's come up."

After several attempts to reach Caldwell again I finally succeeded in speaking with him but he was very unresponsive. After an initial spate of "no's" from Caldwell to every question I asked, I sharpened my approach with:

"Do you recall discussing with *anyone* the Gray case?"

Caldwell: "What Gray case?"

Echols: "Dr. William G. Gray."

Caldwell: "What Gray case? You're . . . I know who . . ."

Echols: "Well, I mean . . . okay, the Gray matter, let me put it that way. I said 'case.' Excuse me. Let me, you know, for the sake of semantics be . . ."

Caldwell: "I mean, this is all about semantics, Mike. But what I'm saying is that we have not had a case in Roanoke City that we have prosecuted Dr. Gray at all."

Echols: " Have you had anyone come to you expressing concern about Dr. Gray and what he was allegedly doing with his clients?"

Caldwell: "To the best of my recollection I do not remember anybody coming to me about that."

Echols: " Do you recall anyone in your office discussing it?"

Caldwell: "No, I do not."

Echols: " I thank you very much, sir."

Caldwell: " Thank you."

☦ ☦ ☦

When told of Caldwell's response to questions about Dr. Gray, Randy Leach laughed and said: "Well, I know they've been approached about him! We had some misdemeanor cases against [Gray] in Roanoke County. The allegations were that most of the stuff happened in Roanoke City, but they were never prosecuted in Roanoke City. I don't know why.

"All I can tell you is that there were allegations there and there never were charges brought. It may be because of the same problem we had when we were trying to prosecute Leyva. We had a bunch of disturbed kids. And let me tell you: In Tony Leyva's case we had some kids that were disturbed and everything else!

"But in Dr. Gray's case it was a whole lot worse. Most of the kids had criminal records and all this other stuff. And they were just very difficult witnesses.

"Gray is your classic pedophile: He picks his victims well and he's able to turn the tables on them. Gray is a brilliant man. Leyva was kind of stupid. . . . It's amazing that [Gray] can pick the kids that have troubles that have been diagnosed, have them come to him for treatment, sexually abuse them, and then all he does is turn around and say: 'Look, these kids were using me, they're troubled kids.'

"We tried [to prosecute Gray] here in the county. I don't know what happened in Roanoke City unless they just looked at it in terms of, 'Oh, come on! We've got a bunch of guys here that are convicted felons and everything else, and they're going to turn around and point the finger at this psychiatrist and say 'He's the one that's at fault.'

"It works very well, when you look at 'beyond a reasonable doubt.' . . . So, I can't tell you that the Roanoke City prosecutors didn't look at it in that

Chapter 19

light. All I know is that I tried to prosecute Gray with one kid here because nothing happened in Roanoke County except two or three isolated incidents with that one boy. And I tried to do the same thing I did with Leyva: I tried to get some other kids to come in and bolster it and the judge wouldn't let me do it. My charge got dismissed and then this thing with Gray took off up to Franklin County, and they tried it up there because he had a house at Smith Mountain Lake where he took the boys."

Randy Leach was asked if—similar to what Franklin County prosecutors did—he would have struck a plea bargain with Dr. Gray to turn in his medical license in exchange for no criminal prosecution. Randy vigorously responded, "Who? Gray? Not me! I don't do bargains like that!

"That way, if we turn around and we get another ten people to come in we're not going to tie our hands. Dr. Gray didn't want to sign that [the Franklin County agreement] without us putting our signature on it and we said we're not going to do it. That was kind of a major stumbling block.

"Now, if somebody walked in tomorrow morning and we could prove a case and we had more than we had before, we'll prosecute [Gray]. That's just the way we are. So, we're not going to sign away our rights to prosecute anything he may have done up to today. Just in case something happens and we can prove it."

✞ ✞ ✞

Darrell Wayne Sharp was very surprised and shocked when in 1993 he first learned of Dr. Gray's alleged pedophilia. And it was a further shock to the young man to learn that Gray was Jenny Montgomery's brother-in-law. When asked his feelings about having been assigned by Montgomery in 1988 to be evaluated by Gray, Darrell Wayne said: "She ought to have been aware of it and what she should have done is not even took any of us around him or into his office knowing that had happened!"

After learning that in 1988 Detective Hudson and Ann Martin were both aware of Gray's predilection to molest his juvenile male clients, Darrell Wayne added: "Well, number one, it looks to me like [Jenny] definitely should have known! I mean, if law enforcement knew, that's where she took a wrong step...."

Darrell Wayne remembers well being taken to Dr. Gray's office by John Terry for an evaluation. "Dr. Gray's office was one of these old houses in downtown Roanoke. You know how most lawyers will take an old house and fix it up as an office with leather chairs and things? Well, his office was fixed up like that with your old English-style furniture. The outside looks nice, but when you walk inside the wood and fixtures and everything looks real nice and it's appealing and so, well, 'Hey, this guy ain't doin' half bad,' you know! . . .

"The time that I talked to Dr. Gray, I thought he was being professional about it because he never made any advances toward me. I was in there for probably twenty minutes or half an hour, and about the only thing I can say about it is he done his job.

"But the funniest thing happened. Out of all of us that talked to Dr. Gray the only one that received medicine and the one that was in there the longest was Mark Crump. He was in there for a good hour! And when he come out he had the awfullest handful of pills that ever was. . . ."

Of his evaluation session with Dr. Gray, arranged by Jenny Montgomery, Robert Earls recalled: "It was like he wasn't asking nothing to try and help me. In other words, it was like he was just asking me information for himself . . . like to entertain himself with . . . like he didn't care about me or my feelings. That was all there was to it! He was just asking me questions about all the details of the sex Tony Leyva did with me.

"And he seemed extra interested when I mentioned about how Tony Leyva always wanted to do '69' with me. He asked me if I liked that, and I told him that that's the way *he* liked it with me, but I told him I didn't like it [and] always quit it before Tony would come. Then he asked me about anal sex, and I told him about the one time when I was about thirteen when Tony Leyva brought up to me that he wanted to do anal sex with me, but that I didn't like it and I stopped it.

"I could tell that it really didn't matter to him how I felt. [Dr. Gray] just wanted to know the information about the sex so he could tell somebody else . . . or, maybe, it was for his own personal reasons."

☩ ☩ ☩

Bonnie Beatty is a deputy sheriff dealing with sexual assault cases in Franklin County, Virginia, just to the southwest of Roanoke County, who conducted the local investigation of Dr. Gray. "The boys Gray [was found by the medical board to have] sexually assaulted he came to know at thirteen to fifteen years of age," Bonnie explained. "And he started doing it to them right then when they first began being counseled by him. They're all from dysfunctional families and they were taken into custody or put into regional homes. And they were geared at that point in time to be counseled and Dr. Gray was their counselor. And so that's how they got in with Dr. Gray and the abuse began . . . in some cases as far back at the middle 1980s. Most of what I investigated on him was aggravated sexual battery . . . oral sodomy. He liked blow jobs. And another thing, too, was mutual masturbation."

When she had completed her solo investigation Bonnie turned the results over to Franklin County Commonwealth's Attorney Clifford Hapgood, who, later, worked out a plea bargain for Dr. Gray with his attorneys. Said Bonnie: "I understand that there is a condition of the agreement with Roanoke City and Franklin County that—if any new victims surfaced—they would not pursue that. In other words, once [Dr. Gray] signed to give up his medical practice he would not be prosecuted for sexually assaulting these juvenile male patients of his."

When Bonnie was asked how that could hold up legally if new victims did surface, she laughed and said sarcastically, "Well, I'm just a lowly county employee. I don't even come out of the wall unless they ask me to. You see, I'm bound legally to do certain things and I'll sit and squirm because I got to keep my mouth shut.

"I know just prior to our criminal court hearing Dr. Gray and his attorney had 168 witnesses subpoenaed and going through that list of names there was only a handful of what I would say would equal Dr. Gray in his professional life as a peer. All the others were . . . gays and drag queens and street kids. But in all fairness, we may be short-changing the [Franklin County] Commonwealth's Attorney. If you were a betting man, would you not bet on a sure thing? That's basically what he was doing.

". . . Personally, I think we could have gone to court in Chatham [on a change of venue] and convinced a jury of Pittsylvania County people that this man did what the boys were alleging that he had done. . . .

"But like I say—not being an attorney and not seeing all the legalities throughout the trial and down the road, I would hate to second guess or even try to say somebody screwed up. . . . The main goal at that time was to take that medical license away from Gray, that shield that allowed him the opportunity to have these young boys come to him and then him to have that opportunity to sexually assault them. And I guess, looking at that, that was a sure thing, that he would give up his license in Virginia indefinitely.*

---

*Dr. Gray and his attorneys felt that by his "voluntarily"—i.e., even though under a court order, not at the order of the Virginia Medical Board—surrendering his Virginia medical license, he would be able to reapply for one in another state. However, authorities with the medical board in Virginia did not want this to happen. They knew that if they held hearings, found against Gray, and then took his license from him, the man would be unable to apply for a medical license in another state.

". . . I'd been hearing off and on through the years about Dr. Gray. There was a lot of smoke but not enough fire. He was the only child psychiatrist in the area who specialized in adolescents with sexual problems. [laughs] Right, leave out sexual . . . he was about the only one in this whole southwest part of Virginia who would deal with hard-core risks, really troubled adolescents."

✝ ✝ ✝

In March 1993 one of Dr. Gray's attorneys, Robert P. "Pat" Doherty, Jr., of Roanoke, was asked for an interview over the phone regarding his client but he declined. Nevertheless, he gave me almost ten minutes of detailed information about his client's problems with the Virginia Board of Medicine as well as with Roanoke-area law enforcement: "Dr. Gray was licensed to practice medicine in the Commonwealth of Virginia, and in late 1991 allegations were made to the Board of Medicine that he had sexual relations with some of his young male patients. And then there were other allegations made concerning sloppy record keeping, improper prescription of antibiotics, and something about blood gases and so on. . . . I mean, a lot of technical things that would affect a physician's license. Round about that same time the Board of Medicine coordinated with the local Commonwealth's Attorneys that were in the jurisdiction where Dr. Gray practiced in Roanoke County and in Roanoke City and in Franklin County[.] . . . The Roanoke County prosecutor obtained misdemeanor criminal warrants against Dr. Gray alleging misdemeanor sexual battery charges against the one person who was a juvenile.

"The allegations—some of them dealt with adults, some with juveniles—were tried in the Roanoke County Juvenile and Domestic Relations District Court back in February or March of 1992 and Gray was acquitted. . . . About that same time the Board of Medicine temporarily suspended Dr. Gray's license because the allegations were so serious that they figured that they better find out what was going on before they allow him to practice.

"So, about May or June of '92 Dr. Gray was indicted in Franklin County for sixteen separate counts of forcible sodomy, both oral and anal. Some involved the juvenile who brought the Roanoke County misdemeanor charges. The remainder of those, I think, dealt with adults.

"However, we never did get precisely enough information, a bill of particulars on each and every one of the indictments because this had occurred while some of these adults were juveniles also. It was planned that two different complainants were to be tried initially. At this same time the Board of Medicine started their hearings which . . . were televised because of the seriousness of the criminal charges concerning allegations made by five or six or seven former patients.

". . . I did not represent [Gray] before the Medical Board, however, I was one of the lawyers involved in the case simply because we were all dealing with the same information so I became a counsel in the Medical Board hearings.

"I only attended one hearing just to get some impression of what the witnesses were like. One of my partners attended another hearing to get the impression of certain witnesses. Then I made the argument on behalf of Dr. Gray to the Medical Board that the . . . Board's hearings should be continued until the criminal cases were completed so he would be able to properly defend himself in the criminal cases, and we wouldn't try the case on television before the cases even came to trial.

"And, so, the trial in the first two indictments was scheduled to commence sometime near the end of January [1993] . . . we blocked off a week or more for those two indictments. And prior to having the trial—after both sides had summoned a hundred plus witnesses—both sides had witnesses who would flip-flop on them and say one thing one day and say something else a different day. A plea agreement was worked out [which] called for Dr. Gray to permanently surrender his license to practice medicine in the Commonwealth of Virginia in return for which the [Franklin County] Commonwealth's Attorney would not prosecute.

"And there were several other jurisdictions who agreed that they had no pending charges against him or anything. . . . [As] far as I was concerned, that was the end of the matter. However, . . . several weeks later, I was notified that the Board of Medicine was continuing its hearings. And I expressed my opinion to Dr. Gray that having surrendered his license under court order and having it accepted by the prosecutor, that the Board of Medicine, who simply regulates people's licenses, no longer has jurisdiction over the man. [But] the board saw it differently so John Grad [Gray's other attorney] filed some legal action to stop the hearings.

". . . The matter came to hearing on that question in Franklin County on [March 1, 1993,] and the judge transferred the venue up to Roanoke City . . . because that is where the next scheduled hearing of the Board of Medicine will be. And the judge . . . ruled that he was without jurisdiction to enjoin them. And so . . . and I was involved in both of those arguments simply because of the distance involved between Alexandria where John

Grad is and here [Roanoke]. . . . In a telephone conversation to John Grad . . . I told him . . . good luck on your Medical Board hearing, I mean, I'm not going to be there and won't play any part in it.

"Now," Mr. Doherty finally caught his breath, "having told you all that, I am reluctant to discuss the merits or the facts of an ongoing case, certainly without client permission, and in my particular opinion without the permission of the lawyer who is handling the matter, which would be John Grad. And so, I will be glad to—assuming nobody has an objection—. . . answer your questions or talk to you again some other time. But for . . . now I don't feel comfortable discussing the case."

I made further attempts to reach Mr. Doherty but was unsuccessful.

✝ ✝ ✝

On November 10, 1993, the Virginia Board of Medicine permanently revoked Dr. William G. Gray's license to practice medicine in that state. The order was signed by Hilary H. Connor, M.D., Executive Director of the Virginia Board of Medicine, who cited the following reasons: " . . . numerous prescriptions for [one] Patient . . . for various controlled substances . . . for which there is no documentation . . ."; for three other patients overprescriptions of "various controlled substances . . . for which there is no documentation in the patients' medical records of any examinations performed or of the specific medications prescribed"; " . . . clear and convincing evidence that from 1983 to 1992, Dr. Gray provided . . . housing, food, money . . . to patients . . . as a *quid pro quo* for sexual favors . . ."; and " . . . clear and convincing evidence that from 1983 to 1992, Dr. Gray unethically exploited the physician/patient relationship by engaging in sexual activities with patients. . . ."

20

"Brother Tony knew how to treat us and love us to get to us."

On October 25, 1988, Mario "Tony" Leyva, Edward Rias Morris, and Freddie M. Herring surrendered to officials at the United States Bureau of Prisons Federal Correctional Facility (FCI) at Butner, North Carolina. Morris and Herring were eventually transferred to serve part of their time at the FCI in Danbury, Connecticut. At one point Morris was sent to the FCI in Milan, Michigan.

But Leyva has been through a number of federal prisons and two federal (prison) medical facilities. In 1989 the U.S. Bureau of Prisons transferred him to the FCI in Ashland, Kentucky. This was where he attempted to orally sodomize a nineteen-year-old fellow prisoner whom, he claims, he had been trying to convert from Islam by studying the Bible with him. Other prisoners threw scalding water on him, burning Leyva so badly that he had to be transferred to the Federal Medical Facility in Springfield, Missouri, for extensive treatment and skin grafts.

After recovering from his burns, Tony was transferred to the FCI in Texarkana, Texas, where he was allowed to marry his second wife on November 14, 1992. However, the next month a package of child pornography he had ordered arrived and he received a disciplinary transfer to the FCI at La Tuna, Texas, just outside of El Paso.

In February 1993, Leyva was transferred to the new federal prison at Florence, Colorado, where he spent five months before being moved briefly to the FCI in El Reno, Oklahoma.

After twelve days, in mid-July 1993, Leyva was sent to the legendary maximum security federal prison Atlanta, Georgia.

Two months later, Leyva was transferred again, this time to the Tallahassee, Florida FCI.

In 1994, after being stabbed by another inmate at Tallahassee, Leyva was transferred to the Federal Medical Facility in Lexington, Kentucky, for treatment.

In 1995, Leyva was returned to the FCI at Tallahassee, but placed in protective custody where—at least for the time being—he continues to write his *Eschatology Digest*, mailing it off to his mother in North Carolina for her to publish and mail out with requests for contributions for their ministry.

However, the money received is used to pay Leyva's attorney, Daniel F. Crandall of Roanoke, for his efforts to convince both Virginia officials to allow his client to serve his state sentence concurrently with his federal sentence (Roanoke County Assistant Commonwealth's Attorney Randy Leach steadfastly refuses to allow this) and the U.S. Parole Commission to grant Leyva an early parole from federal prison. However, since Leyva and his mother do not inform *Digest* recipients that their contributions are used for this purpose, being involved with the *Digest* is technically not allowed under prison regulations. I have brought this to the attention of prison authorities who tell me that an investigator is actively looking into it.

Even though Federal District Judge James C. Turk of Roanoke, Virginia, requested that the U.S. Bureau of Prisons to have Tony Leyva, Ed Morris, and Freddie Herring serve their full sentences without parole, this request could not be fulfilled by the bureau since such decisions are based on the relevant sentencing law and are in the hands of the U.S. Parole Commission in Chevy Chase, Maryland.

Judge Turk also ordered that he be informed in advance of any parole hearings for the three. According to Turk's communications with me, this has never happened. Therefore, with no notification to Judge Turk or any victims or witnesses, Freddie Herring was released early on parole to Columbus, Georgia, in July 1993. Also with no notification to Judge Turk or the others, Edward Morris was released on early "compassionate parole" in December 1993 due to being diagnosed with a terminal disease.

As his own parole hearing, set for late May 1995, approached, Brother Tony thought it prudent to write to Macalynn and her sons. All three letters were dated May 1, 1995, but only two survive: When Jason received his, so angry was he at the duplicitous tone that he immediately tore it in pieces and threw it away.

In part, Kenny's less than one-page letter read:

God Bless You Kenny;
Greetings to you in Jesus' Name!

    I know you're probably shocked and surprised to hear from me; but it seems God is tugging at the heart strings of *His* people everywhere, in these "last days," in preparation for our (all of us) soon "Home Going."

    It is of necessity that I write, letting you know that I have accepted full responsibility for all that happened (as I so stated in the last court session) and particularly am writing to ask you to forgive me for any and all wrongs in word or in deed against you. I really humbly apologize and pray for your forgiveness.

    It would truly bless me to see us all together as a huge "Jesus Family," worshipping God, one day soon.

    I wish you the very best and assure you that there has not been one day pass in six and a half years, but that I have prayed for you, Jason, and your mother. I pray for all your'e [*sic*] happiness: I really do mean it!

Because He Lives, Love, Bro. Tony

[At the bottom of the letter, Brother Tony drew a "smiley face" and under it, wrote, "Jesus is Lord!"]

Macalynn did not feel blessed to receive her two-page letter from her sons' abuser. In fact, so disingenuous was the letter and so angry was Macalynn that she sent a copy of it along with a copy of Kenny's letter to the United States Parole Commission for their consideration at Leyva's parole hearing. Following are some excerpts:

Sis. Macalynn & Family

God Bless You, Dear and Precious Sis. Macalynn, Husband, Family;
5/1/95

    Greetings, blessings and peace to you and yours in the Mighty Name of the Lord and Saviour, Jesus Christ. I trust this letter finds all well and happy in *Him!* As for me, by faith, "... *IT IS WELL!* (II Kings 4:26B). ...

    Sis. Macalynn, I won't even go back in time to detail incidents and conversation of the past (the majority of which I believe were fabricated by jealous, envious or contentious people—as I read the names listed—but—as it stands, regardless of what all was or wasn't said or done, I accept all responsibility—and can only ask that you forgive me for anything ever said and/or done. ...

It hurts me to think I've ever hurt anyone, and even as much have an enemy. It would bless me beyond imagination to see all of us in worship of the Lord together in these "Last Days." Please accept my humble apologies—and—with a new, clean slate, continue on as a "Jesus Family." . . .

I believe God is working to heal all the old hurts and wounds. I've had a few He's needed to heal myself—too many to innumerate [sic].

My "VISION" of the work for God has never ceased—and in numerous "VISITATIONS" He has revealed some awesome things—and I have "VOWED" to believe He even called/CHOSE/ORDAINED me to be—in fact, as of today, God has put me on a forty-day (water only) Fast [and] I'll certainly need His strength to do it. I have heard from Heaven and know a deeper walk and relationship than ever before in my life.

God has given me over three hundred saved, and over one hundred fifty Baptized in the Holy Ghost these six and one-half years—not to mention several hundreds discipled in Him. We communicate monthly (or thereabouts) with 300–400 on a special mailing list—many healings and miracles in these prison services & classes.

I spent the first 2.9 years authoring (at His instruction) a 4-year, 18-volume, avuncular [sic] Bible College Curriculum. And I recently took 1.6 years authoring a 1-year (52 weeks) Bible Correspondence Course—still lots of editing work to do on all of it. . . .

Some day maybe I'll be able to share with you of why [sic] there was ever a "case" [against me] in the first place—you will be surprised of the "CUBAN" connection—and even two deaths to keep the lid on things*—but for now Thanks again, Sis. Macalynn; you've restored my faith in "Christian Love and Unity" and Forgiveness! Thanks!

Because He Lives, Love, Bro. Tony

[At the bottom of the letter Brother Tony drew another "smiley face" and under it wrote, "Jesus is Lord!"]

On May 30, 1995, Brother Tony had his latest parole hearing before the United States Parole Commission, at the Tallahassee FCI. Two weeks later the commission announced that they had denied Leyva's request for early parole and that his next hearing will be in May 1998.

A Bureau of Prisons official told me that Leyva is unlikely to be paroled early because his prison record is poor: "He's been transferred a record number of times. Every time he arrives at a new prison he tells the

---

*A possible reference to the murder of Patti Casey and suicide of her estranged husband, Jimmy

inmates that he's a convicted child molester, but that it's not his fault. He tells them that what happened was all a part of God's plan. Then he starts preaching to them."

So, unless the Parole Commission decides to release Tony Leyva early over the concerns expressed by Judge Turk and prison psychologists, the U.S. Department of Justice, and protests from his hundreds of victims and their families, the earliest that he will be released from federal prison will be sometime after October 20, 1998.

And when Tony Leyva is finally paroled from federal prison, he will still have to serve two and a half years in a Virginia state prison for orally sodomizing boys there; and already there have been threats made against him by several current Virginia prison inmates, including one of Leyva's earliest victims, himself now incarcerated for sexually assaulting young boys.

Although I and some of the victims and their parents have requested by phone and in writing that the exact locations of Freddie Herring and Ed Morris be revealed, Michael A. Stover, General Counsel for the U.S. Parole Commission has refused, stating in writing that the release of such information would require ". . . the balancing of a precisely articulated public interest that would be served by the release of the information requested, against the privacy interest every individual has in not having government file information released."

In late 1995 I located Freddie Herring, who was listed under his own name in the Columbus (Georgia) phone book with an address near the old red brick church on 38th Street. I phoned to ask for an interview, but he would only say, "I don't want to discuss the case, Mr. Echols. All of that happened a long time ago and it's behind me now." I could not find Ed Morris.

✝ ✝ ✝

After Dr. Gray lost his license to practice medicine in Virginia, the North Carolina Medical Board revoked his license to practice there. Then, in 1994, Dr. Gray contacted the California licensing board and (according to a report in the *Roanoke Times & World News* on July 20, 1994) "was allowed to renew his license in California." But California Supervising Deputy Attorney General Jana Tuton in Sacramento says "she has a letter from Gray's attorney promising he won't practice there 'until there's a final ruling in Virginia.' " (Although he no longer resides in Virginia, Dr. Gray is technically but not aggressively, says his attorney, John Grad, fighting the revocation of his Virginia medical license.)

According to Gray's attorney, John Grad, and reporter Doug Pardue of the *Roanoke Times & World News,* the last they heard about Dr. Gray was that in 1993 in Micronesia he attempted to use his California medical license to get licensed to practice psychiatry there. First he tried the Commonwealth of Northern Mariana, but when officials learned of the Virginia Medical Board's permanent revocation of his license, they squelched his plan to practice psychiatry there.

Next he went to the Island of Palau, but that effort also failed and his application to work with troubled teenagers at Palau Memorial Hospital was turned down.

✝ ✝ ✝

Despite what he's been through, Kenny Embert's Christian faith remains: "Today I mainly just go to church, listen to the preacher, and pray. There's no way of my getting out of that. But I don't want to get involved any more than that. I've been on the inside of things and on the outside and you've got preachers falling like flies." Today Kenny is a happily employed school bus driver who enjoys time to himself with his dog and several cats and his new girlfriend and her little girl.

Kenny's brother, Jason, is in the U.S. Army and has served in South Korea. Jason was happily married in July 1995. His wife will graduate from college in 1997. Jason left the army in 1996 and plans to use the college tuition money which he earned through his army service to study to become a registered nurse.

Both boys feel that the worst of their ordeal is now over. They experience very few flashbacks or bad memories.

Macalynn Embert ruminated, shook her head, and said, "I've found out so much about Tony Leyva that it'd take me forever to try and understand it all! I still have nightmares about him! They haven't gone totally away. I hope they do, though!

"So much of it just comes in flashbacks.... Like when I walked in and caught Ed and Bubba [Gordon] having sex together. So much of it was in that two-week span at the last. Nobody will ever understand how much hell I went through there at the last when I found out what Tony done to my two boys!"

Today Macalynn is happily married to an easy-going, retired Baptist preacher twelve years her senior who, to her joy, firmly but lovingly wears the pants in the family. She is a volunteer chaplain for the Texas Department of Corrections.

✝ ✝ ✝

Said Tony's Roanoke preacher friend James R. Carter, "Well, [Tony] come back to me after this thing happened, after he got in trouble, and I had warned him on a couple of occasions and he said, 'You told me it would happen, and it did.' "

And when Carter was asked in late 1993 if Tony still had any supporters remaining in the Roanoke, Virginia, area, he replied: "I don't know of anybody that is now."

✝ ✝ ✝

Former Roanoke County CPS worker Ann Martin was asked for her overview of the Leyva case and she went into it at great though very interesting length:

"Well, for me it was a textbook case. The victims were kids who were in trouble, kids who came from broken homes, not real well-to-do families, that particular type of thing who Mr. Leyva was then able to choose as his victims because of those factors. You know, being that he was a religious man and it involved a lot of pseudo-revival kinds of things, a lot of the families just couldn't believe it. I would say that in this area here today [1993] you would still have a division between the people who do not believe it at all and feel like the government railroaded a prophet of God and those that say, 'Well, yeah, he did it.'

"We found that there were kids involved from all up and down the eastern seaboard, all the way over to Louisiana, and even into the Caribbean islands. . . . it was pretty amazing to me! I mean, here was a whole ring of people involved in the ministry and they were all classic pedophiles, recruiting the boys and using them and swapping them and then when they got out of the age range that they preferred, they just dumped them. And they were very manipulative, using gifts and promises and other typical things to get these kids to do what they wanted them to.

"I think that a lot of these kids got messed up even more than if they had just grown up in the troubled families they were already in. And so, you know, Mr. Leyva himself to the bitter end never believed that he did anything wrong! Never! And wants to come out of prison and do it again, apparently!

"But I think back on all of the interviews that we did of the victims in our area—I'd say about ten different boys myself; Hudson did more; I really can't remember exactly how many—but when we worked it in the county we at first thought we had just one victim.

"But then we got Mark back here from Georgia and when we started talking to him, that led us to another and another and another in jurisdictions all over the southeastern part of this country! We contacted the FBI and said, 'We think we have something pretty big here! . . .

"Ours was a drawn-out case and it was real hard to hold our victims together. And when we did [get them together], they were a mess! But I think as far as [Roanoke] County being aggressive in handling it, we did all we could with what we had. And we were able to get a conviction and this enabled the federal government to go forward with their case. We were aware that there were victims from all over the place. A lot of them we had were from outside the area, like from North Carolina and Delaware and Georgia. And, you know, it was really interesting to see how over decades it went on . . . we saw grown men who had been molested when they were young kids themselves! Well into their thirties and some up in their forties!

"Me and [Garrick Hudson] took Anthony Grooms . . . out to dinner and he talked about it happening to him when he was just twelve in a church office. It was real interesting talking with him because his parents had tried to do something about it back then and I can remember him crying in the restaurant as he told us about what happened.

"It was really hard to hear it coming from him because he was just a good ol' boy, red-neck kind of fellow, and to hear him say what it had done to him, well, we knew we had to try and stop Leyva. We knew we had to do everything we could do to make a case. And we did! It makes me feel good that I have been able to do something about Tony Leyva, so maybe I will have saved somebody else from being molested down the road."

✝ ✝ ✝

As I was researching this book, some people in city, county, state, and federal law enforcement agencies tried to keep from the public certain details of the case against Tony Leyva, Ed Morris, Freddie Herring, Dr. William Gray, and Jimmy Casey. However, Randy Leach did everything that he could to circumvent these efforts. Therefore, as a public servant, it bears repeating what Leach told me one day: "I'm certainly not going to cover anything up. I don't understand why anybody would want to hold back the facts in these cases. As a matter of fact, I think all of the facts should be out there for the people to know what really happened!"

Chapter 20

This Presbyterian minister's son was truly brought up right for, beginning with his trial preparation and continuing well afterward, Randy Leach showed deep concern for the victims of Tony Leyva whom he came to know, particularly Mark Crump and most especially after Mark's mother was killed by Jimmy Casey. Sadly, Randy remarked: "After Jimmy's suicide, that's the last time that we ever heard from Mark because he never called us. We tried to find him a couple of times. No request for counseling, nothing else. We tried to tell him, 'We'll help you any way we can, give us a call.' And we haven't laid eyes on him . . . since. . . . We just don't know where he went."

☦ ☦ ☦

Another person who continues the good fight against sexual abuse and assault in the Roanoke area is Franklin County Sheriff's Deputy Bonnie Beatty, who doggedly investigated Dr. Gray. She said: "Looking back, I wonder how Dr. Gray got away with it for so long. . . . Granted, we didn't have the strongest victims in the world. Maybe we're underestimating our victims. But on the other side of the coin you're dealing with a highly intelligent man who has got lots of money.

"However, there again it's like 4-H counselors and assistant recreation directors and such; there's smoke but no fire. . . . Just give me one kid . . . to come in and sit down and talk to me and give me names. Let me handle it from there. Let me talk to them. I mean, if [the assaults] occurred in Franklin County, fine: don't tamper with that. Let me deal with it. And that's a problem. . . . I've got other jurisdictions who want to get in and get all the information out of the victims.

"And I've even run into a jurisdiction where a kid said something happened in Franklin County, but he didn't want to go to court, he didn't want to testify, so therefore the jurisdiction didn't report it to me! When I discovered that I hit the ceiling! Now, that's all there was to it! I went over to that county and I talked to their supervisor and I said, 'I want to tell you something!' . . . If it happened in Franklin County and it's reported to you, you report it to me! Give me my chance with this individual! . . .

"You know, let [the victim] tell me they don't want to pursue it. So, that's what I'm running into, but then I'm only one person in this area that handles sexual assault cases. Nobody else does. Quite frankly, I'm spread awfully thin. As a matter of fact, just working on the Gray case I don't feel that I had the time to do it justice. If that's all I had to deal with and all I had to work with, I would have come up with four or five boxloads of evidence instead of just one.

"But with my other caseload, I couldn't handle it. . . . That's why I told my supervisors that this is the last [big case] that I'm going to deal with by myself. Bring somebody in to take over my caseload, my already existing caseload. So that's where we are bogged down as far as being law enforcement officers. We are limited as far as our time and energies and we cannot get into it because of our caseloads. Nobody else wants to deal with these kinds of cases anyway, I'll tell you that! Sexual assault cases turn them off!

"In law enforcement, everybody shuns . . . these kinds of cases . . . especially the men. Absolutely. I'm spoiled in my job, I know that. But then they all want to keep me happy because then they won't have to deal with it. They don't *want* to deal with it. They don't *want* to do it. And half the time they don't even know what I am doing! All they know is that I'm making cases, we're getting convictions, and I'm out here going a mile a minute.

"After eighteen years I've established myself in that I don't care who you are, if there is a complaint brought to me and there's enough probable cause, then I'm going for it! I had to charge one of our uniformed officers with sexual assault on a female. Therefore, I'm not the most popular person around the department or around the county. But that's the way it is!"

✝ ✝ ✝

When Mark was last interviewed in 1993 he was asked how his life was going: "I'll tell you right now, it's fucked it up and I have *no* idea!"

Mark very definitely feels that Tony, Ed, and Freddie did not get enough time in prison: "I wish the motherfuckers would die in there! If I had them all in front of me and I had an Uzi? I'd blow them all away! They fucked up my life . . . you can damn well guarantee it!"

And even though he feels that he might benefit from some counseling, Mark said, "After Dr. Gray, I can't trust nobody, no more! My wife [whom he married in 1992] is the best I've got and she understands me. I'm going to make it in spite of everything I've been through. But without her I never will make it."

✝ ✝ ✝

Chapter 20

Since his involvement with Tony Leyva, R. C. Roundtree of New Orleans has been in a great deal of trouble; like Mark, he blames it on his seduction and molestation by Leyva. When I interviewed R.C. in 1989, he said, "I'm seventeen years old now. This stuff with Tony Leyva happened when I was thirteen. Now, today, for me there is no such thing as God. All of the preachers are liars. Today I can't get along with a preacher for nothing in the world!

"Six months after what happened between Tony Leyva and me, I went to jail for one year for theft, breaking and entering, all kinds of stuff. Every time I go by a preacher and he tells me something about the Lord loves me, I tense up. It's just how I feel about preachers now!

"I was in this group home, but I left there and left all my clothes there and then somebody snatched them up. So now I ain't got no clothes to wear. Today, most of the time, I just float around all day long. I don't look for trouble no more, though. I might be the poorest person in the world, but I won't touch nobody else's property. I stay by my mama or with my girlfriend or play football or basketball, ya know, walk around . . . something to keep myself occupied.

"I've thought about finishing school, but things are not going right for me now. My mother's in the hospital and my family is mad at me. Mama, she had a nervous breakdown 'cause of me fighting almost everyday out in front of the house.

"[Leyva] was a preacher had everybody fooled! He had *me* fooled! Until I found out what he was really about. They wouldn't have wanted me to come to court 'cause if I'd seen his face and if he'd have told me 'I never did this,' I'd have jumped off the stand and jumped on him!"

✝ ✝ ✝

A few weeks after Tony Leyva's sentencing in federal court in Roanoke, Virginia, I interviewed sixteen-year-old Rusty Sims in his bedroom in his family's comfortable middle-class Louisiana home. Said he: "To tell you the truth, tonight talking to you was the first time that I really talked to anybody about it. The FBI asked me all kinds of questions and I never answered. I answered truthfully, but I didn't answer because, still, I admit there was embarrassment. As much as I knew they were trying to help, . . . I had a lot of pride, and I was very ashamed. Like I said, everything I said to them was true. I just didn't tell them everything.

"I can say that I was concerned for everybody out there to whom this happened. Hopefully, it will never happen to them again. It's a bad experience and it's something I don't want to live with, but I have to. I can't get away from it! And I think it's the best thing for everybody to know what happened.

"I ran from the Lord for a good while. I didn't know if I understood why it was going on and I guess in the past few weeks, I really started looking back towards God and realizing that it wasn't Him who did it. Even tonight, me and my girlfriend made new commitments to fulfill, because I still love God and if I do become a preacher, I'll be a straight preacher and I will preach the Word like it's supposed to be preached and not go around molesting little boys or little girls.

"Because, from my own experience, I would never want to put anybody . . . adults, kids, *anybody* through the kind of stuff that I was put through. It was a horrible experience! I was just ten years old when Tony started doing that stuff with me! . . .

"As for my background, all I can say is today I've got good parents. As you can see, we're a lot better off than most other people. I don't think there's anybody else who has as much love in their home as we do. I'm not speaking that we're real rich and stuff, but we're not hurting. It was just that back then Tony Leyva knew how to treat us and love us to get to us. Yes he did!"

✝ ✝ ✝

Darrell Wayne Sharp's mother, Martha, was quite upset that Jenny Montgomery and the U.S. Attorney's Office in Roanoke never fulfilled their promises for HIV/AIDS screening for the victims, counseling for the victims and their families, and job training for the victims, at least those who were federal witnesses.

Said Martha during a phone interview in 1993, "You see, Tony Leyva and his bunch wanted to really seal this whole thing in . . . to stop all the stories about him. Some people might tell you different, but pretty much I've kept my mouth shut until now. But, now, I ain't keeping it shut no longer. When my boy Darrell Wayne left us to travel with Tony Leyva, you couldn't ask for a finer young man. I mean, he was well respected [by] everybody. But after he spent time with Tony Leyva and that bunch and then come back home, it was just like he resented us. We had to go into therapy and stuff, and I don't regret that one day that I sit here! I'm behind Darrell Wayne 100 percent! What I regret is what happened to Darrell Wayne with them perverts! . . .

"I think that the government should set up a free clinic and help all of the families with counseling and such and then turn around and sue [Leyva, Morris, and Herring] and make them pay for all that they have done. Lord knows they took in enough money when they were running around preaching and molesting kids!

"And I don't think [the evangelists] deserve counseling there in prison. They're getting it and the boys they molested are not! I think they should be denied it and go to prison and serve their time just like any other criminal. I'd like to see all three hung on a cross and tortured. That's mean, I know . . . but they hurt my boy bad.

"My son Darrell Wayne was sexually abused by all three of them. . . . Tony Leyva gave him money to keep quiet and when he wouldn't keep quiet, he threatened him about telling what he done to him. Darrell Wayne even come to me and said, 'If you and I testify, we're dead.' Now, that was the threat that Tony Leyva made. And I have had phone calls in the middle of the night where people will just breathe. They don't say nothin', but it bothers me nonetheless.

"And if they put Tony Leyva behind bars for the rest of his life, then so be it. I wanna see it! I wanna see justice! . . .

"But if my oldest boy met Tony Leyva on the street, he'd kill him in a minute. It [would] never do that man to even set foot around my boy after what he done to his little brother. . . . He'd blow [Leyva] away! I'm honest. The Bible says they're worthy of death and that's the way I feel. That's the Word. I've got a right to stand up for the Word! I think it should be a capital punishment and do it by the electric chair. That's my feelings. I don't even have to think about it!"

☦ ☦ ☦

Susan Plunkett has experienced some real spiritual problems since learning that what she had long suspected had indeed been done to her sons by Tony Leyva. As she put it: "The Lord says to join yourselves with other Christian brothers. . . . But how do you know who is the Christian? How do you know who's your brother or who's your sister or who's really dedicated or who's just there to sexually abuse your kids? You don't know that anymore! You just don't know! The only thing that I can do to get back with the Lord is stay at home and read my Bible and let him reveal to me what he wants to reveal to me, and keep my mind off of other people and what's going on.

"All those boys who they abused, mine included, they were ashamed for their parents to know what was happening . . . and they just didn't know how to go about it. It's hurt them so bad that it's going to be hard to win them back over to God. How are they ever going to trust anymore?

"Because of Tony Leyva, I'm a long ways in my Christianity from where I was. I'm a long ways from God. I dropped out of the churches because I didn't trust nobody; I didn't trust the preachers. I still trust God. I still believe in God. But I don't pray like I did. I don't read my Bible like I did. It's still hurting my Christianity and I'm concerned for my own salvation. Hey, I don't want to drift so far away from my faith that I can't find my way back!

"This whole thing has really hurt Robert and Timothy [Earls]. At one time, my sons were good boys; they would never sit down to a meal without praying; they read their Bibles; they always prayed at night before they went to bed; I always kept them in church.

"But after going with Tony Leyva, they have never went to a church with me again; they never went to another revival meeting with me. So, it's really hurt them. This concerns me about my walk with the Lord, 'cause, you know, He says that when He saves you, He'll save your household. But you also have to pray for your children, you pray for your household. It's really been a lot on me. Really, it's been torture to me."

✝ ✝ ✝

In April 1993 Anthony Grooms went to the office of the daily local newspaper in Hendersonville, North Carolina, the home of Tony Leyva's mother and his second wife. At the *Hendersonville Citizen-Times* David checked their microfilm records of editions published from two weeks before Tony Leyva's state trial and conviction in Roanoke, to two weeks following his plea bargain in federal court. He found only one article and one interesting development: the microfilm containing that article had been damaged badly by some unknown liquid making the piece illegible. And the *Citizen-Times* staff had no idea how that had happened.

✝ ✝ ✝

Randy Leach was asked how Roanoke County, Virginia's experiences with prosecuting Tony Leyva and the attempts to prosecute Dr. Gray have affected their approach to child sex abuse cases: "We're always looking for it! If somebody brings a complaint to us about any kind of child abuse, we're always concerned. We know that there's enough of this stuff that goes on that we will look at it hard. And the police department in the county looks for it. The old sheriff's department did, too!

"The problem is that I'm not sure the people, the citizens that have kids that are out there and get preyed on, . . . are aware of it. You know, it's like always: 'It can't happen to us.' It's that kind of attitude.

"You know, they bring it to me—nothing shocks me anymore, after Leyva and some other stuff . . . but it's brought to me and by then there's not a whole lot that I can do. I mean, I'm not the one who can go out and prevent it. The police are out there all the time telling people, 'Look out for this, look out for that' about people getting involved with kids.

"But I'm not sure the citizens realize that this kind of stuff happens in Roanoke County, in Roanoke City, in Salem, all over! I'm just not sure that they're sufficiently aware of it. . . .

"It's really scary because we recognize it and by the time we see it and investigate it and go to court to prove it, it's already happened. At that point you can't stop it. You know, the thing is you've got to convince parents that they've got to be aware that there are people out there like this and they have to protect their children! It's *their* responsibility!

"But people . . . well, people just don't understand that it goes on all the time. They'd rather ignore it. They'd just rather ignore it."

✝ ✝ ✝

When I interviewed Darrell Wayne Sharp by phone in 1993, he mentioned one of his fellow victims, Benny Simpson. Simpson was one of the boys who refused to testify in either state or federal proceedings against Leyva who, it was rumored, paid the boy off to keep him quiet.

Darrell Wayne recalled: "Benny was on Tony's side. And to this day he still supports him. And here's the funny thing. After the trial and everything me and Mark [Crump], we kind of stayed in touch and helped each other with support and stuff.

"Mark knew where Benny lived, and we went riding around the neighborhood and we found Benny. Well, Mark asked him, 'Do you want to go for a ride?' And me, him, and Benny all went ridin' and Mark was asking Benny about things and stuff and Benny said, 'I let happen to me what I wanted to let happen to me.'

"I just said 'okay' and drove on and kept my mouth shut.

"But through the years it seems like me and Mark was the only ones that tried to keep in touch with Betty Fitzgerald, the federal witness coordinator. Me and him was the only ones even tried to keep in touch with [the U.S. Attorney's office]. We promised them we would and we told them how we was doing and everything. It's my understanding that Mark got married. It was an older lady, but it don't make no difference to me. Long as Mark's happy, that's the main point."

In 1991, Darrell Wayne Sharp was happily married, a father, a hard worker, and owner of a nice house outside of Roanoke. At the mention of his children, his work, and the house, Darrell Wayne smiled broadly and said, "Yeah, I been busy!

"I'm just basically doing pretty good. I'm just lettin' the past rest. That's about the best thing I can do . . . go on with my life and not dwell on it because just to bring it back up I'd be sitting and moping and everything."

However, at the mention of Herring and Morris being out of prison and the date for Tony Leyva's first parole hearing then rapidly approaching, Darrell Wayne got very upset, convinced as he was that the three would seduce and sexually assault still more children. "They need to be stopped! I mean, you stop and think, this sort of thing is happening every day. It's happening to children every day! It puts a bearing on their life. And these guys say, 'Well, we're really not doing them no harm.'

"Hell, if you want to have sex with another male, go find an adult. Leave the kids alone! You shouldn't even cross their boundaries! What the government needs to do is step in and make stronger laws on this. They need to be doing more than just slapping them on the wrist and saying, 'Okay, you're guilty. You go to jail for a little bit and then you're free.' That's bull!"

In 1992, Darrell Wayne and his wife began a slow slide into increasingly serious emotional problems exacerbated by drug abuse. By 1993, they had lost custody of their children because of neglect and physical abuse. The courts placed the children with Darrell Wayne's mother. At the end of 1995, she told me by phone how sad she was about Darrell Wayne's troubles: "They're greater than anybody else in our family's ever seen. And I blame Tony Leyva and that bunch for every bit of it!

"Back when them trials for Leyva and that bunch was going on, Darrell Wayne wanted to go get counseling. What happened to him was hurting him something awful. And they [Assistant U.S. Attorney Jenny Montgomery] promised him and the others that they'd get counseling. But him and the others never got any! All they got for their troubles was lip service!"

✝ ✝ ✝

Even in prison M. I. Leyva—the former Super Christian, Brother Tony Leyva—is still ingratiating himself with the gullible faithful with his own peculiar brand of Pentecostal preaching.

According to an official at his most recent prison, the Federal Correctional Institute in Tallahassee, Florida, Tony Leyva is still writing for the *Eschatology Digest*; his second wife, Sherry Lynn, and mother, Ada, are still sending it out; and many of those receiving it send them money, much of it going to attorney Daniel F. Crandall to further his efforts to get Brother Tony out early without having to return to Virginia to serve any time there—something which Randy Leach assures me just won't happen!

And Sherry and Ada are busily making plans for that day when their husband and son eventually gets out of prison—a day that almost one thousand young men and their families fervently hope never comes.

Epilogue

NAMBLA Revisited, the Author's Travails, Pedophiles, Pederasts' Assaults, and Helping and Protecting Children

For more than a decade now I have kept tabs on the North American Man/Boy Love Association (NAMBLA) and its members. My experiences have convinced me beyond the shadow of a doubt that on a regular basis throughout the United States, Canada, Mexico, and many other countries NAMBLA members seduce and sexually assault boys from age three through their late teens, doing absolutely unbelievable harm to them. Also, at the very least I am convinced that NAMBLA's meetings and publications—particularly the nearly five thousand monthly copies of each issue of the *NAMBLA Bulletin* as well as its newer and equally damnable publication *Gayme* (aimed at ephebophiles and with suggestive nude photographs of teenage boys) serve to affirm and validate the sick, criminal sexual assaults on children committed by many of their pederast readers.

When my first book, *I Know My First Name Is Steven*, was published in December 1991, it garnered major national media interest due to my "Author's Epilogue," particularly the five pages constituting the first detailed public "outing" of NAMBLA, which FBI Behavioral Sciences Unit Supervisory Special Agent Kenneth Lanning calls "the most dangerous organization of pedophiles in the U.S." In that epilogue I described my first infiltration of NAMBLA in New York City in April 1985, when their then National Membership Secretary, Robert (Bob) Rhodes—an attorney with the Veterans Administration in New Jersey—unwittingly brought me as his guest to a private meeting of the group's leading officers.

I first become aware of NAMBLA through *Time* magazine's January 17, 1983 article entitled "A New Furor Over Pedophilia," the first major national publication to report on the group. There it was reported that in a 1981 child molestation case on Long Island several of those arrested were NAMBLA members including ". . . a New York City neurologist, an Ohio politician, and a California physicist." The piece also reported that in New Jersey in 1982, police "picked up on various child-sex charges . . . a computer salesman, a department store manager, a bank official, and a male nurse," two of whom were NAMBLA members. In that article a psychiatrist and a clinical psychologist with a decade's experience treating pedophiles confirmed: (1) most pedophiles feel a need to dominate and therefore go after children, since that provides them with the greatest power differential; (2) most pedophiles were themselves sexually abused as children; and (3) most pedophiles idealize their sex abuse as a child so that what they are doing seems normal to them. The article stated: "To hear many pedophiles tell it, they are actually protecting the child by isolating him in a warm, romantic setting, where he gets the love that parents and peers refuse to give. . . .

"As the emergence of NAMBLA shows, pedophiles have learned to package their desires in the language of free sexual expression and the children's rights movement. But no matter how sanitized, it is still the systematic exploitation of the weak and immature by the powerful and disturbed." About a NAMBLA press conference the article said: "For parents watching excerpts from the press conference on television, it was yet another appalling development on the sexual front: a group devoted to child molesters' lib."

✝ ✝ ✝

In April 1985, I was living near Idaho Springs, Colorado. During the previous year I had written twice to NAMBLA at their New York post office box by using my real name and address and describing myself as a successful travel writer (I was not) with a nine-year-old foster son living with me with whom I was having sex (also not true) and that I was considering donating a large sum of money to NAMBLA (no way). I asked to meet some NAMBLA members the next time I was in New York on business.

My letters went unanswered until April 12, 1985, when I was in New York City and received a phone call at my hotel room from Bob Rhodes inviting me to join him at that evening's meeting of the slick-paper *Bulletin*'s collective.

Rhodes requested that I rendezvous with him at the group's mail box at the U.S. Post Office Midtown Station. There a grossly overweight, plum-shaped man in his late thirties, wearing horn-rimmed spectacles approached me, stuck out his hand, and in a high voice announced, "Hi! I'm Bob Rhodes, Mr. Echols."

We rode the subway to *Bulletin* editor Renato Corazza's fifth-floor apartment at 222 East 10th Street. There Rhodes introduced me to NAMBLA Founder and President David Thorstad, an editor in the publishing business; NAMBLA Treasurer Peter Melzer, a tenured physics teacher at the Bronx High School of Science; collective member Peter Reed, a teacher in the New York public schools; and Corazza, a teacher of Italian and an artist.

Even though Rhodes and the others had never met me before, they welcomed me as a brother. They immediately began discussing their sexual experiences with boys and reading recently received correspondence from NAMBLA members about their own sexual liaisons with boys, many of whom were incarcerated for sexually assaulting boys. These letters included the members' names, addresses, and gave the writers' occupations, many of which were obviously positions working with children, a sort of odd braggadocio.

I soon realized that by joining NAMBLA I could provide myself with a rich, continuous source of information about NAMBLA by receiving the *Bulletin* and other organization mailings; I therefore did so. But in completing the transaction I inadvertently referred to one of those present as a "pedophile" whereupon Rhodes sharply corrected me with: "Pedophile is an unfortunate choice of a word; we would prefer 'boy lover'."

This is a very clear and important distinction which NAMBLA members constantly draw about themselves: In no way do they see themselves as "child molesters," "pedophiles," or "pederasts." Indeed, they regard such terms as very pejorative and they repeatedly stress that they are "boy lovers." As such they view themselves as completely benign and very loving of boys in a positive sense. In short, NAMBLA members see the world and themselves through the ultimate rose-tinted glasses!

Later that evening Melzer and Rhodes asked me to help sort by address the April mailing of over four hundred pre-addressed copies of the *Bulletin*, each destined for a member in towns and cities all across the U.S. as well as overseas. They were already sealed in plain brown nine-by-twelve-inch envelopes marked in bold black type "First Class," and with a return address reading simply, "P.O. Box 174, Midtown Station, New York, NY 10018."

Some *Bulletin*s were addressed to just a post office box or street address, but as I sorted I made mental notes of the approximately one-third that did have names, most especially those followed by titles which clearly indicated that the recipient had a professional position of trust with children, boys in particular: boy choir directors, YMCA officials, Boy Scout leaders, priests, ministers, rabbis, teachers, coaches, and others.

It would be helpful for law enforcement personnel and other professionals who genuinely care about the welfare of children to note the style of the *Bulletin*'s return address and manner of mailing, should they see anyone receiving it or letters or other material emanating from NAMBLA's New York headquarters.

As the evening deepened I wove my "autobiography" as a pedophile and travel writer to the point that those present seemed to be taken in hook, line, and sinker. With encouragement from the others, Melzer handed me a small metal file box with cards containing NAMBLA's membership and financial records and encouraged me to freely look through them. As I perused the cards I saw the names of several prominent individuals along with the amounts they contributed, such as the poet Allen Ginsberg* and an internationally known novelist. I was then invited to join NAMBLA and to purchase back issues of the *Bulletin*. I happily accepted, joined, and selected a dozen issues to take with me, my membership promising my monthly receipt of future issues.

Once back in Colorado, I read and made copious notes from my newly-acquired *Bulletin* library. And I also contacted the FBI in Denver to tell them of my meeting in New York. Two agents who came up to Idaho Springs to talk with me showed me photographs of several missing boys whom they felt NAMBLA members might be involved with; however, I could not identify any as being boys whose photographs NAMBLA members had showed around. For the next couple of years I continued sending in my annual dues and NAMBLA continued sending me the *Bulletin*. But

---

*For years Ginsberg has proudly proclaimed his membership in NAMBLA as well as his sexual attraction to young boys. He was featured at the 1989 NAMBLA National Conference where he read his poem "Sweet Boy, Gimme Yr Ass" from his self-described "pederast rhapsody" poetry collection, *Mind Breaths,* a third of which are graphic poems about sex with boys. In that particular poem, Ginsberg asks " . . . ever slept with a man before?" And then he goes into explicit detail about just what he would do with a young boy in bed. Ginsberg has been quoted as being a member and supporter of NAMBLA in the following publications: *Harper's Magazine,* January 1990 (article by Tom Lofton), the *Advocate,* March 26, 1991; *NAMBLA Bulletin,* October 1991, and the *San Francisco Examiner,* September 16, 1994 (article by Barry Walters).

Rhodes and his fellows didn't appreciate whom they had entertained and allowed to join NAMBLA on April 12, 1985, until December 1991.

When *I Know My First Name Is Steven* was published, I was living with a friend in the San Francisco Bay Area. On a day trip to San Francisco on December 2, I recalled that there was a NAMBLA chapter in the city. Picking up a copy of the gay and lesbian newspaper *Bay Times,* I checked their "Calendar of Events." Under Saturday, December 7, I found:

> NAMBLA (North American Man/Boy Love Assoc.) will hold its next monthly public meeting 3 to 5 P.M. at the Potrero Hill Neighborhood Public Library, 20th and Connecticut Streets, San Francisco. For information call 415/564-2602 or write NAMBLA, 537 Jones St. #8418, San Francisco, CA 94102

This offered me an opportunity I could ill afford to miss: I had let my NAMBLA membership lapse and with it my subscription to the *Bulletin*. I went to San Francisco's largest gay and lesbian book store, A Different Light, on Castro Street, to see if they carried the *Bulletin*. They did and I got a copy of the October 1991 issue to read about what NAMBLA had been up to lately.

This issue contained the usual member-submitted photographs of boys, including a full-page cover shot of a naked twelve-year-old African-American boy; news articles of interest to pedophiles ("Gay Attorney Faces Jail for Helping Boy-Lover" and "Man/Boy Lovers Organize in Finland"); a photograph and article about NAMBLA's most prominent member ("Poet Allen Ginsberg—'Celebrating the Love of Children' "); a first-person piece "by a prisoner jailed for consensual sex with boys" in the "from the Belly of the Beast" column; racy book reviews in "The Boy-Love Bookshelf" column; and the "Boys in the Media" column with current details about films, TV shows, and the theater, featuring boy actors from Ricky Shroder to Macaulay Culkin, as well as a notice that encouraged members to call for a New York State Social Services catalogue of kids needing adoption ("for your very own copy call 1-800-[etc.]"); and the lead articles, "NAMBLA Should Support an Age of Consent of Twelve Years" and "Staying Safe and Happy as a Man/Boy Lover: Guidelines Developed by NAMBLA Activists for Surviving in an Insane World."

In the "Calendar," I confirmed the date, time, and location of the San Francisco chapter's December meeting, right alongside information about the Horatio Alger Chapter's meeting in New York City. Thus informed—

but with a different name and background, and hopefully no one from the 1985 New York meeting present—I planned to once again "become" a pedophile and infiltrate NAMBLA.

Saturday morning, December 7, 1991, Mike Echols—a.k.a. James Hankins, "a closet pedophile from East Texas with a background in advertising, writing, and fund raising"—took a BART train from Concord to San Francisco.

Wanting to arrive after most NAMBLA members had assembled—to make it easier for me to spot any New York members who could identify me—I walked into the library a bit after three o'clock, asked the librarian where the NAMBLA meeting was being held, and was kindly directed to go through the crowded children's reading room and up the stairs leading to the rest rooms and the second-floor meeting room. When I entered the room I saw a handful of men ranging in age from the late twenties to the early seventies, some wearing stylish clothes, others in worn jeans, sweat shirts, and stained sneakers. A frustrated firebrand left-winger held sway, wildly waving his arms and ranting and raving about how "NAMBLA has to find more radical members who are willing to take the streets to organize our brothers to end age-of-consent laws and free all boys to have sex with whomever they please!"

I later learned that this was Nicholas Alan Palmer, a self-acknowledged member of the Revolutionary Workers League who had chaired the controversial fifteenth Annual NAMBLA National Conference in San Francisco the previous month at the Women's Building which NAMBLA had rented under somewhat false pretenses.*

After I had been at the meeting for a minute or so, a tall, gaunt fellow in his forties—Derek Prince by name, I later learned, and as dark a character as ever you would wish to avoid—motioned me to a chair beside him. As I sat down I continued to carefully scan the assembled faces for what I hoped would not be a familiar one. I was relieved to see that there were none.

Unlike my New York infiltration, this time I brought along a con-

---

*The day before it began, the Women's Building's executive director Regina Gabrielle discovered what NAMBLA stood for and wrote a blistering letter trashing NAMBLA which she posted all over the building. In part it stated: "The Women's Building does not advocate, endorse, or support the philosophy of NAMBLA. The Women's Building must clearly look at our current policies and procedures in regard to our rentals. In upholding the First Amendment the Women's Building made a serious error with consequences impacting the rights and protection of children."

cealed cassette tape recorder and extra blank tapes in my windbreaker's large outside pocket to record the meeting. Each time a full tape softly clicked my recorder off, I felt it and was able to reach into my pocket and surreptitiously turn it over or put in a new tape so dexterously that no one was ever the wiser.

Those men attending this NAMBLA meeting were:

Floyd Lemuel Conway, Jr., a balding, very articulate man in his late fifties to early sixties who claimed to be an economist with "a prominent San Francisco law firm" and said that he was gay but preferred teenage boys as sexual partners;

"Bill" [I later learned he was actually Nicholas Alan Palmer] clean cut, nicely dressed, apparently well-educated and respected NAMBLA member of about thirty, who notwithstanding the topics discussed—e.g., an age of consent of three years, and allowing ten-year-old boys to decide if they wanted to have anal sex—discussed them "logically" and methodically;

Derek Prince (described in detail in this Epilogue);

Joel, a short, stocky man in his thirties, a visiting Roman Catholic monk (he showed us an ID) who walked with a pronounced limp in his left leg and who told us he was on a three-month sabbatical from his order's house in east Los Angeles, where he said he worked "with young teenage Chicano boys . . . I like them the best." Joel would go back, "since my order's not cloistered; therefore I can be with the boys when I want to";

Lester, a slouching, always smiling, self-acknowledged grandfather in his sixties who didn't say much at all;

Hans, a very amiable, well-dressed grandfather in his late sixties who spoke with a German accent, who arrived late accompanied by his lover, George, and brought along soft drinks for everyone;

George, Hans's lover, in his late forties, who walked with a moderate limp and was as jovial as his partner was amiable;

Roger, a quiet, balding, unassuming man in his late thirties who said he taught public school in San Francisco;

Kris, a nervous, boyish-looking blond man in his mid-thirties who said that he was freshly out of San Quentin Prison "for sex charges involving a boy," and who admitted, "I'm on parole for another year, but I'm doing minors again" and then told us that two brothers aged twelve and thirteen had run away from home and were now living with him. He asked for our help in hiding them out when his parole officer came calling the following Monday. Several of the men at the table volunteered;

Donnie, a droopy-looking guy in his early forties with a perpetual silly smile on his face.

Soon Floyd wrested control of the meeting from Palmer, pulled out a copy of the October 1991 *Bulletin*, and remarked that we needed to discuss important topics raised in it.

Most agreed with the article "NAMBLA Should Support an Age of Consent of Twelve Years," particularly the position that, "A young person of either sex, between the ages of 8 and 12 years, should be allowed to consent to the erotic acts of fondling, fellatio, and genital orgasm, both active and passive."

But when it came to the lengthy article "Staying Safe and Happy as a Man/Boy Lover: Guidelines Developed by NAMBLA Activists for Surviving in an Insane World," there was disagreement. The statement "Because of the hysteria and the harsh penalties involved for man and boy alike, an argument can be made for not having sex with boys in the U.S. at this time . . ." was called "timid [and] not in keeping with what we stand for" by Palmer. But the young socialist added that he approved of the article's followup remark: "If you decide not to have sex with boys under [the age of] consent, it should be a reasoned choice and not be denial of your sexuality."

Almost all present voiced agreement with the article's craftily worded caution: "If you have sexual relationships with boys, experience tells us [to] develop a positive relationship with your partner's family. . . . Discuss the possibility of police interrogation with your partner. . . . Be sensitive to the boy's family and community. . . . Never discuss the specifics of an illegal relationship with therapists or social workers [because] the law requires these people to report sex with minors to the public authorities [and] sadly many are prepared to violate the trust of their clients."

Also, virtually everyone present acknowledged what for them passed as the article's crudely stated yet bizarrely responsible advice: "Always practice safe sex, and encourage your partner to do the same. No matter who you are having sex with, don't let cum get in the ass, mouth, or open cuts. If you fuck, use a condom."

For the average person, it is most difficult to fathom the article's advice: "If you are a boy in a relationship with a man you have the right to decide whether you and your friend share sex. . . . If a man wants to have sex with you and you don't want sex with him, say so. On the other hand, you should also feel free to initiate sex. . . . If the police want to talk to you, say no. You do not have to talk to the police and they cannot force you to go with them, unless you are under arrest. Unfortunately, many people in our society misunderstand man/boy love."

James Hankins couldn't resist mentioning his alter-ego's just-published book, *I Know My First Name Is Steven*, and my Author's Epilogue which exposed NAMBLA to the nation. None of those present had read the book, but all expressed incredulity and shocked indignation when Hankins quoted the book's author as saying that the very first time NAMBLA officials met him they had given him access to the group's membership and mailing lists. Also, in his guise as a fund raiser, James Hankins suggested that the chapter put together and sell a calendar of semi-nude boys, something which made a hit with those present.

Considering the group's warm, unwitting acceptance of me in New York City and now in San Francisco as James Hankins, it was especially ironic when Floyd reassured first-time attenders and potential members—Hankins included—that such could never happen by pointing out and quoting one last item in the lengthy article "Staying Safe and Happy as a Man/Boy Lover," where under the heading "Your safety as a member of NAMBLA," it was incorrectly and disingenuously stated:

> NAMBLA is a legal organization that advocates changes in the law. We do not break the law or advocate that others break it. Our publications and meetings are protected by the constitutional rights to freedom of speech and assembly. The NAMBLA mailing list is private and is kept secured. It is never released or shared.
>
> Our sense of self-worth and dignity is our best protection against the police state in which we live. The slight risk of joining together with the other man/boy lovers is more than balanced by the opportunity to support each other and stay informed. Being involved in NAMBLA helps prepare you for the challenges we all face.

At this point, Hans arrived with soft drinks. During our break to enjoy them Derek Prince introduced himself to me and proceeded to tell me what at first seemed a truly tall but very sickening tale: In the 1950s his American-born father immigrated from Houston, Texas, to Iran, where he went to work as a drilling engineer in the shah's oil fields. There he met and married the daughter of a wealthy Iranian family, Derek's mother.

Later, the shah appointed Derek's father second-in-command of his notoriously brutal secret police, Sabak. Noticing my incredulity, Derek pulled from a pocket of his cashmere overcoat a folded, official-looking document. Carefully, he unfolded it to reveal a text in what appeared to Farsi, his youthful photograph affixed thereto, his name written in English, and what he said was the Pavlev family crest in raised gold at the top along with the late Shah of Iran's signature at the bottom. This, Derek said, was his Sabak identification document. Then he pointed to the pin in his overcoat's lapel, diamond-studded with the same crest as the document: "A gift," he smiled, "presented to me in 1975 by His Majesty, the shah himself."

Derek waxed nostalgic as he recalled his days in prerevolutionary Iran while in his late teens and twenties: "My father would give me the young sons of the shah's enemies he had rounded up," Derek smiled a sickening, depraved smile and continued, "and let me do anything I wanted to with them: Fuck them, make them go down on me, slap them around! Two or three at a time! And some were as young as ten!" I thought I would gag, and when the meeting resumed my head was still reeling from what I had heard from this most sinister NAMBLA member I have ever met.

In fact, even the general NAMBLA membership came to the same conclusion about Derek Prince at their sixteenth Annual General Membership Conference in Chicago the next summer. The September 1992 *Bulletin* reported: "The conference considered at length . . . the nomination of Derek Prince to the Steering Committee. Prince, who has been involved in the San Francisco chapter, stated that he deserved this distinction based on his efforts in behalf of NAMBLA. Others raised concerns about ties Prince claims to have to the former Shah of Iran and his brutal police apparatus . . . the nomination did not receive a majority vote [and] Prince announced that he would therefore leave NAMBLA."

When the meeting ended, Floyd, Derek, and Bill invited me to join them and a few others at Farley's Coffee House several blocks away on 18th Street. I accepted their invitation.

Several minutes later, as seven of us walked together down 20th Street near Daniel Webster Elementary School, talk turned to how one could "safely" pick up boys there. Limping along, Brother Joel rhapsodized about how he frequently met and befriended "lonely boys who have nobody to care about them" in his ministry at a public school playground in east Los Angeles, adding, "If they're poor and don't have much, once you've been nice to them and done things for them, they trust you and sometimes they'll even go to bed with you."

✝ ✝ ✝

Later, I phoned Luis Velasquez with the Hispanic Ministry Office of the Roman Catholic Archdiocese of Los Angeles and described "Joel" to him, detailing what the man had said about his work in east Los Angeles. I did this both to assist me in having Velasquez identify this person to me—if he would do so—and to protect vulnerable youths by warning the archdiocese.

Several days later Velasquez phoned back and told me that a man matching "Joel's" description had been reported to the archdiocesan offices by several of their churches in east Los Angeles. However, he went on to say, "Joel"—or whatever his name—was not a brother or priest of the Roman Catholic Church and that he might be connected with one of several small fringe churches that frequently include the word "Catholic" in their name in order to mislead the public.

✝ ✝ ✝

After my December 7, 1991, NAMBLA meeting, when we got to Farley's Coffee House we pushed a couple of tables together and then went to the counter to order pastries along with cappuccino, espresso, latte, and mocha before returning to our table to talk about boys. Derek told how he had a fourteen-year-old "lover" who spent a good deal of time "and most weekends" with him at his home. This gaunt Machiavellian pederast bragged about his steady income from the Houston apartment complex which his late father left to him, saying this allowed him to do and buy things for the boy that the lad's single mother "couldn't even dream of."

The November–December 1991 *Bulletin* contained coverage of the fifteenth Annual NAMBLA General Membership Conference held in November, reporting ". . . 60–70 attenders (though never that many in one place at one time) was [sic] somewhat quirky due to the participation of Revolutionary Workers League, a Trotskyite group centered in the Detroit area. RWL is supportive of gay rights in general and NAMBLA in particular." And it remarked the RWL supporter Nicholas Alan Palmer "did a marvelous job chairing the meeting."

This issue also had a pornographic boy-love piece titled "Howling at the Moon" ("I sucked his cock when I was ten!" etc.); "The Entrapments Quiz" featuring an update on how law enforcement tries to snare unwitting pedophiles ("By far, most of those who respond to the cop's kiddie-porn schemes are: a, NAMBLA members; b, isolated pedophiles; c, other cops running their own entrapment schemes."); an article headlined "New Report Shows Homophobia Rampant in UK Man/Boy Sex Cases"; the usual collection of letters from active and frustrated pederasts; and a piece by NAMBLA treasurer Peter Melzer on the back cover, "The Best of Times, The Worst of Times," which provided an update on NAMBLA by stating:

> Many good things are happening. Memberships have increased dramatically. Book store distributions of the *Bulletin* are also up. The quality of the *Bulletin* has improved and our *Journal** is finally on its way. To top things off, we have just put on a very successful conference in San Francisco and received TV coverage free of the usual calumny. NAMBLA's name is recognized in many areas, and our message is being heard by more people.
>
> Nevertheless, if our views are to gain respect, and if we are to be more effective, we need to grow. We need to mount new initiatives. These will require substantial funds.
>
> Right now, our immediate needs are to continue a vigorous and expanded advertising campaign. We need to reach out to the South and Midwest where we are underrepresented. Prisoners incarcerated for consensual relationships [with boys] are a holy cause. We must continue to support them with free subscriptions [to the *Bulletin*] . . .
>
> If NAMBLA is to grow, it will ultimately need office space. This will be especially expensive [and] we cannot grow without money, and to get money, we need to grow. . . .
>
> We want everyone to live for a very long time, but the sad fact is that we all eventually die.
>
> Organizations, especially great ones like NAMBLA, can live far longer than human beings. Having survived for the past thirteen years despite overwhelming odds, it is not inconceivable that we will thrive for another one hundred years. Make out your will to NAMBLA and let us know about it. Do it now, no matter how young you are. None of us may be around when the great beyond beckons, but a vigorous and dedicated organization will still be around to make your ideals live on. Zymurgy is the name of the corporation to which formal wills should be made out. The address is the same as for NAMBLA. The symbolism of this unusual name can be found by looking it up in the dictionary.†

---

*The *NAMBLA Journal* is an infrequently published, trade paperback book with rather esoteric boy-love pieces written by "prominent" pederasts and pedophiles.

†In the *Concise Oxford Dictionary* "zymurgy" is defined as "n., branch of applied chemistry dealing with use of fermentation in brewing, etc."

My West Coast scam on NAMBLA gathered considerable steam on Wednesday, December 18, 1991, when I went to KRON-TV, NBC's San Francisco affiliate, and met with the station's investigative news team, Target 4: Jon Dann, producer; Greg Lyon, reporter; and Craig Franklin, cameraman. After hearing my story, viewing copies of the *Bulletin*, and listening to my audio tapes of the December 7 meeting, they asked me if I would be willing to attend the NAMBLA San Francisco chapter's next scheduled meeting at the Potrero Hill Library on January 4, 1992, with a hidden camera.

Saturday, January 4, dawned cloudy and cool as I took BART from Concord into San Francisco. I arrived at KRON's studios about 1 P.M. so that the four of us could check our signals and brief each other. Franklin had outfitted their smallest video camera-recorder with a state-of-the-art high-tech Elmo spy lens. Using fiber optics he had connected the lens—well-hidden as part of a notebook binder—to the video camera which he had placed in the bottom of Jon Dann's old leather briefcase with books, newspapers, and other items stuffed on top of it. Next, Lyon wired me with a tiny microphone matching the top button of my shirt—the existing button removed with a razor blade—and ran the wire inside my shirt and then up to an inside jacket pocket where he placed a tiny audio recorder and connected the wire.

An hour later I rode with Dann, Franklin, and Lyon in an unmarked KRON-TV van to within a few blocks of the Potrero Hill Library, where they turned on the video and audio recorders and I got out to walk the rest of the way while they shadowed me and then parked just across and down the street from the library. As I walked up to the front entrance several other attendees from the December meeting greeted me warmly. Prince went inside the library, where he got the key to the outside entrance to the second floor. Returning, he unlocked the door, and as he stepped inside and turned on the stairwell light, I remarked, "Lights! Action! Camera!" Prince briefly froze and replied—and was recorded saying—"I certainly hope not!" (Of course, he suspected nothing at the time: however, Dann, Franklin, Lyon, and I all had quite a laugh about it back at the studio.)

By a bit past three o'clock, there were about a dozen NAMBLA members and guests present, most the same ones who had attended the December 7 meeting. Floyd moderated this meeting, conducting it in an orderly, almost parliamentary fashion with seemingly reasoned rhetoric, much unlike the "holy war" approach by Palmer (who was absent). Soon a gentleman in his early sixties, very expensively dressed and dripping with gold and diamond jewelry, entered the meeting room and spoke privately with Floyd before standing to one side to quietly observe most of the meeting. Later, Franklin and Lyon told me that they had seen him drive up in a BMW, had taken down his license number, and—suspecting he was headed to the NAMBLA meeting—had videotaped his arrival. (Later, Lyon told me that he was a prominent citizen of San Francisco whose name he could not reveal.)

At KRON early that afternoon Lyon and the others decided that they would enter the meeting room a few minutes before the meeting's scheduled end at 5:00 P.M. However, when Jon Dann saw the man in the BMW depart at 4:30, he decided to enter then in case the meeting might be breaking up early.

Suddenly and without warning, those of us seated in the second-floor meeting room heard heavy footsteps on the stairs and—as shown on the video and audio tape—all conversation stopped. Everyone turned and stared at the stairs, on the hidden video tape Greg Lyon can be seen popping up over the stair rail, closely followed by Craig Franklin taping it all with a large KRON-TV video camera and Jon Dann behind him in a baseball cap.

Greg Lyon said, "Excuse me, gentlemen. I'm Greg Lyon with Channel 4. Is this the meeting of NAMBLA? If so, I'd like to ask you some questions if I could . . . if there's anybody willing to be a spokesperson."

After a moment's shocked pause, almost every one of those attending this NAMBLA meeting sprang to their feet, snatched up their coats, and scuttled away like cockroaches through the exit opposite the one that Greg Lyon had entered, using the stairs leading down to the Children's Reading Room.

The only person who hung around to speak with Greg Lyon on camera was Floyd. He told Lyon that KRON was "engaging in gestapo tactics" by barging into NAMBLA's library meeting and that no NAMBLA members had ever been arrested in San Francisco on charges of molesting a child. However, ten days later—when KRON broadcast a portion of Floyd's brief conversation with Lyon—Oakland police phoned Lyon with news that the man was actually Floyd Lemuel Conway, Jr., and that they had an outstanding warrant for his arrest on charges of orally copulating with a minor boy in Oakland's Lake Merritt Park. Understandably, even though Floyd promised to call Greg Lyon and come to the station for an interview, he never did.

In a later KRON piece on NAMBLA, San Francisco Police Sergeant

Tom Eisenmann of the Child Sex Abuse Unit said that from 1989 to 1992, his department has arrested twelve men who were either NAMBLA members or closely connected to the organization.

At the December 7, 1991, meeting Nicholas Alan Palmer had given me his home phone number and encouraged me to keep in touch with him. Since then I had had a couple of phone conversations with him in which I curried a relationship. Before KRON telecast their initial NAMBLA story on January 13, 1992, I renewed these contacts as a further entrée to Palmer. After his return from Michigan on January 5, I phoned Palmer to express indignation at KRON's coming into the NAMBLA chapter meeting uninvited. He had already heard about it from Floyd and was very incensed about, as he put it, "this breach of journalistic etiquette."

Greg Lyon and Jon Dann had been disappointed that Palmer had not been at the January 4 meeting. When I phoned them after speaking with Palmer, they asked me to arrange a meeting with him so that they could secretly videotape it for use in their ongoing coverage of NAMBLA. I called Palmer again and he invited me to attend a gay and lesbian protest at San Francisco Mayor Frank Jordan's inauguration on Wednesday, January 8, 1992; I used this as a pretext to invite him to join me in San Francisco for something to eat prior to the demonstration.

At 6:30 P.M. on January 8, we met for burgers at the Civic Center Burger King while nearby a KRON cameraman secretly videotaped our meeting and conversation and then followed us to the demonstration where another KRON cameraman covered Palmer's participation in the protest.

My second one-on-one television scam against Palmer occurred at the request of Krista Bradford, a producer who was with Geraldo Rivera's nationally syndicated tabloid television show "NOW It Can Be Told." The folks at KRON had alerted her to the developing and yet to be televised NAMBLA story and she had asked them to have me phone her. When I did so she asked me to work with her on a segment about NAMBLA, to which I happily agreed.

Krista flew into San Francisco the next weekend; in the meantime I set up another meeting with Palmer at the Sabina India Restaurant on Webster Street in Oakland for Saturday, January 11, so that she and her crew could position themselves as diners at a nearby table and secretly videotape the meeting.

Due to my then being on the lam from dishonest law enforcement authorities in Clear Creek County, Colorado—detailed elsewhere in this Epilogue—Krista made arrangements for me to wear a wig and receive the services of a makeup artist to alter my appearance for her planned full-face interview of me the day after the hidden camera taping at the restaurant.

On Saturday morning, I traveled on the BART into San Francisco, selected a curly red wig at a wig company on Bryant Street, and at three o'clock met Krista and her crew at her sister's apartment on Nob Hill to plan our scam and my interview. About 4:30 P.M. I took a cab to A Different Light bookstore and purchased a gay picture calendar of almost-naked older teenage boys to facilitate my scam against Palmer that evening. This was in reference to my suggestion at the December 7 meeting that NAMBLA put together and sell a similar calendar of much younger boys as a fund raiser.

I took the BART from the 24th Street Station in San Francisco to the 12th Street Station in Oakland while Krista and her crew traveled to the restaurant in their van. They planned to arrive ahead of Palmer and surreptitiously arrange for a suitable table from which they could easily tape my meeting with Palmer.

Everything worked out perfectly: Krista and crew sat nearby and recorded it all as this member of NAMBLA's national board of directors told me how he had just that morning participated in a two-hour conference-call meeting with the other directors, during which they discussed a number of issues. Palmer then handed me the organization's detailed agenda sent to him beforehand via Federal Express.

I have to admit that my hands trembled a bit as I held this and read through its contents loudly so that the audio transmitter Krista had me wearing could pick it up. It did.

One item concerned NAMBLA's need to have their attorney deal with legal issues surrounding the $400,000 estate of a boy lover and NAMBLA member in Baltimore who had died of AIDS and —much to the displeasure of his family—bequeathed it all to NAMBLA. The man's family challenged the will and, understandably, NAMBLA planned to fight to keep their inheritance. Another matter concerned plans to launch a NAMBLA chapter in Dallas, Texas. Palmer told me that "unfortunately" this plan was not welcomed by Dallas's gay and lesbian leaders.

In the "NOW It Can Be Told" segment that Krista produced and aired, during our dinner Palmer can be heard bragging: "What's nice about being in a revolutionary organization [like NAMBLA] is that I can be completely open and honest and say anything to anyone. Well, there are cops that are NAMBLA members. We have dozens and dozens of members in prison. I mean, nothing new there! I've got a record [and] I'm the spokesperson, you know! I'm the only spokesperson we've got!" Then, speaking about Floyd Conway's legal problems, Palmer confirmed that "the boy he got in trouble with he met in a park."

As we were leaving the restaurant Palmer gave me advice on where I could go to pick up boys for sex in Oakland: "If you like video games, I'll let you in on a secret. Go down 15th toward Broadway. It's on the left. It's got a green sign. It's The Oak Tree. The crowd is, of course, almost all boys, like almost all Asian from six to nineteen. You know, I had like a game of escalating smiles with this gorgeous boy [and] he got me all excited." The "NOW It Can Be Told" segment featured an on-camera visit to The Oak Tree Arcade by Krista. It was indeed filled with scores of young boys playing electronic video games.

On Monday, January 13, 1992, KRON-TV began its exclusive reports which revealed the San Francisco NAMBLA chapter's regular meetings at the Potrero Hill Neighborhood Public Library as well as details about its members' criminal backgrounds and the organization itself. All around the San Francisco Bay Area people were riveted to their television sets as the story unfolded daily—on every single KRON newscast—over the next eighteen days!

Before my part in any of this was televised or known publicly, Palmer phoned Greg Lyon the morning of January 15, identified himself as "Alan Davis, a spokesperson for NAMBLA," and asked to come to the station to present NAMBLA's side of the escalating controversy. Greg then phoned me and asked if I would come into the studio to identify Palmer on camera. Therefore, when "Alan Davis" was being shown into the KRON news department's conference room by Greg Lyon, I was sitting in the station's canteen awaiting my cue.

During his interview of "Davis," Lyon asked: "Is there an age below which a child is unable to give consent and, therefore, below which there should be no sexual relationships?"

"Davis" hemmed and hawed and tried to avert the question. Lyon followed up with: "Could sex with a five-year-old conceivably be okay?"

At this "Davis" answered: "I think that children at any age know what they like and don't like."

Shortly thereafter I walked in and identified "Davis" as Nicholas Alan Palmer on camera. Totally flustered, he mumbled a "thank you" and in a seeming daze left the station.

As a result of KRON's coverage the public castigated the San Francisco Library Board for allowing its facilities to be used for NAMBLA meetings; two weeks after the memorable January 4 meeting the same meeting room hosted a group of nearly fifty very angry parents. Said one unidentified mother on camera: "I cannot believe that this kind of thing has gone on for two years. I'm very upset! I have a ten-year-old boy and I cannot allow him to walk freely down the street because of stuff like this!"

A very visibly upset mother added, "I don't care where they meet! They shouldn't meet [at all]! They're breaking the law! It's scary when they meet about molesting young people. It's wrong!"

Robin Acker, a mother from the Potrero Hill neighborhood, summed it up very rationally: "I was shocked that the library would allow a group like this to meet in the library: shocked not only that they would do it, but that they didn't let the community know that it was going on so that the community could take steps to protect the children in the neighborhood!"

During the series of newscasts Greg Lyon, other journalists at KRON, and several professionals and community leaders pointed out that whereas NAMBLA repeatedly invoked the protection of the gay and lesbian community in advocating their right to have sex with boys, the majority of this community vehemently rejected the group's efforts to ride on their coattails.

Included in KRON's reporting was the story and a home video of one Joe Power, who claimed to be a NAMBLA spokesperson. He said on camera before a Bay Area meeting of professionals dealing with the sexual abuse of children: "We're not going to change. All the therapy in the world is not going to change a boy lover into something else." Indeed. Mr. Power was later arrested by Sunnyvale (California) police for having oral sex with a fourteen-year-old boy, convicted, and sentenced to prison.

Then the report told the story of Jeff White, a convicted pederast who had been confirmed as being HIV-positive. According to San Francisco Police Sergeant Tom Eisenmann, when he arrested White the police found a list of 139 young boys who had been his victims, from ages five on up, with the average being nine years old. In his mug shot, White was shown wearing a blue San Francisco NAMBLA chapter T-shirt.

Another lead by KRON's Greg Lyon involved the discovery by Detective Tim Painter, of the Livermore (California) Police Department, that several NAMBLA members had gotten together to operate an orphanage for boys in Thailand. The rules allowed those who supported the facility to check boys out for sex when they came to Thailand on sex tours. Seven of these men are now in prison. Detective Painter also remarked how NAMBLA members built confidence and trust with the sons of single mothers in Livermore and "took [the boys] on trips for the purpose of breaking down their resistance to sexual advances."

Media interest in the story grew tremendously and CNN's talk show "Sonia Live" asked me to appear on the January 17, 1992 show via satellite uplink from San Francisco along with NAMBLA member Roy Radow from New York. I accepted. Also, CNN and CNN Headline News covered the story and their San Francisco Bureau interviewed me and telecast the interview worldwide January 16 and 17. But on the morning of January 17, I was warned by a CNN producer that I would be arrested by Colorado authorities (explained later in this Epilogue) if I came into CNN's San Francisco bureau to appear on "Sonia Live" and I prudently canceled my appearance.

But Nicholas Alan Palmer's downfall came soon after Lyon's televised interview in which I identified him on camera. Several days later Palmer was arrested and booked into Oakland Jail on a charge of molesting a child under the age of eighteen. It later turned out that this was related to Palmer's troubles during the summer of 1991, when he was convicted for "soliciting a lewd act in public" in a case involving a nine-year-old boy to whom he was teaching piano. He had tried to get the child to remove his clothes so that he "could feel what it is like to have oral sex with a man."

Two weeks later Palmer appeared in court on charges that he had violated a condition of his probation on that conviction prohibiting his having any contact with children under the age of fourteen: He had recently been teaching piano to an eight-year-old boy whose parents saw KRON's report and called Oakland police. Palmer was again released on probation with the added stipulations that he not have *any* contact with children under the age of sixteen and that he was never to have any pornography (including the *NAMBLA Bulletin*) in his possession, and that he could be stopped and searched *any* time, *any* place for such material.

On January 20, 1992, NAMBLA held what it called a "press conference" in front of KRON-TV's offices and studios. None of those who attended NAMBLA's January 4 meeting were present; but *Bulletin* editor Bill Andriette from Boston and NAMBLA supporter and attorney Eileen Schiff of Detroit spoke on camera attacking KRON for their "witch hunt" approach to the organization and defending NAMBLA members' "rights" to have "consensual sex with minors."

Contrary to NAMBLA's repeated public assertions, neither KRON, Geraldo Rivera's "NOW It Can Be Told," CNN, nor any other electronic or print journalists whom I helped on this story about NAMBLA have ever paid me; indeed, I would not have accepted it had they offered. The only money I received was for minimal out-of-pocket expenses involved with travel and for dinners with Palmer or else to purchase NAMBLA publications and other printed material for use in these stories.

(The complete story of my exposure of NAMBLA's San Francisco chapter—including Renato Corazza's defense of the group—was best told in the lengthy article "Victory for a Shadowy Crusader" by Scott Harris in the March 10, 1992, *Los Angeles Times*.)

✝ ✝ ✝

The September 1991 issue of *Playboy* carried an essay written by *NAMBLA Bulletin* editor Bill Andriette, whom *Playboy* identified simply as "features editor of *The Guide,* a Boston-based gay magazine." Titled "Are You a Child Pornographer?" the one-page piece gave a broad, somewhat Draconian, and not altogether honest view of the 1990 Federal Comprehensive Crime Act, which makes it illegal for a person to possess as few as three books, magazines, videos, and other materials, showing children under the age of eighteen "engaging in sexually explicit conduct . . . real or simulated."

However, for those who know of Andriette's connection to NAMBLA —and *Playboy*'s staff assured me that they did not—two paragraphs in his essay are clearly indicative of NAMBLA's major ongoing concerns. Weaving another of NAMBLA's attempts at legitimizing itself, Andriette wrote:

> In some cases, [federal] agents succeeded in finding evidence of ongoing sexual abuse—trophy shots of victims—and under the new law, possession of those photographs is as serious a crime as actual abuse.
>
> The new law broadens [this] definition of sexually explicit conduct to include "lascivious exhibitions of the genitals or pubic areas." In other words, it now says that simple child nudity may be illegal. It allows for no distinction between the sweaty collection of a pervert or pederast and the coffee-table art of a responsible parent.

Many pedophiles take nude or sexually explicit photographs of their young victims and then pass them around to one another as an important, integral part of validating their sexual conquests.

Indeed, this was something that I witnessed repeatedly at private gatherings of NAMBLA members following their regular monthly public meetings. And, too, most pedophiles place great value on these photos to enhance their solitary masturbatory sessions.

Epilogue 341

✝ ✝ ✝

Before my San Francisco infiltration of NAMBLA's operations, callers to NAMBLA's headquarters' telephone number in New York City could get a real earful from member Renato Corazza:

> Hello. This is NAMBLA, the North American Man/Boy Love Association in New York. For information, membership applications, or to order books, please write to NAMBLA, P.O. Box 174, Midtown Station, New York, New York 10018.
> In New York the Horatio Alger chapter meets from 3:00 to 5:00 P.M. on the first Saturday of each month at 250 West 54th Street, eleventh floor, in Manhattan.
> In San Francisco our chapter meets from 3:00 to 5:00 P.M. on the first Saturday of each month at the Potrero Hill Public Library, upstairs meeting room, on Twentieth and Connecticut Streets in San Francisco.
> For any other matter please leave a message at the beep. We will call you back as soon as possible, but we'll, uh, have to do it collect.
> In the meanwhile, if you are a boy, do not despair, be true to your feelings. Times will change and your repression will end. If you are a man, be safe, be brave. And above all, be proud to be a boy lover. In either case, thanks for calling and call us again. Our line is open twenty-four hours. Thank you.

But since March 1992 the message on NAMBLA's answering device has become simple and to the point: The number is identified as belonging to NAMBLA, their mail address is given, and that is it. Period.

✝ ✝ ✝

In the summer of 1994, a shocking feature documentary film about NAMBLA and its members, *Chicken Hawk*, was released in movie theaters across the U.S. It had been produced by New York University graduate film student Adi Sideman who told me that he did extensive interviews with NAMBLA members Renato Corazza, Peter Melzer, Robert Rhodes, Leyland Stevenson, and many others. In the film he allowed them to talk freely about how positive they felt about themselves as boy lovers; one nineteen-year-old Maryland pedophile spoke so expansively that the FBI connected him with several abductions and related molestations and obtained warrants for his arrest.

New York Newsday headlined its review of *Chicken Hawk* with "Pedophiles Rationalizing Irrationality," and staff writer John Anderson began with: "Leyland Stevenson, who spent several years in prison for the distribution of child pornography, is probably the scariest of the pedophiles who populate Adi Sideman's *Chicken Hawk*. Smiling beatifically, wheedling his way into children's confidence as he cruises the strip malls, he recalls his sexual encounters with a joy that's unconfined, and thoroughly monstrous."

Seconded reviewer Gary Indiana in the *Village Voice*: "Indeed the creepiest member of the group, Leyland Stevenson recounts a 'camping trip' with a little friend that culminated in anal intercourse. This episode was so natural and joyous that 'no lubrication was required.'"

And reviewer Stephen Holden in the *New York Times* confirmed these views with his succinct statement: "The film's most outspoken and vivid personality, Leyland Stevenson, was imprisoned several years ago for distributing child pornography. He describes his sexual relations with boys in the quasi-religious language of a persecuted fanatic. He even allows the camera to show him cruising in a suburban mini-mall. And his creepy grandiosity casts a clammy chill over the film."

At the mall Stevenson spots a young adolescent boy he would like to bed, walks over to him, and flirts with the boy. After a brief one-sided conversation, the pederast walks away talking glowingly about the boy's infatuation with *him* (Stevenson) by manufacturing a meaningful relationship out of what were actually the boy's disinterested responses to Stevenson's inane questions: a bizarre fabrication by this spooky, menacing predator!

Wrote *Village Voice* reviewer Gary Indiana about the scene: "We see the stout, beaming pederast striking up a conversation with some teens outside a convenience store; into this innocuous brief encounter, he reads a ridiculously elaborate sexual subtext. What we have here is the absurd stuff of obsessive love, and, more alarmingly, the deluded *raison d'être* of the stalker."

In another scene, NAMBLA member Peter Melzer, the Bronx Science physics teacher I had met at the meeting in 1985, laments his fate at having been removed from the classroom. Standing on the balcony of his high-rise apartment and gazing out on a nearby school playground full of boys, Melzer tells Sideman, "I feel like Moses overlooking the promised land but unable to enter."*

---

*In March 1993, after I provided information to him about my San Francisco scam on NAMBLA, WNBC-TV reporter Jonathan Miller in New York City walked into a NAMBLA meeting in a public room at CitiCorp Bank's Midtown Headquarters. After the story aired, the school board put Melzer in a desk job.

Epilogue

The release of *Chicken Hawk* caused a major split between those NAMBLA members who correctly saw it as offering the worst possible public perception of the group, and others like Stevenson, who are so enamored of their sexual lusts that they get narcissistic enjoyment seeing and hearing themselves and their fellow pederasts on the screen talking about sex with boys.

✝ ✝ ✝

Even in England people are taking note of NAMBLA and its *Bulletin* and the problem of child kidnapping and sexual abuse:

The miniseries *I Know My First Name Is Steven*—based on my first book of the same title—was telecast in over one hundred countries, but nowhere was it received with more interest and acclaim than in the United Kingdom, where BBC-1 premiered it in 1990. The person responsible for that broadcast—and for the 1993 rebroadcast—is Mark Dietch, BBC-1 Editor. In February 1993, Mark visited me for two days in Carmel, California. During that time I showed him some issues of the *NAMBLA Bulletin*, including the September 1992 issue whose back cover featured a photo of ten-year-old Prince William and his parents, Prince Charles and Princess Diana. And at Mark's request I made a copy for him to show associates back in London.

Said Mark about his feelings on seeing this: "It is so extreme that my reaction when I first saw it was deep shock, really. It never occurred to me before, but it put the whole thing in perspective for me to see a young male member of the Royal Family as the subject of the sick sexual longings by the pedophile members of NAMBLA. It really did show me to what lengths pedophiles will go, even if it's not a physical thing, just the idea of Prince William being the subject of sexual longing by these perverted people makes me feel sick, really! No one is safe from this kind of abhorrent sexual desire!'

After his return to London, I asked Mark what was the reaction of his associates at the BBC to this distasteful *Bulletin*. "Amazement, really," Mark exclaimed. "I mean, it's something that has never happened before. We just never have thought of it in those ways. You know, you can see movie stars—you know, it doesn't make it defensible—but you can see how some of the younger film actors could be seen as attractive fantasy fodder to pedophiles. But a young child in the Royal Family? The thought just never occurred to us. We don't put our Royal Family up on pedestals, but having the young prince as a sexual object, that is something that had never, ever occurred to us. And it was a new, totally new and frightening concept. 'Shocked' was the single most-used word that I heard. One just can't begin to get into the mind of somebody who is thinking that way."

Mark concluded: "After I first saw *I Know My First Name Is Steven* I had a similar reaction because I had come to know the boy through the course of the program, and I suppose in many ways it's a similar reaction. And while we don't know Prince William, he is part of our culture and for pedophiles to have those same, very sick, sinister thoughts about Prince William and Prince Harry, we find it deeply shocking."

✝ ✝ ✝

In the state of Washington, a law has been passed mandating police to notify the public via news release when a sex offender is released into the community. On October 2, 1992, one such release was put out by the Tacoma Police Department and involved a member of NAMBLA:

> The California Department of Corrections advised the Tacoma Police Department that a sexual offender with a high risk of reoffending, will be released on parole October 2, 1992. The subject in question has advised his parole officer that he will be living in Tacoma, Washington.
>
> This subject, identified as a Jonathan M. Tampico, is a white male, 5'5" in height, 105 pounds with brown hair and a brown beard and mustache, born 02-14-50.
>
> Mr. Tampico was convicted of sexually molesting a twelve-year-old boy in California. While in prison, Tampico received no sexual deviancy treatment and is considered at high risk of reoffending.
>
> Mr. Tampico is a photographer by trade. He is a member of NAMBLA (North American Man/Boy Love Association). The philosophy of this group is that there is nothing wrong with sexual activity between adult males and young boys. The group aggressively recruits and grooms young males, ages 5 to 14, for eventual sexual activities. Mr. Tampico was the photographer for the NAMBLA group and one of its leaders.

In May 1989, a search was executed by California authorities on Jonathan Tampico's home. During this search a manuscript was found for a book entitled "The Survival Manual: The Man's Guide to Staying Safe in Man/Boy Sexual Relationships." This work repeatedly refers to NAMBLA and is a "how to" book for pederasts. It details safe places in which to engage in sex acts with boys, such as parks, friends' houses, and secretly rented apartments and vehicles. It advises the "boy lover," should he be caught, how to flee the country, secure false identities, have money transferred to other countries, and even how to flee with the boy who is the object of his sexual attention.

This manuscript also details methods used by the FBI, U.S. Customs, and police and how the boy lover can protect himself from them. The book is believed to have been written by a man presently serving time in a Massachusetts prison for molesting boys.

Interestingly, there are many similarities between this manuscript and the shocking article in the October 1991 *NAMBLA Bulletin*, "Staying Safe and Happy as a Man/Boy Lover: Guidelines Developed by NAMBLA Activists for Surviving in an Insane World."

✝ ✝ ✝

Canadian law enforcement is now seriously addressing the risks posed by NAMBLA members. Noreen Wolff—who provided me with the foregoing material—is a detective with the Intelligence Unit of the Vancouver Police Department in Vancouver, British Columbia. Since July 1992, when she executed a search warrant on the apartment of a suspected pedophile and found numerous copies of the *NAMBLA Bulletin* along with child pornography, she has been gathering information on NAMBLA.

At one time NAMBLA had a chapter in Toronto—their only known Canadian chapter—but it is no longer functioning, no doubt thanks to increased vigilance by local law enforcement and the Royal Canadian Mounted Police. Today NAMBLA is attempting to intensify its presence in Canada through increased sales of the *Bulletin* in gay and lesbian bookstores as well as in other magazine and bookshops. Said Detective Wolff, "The people who subscribe to the *NAMBLA Bulletin* are the type of people who are going to molest children. Those who purchase the *Bulletin* [in bookstores] want to meet others who are like minded [since] it glorifies sex with children and those with pedophilic tendencies.

"Commercial publications such as the *Bulletin* are presently being seized by Canadian customs when they are discovered and while the pictures in it are in themselves not [legally] pornographic, the whole context of what NAMBLA promotes is the sexual molestation of children."

In 1993 the Canadian Parliament passed a law banning the importation or possession of the *NAMBLA Bulletin*, labeling it as child pornography.

And in the summer of 1994 there was a first conviction under this law—and a ninety-day jail sentence—for a man who simply had a copy of the *Bulletin* in his possession.

Detective Wolff also provided me with information on another earlier police item dealing with a NAMBLA member: On March 8, 1989, pedophile Richard Helwig crossed the border at San Ysidro, California, in a motorhome on his way home from his annual winter stay in Mexico. The man appeared nervous to U.S. Immigration Inspector Carlos Quevedo and was therefore referred to a secondary customs inspection station. During that search U.S. Customs Inspector Mark Chapman found a blue metal box with sixty photographs of nude children inside along with a photo album with an additional seventy-one photographs of nude children. And behind that cache were still more photographs with children exposing their genitals; copies of the *Bulletin*; and twenty videotapes of children's shows interspersed with adult pornographic material, apparently to be used as lures to entice children into believing that such sexual behavior was acceptable.

The agents did a criminal check on Helwig and discovered a long history of arrests for criminal sexual molestation of children, but that time after time the charges had been reduced or dismissed. And when Customs agents opened Helwig's address book they found notations about age of consent laws for boys and girls in different countries, information about laws regarding what constitutes child pornography, and Helwig's U.S. address, which was identical to that of the NAMBLA's San Francisco chapter, an address which was the subject of search warrant by San Francisco Police in October 1987.

On March 9, 1989, Richard Helwig appeared before a U.S. Magistrate and was charged with "transportation of materials involving the sexual exploitation of children." His bail was set at ten thousand dollars and the following day, with a friend from San Francisco co-signing his bond, he posted 10 percent in cash and was released.

Five days later the federal grand jury for the Southern District of California indicted Helwig on one count of "transportation of materials involving the sexual exploitation of children" and recommended an increase of his bail to $500,000. Subsequently, several rolls of film which had been found in Helwig's motorhome were developed and a previously unseen video tape found there was viewed. Virtually all of this material contained hard-core child pornography apparently made by Helwig.

When Helwig failed to make either of his two scheduled court appearances the federal magistrate issued a bench warrant for his arrest. On March 28, 1989, he was surprised and arrested by U.S. Customs agents and federal marshals when he arrived at an address in Tucson, Arizona. In addition to the initial charge, Helwig was also charged with bail jumping plus sexually exploiting children. He pled guilty to bail jumping and was tried and found guilty of the other charges. On January 29, 1990, U.S. District Judge William B. Enright—calling the case "one of the greatest tragedies I have seen"—sentenced Helwig to a total of fourteen years in federal prison and, referring to the fact that Helwig has AIDS, remarked, "in the natural events, Mr. Helwig, you won't be coming out of prison."

✝ ✝ ✝

For years NAMBLA has received a free ride on the coattails of the gay and lesbian community. However, the tide has now turned for this nefarious, egregious group of child molesters and left them high and dry. In 1992 at the time of the NAMBLA debacle over their meetings at the Potrero Hill Public Library, about 60 percent of San Francisco's gay and lesbian community spoke out against them. But today with the national release of the film *Chicken Hawk* and the attendant brouhaha, all across the United States gays and lesbians are loudly saying "NO!" to NAMBLA.

The September 1994 issue of the national gay and lesbian magazine *Out* featured a seventeen-page article about NAMBLA entitled "The Men from the Boys" which is the most informative such article I have ever seen. The piece's author, Jesse Green, interviewed many NAMBLA members including Leyland Stevenson, Bob Rhodes, Bill Andriette, Renato Corazza, as well as recognized spokespeople in the gay and lesbian community. In trying to dismiss concerns about men having sex with boys, he quotes Rhodes as saying: "Any sex that doesn't interest you, you find ridiculous or disgusting. Beyond that, it's no more inherently pathological than any other orientation." To which author Green offers this commentary: "The way he describes it, pedophilia sounds like macramé: a harmless odd hobby."

Green ends his article with this statement against NAMBLA's position and tactics: "NAMBLA never wants to take no for an answer. But we need not let ourselves be coerced, nor let a smile imply consent. The gay community, such as it is, is now old enough to be allowed to choose for itself whom it will get in bed with and whom it will decline."

The September/October 1994 issue of another national gay and lesbian magazine, *10 Percent*, came out with a six-page cover story entitled "Nixing NAMBLA: Turning a Critical Eye on Man-Boy Love." Some excerpts from this critical piece include: "So what is NAMBLA really all about? Sex with children, for one thing. The *NAMBLA Bulletin* claims it doesn't 'advocate or counsel the violation of [existing] laws,' but with its porn stories and sexually charged photos of boys, that's a little like saying *Playboy* doesn't advocate the practice of heterosexual sex."

In discussing the gay and lesbian community's view of NAMBLA the article stated: "Beyond the gay ghettos in large cities such as New York and San Francisco, NAMBLA has never enjoyed the support of many lesbians and gay men. [According to Andrew Barrer, senior adviser to President Clinton's National AIDS Policy Coordinator] 'I've been [a gay] activist for twenty years, and [NAMBLA has] never been on the radar of the people who forged the movement. That's a joke if they think that they've been sold down the river. They were never on the boat in the first place.' "

† † †

On September 9, 1994, NAMBLA members Bill Andriette, Peter Melzer, and Robert Rhodes filed papers and incorporated the organization as a "nonprofit educational corporation" with the name "Zymurgy" under the laws of the State of New York.

In the summer of 1995, New York Attorney General Dennis Vacco filed suit to dissolve the incorporation, claiming that the incorporation papers contained a "fraudulent representation and concealment of material fact" and that the corporation's true purpose was "to encourage and promote criminal relationships between adult males and boys." Further, Vacco alleged, the three NAMBLA members perjured themselves when they swore that the organization had never existed under any other name.

In August of 1995, New York State Supreme Court Judge Robert D. Lippmann ruled in favor of Zymurgy on a technicality: NAMBLA members "advocate the *right*" to sex between men and boys and, since for legal purposes, the right to *advocate* is something which must be allowed, he dismissed the attorney general's suit.

But in New York State the Supreme Court is not the ultimate legal authority and Vacco appealed Judge Lippmann's ruling. Now NAMBLA is using the *NAMBLA Bulletin* and other mailings to members to raise funds for the "Zymurgy Defense Fund," disingenuously comparing the legal fight to that of 1960s civil rights marchers.

On February 5, 1996, Rhodes sent a form letter to NAMBLA members asking them to help in the legal defense of Zymurgy by sending money to NAMBLA attorney Lawrence Stanley in New York City.

✝ ✝ ✝

"We work to organize support for boys and men who have or desire consensual sexual and emotional relationships and to educate society on their positive nature." For almost two decades this bizarre statement has graced the second page of each *NAMBLA Bulletin*. Today I am happy to report that NAMBLA is severely limited in their ability to spread this dangerous, skewed gospel.

When pedophiles and pederasts feel safe enough to meet publicly with each other without fear of being identified as the child molesters they really are, such networking gives them the moral courage to act out their sick, damnable fantasies of sexually molesting children, the opportunity to teach each other how and where to locate the most vulnerable young victims, and the opportunity to learn from each other just how to perpetrate their criminally deviant behavior to avoid detection. But no longer does the group hold public meetings, for even gay and lesbian organizations from New York to Los Angeles now refuse to rent meeting space to them. But everyone who is truly and genuinely concerned about the welfare of children must remain vigilant to prevent a resurgence of NAMBLA.

I *do not* advocate passing laws to make NAMBLA's or any other such groups' public meetings or publications illegal, because to do so would compromise our nation's freedoms and constitutionally guaranteed rights. However, by the very nature of what NAMBLA's members do to children, the playing field could be made more level by their ranks being drastically cut if the police, the public, and television, radio, and print journalists kept tabs on their meetings, activities, publications. This would cause most NAMBLA members and potential NAMBLA members to think twice before participating in anything sponsored by the group.

Nor do I advocate that any harm be done to members of NAMBLA or their property, but I point out that an informed public—police, teachers, social workers, parents, children, indeed everyone concerned about the safety and welfare of children—should remain aware of the potential danger that NAMBLA, its members, and all pedophiles and pederasts pose to children.

✝ ✝ ✝

As the reader should know by now, I am no stranger to controversy. Regarding my life as a freelance investigative journalist, my Episcopal priest,

Fr. Carl R. Hansen, refers to me as a lightning rod and this modus vivendi was quite evident in 1984 when I lived in Clear Creek County, Colorado, and worked as a reporter for the weekly paper the *Clear Creek Courant*.

That fall my auto mechanic, Roger Holman, told me that on several occasions during the early morning hours, he had seen large trucks driving up the dead end road by his house which leads to the old Colorado School of Mines Experimental Mine on the west side of Idaho Springs. He said a friend of his had told him that the trucks were carrying nuclear waste from the Rocky Flats Nuclear Weapons Plant thirty miles away, waste which was being dumped in the shafts of the supposedly abandoned mine. I told this to my editor, Cary Stiff, and he asked me to research the story, and write a rough-draft article, and then he gave me the paper's camera and told me to photograph whatever evidence I could find.

In researching the story I spoke with a former driver of one of the trucks who confirmed Roger's story. With my interest really piqued, before dawn one Saturday morning I went over the locked main gate of the mine with the camera. Hiking to the top of the hill over the main mine shaft, I found and photographed a travel trailer with electronic testing equipment in crates—all labeled as belonging to the U.S. Department of Energy (DOE)—directly over the mine's main shaft. Coaxial cables ran from the trailer and crated equipment into half a dozen shafts, as an electronic hum emanated from inside the trailer.

I took the camera back to Stiff, he developed the film and made contact sheets from the negatives in my presence, we examined them together, and he told me to continue my work on the piece.

I researched the story—including speaking surreptitiously on the phone with an Army major at the Pentagon whose name and phone number had been on the crate's labels (Was *he* angry!)—and then wrote a rough draft and gave it to Stiff. He stalled me for several weeks, then refused to publish the story or photographs and told me to keep my mouth shut about it all. Except for my telling two acquaintances—fellow freelance writer Sarah Nelson and Silver Plume bookstore owner and political activist, Tom Young—I did keep my mouth shut because I was busy finishing my first book.

In July 1984, I had subleased office space in an old bank building in Idaho Springs in which to write my book, *I Know My First Name Is Steven*. County Tax Assessor Ned Biggs also had subleased space there for his private CPA practice. Several months later, when Biggs found out that I was "writing about a pedophile"—i.e., Steven's kidnapper, Kenneth Eugene

Parnell—he told me he did not like that and that he wanted me to move out. I refused. He then tried to get the landlord, attorney Ed Shindel, to kick me out. Shindel would not do so. And Biggs even told his part-time secretary, Barbara Walker—who occasionally worked for me—that he was so mad that I would not move out that he was going to put me out himself and that I would "live to regret it."

In February 1985, Biggs took matters into his own hands: he boxed up my interview tapes and almost completed manuscript, and hid them from me, and—even though he had no legal right to do so—changed the locks on the building and posted signs telling me to stay out.

I tried unsuccessfully to get the Idaho Springs police to help me to recover my tapes and manuscript, but when they refused to do so I went to the old bank, pushed open the back door which Biggs had previously kicked in while in a rage and never repaired, repossessed my property, and resumed my writing at my cabin.

Soon thereafter I began experiencing a series of harassing incidents: two arson attempts were made on my rural cabin; brass screws were repeatedly driven into my car's tires; I was shot at twice (returning fire with my newly purchased pistol the second time); my car was stolen and several days later found "professionally torched" (so said County Undersheriff Dave Sikes); and my rural mail box was blown up with a pipe bomb.

After this last incident, my friend Richard Love showed up with a truck, insisting that I move to "some place safe . . . like my condo in Denver," and with his help I did so.

I was eventually charged, tried, and convicted of breaking and entering, criminal mischief, and criminal impersonation for my repossessing my own tapes and manuscript. Clear Creek County District Judge W. Terry Ruckreigle presided over my trial in a biased fashion: in July 1986 he declared Ms. Walker a material witness for my defense (i.e., legally required to be present if I was tried), and then—when her young son was hospitalized as my trial began in December 1986—reversed himself so that my trial would not be delayed. Thus he denied my right to have the benefit of Ms. Walker's testimony against Biggs.

Unbelievably, I was convicted and at my sentencing hearing in June 1987—contrary to Clear Creek County Chief Probation Officer Tom Bennington's recommendation of probation—Ruckreigle sentenced me to two years locked up in community corrections and, refusing to continue my bond, had me jailed immediately. Ten days later I was mysteriously attacked from behind, knocked unconscious, and taken from the jail by ambulance to Lutheran Medical Center in Denver, where I was treated for ten days for incontinence, a brain concussion, and a serious back injury.*

Back in 1984, soon after I told the nuclear waste story to Sarah Nelson, she came by a large sum of money and moved to Alaska to live with her adult son. Over the next few years Tom Young tried to find out what really was going on up at the abandoned mine.

In October 1987, Tom and his Labrador retriever, Gus, disappeared without a trace. In June 1988, a friend of Tom's, Keith Reinhard—a sports writer for the *Daily Herald* in Arlington Heights, Illinois—took a sabbatical, moved to Silver Plume, and began researching and writing a book about Tom's disappearance and soon phoned his wife, Carolyn, and told her, "I'm working on a big story!" On August 7, 1988, Keith went for an afternoon hike in the mountains, but failed to return. Two weeks later during the massive search for him, the remains of Tom and Gus, both shot to death, were found two miles outside Silver Plume, ten months after they had disappeared. Keith remains missing to this day.

The Clear Creek coroner ruled Tom's death a suicide. Six months later the Colorado Bureau of Investigation examined the evidence and found that—whereas Tom's .25 caliber pistol was discovered near his body—Tom and Gus had been shot to death with multiple rounds from a .45 caliber weapon. Tom's death was reclassified as an unsolved homicide and remains so in 1996.

During the 1989–90 television season, NBC Television's "Unsolved Mysteries" presented a segment detailing this story. In 1991, I spoke with the segment's field producer, Todd Miller, and he told me that his experiences in Clear Creek County dealing with local law enforcement in researching and filming the story were the strangest he had ever experienced with "Unsolved Mysteries."

In June of 1989, over seventy FBI agents swooped down on Rocky Flats with its nearly twenty tons of plutonium—more than at any other nuclear plant in the U.S.—and seized two trailer-truck loads of documents from the plant's operator, defense contractor Rockwell International. The

---

*At that time (1987), my newspaper articles against child molesters were well known in Clear Creek County. In 1992, Albert J. Boro, Jr., my attorney in San Francisco who was then working to try and get a pardon or commutation of my sentence from Colorado Governor Roy Romer—a major formal effort by Al which Romer's office never did take seriously—obtained documents which showed that I had been jailed in the only cell block which housed child molesters; and my having "fallen to the floor" was reported to a jailer by one of these molesters.

resulting massive investigation led a federal grand jury in Denver to recommend criminal indictments of several Rockwell International executives and several high-level officials of the Department of Energy (DOE). And a subsequent study of this illegal dumping by the Environmental Protection Agency estimated that a decades-long cleanup of the nuclear and toxic waste would cost 200 to 300 million dollars.

In March of 1992, Denver U.S. Attorney Michael Norton overruled the grand jury's recommendations and arranged a sweetheart plea bargain for Rockwell International in which no individuals (even with the DOE) were indicted and Rockwell alone agreed to pay an 18.5 million dollar fine for illegally dumping nuclear and toxic wastes.

Back in June 1989, while my conviction was still on appeal to the Colorado Court of Appeals, Judge Ruckreigle arbitrarily revoked my appeal bond and ordered me to turn myself in to the Clear Creek County Jail, the same jail where I had been attacked two years earlier. Instead, in fear for my life due to that attack as well as Tom Young's death and Keith Reinhart's disappearance, I fled Colorado on July 23, 1989, and drove to a friend's home in El Paso.

I remained on the lam for the next four years, living with friends in Texas and California, including a year in an apartment of my own between Houston and Galveston (the exception being seven months I spent jailed in Houston, in 1990, on Judge Ruckreigle's bench warrant). When I was released from jail, the Texas appellate court asked Clear Creek County authorities to guarantee my safety were I turned over to them, but they refused to do so, and so Texas refused to issue them a warrant (as required) for my arrest.

However, in September 1991 deputies from the Clear Creek County Sheriff's Department flew to Houston and surreptitiously tried to kidnap me and spirit me back to Colorado. This prompted me to flee to Dallas and, shortly thereafter, northern California.

In July 1992, I provided my information about my story of the nuclear waste dumping at the Experimental Mine to KUSA-TV, the ABC-TV affiliate in Denver. At the time I was living in California and the station interviewed me on camera via satellite uplink from CNN in San Francisco. On August 17, 1992, they wrote to me, saying:

> Thank you very much for calling us with the information about strange events at the Experimental Mine in Idaho Springs during the mid-1980's. I have been pursuing the lead and have confirmed many of the details of your story.

There was, indeed, a research project at the Mine dealing with the storage of nuclear waste. It was part of the Energy Department's program which eventually led to the selection of Yucca Mountain as the nation's high-level nuclear waste depository. I am trying to determine whether the work in Idaho Springs involved radioactive materials, as your information would suggest.

There was also a second research project, sponsored by the U.S. Army. It may have involved classified material, which could account for the "wall of silence" which you and other residents of the town encountered.

It is strange that these research projects went unnoticed by the Denver news media for the last decade. I think our audience may find them interesting. Thank you for bringing them to my attention.

Sincerely,
(signed) John Fosholt
9KUSA Investigative Team

On July 13, 1993—due to strong pressure from Clear Creek County authorities—the FBI finally located me living in Carmel, California, and I was arrested and jailed. I had lived there for eighteen months with considerable help and protection from Fr. Carl R. Hansen and many members of All Saints' Episcopal Church, my literary agent, and many friends in the media around the country. By the time I was arrested I had told well over one hundred people my location.

For over two months I was jailed in Salinas while I fought extradition back to Clear Creek County; but finally, in late September, I was extradited to Colorado—but not to the Clear Creek County Jail: I was locked up in the Summit County Jail in Breckinridge. There, on November 1, 1993, Judge Ruckreigle heard testimony from many supporters before he sentenced me to two years in a Colorado prison, a hearing covered by reporters from both of Denver's major daily newspapers, the *Denver Post* and the *Rocky Mountain News*. However, due to the almost nine months that I had spent jailed first in Texas and then in California fighting extradition, I was released on parole on November 11, 1993.

But my problems were not over: Even though California Parole authorities were willing to accept my being paroled back there, Colorado Parole authorities refused to cooperate and treated me as a dangerous ex-convict, insisting that I remain in Colorado, that I wear an electronic monitoring device on my ankle, that I be under a highly restrictive curfew, and that I be subjected to frequent urinalysis for drugs and alcohol although there has never, ever been the hint of my having any problems with either.

Epilogue

On January 6, 1994, Colorado Parole authorities arrested me on trumped-up charges of parole violation and jailed me. With the help of first one then another attorney, I fought this. However, I was sent back to prison where I did two on-camera interviews for the news departments of Denver TV stations KMGH (CBS) and KUSA (ABC). These reports revealed embarrassing details of several allegations of malfeasance by Colorado parole and prison officials, skewed efforts by law enforcement in Arapahoe County to investigate a major mass murder (including neglecting a major street gang's involvement in the crime), and the sale of illegal drugs to prison inmates by a high-ranking officer with the Colorado Department of Corrections.

At this point Colorado prison officials decided to release me to return to California: On May 3, 1994—with security assistance by prison officials—my friend Richard Love again helped to save my life, this time by spiriting me out of Colorado and back to California on two separate flights under two separate aliases.

✝ ✝ ✝

In 1990 the 1,400 residents of the remote ranching community of Boulder, Montana, were forced to face their own case of a homosexual pedophile running amuck and sexually assaulting scores of local boys for thirty years while he taught in area schools.

In 1956, twenty-nine-year-old Douglas Marks began befriending poor boys at the local high school and arranging for them to take school trips and to attend basketball camps, ". . . students who didn't get many other chances to experience these things," said Jefferson County High School basketball coach Dick Nordon. In the late 1950s three of his early victims confirmed that this was how Marks found the boys he would molest.

Three years later three more of his students came forward to accuse Marks of molesting them, and the school board forced him to take an indefinite leave from the high school where he and one of the students were living in a school dormitory for out-of-town, single teachers.

But, as it still happens in many such cases, this teacher soon got another teaching job, this one in Clancy, just twenty miles away, a town where his prominent family owned a lumber mill. Then, incredibly, in 1965 the Boulder school system rehired Marks as a teacher because, said school board member Wahle Phelen, "he was a wonderful teacher and highly thought of—even though there were doubts about his morals."

Finally, in 1990 the father of a boy in Marks's elementary school class went to a Jefferson County Sheriff's Deputy with a complaint that Marks had sexually assaulted his son, and the parent found a receptive ear: As a young boy in 1965 that same deputy had been sexually assaulted by Marks.

On July 9, 1990, Douglas Marks pled guilty to four counts of felony sexual assaults on four different elementary school boys. Sitting in the courtroom were the fathers of two of those boys who said that they, too, had been sexually assaulted by Marks many years before.

Unbelievably, this teacher was so revered for his "good works" that two sections of the local high school were dedicated to him, and wall plaques—quietly removed after his plea—extolled "his years of service to the community." But court records cite twenty-two molestation accusations going back to 1956, accusations which were never addressed and which by 1990 were too old to prosecute, even though County Attorney Rick Llewellyn says that thus far he has found forty-five victims.

Douglas Marks's sexual abuse of young boys was finally stopped on November 13, 1990, when the sixty-three-year-old former teacher was sentenced to forty years in prison, thus ending a trail of crime and government inaction going back thirty-five years. The school board is now attempting to help heal the extensive emotional damage done by Marks by setting aside money to provide counseling "for any victims who request it." And they hired investigators to check allegations that for years some teachers and other school officials ignored complaints about Marks.

✝ ✝ ✝

When it comes to clergy sexually abusing children, the Roman Catholic Church usually comes to mind. Its pedophile priests and brothers in religious orders are easily identified when caught and receive more blame for sexually assaulting children than ministers from other sects. This problem is only now beginning to be addressed, thanks in great part to the definitive book about such sexual abuse, *Lead Us Not Into Temptation: Catholic Priests and the Sexual Abuse of Children* by Jason Berry (New York: Doubleday, 1992) Slowly, the Roman Catholic Church is starting to "get it" when it comes to protecting children from pedophile priests.

Wrote Berry: "Between 1983 and 1987, more than two hundred priests or religious brothers [in the United States] were reported to the Vatican Embassy for sexually abusing youngsters, in most cases teenage boys—an average of nearly one accusation a week in those four years alone. In the decade of 1982 to 1992, approximately four hundred priests were reported to church or civil authorities for molesting youths. The vast majority of these men had multiple victims. By 1992, the church's financial losses—in victims' settlements, legal expenses, and medical treatment of clergy—had reached an estimated $400 million (p. ix)."

Like those Pentecostal faithful who turned to Brother Tony for religious instruction and spiritual guidance, many Catholics unwittingly turned to priests who secretly preyed on their children. In his book Berry detailed the case of Fr. Gilbert Gauthe, a priest who in the 1980s brutally sexually assaulted scores of altar boys in the Diocese of Lafayette, Louisiana, before being caught and successfully prosecuted. Berry's account of the esteem in which Gauthe was held could also describe Brother Tony: "His crimes were magnified by his vocation. As a priest he occupied vaunted status: a server of ritual and symbol of trust, confessor to parent and child, the hand of God baptizing infants, confirming youngsters, performing weddings, burying the dead (p. 28)."

Like Gauthe, few Roman Catholic priests sexually assaulting children have attracted as much media attention as did Fr. James R. Porter, who began his career as a pedophile at the age of eighteen when he molested a thirteen-year-old boy on a playground in his home town of Revere, Massachusetts.

Porter went to seminary in the late 1950s and spent his summers molesting children at a church-run summer camp. After he was ordained, he was assigned to St. Mary's Church in North Attleboro, Massachusetts, where in just three years he sexually assaulted over one hundred boys and girls, even though several parents repeatedly reported the assaults to other priests and then to Bishop James Connolly of the Diocese of Fall River, Massachusetts.

Following his transfer to Sacred Heart Church in Fall River, in August 1963, Fr. Porter sexually assaulted still more children and was again reported to the bishop. The church responded by assigning Porter to St. James Church in New Bedford, Massachusetts, where over the next two years he sexually assaulted still more children.

After being caught, in 1967 he was sent for treatment to the Servants of the Paraclete in Jemez Springs, New Mexico. The facility frequently released Porter to say Mass in churches in New Mexico and Texas where he preyed on still more innocent boys and girls and was reported to the Servants of the Paraclete, who dutifully note in Porter's record that he had succumbed to "his old failings."

In 1969 the servants of the Paraclete gave Fr. Porter a recommendation which enabled him to be sent to St. Phillip's Church in Bemidji, Minnesota, where he sexually assaulted a couple of dozen more children, got caught, and was reported again.

In 1974 Porter asked for and was given a release from the priesthood by the Vatican. In 1976 he was married at St. Casimir's Church in St. Paul, Minnesota, had children of his own, and by 1980 had sexually assaulted several boys in his new neighborhood. But during the 1980s Porter sexually assaulted the two young teenage sisters who babysat for his children.

In September of 1989, one of Porter's first victims, Frank L. Fitzpatrick of North Attlebora, recalled his repressed memories of being raped by Porter and began searching for other victims and for Porter himself, whom he found that November living in Minnesota.

During the first of his several calls to Porter, Fitzpatrick directly confronted his abuser about having raped him as a boy. Porter admitted to sexually abusing many children in general, but claimed to be unable to recall any of his victims by name because of a memory loss due to his having received electroconvulsive shock therapy. Then, with a laugh, he said that he didn't know why he had sexually assaulted his young victims.

In December of 1990, Fitzpatrick made official criminal complaints about Porter's sexual assaults on him to North Attleboro police and the Bristol County (Massachusetts) District Attorney, and gave them copies of his taped phone conversations with Porter.

After local and area media exposure of Porter by Fitzpatrick and the steadily increasing legion of Porter's former victims, in July 1992 ABC Television's "Prime Time Live" told the story on a show featuring Fitzpatrick and twenty-five of the former priest's victims who detailed their assaults by Porter.

Finally, in December 1993, James R. Porter was held accountable in court for his hundreds of criminal sexual assaults on children in Bristol County, and in a plea bargain he was sentenced to eighteen to twenty years in prison, of which he may serve as few as six.

Today Fitzpatrick has turned his personal tragedy into the nationally known, highly respected, and effective Survivor Connections, Inc., 52 Lyndon Road, Cranston, Rhode Island 02905, phone 401/941-2548: a program devoted to to ". . . people sexually abused by any type of perpetrator, whether the abuse was done to a child or an adult . . ." for ". . . any survivor or pro-survivor, not just those related to clergy sexual assault."

Epilogue

✝ ✝ ✝

I tried repeatedly to interview the head of the Servants of the Paraclete, the Very Reverend Liam J. Hoare, the order's Servant General. In a letter dated April 2, 1993, Fr. Hoare wrote: "While I appreciate the thrusts of your efforts and your desire to receive accurate and positive information, I trust that you will accept the fact that we are presently embroiled in litigation and subject to constraints regarding public statements and interviews. These matters being settled, I would be most pleased to afford you the opportunity of an interview."

Finally, in July 1994, Fr. Hoare and I spoke on the phone, the priest still begging off an interview "until our problems with litigation are behind us." And when I asked just when that might be, he referred me to Albuquerque attorney Bruce Pasternak.

But it will be a long time: Unknown to Fr. Hoare, I already knew of Pasternak and had spoken with him by phone. He had told me that his client list of victims of priests and brothers who had been in treatment at the Servants of the Paraclete was continuing to grow month by month as word of his representation spread from victim to victim. By 1995, Pasternak later told me, this list had grown to "over sixty victims."

Most of the victims were boys nearing puberty or in their early teens when they were seduced and molested by these priests. Some were girls. But all of them had endured years with little more than a cold shoulder from the Servants of the Paraclete or the Archdiocese of Santa Fe and now they longed to see justice on their day in court.

In 1994 the Order still treated pedophile priests, and in our conversation Hoare claimed, "Until recently, no one has understood the problem [of pedophilia]." And when asked about Fr. Porter's treatment at the Servants of the Paraclete, Fr. Hoare remarked, "We simply did the best we could to treat those who came to us for help. And just as it was back then, our most important method of dealing with such psychological aberrations remains prayer."

Even with their major problems from such notoriously failed attempts at treating pedophiles, ephebophiles, and pederasts, in February 1996, Fr. Hoare spoke with me briefly by phone from San Antonio, where he was attending a conference. He said: "[Pedophiles] are not that great a problem in the Church. Among priests and brothers in the Church, pedophiles make up only three percent." And when I asked if his order was still attempting to treat such men, he replied: "Yes, in spite of all the adverse publicity that we have received, we are still treating them."

To sum up the problem of child sexual abuse in the Roman Catholic Church, I again turn to *Lead Us Not Into Temptation*: "The crisis in the Catholic Church lies not with the fraction of priests who molest youngsters but in an ecclesiastical power structure that harbors pedophiles, conceals other sexual behavior patterns among its clerics, and uses strategies of duplicity and counterattack against the victims" (p. xx).

✝ ✝ ✝

Most certainly, the sexual abuse of children and especially boys in religious environments is not restricted to Roman Catholics or Christians. In their 1988 book *Monkey on a Stick: Murder, Madness, and the Hare Krishnas* (San Diego: Harcourt Brace Jovanovich), John Hubner and Lindsey Gruson wrote:

> [At the Hare Krishnas' New Vrindaban temple in West Virginia] the boys were ordered to come to the front of the class [in the boys' *guru kula*, an in-house boarding school for the sons of Krishna devotees] and sit on Sri Galima's [Larry Gardner's] lap. Sri Galima then anally raped them, right in front of the class. Other boys were ordered to stay after class. Sri Galima tied their hands to their desks with duct tape and then assaulted them in the same way.
> At night, Fredrick DeFrancisco, Sri Galima's assistant, crept into the boys' sleeping bags and performed oral sex on them. . . .
> [In November 1986 Devotee Susan Hebel's thirteen-year-old son, Scott, told her] that for the last three years, he and other boys in the guru kula have been sexually molested by Sri Galima and his assistant [DeFrancisco].
> [Hebel confronted New Vrindaban's founder, Keith Ham, saying] "I feel so betrayed . . . all these years, I've given up my children. I sent them to the guru kula when they turned five, trusting that they would be loved and taken care of and would become devotees. I never imagined that anyone would molest them."
> [Ham responded,] "You stupid woman. You don't have any right to say that. Sex is sex. How much sex have you had?"
> In 1987 Marshall County (West Virginia) Sheriff's Department Detective Sergeant Tom Westfall gathered sufficient evidence for warrants to arrest Gardner and DeFrancisco for multiple counts of sexual molestation of children. However, when Westfall arrived at New Vrindaban, commune spokesman Dick Dezio told him that Gardner had fled to India a couple of weeks before and is apparently still there. But DeFrancisco

was arrested, tried, convicted, and sentenced to prison for his sexual assaults on boys in New Vrindaban's guru kula.

Child molestation and abuse has been a severe problem at ISKCON [International Society for Krishna Consciousness] temples around America and in India. [In Los Angeles] a devotee was sentenced to ninety-nine years in prison for molesting children he was supposed to be caring for in the temple's nursery. Other cases have been discovered in Denver and Dallas.

On July 10, 1987, Jagadisha Goswami, ISKCON's minister of education acknowledged the problem in a press release that said in part, "... more than several incidents have occurred in the history of ISKCON's guru kulas when a child or children have been sexually abused by adults or older children. This has also been a serious problem in society at large, and a considerable amount of time and energy has been spent studying the causes and effects. Because of several recent incidents [and] recent discoveries of older incidents in our guru kulas, I have been made aware of the many and serious (especially emotional) problems that abused children usually suffer from, the worst being that they become abusers themselves later on."[1]

✝ ✝ ✝

On April 2, 1992, insurance underwriter Edward Savitz of Philadelphia was charged in the statutory rapes of four minor boys. A few days earlier the Philadelphia D.A. and the city's Health Commissioner issued an extraordinary public health warning about Mr. Savitz, who by then had been in police custody for two days on charges of involuntary deviate sexual intercourse, sexual abuse of children, indecent assault and corruption of the morals of a minor in connection with complaints by two males.

The officials said that Mr. Savitz had AIDS and that he had been infected with HIV for two years before he developed full-blown symptoms. During this time, the officials said, he may have had sex with several hundred teenage boys, and they advised anyone who had contact with Mr. Savitz to seek advice about having an AIDS test.

The police say they have evidence that Mr. Savitz has had contact with high school students and teenage street hustlers since 1979. The evidence includes five thousand photographs of boys or young men, some of them nude, and 312 plastic trash bags filled with soiled socks and underwear.

---

1. John Hubner and Lindsey Gruson, *Monkey on a Stick: Murder, Madness, and the Hare Krishnas* (San Diego: Harcourt Brace Jovanovich, 1988) pp. 344–47, 399, 400.

But health officials soon began playing down the risk that Mr. Savitz may have passed on his infection. They said that most of Mr. Savitz's activities appear to have involved oral sex and the acting out of fetishes. According to them, both activities pose little or no risk of spreading AIDS.

Savitz was released in April 1992 on three million dollars bail, but later was rearrested after two more minors came forward with similar allegations. Bail was set at twenty million dollars, but Barnaby C. Wittels, Savitz's lawyer, filed an appeal seeking to reduce the amount. He was successful and Mr. Savitz was released, but within months he was suffering from an advanced case of AIDS. He went into a convalescent home where he died a year later before facing trial.

✝ ✝ ✝

After school on Wednesday, May 5, 1993, second graders Steve Branch, Christopher Byers, and Michael Moore got on their bicycles and rode off into their West Memphis, Arkansas, neighborhood to enjoy life as only eight-year-old boys can: playing and exploring and making believe. But when they hadn't returned home by seven o'clock, their parents began calling neighbors, notified the police, and a search was mounted in this small city along the storied Mississippi River, but that night passed without searchers finding any sign of the boys.

Beginning at seven the following morning, men on all-terrain vehicles began searching an area known locally as Robin Hood Park, a swampy place full of brush, trees, vines, bike trails, snakes, and a bayou filled with turtles and such: an irresistible lure for inquisitive, fun-loving, full-of-life little boys. As noon approached and the temperature climbed into the high eighties with a moderate humidity, they continued scouring the area for the three young friends but found no sign of them.

Then, about 1:30 P.M., a discovery worse than any of the boys' parents, siblings, friends, or even the police and other searchers could ever have imagined was made: Steve, Christopher, and Michael's bodies were found within ten feet of each other and submerged in Ten Mile Bayou. Each had been bound by their hands and feet, raped, and savagely beaten to death, and then sexually mutilated.

John Beifuss of the *Commercial Appeal* in Memphis, Tennessee, wrote of the boys most eloquently:

They had funny nicknames like "Wormer" (" 'cause he was such a squirmer" said a friend of the Byers family) and "Bubba." They swam like fish and kicked like Ninja Turtles. They had smarts and heart and smiles and wiles.

They lived in the same northeastern neighborhood near the interstate and swampy Robin Hood Park. The were in second grade together at Weaver Elementary School. They were in the same Cub Scout pack at Holy Cross Episcopal Church, where the Moores were members, and all had passed the rank of "Wolf."

On Friday, June 4, three teenagers were arrested by West Memphis Police and charged in the three young boys' sex-torture murders: Jason Baldwin, sixteen; Jessie Lloyd Misskelley, seventeen; and Michael Wayne Echols (no relation to the author), eighteen, the purported ring-leader and a self-described devil worshiper whom many acquaintances described as "very frightening" and "dangerous."

Even though two were minors, all three were tried as adults. Baldwin and Misskelley were sentenced to life in prison with no possibility of parole and Echols was sentenced to death.[2]

✝ ✝ ✝

Although they can't exactly put their finger on why, many artistic, liberal parents are also concerned about the potential for sexual abuse of their children and have to be on guard.

In *The Day Books of Edward Weston*, there is a loving yet telling fatherly sidelight that this famed American photographer recorded on December 6, 1925, while he and his adolescent son, Brett, were living in Mexico:

> But I know Brett! So full to overflowing with life! He could be ruined by a tight rein or a long face. He needs to explore naturally. He is bound to adventure much, to experience much. He is open-faced, laughter-loving, amenable to suggestion. I hope to help him when he stumbles or give him a gentle kick in the right direction—if I am able to decide which is right, at the time!
>
> I was forced to make a hasty decision when we first arrived. An ob-

---

2. The story of this case is told in the true crime book *The Blood of Innocents* (New York: Pinnacle Books, 1995) by Guy Reel, Marc Perrusquia, and Bartholomew Sullivan.

vious homosexual made pressing overtures to Brett. And what was I to do, with a personal distaste, but no moral objections? If a woman of the right kind had desired him, I would have aided the affair, but to have Brett at thirteen thrown into a perverse relationship, unformed in tendencies as he is, perhaps to be physically drained by this very sophisticated older man, I could not give in to. So the person suddenly disappeared from his life.

With my attitude towards so-called perversions, which is certainly understanding and tolerant, I retained some feeling of guilt over what I had done, for the man was infatuated, and wealthy, would have done for him in ways that I cannot. Well, in three years, I shall not stand in the way of any experience which opportunity may afford him.[3]

In Carmel, California, during the summer of 1994, I asked Brett's younger brother, famed photographer Cole Weston, about this. Said he: "Yes, I have heard about that [incident]. What Dad did was indicative of his feelings and desire to protect us from harm while allowing us to explore life to its fullest."

There was also something that I had heard about another brother, Neil: In 1925, when Neil was seven, Edward Weston took a series of nude photographs of his young son. One in particular—a strikingly artistic frontal nude of Neil's torso—went on to become widely popular and to be reproduced in a number of books. Reports were that this greatly displeased Neil. Remarked Cole, "Yes, that is true. Especially when he got older, Neil was rather upset about that photograph."

I then asked Cole about his son Kim's well-received photography, some of which includes depictions of Kim's nude young son, Zack, then age four, and Cole suggested that I speak with Kim. Kim also lives in Carmel and, in 1995, I spoke with him at length. Kim said:

"In art—whether it's sculpture, painting, or photography—it does not matter whether the nudes are adults or children. However, in photographing children in the nude, I admit that there is a very fine line. In the case of my photographing my son, Zack, since he was my son, it was my decision and I felt that it was proper.

"It's hard for me to describe because photographing my son in the nude was just a part of my life. Primarily, I do nudes—artistic nudes, not prurient or suggestive nudes—and that was the approach I used when I photographed Zack.

---

3. Nancy Newhall, *The Day Books of Edward Weston* (New York: Aperture, 1961), p. 140.

"Indeed, when I first photographed Zack in the nude it was his idea. I was photographing his mother, my wife, Gina, in the nude, and Zack was watching. Then he spontaneously undressed and asked if it was his turn. And it was.

"I think when it gets right down to it, it's a question of morals. My family is made up of artists and for me, photographing artistic nudes is a way of life . . . an honorable, very respectable way of life."

† † †

The world-renowned composer Igor Stravinsky called the Texas Boys Choir "the finest boy choir in the world." In 1996 the choir will celebrate its fiftieth anniversary thanks, in part, to the group's recently retired Executive Director, Jack Noble White, a friend of mine for over thirty-three years and in my opinion one of the finest Christian professionals working with children today.

In 1977 the Board of the Texas Boys Choir asked White to take over the choir in the wake of a scandal involving alleged sexual improprieties with some of the choristers by former staff. For almost two decades this internationally famed composer, arranger, choir master, organist, and children's educator oversaw the operation of the Texas Boys Choir and its staff, including a move to their new home, a multimillion-dollar facility on the banks of the Trinity River in Fort Worth, Texas. Also during this time, Jack's wife, Johanna—a talented educator in her own right—ran the choir school. In addition to his musical duties guiding and conducting the group's national and international concert tours, performances, and recording sessions, Jack taught, counseled, and tutored choir boys. In reference to his tenure with the choir, I interviewed Jack by telephone in October 1994. Jack said:

"In the spirit I exercised throughout my tenure, I chose not to discuss or be privy to events that preceded my arrival. There was an eighteen-month interim before I came, so as far as my having to address that issue head on, that had already been done and actually by that point the Choir had dwindled . . . to a very small number. In fact, one might say that the incidents and subsequent problems practically put the choir under. And by the time that I was approached it was a last-ditch effort to try and truly save the Choir. So, the damage had been done and therefore my immediate efforts were to address rebuilding the Choir.

"I never did look back. In fact, I was intentionally not privy to any details as far as the allegations were concerned. In many cases like this the details aren't as well-known or as widespread as you would think, but you still have to figure that if there was smoke you just have to recognize that there's going to be some suspicion. And this didn't bother me because the very first priority in my mind was the environment at the Choir and I believe that it is from the environment that you build the steps of the academic, spiritual, and the artistic product.

"So, having come straight out of an educational environment I sat down with the board and said, 'Here's the way we will do things: We'll have an open door, we will not have any secrets, and I'm not going to speak about the past. I don't know about the past, but you may ask me anything that you wish as far as the future is concerned.' "

Thus Jack Noble White set out not only to save the Texas Boys Choir, but to chart the future of this premier arts organization and to use his expertise to strive to prevent the problem of even a suspicion of sexual abuse of choir members by a staff member from arising again.

"I think, number one, that you just want to carefully choose the staff. That's tantamount. Obviously, we are a very small staff and most of us have been together since the seventies, so fortunately I don't have a swinging door staff situation to deal with. I think that that would be a nightmare. You make certain that you have got very excellent character references on everybody. And at all of my interviews with potential staff people—even if they are summer counselors—I let them know that we are vigilant about even the hint of any kind of abuse of choir members.

"One of the big 'don't's' for us is for any boy to take advantage of another boy in any way. And the rule there is that if a boy even has knowledge of that, even if he was not involved and does not report it, he's guilty of a major offense.

"Also, I changed the policy of two boys to a room. They are either alone or there are three just because I think there is a safety with three. And I'm not thinking so much of sexual things as I am just sheer emotional or physical abuse, just one boy dominating the other one. So now we put three boys in each room—a senior boy, a middler, and a younger boy—and that sort of defused that.

"In Colorado Springs in our summer training conference at Colorado College we have a slightly enlarged staff and also have junior counselors and we don't close the doors, we don't lock the doors. The boys are normally in a single room there and it's the policy that one boy cannot go into another boy's room and have the door closed and have any kind of goings on . . . mischief or anything indecent seldom occurs with the door open.

"The very first thing that I tell all of the boys at the first of each year is that if anyone does anything to you or says anything to you that doesn't seem right—whether it's me, someone in your family, or anyone else—you have a responsibility to go to somebody that you trust and tell them. That's the biggest safeguard that we have, letting the children know that they have rights and responsibilities. That's our overriding philosophy. We're pretty old-fashioned around here and we teach and practice that there's a certain order to life and a certain decency that pervades everything that we do."

Since the mid seventies I have been privileged to hear the Texas Boys Choir perform under Jack's direction at many, many concerts. On several occasions I traveled with the choir doing photography for them and it was during such a trip in the winter of 1985 that I had the opportunity to talk with a choir member—I'll call him Garrett—with whom I had witnessed a very busy Jack repeatedly take a great deal of time in order to comfort the boy and show him a considerable degree of personal concern, including taking the boy to his room to counsel him privately.

Garrett did not volunteer, nor did I ask, the reasons behind Jack's giving him this extra attention; however, Garrett did tell me that at the time he was dealing with a major personal problem, commenting, "Mr. White has helped me more than anyone else I've ever known! He's been like a father to me!"

This incident confirmed my admiration for Jack's ability with children, but ten years later I was in for a surprise:

In November 1995, Jack and I met in Dallas for a long lunch to go over his contribution to this Epilogue. As we spoke, Jack began telling me the story of a choir member whom he had counseled and helped during the choir's 1985 tour.

Jack said that the boy had been sexually abused several times by a man in his neighborhood who had befriended him but that no one knew anything about it until—while on tour with the choir in San Francisco—Jack received a phone call from the boy's mother back in Texas telling of the discovery of "Garrett's abuse through evidence given to the police by another young victim."

The mother told Jack that she thought that her son—now unwittingly identified to me by Jack as Garrett—should immediately return home. However, Jack countered that he felt that Garrett should make the decision himself and suggested that he bring Garrett to his hotel room and allow Garrett's mother to tell her son what had happened, with Jack present. This was done, Garrett broke down, cried a great deal, and admitted the abuse.

Jack comforted the boy and supported him in his decision to remain on tour with the choir. The boy's mother agreed, and during the choir's remaining weeks on tour Jack made himself available to Garrett whenever he needed to talk, even to the point of affording Garrett regular private time with Jack in his room at the end of each day.

Jack also told me that he was prepared to be an "outcry" witness for Garrett should the boy's testimony be needed in court against his perpetrator. It wasn't—the man pled guilty to sexually assaulting Garrett and the other boy. And, Jack reported, Garrett keeps in regular touch with him.

Jack was as surprised as I at the striking coincidence. Learning the story behind Garrett's comments to me in 1985 served to underscore my life-long respect for Jack Noble White and his extraordinarily perceptive professional approach to working with children!

Also, over the years I have kept Jack informed about my efforts against NAMBLA. We met in March 1993 in Sacramento during the choir's national tour. I asked him about his impressions of the organization and he responded:

"I can respond in two or three different directions, some of them simplistic, some not. The first one is that I don't have to look in a book—well, any other book except for one published by NAMBLA—to know that what they are promoting is wrong. It is wrong legally, it is wrong morally for an adult to involve themselves sexually with a child. Period.

"But then they believe what they believe and base it on their position that perhaps there are a few boys that have been helped by a NAMBLA member's affectionate relationship. Well, I think that this is really grasping at straws. Every aspect about it is illegal, immoral . . . everything but fattening! I mean, it's a moot point because there are organizations that I disagree with that are so much more credible than NAMBLA that this group is just a black void!"

The December 1992 *NAMBLA Bulletin* had a cover featuring a totally nude twelve-year-old boy stretched seductively across a bed below the headline "If It's Christmas, It Must Be Boy Choirs!" The five-page cover story began with, "Christmas is a religiously sanctioned festival of boy-love." Another article in the same issue read: "It is sobering to consider that the vilification directed toward the boy-lover by present-day society has its parallel in King Herod's murderous enmity toward the infant Jesus and toward those who dared acknowledge the holy child's divinity."

When shown this *Bulletin* during our March 1993 meeting, Jack was visibly distressed and he remarked:

"Well, it's just sheer child pornography! And you obviously get into a whole deal because the people who are hung up with child pornography can have all kinds of rotten involvements with children.

"While I would say that the cover was artistically done, it was very definitely not a cover that I think anyone could stomach other than someone like a NAMBLA member and this is where I can't figure out these people. I don't see how they're still not prosecuted because, basically, they are admitting to and encouraging a felony! And I would have to say that I would have very grave doubts about anyone who intentionally subscribed to the *NAMBLA Bulletin.*

"I guess sitting here thinking about it, if there is an element of truth in what NAMBLA believes—any element of truth that I would agree with— it is that children do need affection. And I would hate to see children denied affection because someone was afraid it would escalate into something sick like what NAMBLA encourages. So I think that there is that element, just that little element of truth, but it then becomes black and white to me that children do not need sexual contact with adults at all ... that the affection is one thing, but that if an adult is showing a child affection for his own personal gratification, then that's wrong! That's very wrong! In fact, to me that is just mind-boggling!!

"You see, I think that a lot of people put their sons in the Texas Boys Choir and in our school because of the demands that we make on the boys through our one-on-one efforts with our students and choir members because these parents know that that's what teaches the boys responsibility ... which, in turn, is going to produce a good self image.

"But in practice some schools have very strict guidelines about an adult and a child never being one-on-one and that troubles me because a great deal of my success in dealing with children is the confidentiality that I have afforded the children I work with. However, today what some people want you to do is to say to a child, "You can tell me what you need to tell me, but somebody is going to have to be here when you tell me."

"In other words, there is going to have to be a witness to the confidentiality and that destroys the system that I have used so effectively for so many years. And the child knows that the protection afforded them did not come by rules but by mutual respect for one another. And if an adult betrays that responsibility and trust and confidentiality with a child, they should be dealt with severely. But I would not want my child to be in a circumstance where that confidentiality could not be expressed, could not be practiced. But then all the while you obviously hold the institution or the neighbor or the teacher or whomever to very strict standards of decency and you have the child know that if ever there is anything that seems indecent that they are to blow the whistle on that.

"Most of the time when children want to discuss something concerning them they don't want to do it in a group situation. They want to go to someone, an individual that they trust and they want to talk privately with that person. But it's a difficult, difficult time today and my only hope and prayer is that those people who do work with children and love children in the very proper way—and to work with kids I believe that you do have to love them—that they have the courage to give children instruction, care, and affection that is good and proper.

"I just hate to see it become more and more difficult to practice the art of teaching children because of the improprieties of a few, and yet I certainly believe that those people who do harm children should be sought out and prosecuted. In the case of pedophiles, they are sick and they need to be dealt with firmly. It's obviously something that cannot be overcome because it's a predisposition. And that brings us back to the scary thing about all of this: In our society we have to be aware of and deal firmly with people like those who belong to NAMBLA—those who believe that adults having sex with children is okay—because it is not!"

✝ ✝ ✝

In his book *Scout's Honor: Sexual Abuse in America's Most Trusted Institution*, Patrick Boyle writes:

> Psychiatrist Dr. Gene Abel, one of the nation's leading experts on sex offenders and director of the Behavioral Medicine Institute of Atlanta, estimates that pedophiles make up 1 percent of the population; this works out to 1.8 million pedophiles in the United States.
>
> [And Boyle writes that experts] know that boys are molested almost as often as girls . . . and that they're more reluctant to report it, especially if the abuser was a man.
>
> [According to Boyle, Dr. Abel] found that men who abused boys averaged 150 victims each. The average [victims] for men abusing unrelated girls was twenty.[4]

---

4. Patrick Boyle, *Scout's Honor: Sexual Abuse in America's Most Trusted Institution* (Rocklin, Calif.: Prima Publishing, 1994), pp. 31–32.

When it comes to effective treatment of pedophiles and ephebophiles and pederasts—"effective" meaning adequate enough to protect children from such offenders' obsessive drives to manipulate, coerce, seduce, molest, and, in some cases, even attack their desired sex objects who are younger, weaker, and more naive than themselves—sadly, there are no truly successful programs. In fact, when I interviewed the founders, psychiatrists, psychologists, and other therapists at several of the best-known sex offender treatment programs in the United States, not a single one could provide real proof that his or her program approach afforded an "unsupervised success rate" of more than 15 percent to 20 percent, and in most cases even these figures were little more than estimates and ill-supported by hard data.

Indeed, one nationally recognized program's co-founder told me that his program treating those who have repeatedly sexually assaulted children "successfully treats 85 percent of those placed here" But when I asked how he had arrived at that figure he admitted that those 85 percent had been released into the community for two years or more and had not been totally supervised, but—he quickly added—had not been rearrested for sexually assaulting children. And this in light of the fact that the National Center for Missing and Exploited Children has found that *less than 10 percent of all sex assaults on children are ever reported!*

Sadly, when it comes to pedophiles and ephebophiles and pederasts who have been convicted of sexually assaulting more than one victim, or those who have committed more than one act with a single victim, we have very few options.

Yes, we must recognize that such persons are mentally ill and they must be dealt with as such. But, as painful as it is for these repeat offenders as well as for their families, if we truly care about protecting our children and preventing those who have already been found guilty of child sexual assault in a court of law from reoffending, then we must realize once and for all that today there are no treatment programs or approaches which provide effective therapy for offenders while they remain free in society or after which they can be even safely returned to society. And we must realize that to allow such identified offenders to remain unsupervised in society places inordinate numbers of children at great risk.

In *Scout's Honor,* page 331, Patrick Boyle advises: "The best protection is the most difficult for busy adults to provide: a family life that is supportive and emotionally sound so that a child does not seek attention and affection elsewhere. 'The best way to protect your child,' [FBI agent] Lanning says, 'is to be a good parent.' "

Boyle quotes incarcerated serial child molester Carl Bittenbender, a former Boy Scout leader in several states, as saying: "My message to parents is to care, truly care by being involved in all aspects of their children's lives, and people with my problem will never have an opportunity to abuse their children."

We Americans have long felt that when something is broken we can fix it and when someone is ill we can cure them. In time, I do hope and pray that a truly successful treatment which cures this aberrant problem is discovered. But for now the only thing that we can do is to place identified repeat offenders in secure facilities like prisons and locked, secure mental hospitals. In short, we must treat them humanely, but we must lock them up in order to keep them away from all children until we indeed have a proven treatment that does not place a single child at risk.

Selected Bibliography

Bass, Ellen. *I Like You to Make Jokes with Me But I Don't Want You to Touch Me.* Durham, N.C.: Lollipop Power Books, 1993.

Bass, Ellen, and Laura Davis. *The Courage to Heal.* New York: Harper Perennial, 1994.

Bennett, Jeffrey P. *Breaking the Bonds of Child Abuse: A Guide to Political Action.* 341 Bonnie Circle, Corona, Calif. 91720: Issues in Print, Write Now!, 1995.

Berry, Jason. *Lead Us Not Into Temptation: Catholic Priests and the Sexual Abuse of Children.* New York: Doubleday, 1992.

Boyle, Patrick. *Scout's Honor: Sexual Abuse in America's Most Trusted Institution.* Rocklin, Calif.: Prima Publishing, 1994.

Campagna, Daniel S., and Donald L. Poffenberger. *The Sexual Trafficking in Children.* Dover, Mass.: Auburn House, 1988.

Cooney, Judith. *Coping with Sexual Abuse.* New York: Rosen Publishing Group, 1987.

Crewdson, John. *By Silence Betrayed.* Boston: Little, Brown and Company, 1988.

Dziech, Billie Wright, and Judge Charles B. Schudson. *On Trial: America's Treatment of Sexually Abused Children.* Boston: Beacon Press, 1991.

Hechler, David. *The Battle and the Backlash: The Child Sexual Abuse War.* Lexington, Mass.: Lexington Books, 1988.

Jessie. *Please Tell: A Child's Story about Sexual Abuse.* Center City, Minn.: Hazelden, 1991.
Lloyd, Robin. *For Money or Love: Boy Prostitution in America.* New York: Vanguard Press, 1976.
Reel, Guy, with Marc Perrusquia and Bartholomew Sullivan. *The Blood of Innocents.* New York: Pinnacle Books, 1995.
The Survivor Activist (newsletter). 52 Lyndon Road, Cranston, R.I. 02905.
Townley, Roderick. *Safe and Sound: A Parent's Guide to Child Protection.* New York: Simon & Schuster, 1985.
Treating Abuse Today (magazine). 2722 East Lake Avenue East, Suite 300, Seattle, Wash. 98102.
Whitfield, Charles. *Memory and Abuse.* Deerfield Beach, Fla.: Health Communications, 1995.

The following titles are recommended for male child sexual abuse survivors.

Grubman-Black, Steven D. *Broken Boys/Mending Men: Recovery from Childhood Sexual Abuse.* Blue Ridge Summit, Pa.: Tab Books, 1990.
Hunter, Mic. *Abused Boys: The Neglected Victims of Sexual Abuse.* Lexington, Mass.: Lexington Books, 1990.
Lew, Mike. *Men Recovering from Incest and Other Sexual Child Abuse.* New York: Harper & Row, 1990.
Tower, Cynthia Crosson. *Secret Scars: A Guide for Survivors of Child Sexual Abuse.* New York: Viking Books, 1988.